Pate Family
Roots in America

Pate Family
Roots in America

Beginning in Colonial Virginia in 1636

With Focus on Thoroughgood
Pate and His Descendants

DR. J. R. PEACOCK

Edited by
A. J. Pate Joel M. Pate

Published by
Carter Pate, LLC

IN MEMORIAM

Obituary of Jimmy Ray Peacock

Published in the *Orlando Sentinel* on August 28, 2011.

PEACOCK, JIMMY RAY, DVM of Clermont, died August 27, 2011 of leukemia. Born July 10, 1929 in DeFuniak Springs, a son of Henry and Grace (Locke) Nowling, he was adopted at age 7 by his step-father, Thomas S. Peacock. His early years were spent in North Florida, graduating from Blountstown High School in 1947 as a 3-year football letterman and class president. He enlisted in the US Air Force in 1948, serving the 40- month span before the Berlin Airlift into the Korean War, as a construction equipment mechanic. He served overseas duty on Amchitka, an Aleutian Island. Jim's family farm experience developed his interest in veterinary medicine. He completed pre-med courses at Florida State University and the University of Florida. He was admitted to Alabama Polytechnic Institute (now Auburn University) in 1954 and received his Doctor of Veterinary Medicine in 1958, graduating with honors. Jim met Margaret Linda Hoadley at the Wesley Foundation at FSU. They were married March 16, 1956, and the Methodist Church was an integral part of their lives. Dr. Peacock joined an established Winter Garden veterinary practice for 6 years, before opening the first Clermont practice in 1964. He left practice in 1976 to inspect for the Fla. Dept. of Agriculture. His retirement years were occupied as a citrus grower, genealogist, investor, furniture refinisher, and avid gardener. He and Margaret spent 15 years camping in isolated areas of Alaska, all of the Canadian Provinces, and all over the U.S. Five summers were spent as volunteers at the Methodist campground at Lake Junaluska, NC. Jim's genealogy experience resulted in the publication of comprehensive works on the Locke, Kirkland and Pate Families. Works of lesser size were prepared on other families. His genealogy collection is housed at the Auburn University Library in Special Collections. Jim was Past President of the Central Florida Veterinary Medical Society, Greater Clermont Chamber of Commerce, South Lake Rotary Club, and was a Trustee of Lake Sumter Community College for 12 years, serving 3 years as Board Chairman. He was active in Boy Scouts, Girl Scouts and youth baseball. He was a member of the First United Methodist Church of Winter Garden and the 1865 Society of Auburn University. Dr. Peacock is survived by his wife of 55 years, Margaret; a daughter, Margaret Marie Locke of Fairfax, VA; a son, Kenneth T. (Lisa) of Minneola; four granddaughters, Laura and Rachel Warnock, Kaelyn and Jayna Peacock; and a brother, Jack H. Peacock of Lebanon, IN. A memorial service will be held on Thursday, September 1 at 4 pm, at First United Methodist Church of Winter Garden. Burial will be at Florida National Cemetery. In lieu of flowers, the family requests memorial contributions to First United Methodist Church, 125 N Lakeview, Winter Garden, FL 34787 or Auburn University Library, Auburn Alabama 36849-5606, or the charity of choice.

FOREWORD

This work by Dr. J R Peacock is his final genealogical research effort. As with his other genealogical publications, Jim did the research and writing and his beloved wife, Margaret, did the manuscript preparation. This book is an exception to that usual arrangement in that, due to failing health, Jim turned to his colleagues to research and write the final chapter. These colleagues were responsible for further preparation, resulting in this book being published. After some delays, the work is now done.

Jim was born Jimmy Ray Nowling on 10 Jul 1929 in DeFuniak Springs, Walton County, Florida, the son of Henry and Grace (Locke) Nowling. He was adopted, at age 7, by his step father, Thomas S. Peacock. Jim's early years were spent in the panhandle area of North Florida. He graduated in 1947 from Blountstown High School in Calhoun County, Florida. He enlisted in the US Air Force in 1948, serving 40 months as a construction equipment mechanic. He was honorably discharged as a Sergeant. One assignment took him to an overseas duty station in Amichitka, an Aleutian Island, Alaska Territory.

Jim did his undergraduate work, including pre-med courses, at both the Florida State University (FSU), Tallahassee, and the University of Florida (UF), Gainesville. In 1954 he was admitted to Alabama Polytechnic Institute (now Auburn University). In 1958 he earned a Doctor of Veterinary Medicine degree, with honors.

Jim met Margaret Linda Hoadley at the Wesley Foundation at FSU. They married in Pinellas County, Florida, 16 March 1956. The Methodist Church was an integral part of their lives.

Jim was a scholarly, multi-talented and passionate man. He had a deep and abiding passion for his Faith, Family, Community Service and Genealogy. He loved family travel, wilderness camping and all creatures, large and small. He was a master gardener, citrus grower and a skilled furniture refinisher.

In his many years of genealogical research, Jim published two books. In the Library of Congress Card Catalog, we find: *Leonard Lock, ca. 1658-1711 and Descendants* © 1998 and *Kirkland family roots: Virginia, South Carolina, Henry County, Alabama* © 2002.

Additionally, Jim wrote and distributed a series of monographs under the title: *Pate Pioneers on the Pee Dee River,* 1987. This 1987 work was, in many respects, the precursor to this work.

After a protracted and difficult battle, Jim succumbed to leukemia on 27 August 2011. He is buried in The Florida National Cemetery near Bushell, Florida. His grave is marked with a typical military style grave marker, with three unique or notable inscriptions: At the top, a Wesleyan cross denoting Jim's Methodist denomination; at the very bottom, is engraved "DVM AUBURN '58" denoting Jim's academic and professional achievement; and above that is another engraving, which reads "OUR PATRIARCH". He was, in fact a Patriarch and mentor to many of us.

Joel Pate, Tallahassee, Florida

PREFACE

This report has two goals. First, to report information that this research has proved on the Pate Families involved. Second, to report what the writer thinks, assumptions, where proof is lacking on the families involved. Readers are cautioned to recognize that all claims are not proved. The justification for a report of this nature is found in the age and health of the writer. The years for research are past. It is time to report what is known and what is thought, for the use of future researchers.

The writer has searched for the origin of a great-grandmother, Caroline "Callie" (Pate) Mitchem (1861-1944) since 1980, some 31 years. Acknowledgement is granted that the intensity of the search has waxed and waned, but the focus has been constant. [See note below by Joel Pate.]

The Pate Family appears in records of the American colonies before the mid-17th Century. Available traditional records are insufficient to justify a report on the origin of the multiple lines of the Pate Family in later Colonial, or American, locations. A number of dedicated researchers have worked jointly and individually with the same results, finding that needed key records are not available.

A new resource has surfaced in the past decade, genetic genealogy, which is provided through DNA testing. The Pate DNA Project was founded by A. J. Pate in 2006, and it was quickly endorsed by the late Jinks Pate-Lee and Joel Pate, the two greatest genealogists in the history of the Pate Family. Their support played a major role in the rapid growth of the Project, which currently has over 220 members. Test results have already advanced Pate Family research, refuting some long-held beliefs while new research challenges have surfaced.

A sufficient number of Pate males have participated in the Pate DNA Project to provide significant information that is not available in traditional records. DNA testing, based on current knowledge, will not provide a family lineage. However, when combined with traditional genealogy, it will provide the information needed to prove some lineages. Some genealogical "dead ends" have now been opened. The results of this Project have greatly advanced our knowledge of Pate Family lineages. An example follows.

DNA testing has established that the three major Pate Family lines which can trace their ancestry to early colonial Virginia in the 17th century are not genetically related. Traditional genealogists and researchers had previously debated the nature of these relationships for decades.

One of these family lines is descended from Thoroughgood Pate who died in Chowan County, North Carolina, in 1713. He had emigrated to Virginia from England ca. 1656. He had lived in Virginia for about 40 years before moving to North Carolina by 1703.

The writer refers to these Virginia family groups as the "Thoroughgood Pate line" and the "James River line", for general identification purposes. Note is added that the James River line likely includes two other Pate Family lines.

Descendants of Thoroughgood Pate, as identified by traditional genealogy, have joined the Pate DNA Project, and they have a distinctive DNA profile which also identifies them through genetic genealogy. The other Pate Family lines have been similarly identified through DNA testing.

Thus, for the first time, we can definitively identify the descendants of Thoroughgood Pate. Further, it can be safely assumed that persons proven by traditional genealogy to be related to tested persons in the Project are also descendants of Thoroughgood Pate.

Traditional records prove Thoroughgood Pate had two sons, and this research identifies them as Charles Pate, who died circa ("ca.") 1769 in Old Dobbs County, North Carolina, and William Pate, who died in Lancaster County, South Carolina ca. 1775. A third son has long been suspected, John Pate, who died in Old Dobbs County, North Carolina ca. 1779. DNA testing on descendants of all three of these men now provides proof for their sibling relationship.

A national Pate Genealogical Convocation was held in Colonial Williamsburg, Virginia, in September 2008. The DNA information presented, as cited above, impressed the writer that a report could be written that would approach the "definitive" state. Thus, this report was launched. The writer's desire is to identify each person in seven generations in the line of Charles Pate d. ca. 1769, with less definition for the descendants of the other two brothers, William and John.

The results have been slow. Additional research was needed in some areas, while health and age issues slowed the project. Note needs to be made that health issues may limit the scope of the report. Perhaps others will be stimulated to continue this work.

The writer has been blessed with co-workers who have advanced the Pate Family knowledge and shared the results. No attempt will be made to list them because all such lists contain omissions. Efforts have been made to recognize most as their work is cited in the narration. Thanks go to all. The writer has completed comprehensive reports for families of other surnames and has noted that reports of this size and complexity are never the work of one person.

This report is presented with the best of intentions. It will prove lineages in some places and offer the writer's opinion of lineages in others. Readers should exercise caution in the use of the latter.

Dr. J. R. Peacock
June 19, 2011

Note by Joel Pate:

Caroline Clara "Callie" Pate 1861-1944, Jim Peacock's great-grandmother was a 4th great-granddaughter of Thoroughgood Pate 1660-1713 and Sarah Chevin 1662.
Her line of descent:
Thoroughgood Pate and Sarah Chevin
Charles Pate and Sarah Howell
Samuel Pate 1730-1795
Bennett Pate 1760
Samuel Pate 1800-1867 and Tirzah Ackridge
Isaiah Pate 1854-1920 and Alcey E. Bray 1836
Carolina Clara "Callie" Pate 1861-1944
+ Abraham W Mitchem
    Alcey Melvina Mitchem
    + David Lee Locke 1874-1950
        Grace Marie Locke 1907–1991
Grace Marie Locke first married Henry Nowling and had two sons with him, Jimmy Ray Nowling and Jack Henry Nowling. In 1938, she divorced Henry Nowling. She subsequently married Thomas S. Peacock, who adopted her son, Jimmy Ray Nowling, and changed his name to Jimmy Ray Peacock (J R Peacock, or Dr. Jim Peacock, DVM).

PROLOGUE

This book is the final legacy of Dr. Jim Peacock in Pate genealogy. It is a monumental work which will stand the test of time and will be an enduring reference and invaluable resource far beyond the lifetimes of all living today.

I first started exchanging emails with Jim in 2006, shortly after founding the Pate DNA Project, and only met him once in person at the Pate Genealogical Convocation in Colonial Williamsburg, Virginia, in 2008.

In May 2011, Jim wrote to me, after reviewing information I had sent him on family lines proven by Y-DNA testing in our Project: "You may be aware that this is the thing that induced me to return to my Pate files. DNA is resolving some questions. Actually, without your contact and information shared, I am sure all of my files would be in Auburn by this date." Before his death, he had donated his genealogical research to Auburn University Library in Auburn, Alabama.

We then exchanged many emails, almost daily, about DNA's disclosures and impact on Pate genealogy. In June 2011, Jim learned that his battle with leukemia was terminal and death was imminent. He wrote: "I do not wish to live this way, but if the medication will give me a few weeks to work, I would be appreciative. God's will isin effect If this comes to a head without more said, the family has no desire to pursue the manuscript you hold. You are free to decide if it is worthy of circulation in this format, otherwise trash it." This was absolutely unthinkable, so I responded: "I value your manuscript as an invaluable and irreplaceable treasure, especially for our Thoroughgood family line. I would be honored to be entrusted with its completion." I took this responsibility with no idea of the difficulties, frustrations, and disappointments that would follow. But those are all past and all the hopes for this book are now being realized.

At that time, Jim was two chapters short of completing his book and unsure if he could complete either. In an act of great courage and determination, he completed Chapter VII in early August, 80 pages in less than two months! During this time, he was often able to work only two or three hours a day, enduring much pain. In late July, his son Kenny had written me: "We're encouraging him to write. It gives him purpose, and the past few weeks he seems happiest when researching and writing." Jim died on August 27, 2011.

After Jim's death, I formed a book committee to oversee the finalization and publishing of the book. Carter Pate, Joel Pate, and Troy Pate agreed to serve on the committee. All subsequent decisions were made by majority votes of the committee, most if not all unanimous. They have been faithful members and steadfast friends all the way through publication.

The final chapter of the book had been left unfinished. The committee had entrusted two different persons in sequence to write this chapter, but after inordinate delays of nearly two years, neither produced a single word. It was at this low point that Joel Pate, the greatest living genealogist of the Pate family, volunteered to finish the chapter. This was particularly unselfish since his ancestry is not in the Thoroughgood Pate family line. Joel McMurray Pate was born in rural Randolph County, Alabama, in 1940, and he is a member of the Thomas Pate family line in the Pate DNA Project. After the chapter was done, the committee was able to move forward with proofreading and editing preceding indexing, and then publication. Much gratitude is owed to Joel for his efforts in completing this book.

Three members of the book committee are descendants of Thoroughgood Pate. But it is truly a remarkable and fortuitous coincidence that they are also each descended from a different son of Thoroughgood (his three known sons).

Our straight-line genealogies follow:

Carter Pate	
Charles Pate	1690 - 1769
Rev. Charles Pate	1729 - 1790
Shadrach Pate	1765 - 1837
Willoughby Pate	1790 - 1834
Nicholas Pate	1822 - 1867
James Henry Pate I	1860 - 1916
James Henry Pate II	1891 - 1942
James Henry Pate III	1926 -
Robert Carter Pate	1954, Wilmington, North Carolina

Troy Pate	
John Pate	1695 - 1779
William Pate	1740 - ? (unproven)
John Pate	1779 - 1830
Benjamin Allen Pate	1806 - 1870
William Henry Pate	1834 - 1915
Joseph Jones Pate	1868 - 1936
Earl Tidwell Pate	1897 - 1971
Edwin Bruce Pate	1947 - 1998
Edwin Troy Pate	1968, Irving, Texas

A. J. Pate	
William Pate	1698 - 1775
Thomas Pate	1755 – 1840 (unproven)
Newell Walton Pate	1811 - 1855
Thomas Benjamin Pate	1835 - 1924
John Benjamin Pate	1872 - 1952
Harlen Jayvan Pate	1905 - 1971
A. J. Pate	1937, Palestine, Texas

Many of the above early dates are speculative and estimated but based on best information available. They should not be used without further proof.

Thoroughgood Pate is proven as our common ancestor through Y-DNA testing in the Pate DNA Project, which places us in the same haplogroup. Through a few mutations in the DNA sequence, the Project has been able to further identify its members as descendants of one of Thoroughgood's three sons. This is an unexpected and very valuable benefit of DNA testing for this family line.

This same benefit is available to any Pate male who has reason to believe that he is a descendant of Thoroughgood Pate. Not only can this ancestry be confirmed by Y-DNA testing, but he will further discover which son of Thoroughgood is his direct ancestor.

A. J. Pate
Houston, Texas
November 1, 2017

Table Of Contents

I

Selected Pate Family Records from England

Available records support the claim that the Pate Family, or Families, in 17th Century Virginia had origins in England. As examples, estate proceedings for Richard Pate, who died in Virginia in 1657, and John Pate, who died in Virginia in 1672, are recorded in official court records of England. These records identify Virginia as the residence of both men and are sufficient proof that the Pate Family represented by them did originate in England. Another Pate Family, represented by Thoroughgood Pate, has been proved to have been staunch members of the Church of England in 17th Century Virginia. Further, Baptist records compiled in 1772 report a long heritage of Anglican Church membership for this family, to be cited in the report on that family.

This research did not pursue an in-depth search of English resources for the Pate Family. However, some records have been observed in published resources that provide background on some of the Pate Families of 17th Century Virginia. Further, the writer was gifted with the England research of Dr. Douglas Kelly in earlier years. The narration to follow is from those resources, and this research did not verify the resulting claims. The claims seem creditable and should be of interest to Pate Family researchers. Citations will be given so that persons with interest may acquire the appropriate records.

The will of Dame Jane Skipwith, written 20 October 1629 and published in *Virginia Gleanings in England* by Lothrop Withington, establishes a relationship between the Pate Family of central England and a number of other families. The will also appears in the *Virginia Historical Magazine*. Valuable footnotes follow the will. This noble Skipwith family resided in the village of Cotes in Leicestershire, England.

Other material is from a paper printed in "Transactions of the Leicestershire Architectural and Archaeological Society", (Vol. IV, 1878, pp. 264-267), Leicestershire, England. This contains Pate Family data from two sources. Zachariah Fenton wrote Pate and Smith genealogical data, as dictated by Lady Abigail Smith, widow of Sir Thomas Smith, Baronet, dated 14 March 1682. Abigail Smith was the daughter of Sir John Pate, who was born 1593 and died 1659.

The will of Edward Pate, of Leicestershire, England, was written 11 April 1597 and proved 18 June 1597. This Edward Pate was a great-grandfather of Lady Abigail Smith. The information she dictated to Zachariah Fenton is comparable to the family information in the will.

The lineage of the Pate and Skipwith families, as listed in these documents, has been placed into lineage charts that are attached to this narrative.

Several surnames appearing in the documents at hand are associated with the Pate Families of early Virginia, and serve to indicate a common origin. Those noted to date include Skipwith, Kemp, Cave, Wimberly, Ashton, Locke, Carr, and Dale.

The will of Dame Jane Skipwith has been an interpretation nightmare for Pate researchers. Study of the documents makes it possible to organize some of Dame Jane's many kin people into families and determine their relationship. Some are impossible because of limited information available at this time. The Dame creates a mass of confusion with the use of the titles of sons and daughters for in-laws, cousins for children of nieces and nephews, and brothers and sisters for in-laws. The actual relationships were well-known at the time the will was written, but over 380 years later, they create difficulty for the modern-day interpreter.

An interpretation and analysis of the will of Dame Jane Skipwith is offered here, with highlighted cautions that errors may exist.

The Pate genealogical information, as given by Lady Abigail Smith, identifies her father, Sir John Pate, and his brother, Edward Pate, as husbands of two daughters of Sir William Skipwith, who married 1) Margaret Cave and 2) Jane Roberts. The latter was Dame Jane Skipwith, testator of the will in study.

Sir John Pate married Elizabeth, and Edward Pate married Anne, daughters of Sir William Skipwith, who died 1610. These daughters were from the first marriage of Sir William. Thus, Dame Jane's relationship to the wives of John and Edward Pate was stepmother, by today's nomenclature.

2

Dame Jane refers to these Pate individuals as her sons John Pate and Edward Pate and her daughters Elizabeth Pate and Anne Pate. The extant records dictated by Abigail Smith provide the basis to interpolate the true relationship. The notes from Lady Abigail state that Edward Pate (who married Anne Skipwith) died without children, and none are implied in Dame Jane's will.

The notes from Lady Abigail indicate that John Pate (m. Elizabeth Skipwith) had five sons and three daughters, who died young and unmarried, and three daughters named Abigail, Frances, and Anne who lived to maturity. Anne was a daughter with Lettice Dilkes, his second wife, their only child. John also had two sons who lived to maturity, but died young and unmarried. John was appointed as a baronet by King Charles I, but with no living male heirs his baronetcy became extinct upon his death. She notes that the wife, Elizabeth, died 17 August 1628, and Sir John married 2) Lettice, daughter of Sir Thomas Dilkes of Maxtock in Warrick. She does not assign children to the respective wives, nor does she name the sons of John. However, the two sons were Henry and Edward, both graduates of Cambridge University and died in their late thirties ca. 1650. John and Elizabeth were married 15 years and had 12 children, as noted on their gravestone.

This point is indicated because Dame Jane's will recognized her son (step-son-in-law), Sir John Pate, and in immediate order, names "My godson Henry Pate .... Edward Pate .... Charles Pate .... Elizabeth Pate .... Amy Pate..." She then proceeds to other surnames. The term godson is only used in reference to Henry Pate. It is of interest to note that the lineage chart on John Pate of Brin reports that he had a grandson named Henry Pate born 1592. That Henry was a cousin to Dame Jane's step-son-in-law, Sir John Pate. The names of Edward, Charles, Elizabeth, and Amy, as listed above, may recognize children of this Henry. Other possibilities are endless.

Dame Jane leaves no legacy to the daughters of Elizabeth (Skipwith) Pate, first wife of Sir John Pate. The only mention of the "daughter Elizabeth Pate" is when she assigns a waistcoat, given her by "daughter Elizabeth Pate", to a niece, Elizabeth Bradshaw. This is as would be expected because Elizabeth Pate died 17 August 1628 and the Dame's will was written 20 October 1629.

Perhaps these Pate names in the will may be children of another Pate Family. That Dame Jane did not name all of John's children is evidenced by the absence of Lady Abigail in the will. She was born 1624, some five years before the will waswritten.

The Pate names of Henry, Edward, and Charles were very prominent in Colonial Virginia and North Carolina. More research needs to be done before placing these names in Dame Jane's will with definition. Information to follow will show that Edward Pate of Eye-Kettleby died 1593 had a son named John Pate, of Brin. This John lived in Leicestershire and had a grandson named Henry Pate, as noted earlier. This Henry may have been the godson of Dame Jane Skipwith. Future research into this area of England may shed some light on the origin and connections of these Pate Families and names.

To understand the relationship of the many surnames listed as kinspeople in the will requires study of Dame Jane's origin. This is listed in the footnotes to the will.

The Dame was the daughter of John Roberts of Wallaston, County Northhampton, who was married to Cassandra, daughter of William Apreece of Washingly, County Huntington. This explains the Uncle Edmund Apreece, named in the will. He would have been her mother's brother, a true uncle by today's nomenclature.

Cassandra (Apreece) Roberts had three later marriages: 2) Adlard Welby of Godfrey, 3) Peter Ashton of Holmear Grange in Spaulding, County Lincoln, and 4) Robert Carr of Aswarby, County Lincoln. The will indicates there were no children of the last marriage.

Dame Jane mentioned only one person named Roberts, Richard Roberts. Perhaps he was a brother born of the same marriage as she, Cassandra Apreece to John Roberts. She does not state a relationship to Richard Roberts.

She names three brothers named Welby -- John, Sir William, and Richard. They would have been half-brothers, of the marriage of her mother, Cassandra, to Adlard Welby.

The brother John Welby appears to have been the father of the Welby nephews in the will named Vincent and William. He appears to have been the father of the Welby nieces named Elizabeth, Jane, Cassandra, and Margery Smith. The brother, Richard Welby, appears to have been the father of the Welby nephews named Adlard, Richard, John, and Edward. The Welby nieces, Dorothy, Elizabeth, Martha, Anne, Frances, Jane, and Susan West, are named as, or appear to be, daughters of Richard.

The brother, William Welby, appears to have had one son named William. Likewise, only one daughter, Susan Josyln, appears in the will. Susan Josyln is interesting. Two given names were not common practice at that time. The name Josyln indicates a

4

marriage to a Josyln. Dame Jane names Susan's daughter, Susan Locke, and a son, Francis Locke. Given the multiple marriages shown by this will, it is easy to assume Susan married 1) a Locke and 2) a Josyln.

The name Francis Locke was popular in a family of that surname who emigrated from England to Pennsylvania, and then to Rowan County, North Carolina. A Francis Locke was a prominent Patriot officer in the Revolutionary War.

Dame Jane does not mention brothers or sisters with the Ashton surname. The footnotes to the will state she had a half-brother, Walter Ashton, and that the nephews in the will, Peter, Edmund, and Walter Ashton, were sons of this Walter. Further, she had two Ashton half-sisters. Mary Ashton married Hawes Apreece and accounts for some of the Apreece cousins. Isabell Ashton married John Bradshaw and accounts for the Bradshaw cousins.

The mention of Dame Jane's brothers and sisters Blewitt probably represent the marriage of a sister or half-sister to a Blewitt. The nieces and nephews Blewitt would be children of such a marriage. There is no record at hand to prove this assumption, nor those immediately following.

The large numbers of Ashhursts, a nephew and several cousins, are also probably children of a sister or half-sister who married an Ashhurst. Likewise, the other surnames given for nieces, nephews, and cousins -- Ives, Wimberly, Hixon, Townly, Barnard, Morrow, and Garyse -- should represent the marriages of Dame Jane's brothers and sisters or half-brothers and half-sisters.

The Dame named a brother, Henry Skipwith. This Henry may represent a brother-in-law. However, the available Skipwith records do not list a brother, so named, for her husband, Sir William Skipwith. Sir William was the son of Henry Skipwith, and he named a son Henry. It would be expected that he had a brother named Henry but a record of this has not been found.

The importance of the documents cited, and the analysis given are emphasized by the name of Richard Pate. Richard Pate died in Virginia 1657. His estate in Gloucester County, Virginia, was administered by his nephew, John Pate. Richard's estate in Lancaster County, Virginia, was administered by Sir Grey Skipwith, according to *Virginia Gleanings in England* by Lothrop Withington. Sir Grey Skipwith was a step-son of Dame Jane Skipwith. There is reason to believe this Richard Pate is the same as Richard Pate, apprenticed at Birmingham, England in 1619 at age 18, as shown in the lineage chart of the Pate Family.

THE LINEAGE OF THE ANCIENT PATE FAMILY OF LEICESTERSHIRE, ENGLAND

1. Edward Pate of Eye-Kettleby, Leicestershire; b. 1503, d. 1593; m. Catherine [?], b. ca. 1510, d. 1593. Served as Master of the Mint to Henry VIII (unproven).
    2. Edward of Eye-Kettleby, b. ca. 1530, d. 19 April 1597; m. Catherine [?], b. ca. 1530, d. 29 September 1593.
        3. Henry -- b. ca. 1553, d. as infant
        3. Elizabeth – b. ca. 1554; m. ca. 1571, George Starkie of Tonge, Leicestershire.
        3. Edmund – b. ca. 1555.
        3. Dorothy – b. ca. 1556; m. [?] Harmon, b. ca. 1562.
        3. Henry - b. 1557, d. 28 February 1603; m. 9 May 1589, Bridget Bussy, b. 8 January 1566, d. ca. 1595; daughter of John Bussy of Haydor, Lincoln County.
            4. Elizabeth, b. 25 August 1591.
            4. Edward - b. 17 August 1592, m. 26 June 1611, Anne Skipwith, b. ca. 1585; daughter of Sir William Skipwith of Cotes, Leicestershire; died without children.
            4. John, Sir, baronet, of Sysonby – b. 6 September 1593, d. 1659, London; m. 5 October 1613, 1) Elizabeth Skipwith, b. 1591, d. 17 August 1628; daughter of Sir William Skipwith of Cotes, sister to Anne, his brother's wife; m. ca. 1639, 2) Lettice Dilkes, b. ca. 1597, d. p. 1659; eldest daughter of Sir Thomas Dilkes of Maxtock Castle, Warwick County.
                5. Henry – b. ca. 1615, d. ca. 1655; d. unmarried. BA, Cambridge, 1638.
                5. Edward – b. 1618, d. ca. 1650; d. unmarried. BA, Cambridge, 1639.
                5. Abigail – b. 1624, d. 25 October 1691; living at Sysonby 1681 as a widow - co-heiress with sister Frances; m. Sir Thomas Smith of Hatherton, Chester County, b. 1622, d. 8 May 1675, London.
                5. Frances – b. 31 March 1627, d. 15 July 1693; m. 11 February 1657, Viscount Charles Carrington,

> of Wooten Wawen, Warwick County, b. ca. 1624, d. 1706. Co-heiress with sister Abigail.
>
> 5. Five sons and three daughters, died young and unmarried. Birthyears and names unknown.
>
> 5. Anne – b. ca. 1640, d. ca. 1662, unmarried. Only child with Lettice Dilkes. (Note 2)
>
> 4. Thomas – b. ca. 1594, d. 1645 in combat at Burton-upon-Trent. 3. John – b. ca. 1558.
>
> 3. Mary – b. ca. 1559, d. bef. 1597; m. 1) Edward Overinge, b. ca. 1557; m. 2) James Wood, b. ca. 1557, d. 1629.
>
> 3. Anne – b. ca. 1561; m. 5 January 1585, Richard Mitton of Shrewsbury in Shropshire, b. ca. 1560.
>
> 3. Ursula – b. ca. 1563; m. Lewis Mitton of Shrewsbury, Shropshire, b. ca. 1561.
>
> 3. Margaret – b. ca. 1565; m. William Atkins, b. ca. 1563.
>
> 3. Frances – b. ca. 1566.

2. John, of Brin, Leicestershire; b. ca. 1535, d. 1588; m. [He]len Saltmarsh, b. ca. 1537; daughter of Thomas Saltmarsh of Epping, Essex County.

> 3. Edward, of Brin - b. 1560, d. bef. 1625; m. Anne Blount, b. ca. 1562, d. 1640; daughter of William Blount of Osbaston, Leicestershire.
>
> > 4. Henry - b. 21 May 1592, d. 1662, MA, Oxford, 1615, m. Jane Hudson, b.ca. 1594; daughter of [?] Hudson of Warwick County.
> >
> > 4. Mary – b. 6 May 1593, d. bef. 1619.
> >
> > 4. John – 1 September 1594, d. 1619. MA, Oxford, 1618.
> >
> > 4. Thomas, of London – b. 2 February 1596, d. 1644; m. 1631, Margaret Jones, b. ca. 1597, d. p. 1651.
> >
> > > 5. Edward, of Ludgate Hill – b. ca. 1632, d. ca. 1700, m. (unknown).
> > >
> > > > 6. Thomas – b. ca. 1652, d. 1703 Virginia. (Note 3)
> > >
> > > 5. John – b. 25 May 1632, d. October 1672 Virginia. MA, Oxford 1652.
> >
> > 4. Edward, of London; b. 17 April 1597, d. 1654; m. (unknown).
> >
> > > 5. John, Rev. – b. 25 May 1632, d. 4 July 1690; m. Elizabeth [?], b. ca. 1634, d. p. 1690.
> > >
> > > > 6. Edward – b. ca. 1657, d. ca. 1731.

6. Thomas – b. ca. 1659, d. 21 February 1723; m.(unknown). 7. John – b. ca. 1685.
   7. Elizabeth – b. ca. 1687.
6. Elizabeth – b. 1 September 1661.
6. Judeth – b. 25 July 1664.
6. Margaret – b. 4 August 1667; m. 11 February 1685, Benjamin Raynor, b. ca. 1660.
6. Anne – b. 29 May 1670.
6. Alice – b. 11 May 1673; m. 13 April 1693, John Dalloway.
5. Henry – b. 1638, d. 29 June 1705; m. Mary [?], b. ca. 1640, d. 1702.
4. James – b. 14 May 1598, d. 1619.
4. Timothy - b. 10 June 1599.
4. Richard - b. 17 January 1601, d. 1657, Virginia. Apprentice at Birmingham, England, 1619. (Note 1)
4. Ellen – b. 24 April 1603.
4. Rebecca – b. 23 September 1604.
4. Anne – b. 15 December 1605.
4. Katherine – b. 16 August 1607, d. 1619.
4. Elizabeth – b. 18 March 1608.
3. Thomas, Esquire - b. ca. 1562, d. 1609; m. Mary Nevell, b. ca. 1564, d. 1632; daughter of Herry Nevell of Grove, Nottinghamshire.
4. Edmund – b. ca. 1587.

NOTES:

1. All research indicates that this Richard Pate emigrated to Colonial Virginia ca. 1636, where he patented 1141 acres for a tobacco plantation in 1650 in Gloucester County.

2. John Pate emigrated to Colonial Virginia in 1651 and inherited his uncle Richard's plantation, adding an additional 1000 acres over the years.

3. Thomas Pate emigrated to Colonial Virginia in 1672 and inherited the plantation that same year on the death of his uncle John.

4. The above notes were first speculated by the late Jinks Pate-Lee, one of the greatest genealogists of the Pate Family. Subsequent research strongly supports her conclusion.

5. There is no known kinship between this family and Thoroughgood Pate.

II

THE PATE FAMILY IN COLONIAL VIRGINIA, 17th CENTURY

An attempt to identify members of any family in 17th Century Virginia must include research of land grant records. Each person who arrived in early Virginia should have created a land grant record. Those who paid their transportation should have received a land grant, and those for whom transportation was paid by another resulted in a land grant for their sponsor. The passage of so many years certainly results in some loss of records, but the Virginia land grants remain the largest source for the names of early settlers in Virginia.

These records are of significant value to researchers of Virginia families, and a cursory background is indicated for the proper interpretation of these records. Persons with more interest in the subject will find the forewords to *Cavaliers and Pioneers* in several volumes to be of value.

The volume of land records held by the Virginia State Archives is impressive. The foreword to *Cavaliers and Pioneers*, by Nell Marion Nugent, Vol. 1, reports that the holdings include 45 volumes of Colonial Patents and 22-1/2 volumes of Northern Neck Grants. The latter pertain to the Fairfax Proprietary; few proprietary records pertain to the 17th Century. The writer reviewed the Northern Neck records in earlier years and recorded only one Pate entry, the will of Thomas Odonell, in which Thur [sic] Pate and Thomas Lund are legatees. This record will be discussed in the narrative on "The Life and Times of Thoroughgood Pate ".

Other resources have been used to supplement the Colonial Grants, as Pate immigrants to Virginia were compiled. These include *Early Virginia Immigrants,* George Greer; *Virginia Colonial Abstracts,* Beverly Fleet, and a number of books by Peter Wilson Coldham. Periodicals found to be helpful in Pate research include

The William and Mary Quarterly and the *Virginia Magazine of Genealogy and History.*

The original governing body for the Virginia Settlement, The London Company, determined that no land would be assigned to Planters or Adventurers until seven years had elapsed. Three types of landowners evolved after the waiting period: the Company, private adventurers, and individual planters. The second group resulted in the large holdings, identified as "Hundreds" and plantations of large size. These tracts were purchased and have been referred to as "Treasury Grants". The individual planters received land based on the shares the individual held in The London Company. Shares cost 12 pounds, 10 shillings, and each shareholder could receive 100 acres per share owned. They also received 2 shares for each person they transported to Virginia.

The London Company fell onto hard times, and the Crown reclaimed the Virginia Proprietary in 1625. The system for distributing land changed. Headright grants were set in place, and this system governed land distribution for the years 1625 to 1699. The term "headright" was used because land was distributed at the rate of 50 acres for each "head" that entered the Colony. The 50 acres were patented to the immigrant if he/she paid for the transportation. The person who paid for the transportation of another received 50 acres for each person transported. Those who came in bondage were entitled to 50 acres, after their indenture was served.

The Treasury Grants of the early years, which resulted in the large tracts known as Hundreds, no longer existed. The only way for wealthy persons to acquire large tracts was by paying for the transportation of a large number of immigrants. One writer claimed that the large landed estates, so characteristic of 18th Century Virginia, did not occur until Treasury Grants were reinstated in 1699.

Efforts to by-pass the intent of the headright system invited fraud. A ship captain could load with emigrants from the streets of London and collect 50 acres of land for each head when he arrived in Virginia. The immigrants could be sold to a planter who needed labor, and some planters then claimed another 50 acres for each head purchased. Controls were inadequate to prevent names from appearing on multiple lists.

An example of names appearing on two lists occurs in two grants to John Pate. He patented 300 acres in Gloucester County on 22 March 1666, and the persons cited for headright land included Jno.

King, Elizabeth White, Mary Bates, and George Stainer. The same four persons were among the headrights for his patent for 1000 acres on the Piscataway River in the Northern Neck on 31 December 1662.

One set of figures viewed in this research equated the cost of transporting a person to the value of 50 acres of land.

Claims were not filed chronologically. The earliest extant patent appears on page 109 of Land Book I, not on page 1. The records are not complete. Records were lost in disasters such as Indian massacres and fires. It is reported that a Charles City Record Book has record of a number of patents for the years 1655 to 1665. None of these are recorded in the land patent books. Certainly, the wear and tear of time limited the survival of some records.

Headrights may have actually entered the Colony long before the patent date. Archival personnel have cited periods of 15-20 years before some patents were claimed. An example was cited of a planter who claimed headright land for three wives at one time, imported over a period of years. One can only wonder if the man had accumulated all of the wives he wanted or all of the land he wanted!

Escheatment of land, or the return of land to the Crown, was common. The patentee had no time limit to file for the patent. Nor were they limited in the use of land vouchers. Many sold them, gambled with them, devised them to heirs, etc. However, once the holder of the certificate, or voucher, received the patent, he had three years to seat on the land and pay quit rents. Failure of either resulted in escheatment of the land by the Crown. Further, land previously patented was returned to the Crown when a land holder died without an heir-at-law or when he was convicted of a felony. Escheatment resulted in a term, "Escheatment by Inquisition", that will be discussed in the report on Thoroughgood Pate.

This background on the headright land system is of value. But, perhaps, it is of more practical value to note four items in the land records. First, the name of the patentee is always listed. This is the person who paid for the transportation of the headright, or the one who acquired the patent rights from one who was the sponsor. The headright may have had no personal relationship with the patentee. Second, the name of the headright, which is of value if the person was your ancestor. The third item is the location of the land in the patent, which may or may not be informative. The headright may never have visited the land or lived near the land. Fourth, the year the patent was granted establishes a date by which the headright was in Virginia, but it was not necessarily the date the headright entered the Colony.

The Crown ordered a census be made of all persons in Virginia in 1625. No Pate was on that enumeration. Thus, it can be said that all Pates arrived after 1625 and before the date on the patent. Someone has recently reported that John Peate was listed on this record. Perhaps this research missed his name when reviewing this record in past years. However, the name failed to come up when inserted, recently, into the Internet access to this census. And he was likely not a Pate in any case.

The survival rate for initial settlers was not good. Mary Lewis Ulmer, a past director of Clayton Genealogical Library, Houston, Texas, led seminars on Virginia research in past years. Her figures for survival in early Virginia are appalling. Between 1607 and 1616, 1,650 persons came to the Colony. One thousand of these died, and 300 returned to England. Only 350 remained in the Colony. One can only wonder of the living conditions in England that prompted persons to continue to migrate to the colonies in the face of such survival records.

Researchers must recognize that the presence of a name on the headright lists does not provide assurance that the person survived or was survived by heirs. Richard Fowler was a Pate researcher of past years. He published his Fowler family and addressed the number of early Fowler immigrants who were not survived by heirs. He identified 12 Fowler men in 17th Century Virginia. Only three of these were survived by heirs, and one of the three had no male heirs to perpetuate the surname. He cited reasons for the absence of heirs descending from so many persons, including the high incidence of unfamiliar illnesses, like malaria; the hostility of the natives; the spread-out character of plantation life; and the absence of women.

Certainly, the male to female ratio needs to be noted. One report stressed that the ratio of 6 males to 1 female existed early in the 17th Century. Numerous writers have noted the short widowhood of Virginia widows. Wills of deceased husbands frequently limited estates for wives to their widowhood; they lost the inheritance if or when they remarried. Regardless, widows commonly found their way into another marriage because the male to female ratio was in their favor.

The majority of immigrants to the Colonies were young. Ms. Ulmer, in her seminars, cited 18 as an average age. Indentured servants were commonly 14-16 years of age. Patentees of land grants had to be 21 years, males had to be 21 years to sell land, make a will, to sue or be sued, or make a bond to marry. However, birth certificates were not required! Males over 14 could legally own land, serve on juries, if they were free holders, and witness documents. Only English citizens could own land, but citizenship appears to have been easy to acquire.

There does not appear to have been a flow of settlers into Virginia from the colonies located south of Virginia in the 1600s. No Pates appear to have entered Virginia from the Carolinas. Movement to and from Maryland was common, and Pates were in early Maryland. The possibility of Pates in Virginia having origin in Maryland warrants the following cursory review of the family name in Maryland.

The Crown granted Maryland to the Calvert family as a proprietary in 1632. The Calverts were Catholic, and desired to establish a Colony in the New World where persons of their faith could live and worship without harassment. Charles Calvert stressed complete religious freedom for all who came to his Colony.

The Church of England, the Anglican Church, held tight control over Virginia. A number of Virginia Protestants, of faith other than Anglican, were attracted to Maryland policies and moved. Many of them returned to Virginia.

Early Settlers of Maryland, Gus Skordas, provides land records of immigrants to Maryland. These records differ from Virginia records in that the date cited is the date of arrival in the Colony. These records provide the names of seven persons named Pate in the 17th Century. One, William Pate, came as an indentured servant in 1665. He completed his indenture in 1688 and was eligible for a headright land grant. The other settlers paid for their transportation. They arrived as follows: John Pate - 1663, Nicholas Pate - 1667, Roger Pate - 1671, and Richard Pattee with his wife Elizabeth and daughter Lydia - 1672. The Pattee spelling is assumed to have been a corruption of Pate.

This John Pate was living in St. Mary's County, 18 February 1674, when he was the legatee of the will of Henry Barristis. John was involved in the Maryland spin-off of Bacon's Rebellion in Virginia in 1676. He was charged with inciting Indians to attack settlers in Maryland and was hanged. Any children are unknown. William Pate received payment from the Cecil County Estate of Thomas Carleton, 9 October 1677. He was deceased by 3 May 1680, when his estate was inventoried. No record of heirs was found in this research. No further information is available on Roger Pate or Nicholas Pate.

Richard Pattee did not appear in this cursory review of other Maryland records. Note needs to be made of the Pattey family in early records of Old Rappahannock County, Virginia. The origin of this Virginia family is unknown. Additional comments follow later.

Two quotations from historians of past years need to be recognized. It is not the intent of the writer to discredit the report of either. In reality, both have reputations that would be hard to tarnish by an amateur genealogist.

Dr. Phillip Bruce published several Virginia works. One examined Virginia social life in the 17th Century. Dr. Bruce recognized the Pate Family of Gloucester County, Virginia. He reported that descendants moved away, and the loss of records precludes a discussion of the family lineage. We do not have all of the answers, but the records on hand indicate that far more is known about the Gloucester County Pate Family than Dr. Bruce anticipated.

John Ben Pate, in his *American Geneology* [sic] *of the Pate Family,* credited Dr. Lyon G. Tyler with the claim that all Virginia Pates descended from Major Thomas Pate of Gloucester County, Virginia. Dr. Tyler was a learned and talented person. Perhaps someone attributed this claim to him in error. Research tells us that about ten Pates preceded the arrival of this Thomas Pate to Virginia.

This research has identified 17 or 18 Pate names in Virginia records before 1700. A list of these names, in the chronological order of their first appearance in records, follows, with comments and records on each. The list of records is not all-inclusive. Additional records would be redundant, and not add further definition to this project.

1. Richard Pate - 23 September 1636.
    Richard was a headright for Walter Hatcher, who patented land on the James River. Richard patented several tracts of land on the York River and Poropotank Creek/River in the area known as Gloucester County today.

    He was a member of House of Burgesses in 1653.

    Preogative Court of Canterbury, Administration Book 1657: Letters of Administration on estate of Richard Pate, late in Virginia, issued to John Pate, his brother Edward's son.

Sir Grey Skipwith, the Administrator for estate of Richard Pate in Lancaster County, Virginia, was succeeded by John Pate.

Lineage chart for John Pate of Brin, Leicestershire, England, indicates Richard Pate was a grandson of John of Brin. His father was Edward Pate who married Anne Blount.

Richard Pate was apprenticed to Birmingham, England, in 1619, at 18 years of age.

2. William Pate - 25 October 1637.

Francis Fowler patented 1,000 acres of land in James City, Virginia. The land was located on the west side of Juring Creek. Headrights included William Pate. This research failed to locate additional records on this man.

3. John Pate - 10 October 1651.

Edward Welch patented land on north side of North River on Mockjack Bay. Head- rights included John Pate.

He was again listed as a headright on 16 April 1653 when Jasper Hogkinson patented 50 acres on the Eastern branch of Daniell Tanners Creek. Perhaps these represent a return to England and reentry to the Colony. However, note was made earlier of the use of four people as headrights on two grants to John Pate, who appears to have never left the Colony.

John was the heir-at-law of Richard Pate in 1657.

John acquired the estate of Richard and expanded the holdings. He acquired tracts of land, including land in Old Rappahannock County, New Kent County, King George County, and the Gloucester County area of Poropotank River and York River. Just as John Pate had inherited the estate of Richard Pate, Thomas Pate inherited the estate of John Pate.

Wilson Cary acquired the 1,141 acres that had been patented to Richard Pate and Wingfield Webb after the death of John Pate, Thomas Pate's son in 1706. Cary married Sally Pate, daughter of John Pate and granddaughter of Thomas Pate d. 1703.

John served on the Virginia Council of State, members appointed by the Crown. *English Estates of American Colonists*, by Peter W. Coldham: John Pate of Virginia, bachelor, administration to the brother, Edward Pate (March 1673).

John died without children in 1672. One official Virginia record said he had a widow out of the country.

8 November 1672, Thomas Pate, of Virginia, son of Edward Pate of London, was granted administration on his uncle's estate. Securities were Richard Lee and John Armistead.

17 March 1673, General Court Orders, Inventory of the estate of John Pate: Value of 1221 pounds, 12 shillings, and 23,714 pounds of tobacco.

A professional researcher of earlier years reported another John Pate in 17th Century Virginia records. This man reportedly died in Middlesex County, Virginia 1720. He left a will dated 2 December 1720--7 March 1720, Will Book B 1713-1734, pages 173-174. This will have been read by the writer, and the testator is not John Pate. The name is clearly John Pace. Other records show families named Pate and Pace resided in Middlesex County in this time frame. Any reference readers may see to a will for John Pate in this county, late 17th or early 18th Century should be disregarded.

4. Henry Pate, Elizabeth Pate, Katherine Pate -- 25 March 1656.

The assumption is offered that Elizabeth Pate was the wife of Henry, and Katherine Pate was their daughter. Records to follow support the claim that Henry and Elizabeth were husband and wife.

The three Pates were headrights of Henry Soanes, who patented land in New Kent County on this date. A Tho. Thorowgood was also a headright.

16 April, 1657 - Henry Pate ordered to testify in court, Charles County, Maryland. Additional information will be provided in the following narrative.

22 October 1665 - Henry Pate and Elizabeth Pate were headrights of Christopher Lunn, who patented land in Stafford County. Records show that this Pate Family had a close association with the Lunn/Lund family.

22 December 1682 - Henry Pate and Elizabeth Pate were headrights of Matthew Whitfield, who patented land in Lower Norfolk County, at the head of the South Branch of Elizabeth River in the woods called Sandy Hutton.

Westmoreland County Court Minutes -

Henry Pate registered his mark 14 February 1660.

Henry Pate was one of the Church Wardens for Potomac Parish in Westmore- land County. He served on jury duty and was a respected witness for Lunn family documents.

16

1664 - Rights were granted to a number of persons, including Henry Pate on 3 March 1664. Henry Pate owned land between the Potomac and the Rappahannock Rivers of Westmoreland County.

Will of Thomas Lunn - 29 January 1660/14 February 1661 - Lunn was a merchant. Robert Lunn and William Lunn were his brothers. Christopher Lunn/Lund was his nephew.

Henry Pate was devised the use of the house and land for three years. He was to manage the Lund cattle.

Henry Pate and Thoroughgood Pate owed Lunn money, probably for goods purchased from the merchant.

22 October 1697 - Malachy Thurston patented 200 acres of land in Lower Norfolk County, escheated from Henry Pate by Inquisition.

5. Thoroughgood Pate

1 February 1657 - York County Deeds, Wills, etc. - Inventory of Giles Mode, deceased estate - Thoroughgood Pate and two money debts.

24 February 1658 - Dr. Francis Haddon against estate of Thoroughgood Pate (Haddon had married widow of Giles Mode)...said Pate departed from country. Same date - Thomas Ballard against Thoroughgood Pate - asks security of 361 pounds of tobacco.

12 May 1658 - Charles City Court Orders - Thomas Lignon sued by Howell Pryse (Was Pryse same as Prid/Pritt?) for escape of Thoroughgood Pate, a prisoner.

29 January 1660/14 February 1661 - Will of Thomas Lund, Westmoreland County. Thoroughgood Pate owed accounts to Lund, a merchant. Henry Pate also owed debts and was a legatee of the will.

30 October 1669 - William Taylor patented 1,000 acres in Accomack County. Headrights include Thoroughgood Pate (several other names on this list had been in Virginia several years - David Carr, Thomas Prosser, Thomas Bayly/Baily, Edward Henderson, Thomas Powell.) William Taylor was Sheriff of Old Rappahannock County when Thoroughgood Pate witnessed will of Robert Prid.

23 January 1684/4 February 1685 - Thoroughgood Pate and Jeremiah Thornton witnessed will of Robert Prid. Both proved

the will in court. Thoroughgood Pate signed as "Thorough Good Pate"; Thornton made a mark.

22 August 1682 - Will of Thomas O'Donnell, Stafford County - devised 100 acres to Christopher Lund, 50 acres to "Thur. Pate" and "what he owes me". 11 February 1692- Petitioned Stafford County Court for possession of the 50 acres devised to him by the Will of Thomas Odonell; Court granted wish.

6. Robert Pate - 26 March 1661.

Patent issued to Robert Taliafero and Lawrence Smith for 6300 acres in Rappahannock County. Headrights include Robert Pate.

No additional information available.

7. Mary Pate - 26 June 1663.

Patent to John Martyn for 268 acres in Sittenburne Parish on the north side of the Rappahannock River. Headrights include Mary Pate. There may be some significance to the sponsor of Mary. The Martyns, Kemps, Skipwiths, and Pates had an association that originated in England.

18 March 1662 - 300 acres patented to Roger Perfitt 31 March 1660 and by him given by will to Mary Pate.

8. Alexander Pate - 15 April 1667.

Patent to Edward Humston in Stafford County, 337acres. Headrights include Alexander Pate.

7 August 1667 - Patent to Will Porter in Surry County, 432 acres. Headrights include Alexander Pate.

9. Hannah Pate - 2 October 1676.

Apprenticed in Bristol, England to go to Virginia aboard the vessel *Francis and Mary*, bound to Richard Milshaw for 4 years.

10. Thomas Pate - Died in Virginia, York County, will dated 7 April 1703/25 October 1703, York Deeds and Wills #12, 1702-1706, page 151, more information later. March 1673 - John Pate had a brother Edward, who relinquished administration on estate of John. Thomas succeeded Edward as administrator. See discussion under John Pate No. 3, preceding this entry, for more on the relationships of John Pate of Virginia, Edward Pate of

England and Thomas Pate. Became known as Major Thomas Pate and Colonel Thomas Pate, of Gloucester County.

Some, perhaps all, of his children recorded in Abingdon Parish Registry of Gloucester County.

Served in numerous public offices - House of Burgesses, Justice of Peace, etc. Owned a ferry and ordinary in Yorktown on the York River.

He was the Thomas Pate who purchased land from John Soaper in Old Rappahannock County.

He survived the wrath of Governor Berkeley despite providing shelter to the dying Nathaniel Bacon in Bacon's Rebellion.

Complete Book of Immigrants 1661-1695, Coldham. 16 July 1687 - Deposition of Benjamin Bartlett of London, Gent'l., age 37, swore that Thomas Pate of Poropotank, Gloucester County, Virginia, Merchant, deceased, became indebted by Deed of 19 October 1683 to his father Edward Pate, London, a merchant, from Lord Mayor's Court of London.... Note: The abstract reports Thomas Pate of Gloucester County was a son of Edward Pate of London and died. Perhaps the deposition should have said Edward, the father died! A recently shared item is of value here. Lord Francis Howard was the Royal Governor of Virginia in the late 1600s. His papers at the Virginia State Library include a letter he wrote to Edward Pate, a merchant in London. Footnotes to the letter identify Thomas Pate of Gloucester County, Virginia as a son of this Edward Pate. Further, John Pate, formerly of Virginia, was a brother to this Edward Pate.

11. Elice (Alice?) Pate - 1 June 1678.

Timo. Carter patented 1,000 acres in New Kent County. Headrights include Elice Pate. No additional information.

12. Edward Pate - 16 April 1683 - Mrs. Elizabeth Smith patented 400 acres in St. Stephens Parish, New Kent County. Headrights include Edward Pate.

24 March 1725 - Edward Pate patented 150 acres in Isle of Wight County on south Side of Nottaway River for 15 shillings (apparently a Treasury Grant).

Books by Peter Wilson Coldham cite one Edward Pate as a reported shipper from London to Virginia.

13. James Pate - 23 November 1687.

Military census of Middlesex County – persons capable to serve as footmen and find themselves in arms, includes James Pate.

27 June 1687 - James Pate married Elizabeth Eddington, Christ Church Parish Registry, Middlesex County.

5 October 1691 - Middlesex County - James Pate/Pates gifted a horse to Thomas Thompson, Jr., son of Thomas Thompson, Sr. of Bland Neck, Middlesex County. 11 November 1695 - Middlesex deed - Matthew Kemp to James Pate, 60 acres, part of land where Kemp lived at mouth of Bland's Creek. (This land was part of 900 acres Sir Grey Skipwith conveyed to his daughter-in-law, Elizabeth Kemp.) Records of the Church of Jesus Christ of Latter-Day Saints report Grey Skipwith b. 23 January 1623 in Leicestershire, England, who married Elizabeth Arundel and died in Middlesex County, Virginia, was a son of Henry and Amy (Kemp) Skipwith. Others say he was a son of Sir William Skipwith.

14. Thomas Patty - 2 May 1688.

Old Rappahannock County - Judgment granted to Capt. George Taylor against estate of Thomas Patty, estate in hands of James Harrison.

3 November 1672 - Tho. Patty witnessed document for Charles Tomason and Thos. Pannell.

18 July 1675 - Tho. Patty's land adjoined land of Jno. White.

Richmond County Moore Records (Harbin Moore) - Thomas Patty, Jr. married a daughter of Francis and Ann [?] Moore, moved to Lunenburg County.

The Patty family moved south to South Carolina and Alabama. Given names of Charles and Elijah were common.

15. William Pate - 28 April 1691.

Joshua Storey patented 11,620 acres in New Kent County, headrights include William Pate.

16. William Pates - of the Rappahannock River area of Virginia, died December 1763 or January 1764, as an old man. Included in 17th Century Pates because it is assumed this man lived in 17th Century Virginia, the records to identify him are good, and the sources for those records are not readily available in most places.

This research has found no proof of the origin of this William Pates. One good possibility is the William in the headright of 1691, listed above. Also, the son of Thomas Pate d. 1703 named William was born 16 February 1689, according to the Abingdon Parish Registry. This birth year is acceptable; the son of Thomas would have been 74 years old when this man died.

William filed a claim for 1,800 pounds of tobacco lost in a "Fresh" at the Falmouth warehouse, 28 November 1738.

William Allason was a Scottish merchant who came to Virginia in the mid-1700s, established a store at Falmouth, and eventually opened branches in surrounding counties. His record system was elaborate, and his ledger books have survived. The Virginia Archives has twelve reels of microfilm of the records. He was broker for the planters' products, tobacco, grain, livestock, etc. He credited the customer's account for items sold and debited for purchases they made. He supplied every- thing needed - clothes, cloth, tools, nails, spices, coffins, rum, etc. He sold rum in quantities.

Most customers failed to sell as much as they purchased. Mr. Allason was equipped to provide bonds they could buy to guarantee payment of past due accounts. Most planters fell further behind because of the interest charges, but the merchant seemed to prosper.

Each entry in the ledger book identifies the customer and any family member who accompanied him or her. Thus, on 2 January 1762, William Pates and son Reubin entered the store and purchased a quart of rum. On 17 August 1762, William Pates and son Aaron purchased one linen handkerchief. Mrs. Pates purchased 2 ½ yards of white sheeting, 15 July 1762. A charge was made to the William Pates account, but the ledger entry reads "not to be read over to the Old Gentleman." Apparently, Mr. Pates could not read and would not approve of the purchase. The more we read history, the less things change!

The family apparently never owned land. Mr. Allason paid levies for their tithes to the Parish, but nothing for land. He paid the Fitzhugh family for land rent, and the payments were debited to the William Pates account.

King George County Will Book A 1 provides entry as follows: 7 March 1740.

William Stone died intestate. Administration on his estate was granted to William Pates and his wife Catherine. William and his family later had an association with John Stone. William Pates and John Stone's wife visited the store, 19 February 1762. Jesse Stone visited the store, 3 July 1764, after the death of William Pates, and was identified as the son of the Widow Pates.

Jesse Stone, Aaron Pates, Raunce Pates, Ezekiel Pates, and Reubin Pates shared in the division of the proceeds of the crops for the estate of William Pates, 14 April 1765.

The writer interprets the Allason records and the King George County Will Record as follows: William Pates and his wife Catherine had sons named Aaron, Raunce (Ransom?), Ezekiel, and Reubin. Catherine died, and William remarried to the widow of John Stone, who had a son named Jesse Stone.

The Widow Pates (Stone) died before 14 April 1765, the date when Allason paid John Ballard for making her coffin.

Perhaps William and Catherine also had daughters.

The sons of William and Catherine Pates remained in the area of Stafford and King George counties through 1793.

17. Peet and Peate entries.

5 April 1649 - Capt. John Sibsey patented 80 acres in Lower Norfolk County for transporting two persons: John Peat and Arthur Watson.

29 July 1652 - John Howett patented 650 acres in Northumberland County for transporting 13 persons. The list includes John Peete

The fate of these men is unknown.

The preceding review of the Pate Family in 17th Century Virginia leads to three important questions. Do available records identify a relationship among the Pate immigrants, do any of these relate to the known Pate Family in England, and to where did these Pates or their descendants emigrate from Virginia? An attempt to provide answers to these questions will follow. Emphasis is added that this will be a mix of fact and assumption.

The assumption, based on records from England, cited earlier, has been offered that the earliest Pate immigrant to Virginia, Richard Pate who died 1657, was a grandson of John Pate of Brin, Leicestershire, England. The grandfather was a brother to Edward Pate d. 1597, of Eye-Kettleby, Leicestershire, England. The estate of

Richard Pate was administered by his nephew, John Pate. The records tell us that John was a son of a brother of Richard. Given information from the lineage listed earlier in this report, Henry Pate was the eldest brother of Richard.

John Pate, the nephew of Richard, died in 1672, and his brother, Edward Pate of England, was first granted administration of the estate in the Preogative Court of Canterbury in England. Records, cited earlier, show that Sir Grey Skipwith, of Virginia, was granted administration on Richjard's estate in Lancaster County, Virginia. Both the brother Edward and Sir Grey Skipwith were succeeded in the administration by Thomas Pate, a nephew. It is assumed that Edward was the oldest brother of John, and this Thomas was the oldest son of Edward. Thomas was the man who died in 1703.

The assumption that the Virginia Pate Family of Richard-John-Thomas descended from John Pate of Brin, Leicestershire, England, seems to be sound.

Both Richard and John apparently died without children. Thus, the first two generations of this family in Virginia passed without producing a male heir. Thomas was the prominent Major/Colonel Thomas Pate of Gloucester and York counties, Virginia. He married Elizabeth (surname unknown), and they had children listed in the extant Abingdon Parish Registry. Their children, as listed in the parish registry, were: John born 27 April 1677, Elizabeth born April 1680, Mary christened 27 April 1684, Matthew christened 21 February 1686, and William christened 16 February 1689. Additionally, a daughter, the given name of whom was illegible to the compiler who published this record, was listed with surname of Peate. She was the daughter of Thomas and Elizabeth Peate and was born 12 February 1680. This is assumed to have been the daughter of Thomas and Elizabeth Pate.

The daughter whose name was illegible, may have been Sarah. Research by A. J. Pate into the Lee and Wyatt Families of Virginia revealed the claim that one Sarah Pate, a daughter of Thomas Pate, married Conquest Wyatt in 1669. She, reportedly, was born in Virginia 1652. No records were cited to support the claim, and this writer considers the dates as ill-founded and in error. This research failed to identify any Pate named Thomas in Virginia this early. However, consideration must be granted that one Conquest Wyatt did marry the daughter of Thomas, born 1680, noted above. Middlesex County Orders Book 1673-1680 identifies Robert Young as the guardian of one Conquest Wyatt, 14 October 1678. The age of this Conquest Wyatt was not cited, but he was a minor, and therefore similar in age to the presumed daughter of Thomas Pate born 1680.

A cursory review of records indicates that John remained in Gloucester County. John died in 1706, apparently not survived by male heirs. Matthew had a full life remaining in the Gloucester-New Kent area and was survived by heirs, both sons and daughters. The fate of William is unknown to the writer, unless he was one of the several men named William Pates of the Allason Store records cited earlier, which is very probable. Later generations of this family moved west.

Three days before Thomas wrote his will, April 4, 1703, he executed a deed of gift to Joanna (Joan) Lawson, wife of John Lawson, Deeds and Bonds No. 2, page 100. The gift was his house and lot in Yorktown and recognized the seven years of service Mrs. Lawson had provided him and the care she had provided in his terminal illness. The will, recorded in Gloucester County Deeds, Wills, Orders 1702-1706, page 151, did not recognize any of his children as legatees. Further, trustees for the estate and witnesses to the will did not include persons with the Pate surname. Legacies were left to Margaret Read, the daughter of Robert Read, for 20 shillings or a ring of this value; Tony, his Negro servant, received his freedom; Joan Lawson received liberal gifts of furniture and kitchen ware. Elizabeth, his wife, received one-third of the estate, though it appears to have been heavily depleted; Rowland Pierson received the balance of the estate and was appointed executor of the estate. Other records of interest to this estate are recorded in the will. They are not vital to the overview of Pates in 17th Century Virginia and are omitted here.

One comment on the absence of heirs named in the will needs to be made. This is a report on Pates in 17th Century Virginia, not the history of the Thomas Pate Family.

However, a comment seems to be in order after reading this will. Land is not mentioned in this will. Researchers frequently pass this off with the thought that children had previously received land from the father. Partially correct, but that is not the real. The here is the system of inheritance under English Law at the time, primogeniture and entail. Land was frequently omitted from wills of this timeframe unless it was to descend to someone besides the heir at law. The Yorktown home site was deeded to Joan Lawson three days before he wrote the will. The heir at law, probably the son John, would receive any land that remained if the will did not assign it to the widow. There was no need to identify the heir at law to protect this legacy. It is known that John inherited the Gloucester County plantation because quit rent records show him as the owner in 1704, the year after Thomas died.

Edward Pate, who appears in Virginia records 16 April 1683, had a given name common to the family of Richard, John, and Thomas. He remained in the Gloucester-New Kent counties area until 1725. The assumption is offered that he was a cousin of Thomas Pate died 1703, probably one generation later. Edward patented land on the Nottoway River in Isle of Wight County, 24 March 1725. This appears to have been a Treasury Grant, not a headright grant. The Nottoway River was located in the part of Isle of Wight that became Southampton County in 1749. Edward died in Southampton in 1757 and left a will. He was survived by sons Thomas, Samuel, and Travis.

James Pate married Elizabeth Eddington in Middlesex County in 1687, as cited earlier. The association of James and Matthew Kemp has been noted. Also, it is of record that the Kemp, Skipwith, and Pate Families had a long association in England and Virginia. Middlesex County was formed from Lancaster County in 1674. Note has been made that, when John Pate died in 1672, his estate in Lancaster County was initially managed by Sir Grey Skipwith. The land James acquired from Matthew Kemp was originally owned by Sir Grey Skipwith. An association of James Pate with the Pate Families of Richard, John, and Thomas could be inferred.

Available records do not identify the children of James and Elizabeth. Nor do they tell us if the family remained in Middlesex County, or relocated.

Thomas Patty is listed in this report because the surname may have been a corruption of Pate. Note has been made of a Pattee family in Maryland records. Thomas Patty was in early records of Old Rappahannock County. Colonel Thomas Pate executed at least one deed in Old Rappahannock County. Henry Pate and Thoroughgood Pate were in Old Rappahannock for over two decades.

However, this research was unable to associate Thomas Patty with any of these Pate men. The writer believes Thomas Patty of Old Rappahannock, and later Lunenburg County, did have a relationship to the Patty family of Newberry District, South Carolina, and Cherokee County, Alabama. These families had given names common to the Pate Family -- Elijah, Charles, James, etc.

Henry Pate and Thoroughgood Pate lived in close proximity on land between the Potomac and Rappahannock Rivers. They had associations with the same people - Lunn, O'Donnell, Alexander, Prid, Taylor, etc. The writer believes they were brothers, but available records fail to prove this association. They appear to have been located, initially, in the James River area at the same time. They moved north as settlers began to develop the Rappahannock River area. They were in close proximity in the Northern Neck. Records prove that both sought a change of scenery and relocated to the Dismal Swamp area of Virginia and North Carolina.

The relationship of Thoroughgood Pate, and of Henry, to the other Pate Families of 17th century Virginia has been debated for years. The introduction of DNA testing to genealogy may have resolved this question.

In DNA testing, tested persons are grouped into haplogroups, based on differing values assigned to specific genetic characteristics. The haplogroup identifies the ancient peoples from which the persons descend. Obviously, a person cannot descend from but one ancient group through a direct paternal line. For the time frame of genealogical significance, persons who test into one haplogroup do not have a paternal relationship to persons in other haplogroups.

Descendants of Thoroughgood Pate have tested in Haplogroup I-M223 (formerly I2b1). Other Pates in 17th Century Virginia test in other haplogroups, such as R-M173 and R- M269 for the Pates who settled in the James River area. All of these colonial families had the surname of Pate and appear to have immigrated from England. However, they may have been from different groups of ancient peoples. History proves numerous groups of peoples plundered and settled the British Islands over the centuries, resulting in a mix of genetic backgrounds.

Perhaps Henry had sons, and some of the unplaced Pates in the Rappahannock River area are their descendants. The Pates named Robert and Alexander appear in the Rappahannock River area 1661-1667, when Henry and Thoroughgood were settled there. Alexander also had an association with Stafford County, as did Henry and Thoroughgood. Further, did his given name recognize the Alexander family? Available records have failed to identify a relationship among these names.

Henry Pate and Thoroughgood Pate will be treated in more detail later in this report.

William Pate of the 1638 headright disappeared from records viewed in this search. He could be the source of some of the unplaced Pate men. It seems more probable that he died soon after entering the Colony.

The next chapter in this project will cover the life and times of Thoroughgood Pate.

III

THE LIFE AND TIMES OF THOROUGHGOOD PATE

This is an attempt to trace the life of this man through the locations in which he lived and the activities in which he participated. The desire is to relate his life to the history of his times, to mesh his genealogy with the history in which he lived.

The earliest record for the appearance of Thoroughgood Pate, developed in this research, is dated 1 February 1657. The record is recorded in York County, Virginia Wills, Deeds and Orders Book III, page 22, and was the inventory of the estate of Giles Mode, deceased. Thoroughgood owed the Mode estate two money debts.

Scattered records have been located for this man over some fifty-five years, in several Virginia and North Carolina locations. These include: In Virginia, York County, 1658; Charles City County, 1660; Westmoreland County, 1669 and 1684; Old Rappahannock County, 1685, 1686, 1687, 1691, 1692, and 1693; Stafford County, 1703; Chowan Precinct, North Carolina, and his death in Chowan Precinct in 1713. It is possible that all of these records do not represent a new location. The county lines changed, and new counties were created. This is more important in the Old Rappahannock and Stafford area. A complex court case involving a land dispute in 1693, not involving the Pates, suggests that may be the case.

The opinion is offered that he lived and died in the area that remained Chowan Precinct when Bertie Precinct was formed from Chowan in 1722. His sons established their homes in the area of Chowan that became Bertie Precinct in 1722, of which more will be discussed later.

These records, at their face value, provide no more family information than merely his presence in these places on the dates cited, and his death in 1713. His migrations within Virginia did not cover a long distance. However, any move was a challenge in the rugged, undeveloped country of the 17th Century. Charles City and Stafford counties of Colonial Virginia were approximately one hundred miles apart. Stafford County, Virginia, and Chowan, North Carolina, were separated by less than two hundred miles.

Knowledge of the formation of these counties is of value as one attempts to interpret the records. The original counties in Virginia were formed in 1634. The eight earliest counties were formed around the James River. The north bank of the river, starting at the mouth of the river, provided land for Elizabeth City County, Warwick County, James City County, Charles City County, and Henrico County. Charles River County was located north of James City and Charles City, to the York River. Charles River County was renamed York County in 1643. Westmoreland County was formed north of York, in 1653, from Northumberland County, one of the original eight counties. Old Rappahannock County was founded in 1656 from the eastern part of Westmoreland and Stafford in 1666 from the west of the same. Chowan County, North Carolina, was recognized as a precinct of Albermarle County in 1670. It continued without county status when Thoroughgood Pate settled there before 1703.

Judgmental and character comments on a person who lived 350 years ago should be made with caution. However, it seems safe to say the records of his migration suggest Thoroughgood Pate had a passion for the virgin lands of the American colonies and followed that urge until his death.

He left no will, and probate records were not created to identify his heirs. Records executed after his death prove two sons, Charles and William. Most researchers, including this writer, assign an assumed son named John to Thoroughgood. Available records fail to suggest daughters, though some should be expected. Likewise, records will not prove the children of these sons, but most researchers, including the writer, credit Charles with founding a prolific line of Pates, and available records lead to the assumptive identity of his sons. The assumptive sons of John and William are identified with less definition than those of Charles.

The assumed descendants from the three brothers, Charles, William, and John, have a base in the North Carolina area that began as Craven County. The area evolved into Johnston, Dobbs, Wayne, and Lenoir counties, as new counties were formed.

The preceding serves to highlight the frustration experienced as family researchers attempt to develop the genealogy and history of the Thoroughgood Pate Family. Researchers have labored long to identify the descendants of this man. Unfortunately, frustration continues to reign. Available information continues to raise many questions that have little in the way of definitive answers.

Some of the more common questions resulting from the lack of records follow: Was the man in the record of 1657 the same as the man who died in 1713?

Was he a common debtor or one who had the misfortune of having debts that overshadowed his true character?

Was his wife at his death the second wife? Was he related to Nathaniel Chevin and how?

Was he related to the prominent Pates on the James River of 17th Century Virginia and how?

Was he Welsh, as some traditions report?

Was he related to the other Pate names in early northeastern North Carolina records? What was the origin of his given name?

This report will not provide definitive answers to these questions. Available records are insufficient. However, this report will show some well-thought-out assumptions, based on available records, for the consideration of readers. These are offered in the light of a response received, by the writer, to a query in past years. Correspondence in the 1980s, with a researcher reported to have been an authority on Tidwell family history, resulted in the following response, "I cannot help you and you cannot help me, but misery loves company"! The preceding questions will be considered in that light.

The debate over the relationship of Thoroughgood Pate in the records of 1657 to the man of that name in the record of 1713 has been ongoing for at least 18 years, to the knowledge of the writer. The writer has been on both sides and has finally settled on the side of "one man made both records" about ten years ago. This is the classic case of the futility of debate based on assumptions. No one can be proved correct beyond doubt, and no one can be proved wrong beyond doubt.

Acknowledgement is granted that no one can prove that one man made both records. By the same measure, no one can prove that two men were involved and that seems to be more important. There is record of one Thoroughgood Pate and to duplicate him would require many more non-overlapping records for a second, which no one has located.

The argument for two men in this time frame, as brought to the attention of the writer, is based on two beliefs. First, the life

31

expectancy in the 17th and 18th Centuries was too short for a mature man in 1657 to have lived until 1713. The second belief is that a man of this age would not be expected to father children in the 1690s.

One researcher, in support of the first belief, shared charts prepared by someone who listed the life expectancy for men in the 18th Century colonies as 43 years. There was no information to support the validity of the charts. Regardless, that average may be correct. But, averages fall by the wayside when looking at individuals. Exceptions exist for all averages.

Thoroughgood Pate should have been mature in 1657 when the estate of Giles Mode was inventoried, at least 21 years of age. Note was made earlier that men had to be 21 years old to be sued. However, given the mood of a developing society, he may not have been that old. Someone may have simply said he was of age. Mode had died, Pate owed him money, as did a lot of other persons, and action was taken to collect the just debts for the estate. Perhaps no authority was in the mood to question the action.

Irrespective of the questions, the assumption is offered that he was at least 21 years in 1657, thus born ca. 1635. The birth year of 1635 and death in 1713 reflects a life span of 78 years. A comparison with the life span for other Pate Family members is interesting.

Charles Pate, the proven son of Thoroughgood Pate, has been assigned the birth year of 1690 by more than one researcher. Dobbs County, North Carolina, deed records prove he was alive in 1769. The two dates reflect a life span of 79 years. The birth year could be a year or so later, but the death may have occurred after 1769, how many years is unknown. The anticipated life span seems to be reasonable. The wife of this Charles had the given name of Sarah. The assumption is offered that she may have been the Sarah Pate on the 1790 U. S. Census of Dobbs County. Records lead to the opinion that she was approaching, or over, 80 years of age.

Samuel Pate of Richmond County, North Carolina, an assumed grandson of this Charles Pate, and a son of Thoroughgood Pate d. 1802, was 90 years old on the U. S. Census for 1850, reflecting a birth year of 1760. This birth year is supported by census records earlier in his life. He lived to be 90 and his father, Thoroughgood d. 1802 lived past 72 years of age.

Other records could be cited, but these seem to be sufficient to support the claim that Thoroughgood lived about 78 years. Others in his family enjoyed an equal lifespan.

Numerous writers have made note of the advanced age at which many men married in the early colonies. Few eligible brides were available in the frontier areas, which has been addressed earlier in this report. Marriage at 40-50 years for men was not uncommon. Given the ages and years cited, Thoroughgood would have been 55 years in 1690, when his first son was born. The age is within the bounds of normal male fertility.

The assumption is offered that Thoroughgood Pate was born ca. 1635 in England and died in Chowan County, North Carolina, before 3 September 1713, when the inventory of his estate was filed in Chowan Court.

Terms used to describe the character of Thoroughgood Pate, by earlier researchers, are less than complimentary. Terms such as chronic debtor, ne'er-do-well, etc. seem to be unjustified. Family historians have the responsibility to report the good and bad equally. That responsibility also applies to the character of an ancestor, that they be neither embellished nor degraded. Unfortunately, misinterpretations of records can occur, especially so when records are few in number and often missing. Ancestors lived their lives in their times. It is difficult for researchers living in this century to relate to the times of the 17th Century. A view of those times is in order.

Two available references provide a view of the society in which Thoroughgood Pate lived. One refers to the Northern Neck of Virginia, the other to the Chowan County area of North Carolina. Thoroughgood lived in both. No effort has been made to validate the claims; however, both seem credible.

A description of the people and living styles in Loudoun County, Virginia, around 1725 appears in *"History and Comprehensive Description of Loudoun County, Virginia"*, housed at Alderman Library, University of Virginia. Loudoun County was still within the bounds of Stafford County in 1725. It was located on the Potomac River, upstream from Old Rappahannock County. Records locate the man of this report in Stafford decades before 1725. Conditions in Old Rappahannock, when it was formed in 1657, must have been similar, perhaps even more primitive. The following appears: "[They] ate from wooden trenchers and platters, sat on 3 legged stools or wood blocks, used bear grease in lieu of butter and lard cut food with same knife used to disembowel deer.... furniture was crude, few had any pewter or spoons, used wooden bowls, noggins, horse troughs were used for wash basins, iron pots were owned only by the rich."

An Internet description of North Carolina coastal towns before 1770 describes Chowan County as follows. The town of Edenton was not incorporated until 1723. One visitor, William Byrd of Virginia, recorded his impression of Edenton in 1728. William Byrd was a surveyor and active in the area. He recorded notes on his experiences, and some have survived. He wrote, of Edenton, "They may be 40 or 50 houses, most of them small, and built without expense. A citizen here is counted extravagant, if he has ambition enough to aspire to a brick chimney. Justice herself is but differently lodged, the courthouse having much the flair of a common tobacco house." Obviously, a common tobacco house, whatever that was, did not rank high in the values of William Byrd. Note needs to be made that this was 15 years after the death of Thoroughgood Pate. Conditions observed by William Byrd should have been an improvement over those experienced by Thoroughgood Pate.

Researchers should note the description of the judicial facilities, when complaints are made about illegible, or non-existent, records. Primitive courthouses were common. Further, it is easy to envision that lax enforcement of laws could result in an underage male being treated as an adult. Mr. Byrd wrote that justice was "differently lodged".

Two tragic events marked the closing years of the life of Thoroughgood Pate. A review of the "times" of his life warrants note of both events.

Edward Hyde was sent from England to replace Thomas Cary as the Colony Governor in North Carolina. Cary refused to relinquish the office. Supporters for each took up arms against each other, and the Colony was in a civil war. Crops were not planted, and food became an. Historians refer to the dispute as "Cary's Rebellion." The dispute was settled by the summer season of 1711.

The Tuscarora Indian War erupted in the fall of 1711 and is described by some historians as the worst Indian disturbance to befall North Carolina. The food shortage resulting from Cary's Rebellion compounded the problem, as hundreds of colonists were killed. Groups of the colonists assembled at large plantations and in the towns of Bath and New Bern for protection. Homes and personal property were destroyed, and crops for food were non-existent in some areas. South Carolina militia units, supported by friendly Indians from that Colony, succeeded in bringing peace to the area in the fall of 1713. One report cited twenty settlers were killed on Alligator River in the spring of 1713. This river is across Albamarle

Sound, and a few miles east from the location of the Pate home site. The old man was viewing tragedy and turmoil to the end of his life.

Some researchers have been critical of the minimal amount of personal property Thoroughgood owned at his death. The meager inventory of his estate certainly could reflect his ambitions, or lack of ambitions, and living style. However, it may reflect the tragic events in the last years of his life, as well as the frontier lifestyle of the area.

He seems to have attracted the "debtor" label from records in the York County record book in 1657. A review of those, particularly the Giles Mode estate records, is of interest, York Deeds, Wills and Orders #3 1657-1662, pages 2, 23, 25, 36, 56, 58, 123, and 164.

Giles Mode died by 21 December 1657, when his widow, Jane Mode, was granted administration on the estate. The widow remarried to Francis Haddon before 24 February 1659, when Haddon succeeded her as administrator. The inventory of the estate is recorded on two different pages, page 58 being the most legible.

Thoroughgood Pate was among 25 persons listed as debtors to the Mode estate. He was in impressive company. The names included Lt. Col. William Barber (other records identify him as a justice of the county court), Capt. Hen. Jackson, George Cary (a prominent James River family), Tho. Ballard, William Bell (major landowner), and Jno. Overstreet. This was definitely not a list of ne'er-do-wells.

The entries on page 123 report Thoroughgood had left the county, and Francis Haddon requested an attachment to his estate. One can only wonder if this was a legal maneuver by Haddon in the event Thoroughgood returned, or if he actually owned land in York County. This research failed to find his name in deed indexes. Thomas Ballard also asked for an attachment to the estate of Pate. Ballard was among the 25 debtors to the Mode estate.

The entry on pages 116/117 reports the inventory of the Stephen Page estate. This was filed 16 December 1659. Debtors included Thoroughgood Pate and Arthur Dickson, jointly. The amount of the debt was not listed, and further action on this debt was not found in the records reviewed. Given the condition of the records, a name could have been overlooked. A deposition on page 69, unrelated to this project, reports Arthur Dickson was 30 years of age and had a brother named John Dickson, age 23 years.

The records fail to identify the need for which Thoroughgood borrowed so much money, or when he borrowed it. The most probable cause would be the "cash crop" of Virginia, tobacco. This was in the days before public warehouses, and tobacco inspectors added some stability to marketing the crop. Perhaps he borrowed heavily to produce tobacco and had a crop failure, or lost the crop to decay in transit, neither uncommon in modern times.

It is of interest that several entries in the York books were made by people who had relocated to Rappahannock County. Thoroughgood soon joined them.

A Charles City County record of 20 April 1658 probably marks the departure of Thoroughgood from the James River area, Deeds, Wills and Orders 1655-1665, page 101.

Howell Pryse sued Thomas Ligon because Thoroughgood Pate had escaped from his custody. The record provides little in the way of background. Apparently, Pryse was among persons who had a claim against Pate that could not be satisfied, and Pate had been legally confined to the custody of Thomas Ligon. Other records identify Ligon as the County Surveyor. Perhaps he used legally-confined persons as labor in his work. Pate departed the area, and Pryse sued Ligon to recover his claim against Pate. Caution is issued; the suggested circumstances are assumptive.

Howell Pryse was identified in other records as the past Sheriff of Charles City County. He was active in the importation of immigrants and claimed several tracts of headright land. He was frequently in court, whether as the sheriff or for personal claims is unknown. Regardless, Thoroughgood was gone, and the court held Thomas Ligon responsible to Howell Pryse for the debt cited.

One researcher suggested Thoroughgood fled to the backwoods of Old Rappahannock County and hid from the law. He did move to Old Rappahannock County, and it was frontier and primitive country, though not many miles from the James River. Records show he had an association with William Taylor, who became Sheriff of that county. Therefore, there is question to the claim that he was hiding. Law enforcement officers knew his location.

As noted earlier, available records fail to identify the causes of his financial disaster. One must wonder why so many people loaned so much money to one new to the colony? This report has suggested it involved tobacco in some form, production or marketing. The venture must have had expectations of success by those who loaned him money. That seems important as researchers attempt to define his character. Records on hand provide little information on two of his financiers, Stephen Page and Thomas Ballard. However, Giles

Mode and Howell Pryse had experience in finances. The multiple loans (probably in the form of tobacco) they advanced to him indicate approval of the venture and expectation of success by mature knowledgeable persons.

The next record on Thoroughgood was in Westmoreland County, 29 January 1660. For reference, Westmoreland and Old Rappahannock counties adjoined, both fronting on the Rappahannock River.

The record was the will of Thomas Lund (also spelled Lunn), written 29 January 1660, proved in court 14 October 1660, Deeds and Wills No. 1, 1653-1671, page 137. The inventory of the estate identified a large number of persons who owed money to Lund. Thoroughgood Pate was among those listed. The will, and the Lund family, will be treated in more detail in the report on Henry Pate. For here, it is sufficient to say Thomas Lund was a merchant, but not on the scale of William Allison, identified in the preceding chapter. Merchants of this time sold goods on credit. A name on this list does not imply the person was a chronic debtor. The debt of Thoroughgood was minimal, 4 shillings, 9 pence. Henry Pate was also on this list.

Thoroughgood remained in Old Rappahannock County for two or more decades, appearing in available records five more times. He was a headright for William Taylor, 30 October 1669. This probably results from his earlier entry into Virginia, before his financial troubles started in 1657. William Taylor held this land voucher for over 12 years, which was not unusual, if this did in fact represent his entry into the Colony. Other names on the list are recognized as being in the Colony for years prior to 1669.

As noted, William Taylor resided in Old Rappahannock County, as did Thoroughgood. The land patented, 1000 acres for the transportation of 20 persons, was in Accomack County, across the Chesapeake Bay from the mainland.

Thoroughgood and Jeremiah Thornton were witnesses to the will of Robert Prid, 25 January 1684, in Rappahannock County, Deeds, Wills and Orders No. 6, 1682-1686, page 431. Thornton signed with a mark, while Thoroughgood signed his name "Thorough Good Pate". It is not known if this was his customary style or was the version used by the scribe who transcribed it into the official book. The scribe also used "Thoroughgood Pate" in the proving statement. His signature in the North Carolina Deed Book is written "Thoroughgood Pate".

The will of Robert Prid, on its face, has no information of value for Pate researchers. However, the signature of Thoroughgood is significant. He did not make a mark, rather signed his name and in good form. This suggests he had some level of education. The education level of Henry Pate, with whom Thoroughgood associated, is to be noted later. For here, it can be reported that Henry demonstrated literate skills beyond the basics. The assumption is offered that Thoroughgood was the equal of Henry Pate in this respect.

A discussion of the relationship between Thoroughgood Pate and Henry Pate warrants some background on Henry. The records are more numerous than those for Thoroughgood. Some will be omitted in the interest of space and to avoid redundancy.

Henry Pate was a headright for Henry Soanes, 25 March 1656. Soanes patented 1,600 acres in New Kent County for the transportation of 32 persons. The list included Henry Pate, Elizabeth Pate, and Katherine Pate. Records, to be cited, lead to the assumption that Elizabeth Pate was the wife of Henry Pate and Katherine was their daughter.

This record should approximate the arrival of Henry to Virginia. It has been noted that headrights may never have seen the land described. That may be the case here, but New Kent County was in the general area where new arrivals had to settle. New Kent was formed from York County in 1654. Other records have placed Thoroughgood in York and Charles City counties. The presence of both men in a limited locale, in the same time frame, suggests an association between them. The assumption is offered that both arrived in Virginia 1652-1654 and remained in the James River area for a few years.

One researcher reported viewing a York County Deed that Henry and Thoroughgood had signed as witnesses. A request for a copy of the record, or the citation of the record, was not answered. The records cited earlier in this report seem to be sufficient to state that both resided, initially, in the James River area.

Note is made in other areas of this report of the migration of settlers on both sides of the Potomac River between Maryland and Virginia. The next record on Henry Pate places him in Charles County, Maryland, Maryland Archives Vol. LIII, page 681. Charles County fronted on the Potomac River, opposite to the original area of Westmoreland County, Virginia. Henry was "sopanyed" [subpoenaed] to testify in Charles County Court, 16 April 1657. The record provides no background information, nor the results, or if he even appeared. It is interesting that the date is before the initial debt problems of Thoroughgood and before he escaped the custody of Thomas Ligon.

The will of Thomas Lund places both men in Westmoreland County before 29 January 1660, when it was written. The assumption is offered that Henry checked out the Westmoreland-Charles County area, liked what he saw, and started his home site in Westmoreland County. Thoroughgood joined him, after his escape from the custody of Thomas Ligon. Additional evidence of a Maryland connection is found in the will of Lund. One of the executors of his estate was James Walker of Maryland.

Henry was represented in numerous Westmoreland, Old Rappahannock, and Stafford county records and church records of the area in the 1660s. They are interpreted as proof that he could read and write and was concerned for the needs of the poor. He served as church warden for Potomac Parish, was on jury duty, witnessed records, and served with Christopher Lund as security for the performance of the executor of the Robert Maphe will. A sampling of the records that review his activities include Westmoreland Court Orders 1662-1664, pages 11-13; Court Orders 1663-1664, page 30; and Court Orders 1665-1667, pages 233, 471, 481, 543, 546.

The will of Thomas Lund dated 29 January 1660 and probated 15 October 1660, with the estate inventory of 19 February 1661, provides several items of interest for this report, Deeds, Wills, etc. 1661-1662, pages 31 and 7-8. The references to Thoroughgood Pate have been noted. Henry Pate was given use of Lund land and the house for three years and was appointed to care for the cattle. Christopher Lund, a nephew, was the executor of the will.

Thomas Lund was ill and was returning to England. He had migrated to Virginia by 4 November 1656, when he purchased a large tract of land from David Phillips, Westmoreland Deeds, Wills, etc. 1653-1659, page 114A. This is near the time frame when Thoroughgood and Henry are thought to have entered Virginia.

Lund registered his mark for cattle and hogs, same citation, page 27. The mark was under keel and over keel in the right ear and left ear unmarked. Henry Pate registered his mark 14 February 1660, about two weeks after Lund wrote his will. The mark was a swallowfork in both ears, Deeds, Wills, etc. 1661-1662, page 35. Perhaps Henry knew the provisions of the Lund will and took action to prevent his livestock from being confused with the animals of Lund.

The association of the Lund, Pate, Odonnell, and Alexander Families must be noted. Robert Alexander had land that adjoined Lund and Henry Pate in Westmoreland and was a near neighbor of Lund and the Pates in Stafford County. The possibilities that these families were associated in England should be considered by future researchers.

The headrights of Henry, Elizabeth, and Katherine in 1656, for Henry Soanes, has been noted. Henry and Elizabeth were also headrights for Christopher Lund 22 October 1665. Lund patented 800 acres in Stafford County, near or adjacent to the land of Thomas Odonnell, who devised gifts to Thoroughgood Pate in 1687/1690.

The assumption is offered that Katherine was not listed as a headright for Christopher Lund along with her parents, because she had married Christopher Lund. The close association of the Lund and Pate Families has been noted. The presence of Thomas Lund as a legatee in the will of Thomas Odonnell will be cited later. He was a son of Christopher and Katherine Lund. The Stafford Court Orders 1687-1693, page 102, is record of the appointment of appraisers for the estate of Odonnell, 8 October 1690. Henry Coldstream, the executor of the Odonnell estate, petitioned the court in November with a request that a horse included in the appraisal should have been excluded. He reported the horse, named Turk, had been the property of Christopher Lund and had been bequeathed to Katherine, the widow of Lund. Further, the widow Lund had married Henry Coldstream. The horse had been at the Odonnell property, but was the property of his now wife, the former widow of Christopher Lund, and was not the property of Odonnell. The Court agreed.

Given the association of the two families, that Henry and Elizabeth had a daughter named Katherine, that Christopher Lund had a wife named Katherine, the assumption that Christopher Lund married the daughter of Henry and Elizabeth Pate seems sound.

Henry and Elizabeth were again headrights, 22 October 1682, for land in Lower Norfolk County, Virginia. Acknowledgement is granted that another Henry Pate could have been involved. However, Elizabeth was also listed, and both disappeared from records in the Rapphannock River area. They were headrights for William Whitfield as he patented 650 acres on the lower branch of the Elizabeth River in Lower Norfolk County. This land was near the North Carolina border. This record seems to mark the relocation of Henry and Elizabeth.

It is important to recognize that Stafford County Court Orders for 8 June 1686 listed Henry Pate and Thomas Odonnell among 14 debtors of the estate of John Sims. Perhaps Henry incurred this debt before leaving Stafford, or he remained in Stafford a few years, after serving as a headright for William Whitfield.

Malachy Thurston patented 200 acres in Lower Norfolk County, 28 October 1697. The land was identified as land granted to Henry Pate but escheated from him under escheatment claimed by William Randolph. An interpretation of this record was sought from the Virginia Archives. The opinion rendered was that Henry Pate patented this land but failed to seat on it and pay the quit rents within three years. His failure could result from several reasons. Death without a male heir was a common cause. Randolph never completed his claim, and Thurston acquired the land.

The assumption is offered that Henry and Elizabeth relocated to Lower Norfolk County in the 1680-1690 decade. Henry patented land, but died before he seated on it. His death, based on this record, would have been before 28 October 1697. Another record, to be cited, suggests it may have been nearer to 1691.

As noted, records indicate Katherine married Christopher Lund. Perhaps other children were born to Henry and Elizabeth after they reached Virginia. Some of the other male Pates in the Rappahannock River area could have been their sons, but one must wonder why they did not claim the land that was escheated in Lower Norfolk County. The Virginia Pate names of Alexander and Robert are not placed with families.

The assumption is offered that Henry and Thoroughgood were brothers. They appear to have entered Virginia 1652-1654, as adults. Their possible birth in Virginia is discounted because we have no record of an adult Pate in Virginia early enough to have been their father. Henry died ca. 1691, Thoroughgood died in 1713. They had similar life spans. One researcher suggested that Henry was the father of Thoroughgood. That seems unlikely to the writer, but nothing is proved!

The next record on Thoroughgood Pate, in the Rappahannock River area, was in Stafford County Deeds, Orders, etc., 9 July 1685. Thoroughgood witnessed the sale of livestock by Gerrard Fawkes of Maryland to Edward Maddocks of Stafford County. Andrew Buckner was the other witness. Maddocks and Buckner were active in later records involving Thoroughgood.

Stafford Court Orders 9 July 1687 provides record of activity between Thoroughgood Pate and John Sims. Note was made earlier of the debt of Henry Pate to the estate of John Sims. Depositions by Thomas Atkins and Richard Hemwood report that John Sims, on his deathbed, gave a horse named "Bold Colt" to Thomas Walton, Thoroughgood Pate, and Ralph Walker.

Annie Sims, formerly the widow of Hugh Dowding but then the widow of John Sims, conveyed land left her by Hugh Dowding to Thomas Walker, Phillip Buckner, and Thoroughgood Pate on 20 May 1687, Stafford Orders, etc. This research failed to find any record regarding this land by these three men, singularly or individually. Annie Sims conveyed the same land to Francis Dade two years later. Francis Dade and William Fitzhugh ended up in a complex land dispute over ownership of the land.

The next record of Thoroughgood in the Rappahannock River area was the Stafford County will of Thomas Odonnell, written 23 August 1687 and proved 18 September 1690. This will was filed in Northern Neck Land Office Warrants. The citation is Northern Neck Land Office Wills 1657-1784, page 156. The Odonnell will, and the court records associated with the will, proves an interesting relationship of the Pates and others associated with the will of Odonnell, to be cited.

The will is not as complex as the will of Dame Jane Skipwith, but it does devise legacies to 21 persons. Those receiving land were as follows: Henry Coldstream - 250 acres, Thomas Lund - 100 acres, "Thur" Pate - 50 acres, Wilford Kelly (son of Edmond Kelly) - 50 acres, Isabell Derrick (daughter of Thomas Derrick) - 50 acres, George Brent (son of George Brent) - 200 acres, and 50 acres were to be divided between Henry Coldstream and Thomas Lund. The tracts were identified as "the land where Edmond Kelly liveth" and as "my last purchase", both descriptions referring to the same tract. Mary Glass received 200 acres of land from another tract, "all my land in Quanticutt". Quanticutt was a tract of land Odonnell received from the will of Andrew Watson in 1679.

Proof that Thur was a nickname for Thoroughgood is found in Stafford County Court Orders 1687-1693, pages 215-216. Thoroughgood petitioned the court to have his legacy surveyed out and delivered to him 11 February 1692. His name was spelled "Thur" in the Odonnell will.

Two other records need to be noted before the 11 February 1692 date. While three years apart in time, they seem to be related.

Thoroughgood Pate appeared in Stafford County Court and confessed a debt of 500 pounds of tobacco to William Loxham, 9 September 1690. He was ordered to make payment with costs, Stafford Court Minutes.

William Loxham appeared in Stafford Court 10 February 1693 and presented a Power of Attorney signed by Thoroughgood Pate to authorize him to represent Pate. He testified that Pate owed him a debt for clerk and blacksmith work, and that he owed Samuel Haywood a similar amount. Loxham assigned the debt Pate owed him to Haywood, relieving him of the debt to Haywood.

It is difficult to know the behind-the-scene workings after the passage of some 320 years. It is interesting that the signature of Pate was a mark, although he had signed his name in other records. We have no record of Thoroughgood Pate being in Stafford County this late. Perhaps this was a move by one, or both, of the involved parties to resolve a legal matter in the absence of Pate, and the signature was a case of forgery.

George Brent appeared in court the day before the Odonnell will was proved and, on behalf of his son, urged the court to "fully prove" the will. He made note that the will identified the widow Anna Odonnell and Henry Coldstream as joint executors of the will. The widow had relinquished her rights to Coldstream. The action by Brent suggests he had reservations as to the performance of Coldstream as the sole executor. Henry Coldstream was granted sole administration 11 September 1690, with William Buckner and Edward Maddocks as his securities. John Wheatcraft, Richard Richards, Robert Alexander, and Christopher Richardson were appointed to appraise the estate 8 October 1690.

Ralph Davison, a servant of Thomas Odonnell, requested the court to order Henry Coldstream to pay his wages and costs as established in his contract with Odonnell. The court so ordered. Anna Odonnell, the widow of Thomas Odonnell petitioned the court to stop Coldstream from leasing her dower lands to others. The court soordered.

Thoroughgood Pate brought action against Henry Coldstream to protect his legacy in the Odonnell will, 7 October 1691. A non-suit was declared because Pate failed to appear. He was ordered to pay Coldstream 50 pounds of tobacco and costs.

William Buckner appeared before the court 11 February 1692. He and Edward Maddocks had been security of the performance of

Henry Coldstream in the Odonnell estate. Coldstream had died, and his will, to be located and presented to the court later, appointed Buckner and Maddocks as executors of the Coldstream estate. Buckner reported Henry Coldstream, "late deceased...died remote out of this county". He reported the estate was insolvent, and he was the largest creditor of the estate. The court gave him control of the estate and appointed John Wheatcraft, Robert Richards, and Ralph Walker to be sworn by Robert Alexander as appraisers of theestate.

One can only wonder about the influence of Maddocks and Buckner on this court. Maddocks was given control of the estate in the absence of a will and without proof of the death of Coldstream. Research failed to locate a later recording of thewill.

Edmond Kelly appeared as agent for his son on the same day and asked for the 50 acres legacy for his son, from the Odonnell estate, to be set off. The same action, on the same day, by Thoroughgood Pate has been cited earlier.

Katherine Coldstream appeared before the court 13 September 1692 and requested assistance. She reported her husband died poor and insolvent, leaving her destitute. She prayed for widow's paraphernalia from the estate. She was assigned a bed and furniture. The appraisers had noted 14 June that furniture and a bed, a broad axe, a rug, one mare, and a horse in Maryland had been left out of the appraisal.

The identification of Katherine as the widow of Christopher Lund and present wife of Henry Coldstream on 8 October 1690 has been previously cited.

A search of Stafford Deed indexes did not provide a deed of sale by any of the legatees to the Odonnell land. Lund deeds listed a sale of the 800 acres that Christopher Lund had acquired by patent in 1665, when Henry and Elizabeth Pate served as headrights for him. The land was sold by Thomas Lund and Christopher Lund, assumed to have been sons of Christopher and Katherine Lund.

Records indicate Christopher Lund and Henry Coldstream left wills. This research was unable to locate them. Edmond Kelly died in 1706 and left a will, but no information of value to Pate research was recorded. He did recognize a daughter named Sarah Kelly, but she was too young to have been the wife of Thoroughgood Pate.

Note needs to be made that Henry Coldstream died "remote out of this county" by 11 February 1691. The date is comparable to the time frame in which Henry Pate died in Lower Norfolk County.

The question must be considered, did Coldstream travel to Lower Norfolk because of the death of the father of his wife? "Remote out of this county" implies a trip of some distance. Further, it is noted that Thoroughgood Pate failed to appear in court for his complaint against Henry Coldstream 7 October 1691. One must wonder if he was also absent because of the death of Henry Pate, out of Stafford County.

As with so much of Thoroughgood Pate research, records provide many questions and few answers.

A cursory search of records revealed limited information on Thomas Odonnell. Indexes for Northern Neck Land Grants and Virginia headright grants do not list Thomas Odonell as the patentee of any land. He was not a grantee for a land purchase in the Stafford Deed Indexes. He was a legatee in the will of Andrew Watson of Stafford County 8 June 1679 and served as the executor of that estate. The Watson will have established an association of Odonnell and Watson with Robert Alexander, a long-time associate of the Pates. Several records prove Robert Alexander, the Lund family, and Henry Pate were adjacent land owners in Old Rappahannock County.

John Withers leased a tract of land to William Williams 5 August 1688, Stafford Order, Deed, etc. He identified his mother, formerly Anna Withers, as the present wife of Thomas Odonnell. Perhaps Thomas Odonnell acquired some of his land by marriage to the widow Withers.

An interesting history of the land Watson devised to Odonnell appears in *Northern Neck Land Warrants and Surveys Vol III* by Peggy S. Joyner, pages 97-98. Elizabeth Chapman patented 100 acres of this tract in 1749. The 200 acres had been patented to Henry Holtzclaw initially. He conveyed the land to Andrew Watson, who devised it to Thomas Odonnell in 1679. Odonnell devised it to Mary Glass, who died without heirs, and the 200 acres were returned to the Proprietors, making it available for Elizabeth Chapman.

A search of Stafford Deed Indexes, Grantor and Grantee, for a sale of the 50 acres of land inherited by Thoroughgood, was unsuccessful. Record of the acquisition of any land, or the sale of any land, by Henry Pate was not found. As noted earlier, several records prove Henry owned land, and the Stafford records cited prove Thoroughgood also owned land.

The preceding information seems to respond to the charge of a "debtor lifestyle" for Thoroughgood Pate. He had the motivation to borrow heavily in his young adult years for unidentified ventures that failed. He apparently abandoned those debts, moved to the Northern Neck of Virginia, where he lived quietly for about three decades. He relocated to the undeveloped area of northeast North Carolina in the latter years of the 17th Century. He acquired land in North Carolina on two occasions and had sufficient funds to pay for the land. He died in 1713 as the owner of 126 acres of land and minimal personal property. His personal property may have been limited by the frontier nature of the locale and the difficult conditions resulting from Cary's Rebellion and the Tuscarora Indian War.

Two published descriptions of the lifestyle in those times, cited earlier, suggest his living standards were comparable to those of his peers. Available records indicate that, after his initial financial failure, he apparently managed his affairs in a responsible manner.

Speculation abounds on the origin of the given name of Thoroughgood Pate. Naming patterns is a commonly-recognized tool in genealogy. It does not prove relationships but does support assumptions and provides leads for further research. The most probable source of Thoroughgood Pate's unique given name would result from the marriage of a Thoroughgood female to a male Pate. There are many examples in genealogy where mothers have used their maiden surnames as given names for sons. But no such marriage has been located to date.

A cursory review of records of the Church of Jesus Christ of Latter-Day Saints produced a sizeable file of Thoroughgood family names in areas of England where Pate Families lived. One researcher reports that a Thoroughgood family lived as neighbor to the family of Edward Pate in the ancient Pate home in Eye-Kettleby, Leicestershire, England in the 16th Century. There seems to have been ample opportunity for such a marriage of the two families.

In fact, ca. 1700, Constance Pate married Catlyn Thorogood of Essex County, England, where he was high sheriff in 1729. According to the naming custom indicated above,this couple had a son named Pate Thorogood. This family has no apparent relationship to Thoroughgood Pate, the subject of this project. It is only noted here for therecord.

Earlier researchers advanced the thought that Thoroughgood was related to the prominent Norfolk and Princess Ann County family of Adam Thoroughgood. This family is adequately treated in *Adventurers of Purse and String,* Frederick Dorman, and in *The Virginia Genealogist,* Volume XVI, pages 3-12. Adam of the first generation was in Virginia for the 1624/25 census. He died before 27 April 1640, when his will was probated in Norfolk County. He had one son, Adam of the second generation. The younger Adam died before his will was probated in Norfolk County 1 February 1686. A vast amount of genealogy is available in the cited sources and related families are traced. No recognition of the Pate Family is recorded.

Two items of interest need to be noted here. First, the death of Adam Thoroughgood in the mid-1680s occurred as Henry Pate relocated to Lower Norfolk County. Second, Adam Thoroughgood of the second generation instructed in his will that, if his wife died before their children were educated, a panel of four men would supervise the children. One of the men was Malachy Thurston, the man who patented the land escheated from Henry Pate in Lower Norfolk County. These items may, or may not, be of significance.

Record of entry into Virginia in the 17th Century was located for at least 12 members of the Thoroughgood family. The most interesting of these, to the writer, was Charles Thoroughgood. He was a headright for John Sharpe, 10 October 1655. Note the nearness of this to the arrival date for Thoroughgood Pate, Henry Pate, and Thomas Lund. Sharpe patented 300 acres in Lancaster County, which was in the Rappahannock River area. Thoroughgood Pate named his first-born son Charles Pate, which may recognize Charles Thoroughgood, and it may not!

Research to date does not identify the origin of the given name of Thoroughgood Pate. Perhaps research in England will be more definitive.

Questions regarding the wife of Thoroughgood Pate and her relationship to Nathaniel Chevin will be considered together.

Confusion over the names and number of wives, or wife, results from an error in an old North Carolina resource, *Hathaway's Register,* J. R. B. Hathaway. Hathaway recorded valuable North Carolina genealogy in 1901. Unfortunately, he erred in a deed involving Thoroughgood in his popular work, Volume 1, page 89. The wife of Thoroughgood is reported as Mary Pate. Other resources, abstracts of deeds, report this wife as Sarah, with the descriptive term "my now wife Sarah", Chowan Deed Book W-1, page 47. Researchers were led to believe Mary was the first wife, she died, and the term, "my now wife" means he remarried to Sarah.

Comparison of the citations for these abstracts reveals that both represent the same deed. A copy of the complete record confirmed the wife was Sarah. Apparently, Hathaway mistakenly repeated the given name of the wife in the preceding deed, Mary Williams, in the Pate record. Margaret Hofman abstracted these records years later, and she recorded the wife of Thoroughgood as Sarah.

Interpretation of the term, "my now wife", was sought from the North Carolina Archives. The opinion received explained that the term was frequently used in that timeframe. It does not refer to a new wife, but was only a way of saying "my wife". Reference was made to the repeated use of the term in other deed records of Chowan Precinct. The term appears repetitiously in the old Chowan deeds, too many to be actual references to new wives. As an example, in addition to the Pate record on page 47, the term also appears on pages 45 and 42. The opinion from the Archives is accepted asfactual.

In summary of the preceding, the wife of Thoroughgood had the given name of Sarah, not Mary. She was the only wife of whom we have record. The question of when they married and the relationship to Nathaniel Chevin is more difficult to answer.

Acknowledgement is granted that Thoroughgood could have had an earlier marriage. However, records leave no question that his heir-at-law, the oldest son, at his death in 1713, was Charles Pate. Records seem sufficient to say Charles was born ca. 1690. It is assumed that Thoroughgood and Sarah married prior to, but near, 1690 in Virginia. Any earlier marriage would have been without surviving sons. Records, to be cited, prove Sarah was the mother of a son named William Pate. It is assumed she was the mother of all three sons of Thoroughgood.

The records on Thoroughgood Pate, cited to this point, include only two records that were executed by him. This was his effort to acquire the legacy left him in the will of Thomas Odonell in 1691 and 1692. All other records involving him were executed by other persons. It was the efforts by the Giles Mode estate, Howell Pryse, Stephen Page, and Thomas Ballard to recover debts owed them by Thoroughgood that proved he was in York County in 1657 and Charles City County in 1658. The will and estate inventory of Thomas Lund and the headright grant to William Taylor placed him in Westmoreland County and Old Rappahannock County in 1660 and 1669, respectively. The will of Robert Prid proved his signature and located him in Old Rappahannock County in 1684. The will of Thomas Odonnell placed him in Stafford County in 1687 and 1690. Other records cited for him in Stafford County were initiated by other persons when he was a witness or recipient of gifts.

Thoroughgood executed two land records in Chowan Precinct of North Carolina in 1703. His estate inventory is also recorded there in 1713. However, activity by another party again provides important information on Thoroughgood, and again results in controversy.

Nathaniel Chevin petitioned the Chowan Precinct Court for the guardianship of William Pate, who was identified as the son of Thoroughgood and Sarah Pate, 19 January 1715, Chowan Court Minutes 1715-1719, page 2. The father was deceased, and the mother was unable to provide for the son. Chevin identified himself as godfather and uncle to the boy.

An earlier researcher reported William was 16 years of age at the time. The original record does not list any age for William. This record has been interpreted by some researchers to identify a brother-sister relationship for Chevin and Sarah Pate. Reports have circulated that Thoroughgood married Sarah Chevin. Available records, in the opinion of the writer, do not support either claim. Some background on Nathaniel Chevin is in order.

This research was unable to account for Nathaniel Chevin in the colonies prior to his appearance in Chowan, North Carolina. One researcher reported seeing the surname as a Court Clerk in one of the counties in the Northern Neck of Virginia, but has not shared that citation. The surname does appear in the deed index of Frederick County. However, review of the record reveals the name was Chavers, not Chevin, and the record does not appear to relate to the Chevin family. Deeds of Norfolk County, Virginia, have two entries for William Chevin, Wills and Deeds Book C, pages 3, 5. Attachment was made to the estate of William Chevin for debts 10 April 1652, some forty years before Nathaniel Chevin appeared in the colonies. The record on page 5 reports Chevin was alive but had left the [c] ounty. No further record was found for this man.

The surname fails to appear in the indexes for commonly used resources that identify immigrants to the colonies. These include *Cavaliers and Pioneers*, the several books by Peter Wilson Coldham, Frederick Dorman, and Beverly Fleet. Nor does the surname appear as an immigrant among the headrights in the *Albermarle, North Carolina Warrants and Surveys*.

Review of the International Genealogical Index provides interesting information from England. The Chevin family was well documented in Lincoln County in the 1630-1700 timeframe. They were located in the communities of Coleby, Horbling, and Fellingham. Smaller numbers of the surname were in Yorkshire and Norfolk County. The given names of John, Samuel, William, and Richard were present. One Richard Chevin of Horbling, Lincoln County, had a son named Nathaniel Chevin. He was christened 11 January 1663. The fate of this son is unknown, but the date is comparable to the life span of the man in North Carolina. Caution is advisable as we do not have proof that this is the man who migrated to North Carolina. There was also a younger man of the same name in later records of Horbling.

The Colony of North Carolina was among New World land granted to eight court favorites by King Charles II in 1665. It was a Proprietary, given to the eight Proprietors to develop and govern within bounds set by the Crown. The Proprietors commissioned all officers, who served at the pleasure of the Proprietors. Nathaniel Chevin was one of these officers. He was probably recruited and trained in England and sent to the Colony as an official. Thus, he did not immigrate in the fashion of most settlers to the colonies. This explains his absence from the normal lists of immigrants. He came to the colonies for vocational opportunities, not necessarily from a desire to settle new lands.

Chevin came to Carolina as a clerk. The earliest record of his presence, found in this research, was 18 October 1693, when he witnessed the will of Elizabeth Crossland as a Clerk of Chowan Precinct Court. He progressed to the office of Deputy Lord Proprietor by April 1714. The latter was the highest official in the Colony. He was in endless records until his death in 1720.

The extant St. Paul's Vestry Book of Chowan County documents his participation in the Anglican Church activities. He served as Clerk, Church Warden, and Vestryman until he relocated to Perquimans Precinct in 1708. He served that parish in a similar fashion. For future reference, Thomas Luten and William Wallston also actively served the Chowan Parish Church.

A biographical sketch of Chevin appears in *Dictionary of North Carolina Biography,* William Powell, page 366. The Chevin sketch was prepared by Dr. William S. Price, who has shared thoughts on Chevin with the writer in past years. Note was made that Chevin differed with Governor Charles Eden and fell from favor in government circles. The writer, in earlier writings, interpreted this to mean he ended his life in financial difficulties. That is not the case. He lost his position in governmental circles, but the records involved in the probate of his estate indicate he continued to own multiple properties and was active in some sort of sizeable real estate venture at the time of his death. He devised cash legacies to several persons, including 40 pounds to William Pate.

The will of Nathaniel Chevin was dated 3 March 1720 and probated 17 March 1720, *Secretary of State Wills.* Two legatees are important for this report. The 40-pound legacy to William Pate has been noted. William Pate was identified as a cousin, a term that could apply to a nephew during that time. Chevin's wife, Judith, was deceased. The following quote is important, "Item I give and bequeath to Nathaniel the son of my late wife Judith lately deceased..." The boy was to receive his plantation and the remainder of his estate when he reached the age of 21 years. Later in the will he added, "I give and bequeath to the above named Nath'l, son of my late wife Judith, the sum of 20 pounds..."

The claim has been circulated that the wife Judith had the surname of Coley and that her son was Nathaniel Coley. This may result from a popular abstract of North Carolina Wills, *North Carolina Wills,* Grimes. The Coley name appears in that abstract of the Chevin will. Study of the will indicates an error may have resulted from the interpretation of the quotes cited here.

First, it should be noted that the deceased wife would have been Judith Chevin, not Judith Coley. The word "lately" appears after the name of Judith, in the first quote, and appears to be the source for an error in interpretation, "Judith Coley, deceased". The first letter could easily be interpreted as a C, rather than an L. Comparison with the word "late" in the second quote reveals an identical letter. Comparison with "Loving Friend" in the next to last sentence on the first page results in the same letter.

The T is not crossed in the word lately, but it also is not crossed in late, though there is a faint mark to the right of the T. This record was written in Old English script, very difficult to interpret today. The document nears 300 years of age. Ink fades, and script styles change. The writer does not interpret the surname of the boy or his mother as being in the will. The interpretation is as listed in the quotes cited earlier and seems to be correct.

The will is interpreted as proof that Nathaniel Chevin was not the father of the son of his deceased wife Judith. Judith had a son born before she married Chevin, whether from another marriage or out of wedlock is unknown. Records will show that the boy was known as Nathaniel Chevin in later life.

Additional information is available on Nathaniel Chevin from other wills. The will of John Heckelfield 30 March 1721/8 August 1721; the will of John Jevin 14 May 1734/April 1735; and the will of Elizabeth Jevin, widow of John Jevin, 5 February 1735/8 July 1735.

One researcher has interpreted the name Jevin to have been a corruption of Chevin, that John Jevin was a brother to Nathaniel Chevin. However, the scribe of the will did recognize both surnames, Jevin and Chevin, in the wills. Therefore, that interpretation is questionable. The name is clearly spelled Jevin in both wills. The will of Elizabeth recognizes the nephew of her late husband, Nathaniel Chevin, not Nathaniel Jevin. This nephew is assumed to have been the son of Judith Chevin in the will of Nathaniel Chevin 1719-1720. The writer interprets these records to say John Jevin was a brother to Judith, the wife of Nathaniel Chevin. This is not a Chevin report, and the information cited here seems sufficient to say that the wife of Nathaniel Chevin had no relationship to Thoroughgood Pate.

The following is offered as a summary of records to this point. The assumption is offered that the maiden surname of Judith Chevin was Jevin, and she was a sister of John Jevin. Thoroughgood Pate had no association with Nathaniel Chevin until he moved to Chowan Precinct, North Carolina, as a married man. Both men were faithful to the Anglican Church. Chevin's activity in the church placed him in position to serve as godfather to William Pate, when the latter was christened at St. Paul's. Unfortunately, the Parish Registry is not available to prove this claim.

Note has been made that some have suggested Thoroughgood married a sister of Nathaniel Chevin, Sarah Chevin. Additional comments are in order on this. The assumption has been offered that Chevin came to the colonies as a young clerk, employed by the Lords Proprietor to attend to their affairs. He entered an undeveloped, primitive frontier. It is unlikely that he would have been joined by an unmarried sister, nor does it seem probable that his employer would have permitted such. The writer has differed with some over the character role cast for Thoroughgood. However, reality forces one to recognize the difference in the social status of these men and their ages.

There seems to be little chance that a sister of Chevin, if one did migrate to the colonies, would have married one with the financial means and age of Thoroughgood Pate.

The role of Chevin as uncle to William was not blood related. It was adoptive. Chevin recognized William only for assistance, not both William and Sarah. Surely, if he had such compassion for his blood nephew, he would have shared some of his wealth with his blood sister, if Sarah had in fact been his sister. Further, records indicate Sarah survived Chevin. The will of Chevin did not recognize Sarah for a legacy.

It is the opinion of the writer that the origin of the wife of Thoroughgood Pate is more probable to be found in the Rappahannock River area of the Northern Neck of Virginia. As with other items in the life and times of Thoroughgood Pate, this is an opinion, and many questions continue to be unanswered. As an example, why did Thomas Odonnell devise land to Thoroughgood Pate?

Records have been cited to show that Thoroughgood Pate was associated with a long line of Englishmen with strong allegiance to the Anglican Church. Some family traditions have evolved to claim he was Welsh. This may result from the development of a strong Welsh community on the Pee Dee River in South Carolina.

A group of Welsh Baptists entered the colonies of Pennsylvania and New Jersey as early as 1703. They migrated north and south, and reached the Pee Dee River area of South Carolina by 1736. They acquired a large grant to land along the River, near the North Carolina boundary. They influenced other people in the area to join their Baptist movement, including Anglicans. Pates were apparently among these.

Morgan Edwards was a leader of the Welsh Baptists. He traveled the length and breadth of the American colonies in the Pre-Revolutionary War period in an effort to unify all Baptists and inventory those of the faith. He recorded notes on congregations, church organization, pastors and members. Many of these notes for the Southern colonies survived. They have been published as *Materials Towards a History of the Baptists,* Heritage Press.

A grandson of Thoroughgood Pate, Rev. Charles Pate (b. 1729, d. p.1790), was among the pastors in the Welsh area of South Carolina. Rev. Pate was pastor of Beautyspot Baptist Church, east of present-day Bennettsville, South Carolina, when Morgan Edwards visited the area. He had been associated with Catfish Creek Church, near Welsh Neck on the Pee Dee River, and was baptized at that location. Edwards recorded valuable information on Rev. Pate, much of which will be noted later. For here, it is important to note that he described Charles Pate as now a "Regular Baptist", but was "bred a Churchman "(term used for Anglican Church), in the 1772 timeframe. Thus, he had a family heritage in the Anglican Church.

Thoroughgood Pate was English in origin, not Welsh, and his heritage in the Anglican Faith is well documented. The association of his descendants with the early Welsh Baptists may have resulted in the Welsh family traditions.

Questions have been raised as to a relationship of Thoroughgood and his descendants to other Pates in areas where they lived. Note was made in the narrative on 17th Century Virginia that DNA testing separates Thoroughgood Pate from other Pate families of 17th Century Virginia, genetically. However, his probable physical association, and that of his descendants, with other Pate Families should be recognized.

The association of descendants of Thoroughgood with descendants of Edward Pate who died in Southampton County, Virginia, in 1757 is very probable.

The sons of Thoroughgood removed from the Chowan/Bertie area to the Neuse River of Craven County 1737-1739. This location became Johnston County in 1746, Dobbs County in 1758, and Wayne County in 1779. The sons of Charles Pate, cited above, remained in this area for most of the later county transformation.

Edward Pate of Southampton, identified in the previous narrative, was survived by sons named Thomas, Travis, and Samuel, cited earlier. Travis was the executor of the will of Edward, appearing in the Southampton records as late as 14 December 1758, Southampton Orders 1754-1759, pages 476, 479, 488. He was located in Johnston County, North Carolina, 17 October 1766, Deed Book E-1. The research of Virginia Livingston proves the same man made both records and provides the record from the Southampton Orders Book. Others of the Edward family migrated to Johnston and Wake counties of North Carolina.

This research did not find proof of an actual association between these Pate Families. However, the Thoroughgood line recognized the given names of Travis, Samuel, and Thomas in the generation following Charles and his brothers, William and John. Travis is an unusual name, and use of it seems significant and may recognize the association of the Pate Families in Johnston, Dobbs, and Wake counties.

Samuel Pate and Jacob Pate appeared in the Chowan/Bertie area before Charles and his brothers departed. Jacob owned land on the Moratuck River, near where Thoroughgood and his family lived, Bertie Deed Book B, page 207. Available records do not identify the origins of these men. Perhaps Samuel was of the Southampton Pate Family. It is of interest that Jacob Pate was associated in Chowan Deed records with John Pope and Barnabus McKennie. Ms. Livingston reported John Pope was her direct ancestor and was proved to have been born in Isle of Wight County, Virginia. This research has proof that McKennie had an Isle of Wight background. A similar origin for Samuel and Jacob is probable.

Available records do not identify the date Thoroughgood entered Chowan Precinct, North Carolina. He was there, and established, before 25 August 1703, when he and Sarah sold a tract of land to Nicholas Blackmon, Deed Book W-1, page 47. The number of acres was omitted from the deed, but Blackmon sold the land 1 April 1707 and identified it as 84 acres. The deed executed by Thoroughgood described the sale to include "all my labor in Green Hall by the Beach Neck." It adjoined William Sadler and the Swamp. The deed executed by Blackmon again recognized William Sadler as the adjoining landowner, recognized all houses, fences, etc. Blackmon identified the land as part of a grant to Thomas Luten 22 March 1703. North Carolina Land Grant Book 1, page 121, listed a grant to Thomas Luten of 1,126 acres in 1703. Thoroughgood and Sarah signed the deed by signature, not a mark.

The records suggest Luten sold the 84 acres to Pate after the grant was completed. This research failed to find record of the purchase by Pate. Apparently, Pate was unhappy with the land, or had the opportunity to sell it and knew he could buy additional land from Luten. Luten sold 126 acres to Thoroughgood 4 January 1704, in the same area, by assignment of another patent.

The titles used to describe landmarks in this area are confusing and lead to frustration in an effort to locate Green Hall. However, one researcher provides needed insight. Mattacomack River, a waterway associated with landmarks cited in early Pate records, is recognized as Pembroke Creek today. It is located near the present-day town of Edenton. This seems sufficient to say Green Hall was on the east side of the Chowan River, near Edenton. This area remained in Chowan County when Bertie County was formed in 1722. Records locate his sons on landmarks of Roquist Creek, Salmon Creek, and

Cashie River, west of the Chowan River and near the town of Windsor, which became Bertie County in 1722.

The final record on Thoroughgood was his death in 1713. The inventory of his estate was filed in court 3 September 1713, Secretary of State Wills 1712-1722, page 74. No will was recorded, and no other probate records survived. It is assumed he died intestate. Records to follow will show the 126 acres of land descended to his eldest son, outside of probate, which was the custom under inheritance laws of the time.

The modest estate was inventoried by William Wallston, William Jones, and Phillip Wallston. Note was made earlier of involvement of the Wallston men and Thomas Luten in the activity of the St. Paul's Anglican Church. Numerous land records show Thomas Luten and the Wallston men lived as neighbors to Thoroughgood Pate, and all were active in the Anglican faith.

The value of the estate was 20 pounds, 18 shillings, 8 (or 3) pence. This included the value of four horses, three head of cattle, iron cooking pots, a frying pan, some old pewter, a gun, assorted wedges, hoes and axes, and a pile of lumber. It certainly was not the estate of a wealthy man. But, he was solvent and left a homesite and 126 acres for his heirs. He lived through some of the most trying of times. Raiding Indians killed twenty settlers within miles of his homesite in the year of his death. He had been party to the settlement of a large area of the New World. He is survived by a host of descendants who should respect and regard him with a great deal of gratitude.

Sarah survived Thoroughgood, as proved in the court record executed by Nathaniel Chevin, cited earlier. Her death may be indicated by the sale of the homesite by the son Charles, 9 March 1723, Chowan Deed Book C, page 137.

The report now turns to the sons of Thoroughgood. The son William was identified and proved to have been a son of Thoroughgood and Sarah in the court record executed by Nathaniel Chevin. It is assumed William was the youngest son.

Charles was proved to have been the oldest son of Thoroughgood when he sold the home site in 1722, cited earlier. The land was sold to Robert Hicks. The deed identified the land as 126 acres patented to Thomas Luten and sold by him to Thoroughgood Pate, the father of Charles Pate, and descended to Charles as heir at law of his father. It is assumed that Sarah was his mother.

The writer had advanced the claim that Thoroughgood had a son named Thoroughgood in earlier writings. Continued research has proved this to have been erroneous. The claim resulted from an incorrect interpretation of records. Unfortunately, the written word cannot be retracted! This current research has provided no record, nor opinion, that Thoroughgood had a son named Thoroughgood Pate. However, records do prove he had two sons named Charles and William. The association of John Pate with Charles and William lead to the assumption that John Pate was a third son.

The birthdates for these sons are open for debate. The Chowan County Deed cited earlier proves Charles was the oldest son (being the heir at law). A birth year of ca. 1690, in Virginia, seems appropriate for Charles. The court record executed by Nathaniel Chevin seems to suggest William was the youngest son, born ca. 1698, in Virginia or North Carolina. John is assumed to have been born between these dates, ca. 1695, in Virginia or North Carolina. Readers are free to accept these dates or determine others.

John Pate witnessed a land sale, Ambrose Airs to Thomas Powell, in Bertie (formerly Chowan) 4 December 1726, Deed Book B, page 222. The land was located "at the fork of Cashie River". This places John in the neighborhood of the residences of Charles and William. Records, to be cited, will show John relocated to the Neuse River of Craven County with Charles and William.

This research has no evidence of other sons for Thoroughgood. Note has been made that the Jacob Pate and Samuel Pate of later Chowan-Bertie records appear to have been from other Pate lines in Virginia.

This research failed to find records to identify any daughters of Thoroughgood. It is assumed that John Monk relocated to Craven County with Charles, John, and William. They exchanged land. He may represent a brother-in-law. Records to prove this were not located. Monk families were associated with the Pates in the Northern Neck of Virginia.

Charles Pate was active in Chowan-Bertie land records after the death of his father. Researchers must wonder how the son of one who died with such modest financial holdings could manage success in real estate so soon. He purchased 350 acres only three years after the death of his father, and, shortly after that, acquired a 260-acre land grant. Perhaps the success that eluded his father, in his early manhood, graced the son. Note will be made of the most important of these transactions.

Phillip Wallston and wife Dorothy sold 350 acres of land to Charles Pate 24 September 1717, Chowan Deed Book B, page 590. This tract was located on the Kesiah (Cashie) River, near the home site of Thoroughgood Pate. Charles sold this land in two tracts in later years. The wife of Charles did not sign the deeds, so it is assumed he was unmarried at that time. Charles and Nathaniel Chevin were recognized as adjacent landowners to a 640-acre grant to Richard Rose 21 July 1717. Charles acquired a grant for 260 acres on the north side of Roquist Swamp in 1721, Patent Book 3, page 83. The latter, apparently, became his homesite because he and wife Sarah sold it to Robert Howell 7 October 1740, after they had departed the county. Charles and Sarah were identified as "of Craven County". A list of freeholders living between Solomon Creek and the Cashie River, 9 January 1719, included Charles Pate and William Pate.

Available records failed to identify the marriage date for Charles and Sarah. It is assumed his first-born son was named Charles and was the Rev. Charles Pate acknowledged as pastor of Beautyspot Baptist Church by Morgan Edwards, cited earlier. The notes made by Edwards report Rev. Charles Pate was born 1 May 1729 in Bertie Precinct, North Carolina. The Edwards notes also report that Rev. Pate married Sarah Henderson. These records identify three successive generations of Pate men married to a wife with the given name of Sarah.

The records in the Chowan-Bertie area were fewer in number for William and John. Both were present, and William was identified as a freeholder and served on jury duty. Records of the purchase or sale of land by either were not found.

Valuable land records for the three brothers were found in Craven County. The Neuse River area where they settled was in Craven County for a short time after they arrived. It became Johnston County in 1746.

Available records do not tell us who first migrated to the Neuse River area of Craven, but William acquired a colonial grant to 640 acres of land 17 February 1737. The land was located on the north side of the River, near Pate's Branch, Patent Book 3, Page 368. Current information is that Pate's Branch flows into Stoney Creek, considered by family members to be the ancient seat of the Pate Family in present-day WayneCounty.

William sold this land as follows: 4 April 1738, Charles Pate purchased 301 acres of the grant for 50 pounds, Craven County Deed Book 1, page 10; John Pate purchased 199 acres on 7 April

1738, page 11; John Monk purchased the remaining 140 acres on the same date, page 8. The sale to Charles Pate was witnessed by John Monk and William Pate, the sale to John Pate was witnessed by John Monk and Charles Pate, and the sale to John Monk was witnessed by Charles Pate and John Pate. The grant was for 640 acres, and William sold the entire 640 acres.

The suggestion has been made that John Monk was a brother-in-law to the Pate brothers. Caution is made that proof is not available. The records place three sons, and possibly one daughter, on the north side of the Neuse River in the location that became Wayne County. It is in order to note that other researchers have noted an association of Monk and Pate families in later generations.

The assumption is offered that Charles was born ca. 1690 in the Northern Neck of Virginia and died in Dobbs County, North Carolina, after 1769. He and his children will be treated in detail in the next narrative in this report. An overview of his children is in order here.

Unfortunately, the Dobbs Courthouse burned in 1880, with only one deed index book surviving the fire. The index book provides proof that Charles conveyed land to James Pate in 1758 and in 1769. It is assumed that James was a son of Charles and the last conveyance was in anticipation of death. All other records were lost in the fire. Thus, there are no extant records to prove the children of Charles. Various records lead to the assumption that other sons included Rev. Charles Pate of the Pee Dee River area of South Carolina who disappeared from records after the U. S. Census of 1790; Thoroughgood Pate who died in Richmond County, North Carolina, ca. 1802; and Samuel Pate who died in Kershaw County, South Carolina, after the U. S. Census of 1810. Other sons are possible, but available records are not supportive of such. Available records fail to suggest any daughters.

James, like his father, remained in the Dobbs County area. He died before the U. S. Census for 1790. His assumed widow, Martha, appeared on this census. Various records lead to the assumption that his children included sons named Daniel, Elias, Isham, and James.

Records prove that Thoroughgood Pate d. ca. 1802 had sons named Samuel, Stephen, and Thoroughgood d. 1836. Also, one daughter, Sabra, who married George Wright is proved.

The Baptist Church records compiled by Morgan Edwards identify the children of Rev. Charles Pate in 1772. They were Sarah,

Charles, Mary, Rebecca, Ann, Shadrack, and Joel. This research adds one son, Ananias, to the list. Ananias was born after Morgan Edwards recorded the family.

The sons of Samuel are assigned with less support than is available for his brothers. The writer strongly believes that Samuel, Bennett, Elijah, William, and Jason were among his sons. One named Allen may have been a son, though descendants of Allen claim he was a grandson through Elijah.

Research provides less definition on the other sons of Thoroughgood d. 1713 -- John and William. A large number of people from the Dobbs County area relocated to the area of Cumberland County that later became Moore County. These included three sons of Charles d. p. 1769, Thoroughgood d. 1802, Charles d. p. 1790, and Samuel d. p. 1810. A William Pate was among them, and more will be offered on his identity later.

This concludes the review of the life and times of Thoroughgood Pate d. 1713. The next narrative will treat his children in more detail.

IV

THE PATES OF DOBBS COUNTY, NORTH CAROLINA

The preceding narratives placed the known descendants of Thoroughgood Pate d. 1713 on Stoney Creek, a tributary of the Neuse River, in North Carolina. The site, in 1737- 1740, was located in Craven County. The evolution of this area to Johnston, Dobbs and Wayne counties was followed in the preceding narratives. Additional detail on some later county formation will be of value as this report progresses.

Wayne County was formed from the western part of Dobbs, 18 October 1779. The Stoney Creek area of Old Dobbs became Wayne County at this time. The remainder of Dobbs continued as an entity until 5 December 1791, when that area became Lenoir and Glasgow counties. Glasgow had a brief existence, becoming Greene County 18 November 1799. Each of these county formations is important to Pate Family history.

The area of Old Dobbs County, North Carolina, was home to the generation that followed Thoroughgood Pate d. 1713. The assumption is offered that two of his sons were buried there, though grave sites have not been identified. It was from this base on Stoney Creek that this Pate Family divided and migrated to numerous areas of the undeveloped American colonies, and ultimately, the new nation. Certainly, all members did not migrate. The Pate surname continues to be present in the Stoney Creek area today.

The loss of courthouse records in this area has been a long-standing impediment to the development of family history. Some background is in order.

The courthouse for Johnston County, when the area separated from Craven County in 1746, was established at Kingstown (Kinston today). Kingstown became the county seat of Dobbs when that county was formed in 1758, a new courthouse was formed for the western area that remained Johnston County. Earlier Johnston records were retained by Dobbs County. Likewise, when Wayne was formed in 1779, the Kingstown courthouse retained all existing records and continued as the courthouse for Dobbs County. The dissolution of Dobbs and formation of Lenoir and Glasgow counties in 1791 again resulted in the retention of all existing records at Kingstown, which became the Lenoir County seat.

The Lenoir County courthouse burned in 1878, and a facility established for the temporary storage of records also burned in 1880, with the loss of all records, except one Deed Index Book. The Pate Family members who lived in the part of old Johnston – Dobbs that became Lenoir County lost records for the years 1746-1880. The Pates who lived in the part of old Johnston-Dobbs that became Wayne County lost records for the years 1746-1779, when Wayne was formed. Thus, research is more productive on those who remained in the Stoney Creek area.

The surviving Deed Index Book has been probed by historians, and it does provide some details of value. Grantee and grantor records have been re-created for some 49 deed books. Dates have been assigned to most transactions. Examples: John Pate purchased land from Joseph Griffin in Book 1, between November 1746 and April 1754; and Charles Pate conveyed land to James Pate in Book 7, between April 1765 and April 1769. There are 52 Pate transactions in Deed Books 1-49. One source reports Johnston County records were included in Book 1 through page 400 of Book 5. Dobbs County records were included in Books 5-14. Books 15-49 pertain to Lenoir County entries.

This report will draw conclusions based on records in the surviving Deed Index Book. Acknowledgment is granted that deed books of this time recorded transactions other than land conveyances, such as the sale of slaves, marriage agreements, gifts of any type, etc. No means exists to identify the type of transaction. This research assumes these Pate entries represented land conveyances.

Additional resources found to be of value to this report include some surviving quit rent records of Johnston County, colonial and state land grant records, some surviving tax lists of Dobbs County, militia records, voters list of Dobbs, and District Court records. Some of these were not housed at Kingstown.

Attention also needs to be noted of the loss of records in Moore County, North Carolina. Extant records show that Pates from the old Dobbs County area migrated west, at an early date, to the area of

Cumberland County which became Moore County in 1784. The Cumberland records for this timeframe provide good information, starting in the early 1750s. The Moore County Courthouse burned in 1884, with the loss of all Moore County records. The fate of several Pates in the Moore County area is known because of the survival of Cumberland records and will be provided in this report. However, the loss of Moore County records results in unanswered questions on somepersons.

The preceding background leads to the opinion that research is sufficient to provide a creditable, though assumptive in some areas, report of the descendants of Charles Pate d. ca. 1769. Limited information is available on his brothers, John and William.

DNA testing is a new and very valuable tool in genealogy. Perhaps it can be described as a needed adjunct to traditional genealogical research, though alone it will not develop the history of a family. In conjunction with traditional research, progress is possible on many previously observed "dead ends" and "brickwalls", while many suspected and presumed relationships may be validated.

This is not a dissertation on DNA testing. The writer is not qualified to venture far into this technology. Rather, it is an overview of the correlation of genetic genealogy (DNA testing) with traditional genealogy, and to recognize the complementary value of each to the Thoroughgood Pate Family research.

Some basic background is essential to understand the results cited here. Only males carry the Y-chromosome. It is unique in the reproduction process in that it does not divide. It is passed intact from the male of one generation to a male of a later generation, unlike other chromosomes. The Y-chromosome of a living male does not differ from that of his male ancestors of the same surname.

The locations tested on the Y-chromosome are called markers. Each marker has an identification assigned to it by the scientific community (for example, DYS391). The Y- DNA test provides number values (called alleles) for each marker, which together comprises the haplogroup. These alleles remain constant through generations, even back to when surnames were first adopted. To summarize, Y-DNA passes from father to son along with the family surname, and may remain unchanged through succeeding generations except for infrequent random mutations.

Identification is given the test results on individuals in DNA testing that determines the ancient people, or family group, from which the person descends. These groups are identified as haplogroups which may have origins thousands of years past. Each haplogroup is given a unique identifying code.

There are several family lines in the Pate DNA Project which have been classified into different haplogroups, the major ones being I-M223, R-M173, and R-M269.

It is important to note that there is no relationship between haplogroups, at least in the timeframe of historical records, nor even within the timeframe of our current calendars. Pates can be found in different haplogroups, though the ancestral origins of each are currently unknown.

All descendants of Thoroughgood Pate d. 1713 are in Haplogroup I-M223, having a different family origin from Pates in other haplogroups.

In addition to the broad assignment to a haplogroup, DNA results of the Pate DNA Project may also identify descendants of Thoroughgood to specific sons.

As noted above, a mutation seems to have occurred within the sons of Thoroughgood. The alleles will be the same for all his descendants until such a mutation has occurred. Some Thoroughgood descendants differ at Marker 391, some have 9 alleles and some have 10 alleles. Traditional research at this time identifies all with 9 alleles to be probable descendants of Charles Pate d. ca. 1769. The records to support this relationship are as strong (definitive) as Pate research can determine. As further confirmation, traditional genealogy does not provide any support for a relationship to Charles among any with 10 alleles at Marker 391.

The conclusion is offered that all with 9 alleles at Marker 391 are descendants of Charles Pate d. ca. 1769, a son of Thoroughgood Pate d.1713. Those with 10 alleles at this marker are descendants from Thoroughgood's other two sons, John or William. This ability to differentiate the descendants of Charles from those of John and William is a major genealogical advance.

The known children of Thoroughgood Pate d. 1713, documented earlier, were sons named Charles, born ca. 1690; John, born ca. 1695; and William, born ca. 1698. As noted earlier, these birth years are arbitrary. Records prove the sibling relationship for Charles and William, but that of John had been an assumption, until DNA testing has removed any reasonable doubts as to the father of John, in the opinion of the writer. His father was Thoroughgood, and he was a brother of Charles and William.

The assumption that John Monk was a son-in-law, based on his association with Charles, John, and William, was offered earlier.

The oldest son, Charles, will be identified hereafter as Charles Pate d. ca. 1769. Attaching a year to the given name in families where repetitive use of given names was common serves to maintain identity of individuals in the narration. The death year is more easily identified or confirmed than the birth year in early generations. He and his descendants have been the focus of this research for many years and will remain the object for the remainder of this report.

Cursory information will be offered on the fates of John and William at this point. Hopefully, this will be of value in the differentiation of the children of the three brothers. Information on John and William follows.

JOHN PATE D. CA. 1779,
SON OF THOROUGHGOOD PATE D. 1713

Records document the presence of John Pate on Stoney Creek in Craven County, 7 April 1738, when he purchased 199 acres of land from his brother William Pate, cited earlier. His continued ownership of this land is proved by Johnston County quit rent payments for 199 acres in April 1744 and June 1750. These records are sufficient to say John lived on, and owned land, on Stoney Creek through 1750.

A John Pate moved to the area of Cumberland County, North Carolina, that became Moore County, as did many of his Dobbs County kin and neighbors. He was active in land records of that area. He and William Pate witnessed a land transaction between Joseph Elkins and Thomas Wadsworth, 28 January 1755, Cumberland Deed Book 2, page 60. John Pate purchased 100 acres of land on Lower Little River 11 July 1761 and sold it 28 September 1762, Deed Book 2, pages 138 and 246.

Records to follow suggest this John Pate was a son of the William Pate in area records, who was the son of Thoroughgood Pate d. 1713. Many of his Pate kin from the Johnston/Dobbs area settled on Lower Little River and nearby Crain Creek in this time frame, to be cited later.

Arthur McKey received a grant to 170 acres of land, 26 November 1757, Patent Book 2, page 183. The land was located on Contentnea Creek, adjacent to John Pate's land. Thus, John lived on the Contentnea in Dobbs County by 1757. This waterway is north of Stoney

Creek. It flows through present-day Green and Lenoir counties, in an easterly direction, to join the Neuse River on the east side of Lenoir County. Other land records also place John and persons thought to have been his sons on Contentnea Creek. These include land grants for 109 acres on 3 July 1769, 200 acres on 5 May 1772, and 150 acres on 11 January 1773.

One published resource, *North Carolina Entries of Claims for Land within Dobbs County 1778-1790* by William L. Murphy, identifies Dobbs land grants that were located in the area that became Greene County. Some researchers place John and other Pate men thought to be his sons in the Dobbs County area that became Greene County. They include Pates identified in land transactions: Isaac Pate – 10 March 1780, 100 acres joining his own land and the land of John Pate and William Pate; Elijah Johnston – 14 April 1785, "on south side of the Great Contentnea joining John Pate" (and others); and Enos Ellis – 5 July 1785, 50 acres on the "north side of Contentnea joining Joseph Pate" (and others).

Few county tax lists for this period survive. However, the existing ones add support for the claims that John Pate and his family removed from the Stoney Creek area to the area that became Greene and Lenoir counties. The tax list for 1769 identified Pates named James (son of Charles d. ca. 1769), William, John Sr. (who had a son named Joseph of taxable age), and a John Pot. Perhaps John Pot was John Pate, Jr. This list represented Dobbs before Wayne County separated in 1779.

The Dobbs tax list for 1779, after Wayne County had been separated from Dobbs, listed Pates named Isaac, Joseph, and William. John was absent. The list for 1780, one year later, listed Catherine, Isaac, John, Joseph, and William. John Sr. was absent. Note needs to be made that the descendants of Charles Pate d. ca. 1769 were in newly-formed Wayne County, separate from the family of John. Catherine had a sizeable estate, when compared with others on the list, suggesting that she was mature in age and established with assets. Isaac, John, and William were her near neighbors.

The absence of John Sr. and the presence of Catherine, with a taxable estate, leads this researcher to the assumption that John Sr. was deceased, and Catherine was his widow. Caution is issued that this is an assumption! The death year for John appears to have been ca. 1779. His identity, for this report, now becomes John Pate d. ca. 1779.

Several entries in the Dobbs Deed Index Book suggest land conveyances between John Pate d. ca. 1779 and his family. The most important, for this report, follow: John Pate to John Pate, Jr., Book 5, page 382 - April 1758-April 1761; John Pate to William Pate, Book 5, page 471 – same dates; John Pate to Isaac Pate, Book 7, page 181 – April 1765- April 1769; William Pate to John Pate, Sr., book 10, page 39 – January 1773-May 1775; John Pate to William Pate, Book 10, page 491 – April 1773-1775; and John Pate to Joseph Pate, Book 11, page 51 – January 1777-April 1779. The assumption is offered that these records represent land conveyances between John Pate d. ca. 1779 and his sons.

The conveyance to Joseph Pate in 1777-1779 appears to be the last entry involving John Pate d. ca. 1779. Again, caution is issued that this is an assumption based on subjective information. Later entries for the names of John Pate, John Pate, Sr., and John Pate, Jr. are assumed to refer to the son of John d. ca. 1779 and his son, or a grandson through another son.

The 1754 Johnston County militia records report John Pate, Sr., John Pate, Jr., and William Pate were members of Captain Francis Machelwain's Company, *Colonial Soldiers of the South* by Murtie June Clark. The two named John were the man of this report and his son. The William Pate is assumed to also have been another son of this John. Ages for militia duty varied, but most commonly all males between 16 and 60 years were required to participate. This record, when compared to other records available, leads to the assumption that John Pate, Sr., was near 60 years and his sons John Pate, Jr., and William Pate were over 16 years in 1754. The ages are compatible with the arbitrary birth year for John Sr. and do not conflict with the expected ages for men with land transactions in the Dobbs Deed Index between April 1758 and April 1761.

The preceding records lead to the assumption that John Pate d. ca. 1779 married Catherine [?] and had sons named John Pate, William Pate, Isaac Pate, and Joseph Pate, and perhaps in that order of birth. Other sons are possible, but are not of record in the research performed to date. The names of any daughters are unknown.

The 1790 U. S. Census provides supportive information for this family structure. The following Pate households were listed in Dobbs County: John Sr., John Jr., Sarah, William Sr., William Jr., and Joseph. All but Joseph were listed in adjacent households, which compares favorably with the 1780 tax list. That list reported Joseph in District 7, Catherine, William, Isaac, and John were in District 9. Three of the sons of John d. ca. 1779 on the 1780 tax list are recognized on the 1790 U. S. Census. Isaac is missing, but an Isaac Pate is listed in nearby Beaufort County, over 16 years of age.

A study of tax records, militia records, and the Dobbs land conveyances indicates the four sons assigned to John Pate d. ca. 1779 were born 1738-1754. Thus, Isaac Pate in Beaufort County in 1790 was of the age of grandsons of John, not the age of his sons. He appears to have moved to Richmond County by 1800, where he was enumerated with his Pate kin of that county, and was with his family in Greene County in 1820, 26-45 years of age. This leads to the assumptive identity of Sarah Pate living adjacent to John Sr. and William Sr. on the Dobbs U. S. Census for 1790. She was the widow of Isaac, son of John Pate d. ca. 1779, and brother to John and William.

The preceding narration provides the opinions of the writer on the fate and family of John Pate d. ca. 1779, the son of Thoroughgood Pate d. 1713. As with many other areas of research on this family, it is a mix of records and assumptions. Readers are free to accept or refute the claims.

The report now turns to William Pate, assumed to have been the youngest son of Thoroughgood Pate d. 1713.

WILLIAM PATE D. CA. 1775, SON OF THOROUGHGOOD PATE D. 1713

William was the first of the Pate brothers to acquire land in the area that became Old Dobbs County. He received a Colonial Grant to 640 acres, 17 February 1737, Patent Book 3, page 368. The tract was located on the northeast side of the Neuse River on Pate Branch. This branch is one of the waterways that forms the head of Stoney Creek. He sold the entire tract to his brothers (Charles Pate d. ca. 1769 – 301 acres and John Pate d. ca. 1779 – 199 acres) and to John Monk – 140 acres. The sale to Charles Pate was on 4 April 1738, and the sales to John Pate and John Monk were on 7 April 1738, Craven Deed Book 1, pages 8, 10, 11. It is interesting that John Monk sold 130 acres of his purchase to John Pate in June 1743, Craven Court Minutes 1742-1748.

William applied for another grant for 195 acres ten days before this sale, *North Carolina Colonial Records,* Volume 4, page 349. This research failed to determine how he disposed of this land.

These records provide a definitive start for the report on this son of Thoroughgood Pate d. ca. 1713. Unfortunately, the nature of the report turns from definition to assumption fast.

Important questions on his fate and family escape definition. Available records do identify a William Pate who has been accepted by this research as the son of Thoroughgood Pate d. ca. 1713. However, his proven association with the sons of Charles Pate d. ca. 1769 requires some consideration be given that he was their sibling, rather than their uncle. A review of some records is indicated.

The presence of a William Pate on a 1755 Johnston County militia record has been cited. Since he was listed with John Pate, Sr., and John Pate, Jr., it is assumed that this record listed John Sr. and two of his sons, John Jr. and William. The Dobbs Deed Index Book supports this assumption, in that it has record of land conveyances from John Pate, Sr., to John Pate, Jr., and William Pate within the 1758–1761-year timeframe. This record indicates both sons reached the age of maturity within the cited years. Thus, they would have been of military age in 1755. The assumption is offered that the cited record of 1755 represented John Pate d. ca. 1779 and two of his sons.

Note was made earlier that one William Pate moved to the part of Cumberland County that eventually became Moore County. He is proved by records to have had an association with a number of persons from the old Dobbs County area. They include Pate kinsmen named Thoroughgood, Charles, and Samuel, as well as Nicholas Smith and others. These kinsmen were sons of Charles Pate d. ca. 1769, to be validated later. The question for this report, here, is to determine if this William was their brother or uncle.

Available records fail to provide unquestionable identity for all of the sons of this Charles. It is possible that one named William could have been another of his sons. A review of available records adds some definition to the.

The results of traditional research leave researchers with four good assumptive choices on the sons of this Charles, to be cited later. Further, DNA testing supports this assumption. Note has been made of the mutation at Marker 391 that identifies the sons of Charles, as currently interpreted. All of the participants tested to date with that mutation are descendants of one of the four recognized sons of Charles.

The current interpretation of records of Cumberland County is that William Pate of that area was the son of Thoroughgood Pate

d. ca. 1713 and a brother to Charles Pate d. ca. 1769. Since he disappears from records after the year of 1775, he will be identified as William Pate d. ca. 1775 for the remainder of this report.

William was located in Cumberland County by 16 January 1754. He could have arrived there any time after his Craven County records of 1739-1740. Records suggest he was established there in 1754, when land was surveyed for Phillip Mulkey on the North Fork of Lower Little River. The North Fork was also known as Crains/Cranes Creek. The survey tells us the 200-acre tract was about a mile from William Bates. The assumption is offered that the Pate surname was misinterpreted as Bates. Other records tell us that William Pate lived in this area. Chainbearers for the survey were Thoroughgood Pate d. 1802 and Charles Heard, as reported in the Bladen Survey Book 1753-1754 (Cumberland County separated from Bladen County in 1754.) The index to published Cumberland County Deed Book 1-7 has no other Bates entry.

William Pate and John Pate were witnesses to a land conveyance by Joseph Elkins to Thomas Wadsworth, 28 January 1755, Cumberland Deed Book 2, page 60. William received two land grants in Cumberland County, 14 November 1757 and 1 July 1758. Both were located on Cranes Creek, a tributary of the Lower Little River. The chainbearers for the 1757 grant were Thoroughgood Pate and Thomas Wadsworth. The citation for the 1758 grant was Patent Book 2, page 205. The other citation has been misplaced, as of this writing.

William Mires sold land to John Smith 26 October 1758, located on the Lower Little River. The witnesses included Ruth Pate, Cumberland Deed Book 1, page 295. John Smith was from the Old Dobbs County area. Consideration is given that Ruth Pate was the wife of one of the Pate men in these records. This research has identified the wives of Thoroughgood Pate and Charles Pate of these records, and neither was named Ruth. Most probably, she was the wife of William Pate, but that has not been proved. Note needs to be made that a Samuel Pate of the Virginia Pate Family that settled in the western part of Johnston County had a wife named Ruth. This research failed to find presence of this Pate Family in Cumberland County in this timeframe. It seems unlikely that Ruth Pate in this record was of the Johnston County Pate Family.

William Pate conveyed 75 acres to Sarah Wadsworth 10 March 1760. The tract was identified as part of a grant to William Pate in 1758, Cumberland Deed Book 2, page 93. Sarah Wadsworth conveyed the same 75 acres to John Wadsworth 18 May 1766, and identified it as a part of the Pate grant of 1758, Book 3, page 6. William Pate conveyed the remainder of the 1758 grant (125 acres) to John Wadsworth on the same day, same citation. John Wadsworth conveyed the 200-acre tract to Neil Shaw 12 February 1771, and identified the land as a grant to William Pate in 1758, Book 6, page 185.

The preceding records infer a relationship between William Pate, Sarah Wadsworth, and John Wadsworth. Further, the relationship between Sarah Wadsworth and the Wadsworth men named John and Thomas would be of value in the interpretation of these records. Perhaps Sarah was the wife of one of them. William Pate left the area before the execution of the record of 1771, on which more will be offered later. The 1790 U. S. Census for the Lower Little River area listed John Wadsworth. Thomas Wadsworth and Charles Heard were in South Carolina, where the assumed sons of William Pate lived.

John Pate had purchased land in the Lower Little River-Cranes Creek area. The land had originally been granted to Charles Heard, Deed Book 2, page 138, who served as a chainbearer with Thoroughgood Pate for the Phillip Mulkey survey in 1754. John sold this land 28 September 1762, Book 2, page 246. He acquired 200 acres by grant, located on McDeed Creek of Lower Little River, which adjoined Thomas Wadsworth, survey 11 April 1766. The chainbearers for this survey were Thomas Wadsworth and Mose Williams.

Several entries for Thomas Pate are recorded. The most important for this report follow. He had a survey for 100 acres, 11 November 1772. The land was located on Lower Little River between Thomas Wadsworth and John Pate's lines. Chainbearers were Thomas Wadsworth and John Pate. This appears to be the land he sold 13 October 1782 to Matthew Davis, Deed Book 7, page 98. The location on the deed of sale was identical to the survey. Thomas Pate was identified as a "gamekeeper".

Thomas Pate sold livestock to Matthew Davis, 26 October 1781, Deed Book 7, page 83.

The Cumberland County tax list for 1777 reported Thomas Pate and John Pate were taxable, Thomas for 150 acres and John for 100 acres, *Miscellaneous Ancient Records of Moore County*, R. Wicker.

This research found no record of John in Cumberland or Moore County after the 1777 tax list. Thomas seems to have departed after his sale to Matthew Davis in 1782.

The records already cited here clearly establish an association for the three men named William, John, and Thomas. Citing further records for William, John, and Thomas would be redundant.

Other Cumberland County records (in the area that became Moore County) exist for other Pates. Those for Thoroughgood Pate, Charles Pate, Sarah Pate, and Winefred Pate will be reported in the appropriate areas of this report. A relationship to Sarah Wadsworth and Ruth Pate has been suggested.

William Pate sold the last of his Cumberland County land 19 May 1766, Deed Book 3, page 6. He was living in Anson County, North Carolina, before that date. A North Carolina coroner's inquest for Anson County 15 July 1764 reported that he and Thoroughgood Pate d. 1802 were on a jury to investigate the death of John Rottenberry.

William acquired a patent to 200 acres in Anson County, 22 January 1773, Patent Book 22, page 142. He sold this tract to Jos. Melton, 11 March 1775, Anson Deed Book K, page 319. The location was on the southwest side of the Pee Dee River, on Night's Branch of Little Brown Creek. This waterway arises near the South Carolina border and flows north to join the Pee Dee River north of present-day Wadesboro.

Readers will note that William Pate d. ca. 1775 was associated with Thoroughgood Pate d. 1802, a son of Charles Pate d. ca. 1769, in Cumberland and Anson County records.

Records do not identify the children of William Pate d. ca. 1775. The assumption is offered that they include sons named John Pate, Thomas Pate, and William Pate. Sarah Wadsworth may have been a daughter. John and Thomas were the men of those names in the Cumberland County records, cited earlier. The assumption is also offered that they were the men of those names on the Lancaster County, South Carolina, U. S. Census for 1790. They were listed with a William Pate of their age, who is assumed to have been another son of William Pate d. ca. 1775.

John Pate is documented as a Loyalist in the Revolutionary War, *Loyalists in the Southern Campaign of the Revolutionary War* by Murtie June Clark. He was a member of Major John Harrison's Corps, South Carolina Rangers. Muster rolls document his service in the Camden District area, 24 June 1780 to 24 December 1781. The last entry reported he was "a prisoner with the Rebels". These dates follow his departure from Cumberland County, North Carolina.

Though available records do not prove that the John Pate in the Revolutionary War records and the U. S. Census for 1790 represent the same man, the assumption is offered that the same man made both records. Both records record his presence in the Camden District.

Little Brown Creek, Anson County, North Carolina, where William Pate d. ca. 1775 owned land, is near the South Carolina border. A journey from this location to Lancaster County in 1790 would involve little more than crossing the border.

The 1790 U. S. Census provided scant information, compared to later enumerations. This one tells us that John and William had children represented, probably two sons and two daughters each. Thomas had no children represented in his household.

Speculation and assumptions are generally unwelcomed in a formal family report. Given the loss and/or lack of records on this Pate Family, assumptions are essential to this report. Fortunately, most being used are based on records, not intuition.

Intensive research has been ongoing for years to develop the origin of four Pate men listed on the 1801 tax list of Lincoln County, Georgia. They appear in other county records and church records of the area. They were Thomas Pate, William Pate, James Pate, and Charles Pate. William died in Henry County, Georgia, with his will filed 30 November 1844; James died in Fayette County, Georgia, with his will filed 19 September 1831; and Charles died in Tuscaloosa County, Alabama 20 July 1837, apparently without sons. An elderly Thomas Pate accompanied Charles to Alabama. He was enumerated on the U. S. Census for Tuscaloosa County in 1830 and that of adjoining Pickens County in 1840. A younger Newell Walton Pate lived adjacent to Thomas on both returns.

Men known to descend from William, James, and Newell are in the Pate DNA Project. They test in Haplogroup I-M223 and have 10 alleles at Marker 391. This places them in the Thoroughgood Pate d. 1713 family line and identifies them as descendants of John Pate d. ca. 1779 or William Pate d. ca. 1775, unless Thoroughgood had another son unknown at this time.

The assumption is offered that William who died in Henry County, Georgia, 1844, and Thomas on the Alabama U. S. Censuses for 1830 and 1840, were the men so-named on the 1790 U. S. Census for Lancaster County, South Carolina, and were sons of William Pate d. ca. 1775. The other two men were more probably grandsons of William d. ca. 1775, through either the son John or a son not identified by this research.

Thomas Pate in the 1790 U. S. Census for Lancaster County had no children represented in his household. All males near him on the Alabama U. S. Censuses were born after 1790.

A similar assumption is offered on the fate of some descendants of John Pate d. ca. 1779. A Pate Family of Richmond County, North Carolina, is proved to have migrated to Weakley County, Tennessee, in the 1820s, to be documented later. DNA testing and traditional genealogy prove the Richmond County family descended from Charles Pate d. ca. 1769, of which more will be offered later. The assumption is offered that they were accompanied, or followed, by Pate cousins who settled in the adjoining county of Obion, Tennessee. Descendants of this family have tested and are in Haplogroup I-M223 and have 10 alleles at Marker 391. The assumption is offered that they descend from John Pate d. ca. 1779.

North Carolina families other than Pate also relocated to this area of Tennessee. The Howell family was neighbors to the Pates on Stoney Creek in Old Dobbs County. Howell family information, shared with the writer in past years, documents the migration of this family to Obion and Gibson counties of Tennessee. A letter written by Thomas Charles Davis Howell, a son of Caleb Howell, describes the migration. He was three years old when his family moved from Wayne County to Moore County, North Carolina, about 1817. They moved on to Gibson County, Tennessee, in 1824, where his father died in 1836. Consideration must be given that the Pate Family that settled in Obion County, Tennessee, about 1824 relocated with Caleb Howell. John Brickhouse, who married into the Pate Family of Richmond County, North Carolina, also moved to Gibson County before 1840. The Long family of Columbus County, North Carolina, is reported to have moved to the Obion/ Gibson area of Tennessee and intermarried with the Pate Family located there.

Caution is issued that, as of this writing, proof for neither of the preceding assumptions is available. However, they seem plausible and are supported by records. Further, unknown sons of John d. ca. 1779 and William d. ca. 1775 should be expected.

This completes the report on two sons of Thoroughgood Pate d. 1713, John Pate d. ca. 1779, and William Pate d. ca. 1775. They will not be followed further in this report.

The third son, Charles Pate d. ca. 1769 will be treated next. Subsequent chapters will treat the descendants for each of his four sons.

The early years in the life of Charles Pate d. ca. 1769 were described in the narration on the life and times of his father. This area of the report provides information on his years in the area of North Carolina that became Dobbs County. His sons reached maturity in this area, and they will be identified to the extent available records and DNA testing permit.

The death year attached to his name serves to separate him from the many Pate men named Charles in later generations. Two resources suggest he died about 1769. The Dobbs Deed Index Book reports land conveyances by him to a younger Pate in the 1761-1769 timeframe. Also, he was absent from the extant 1769 Dobbs County tax lists. Acknowledgement is granted that his absence may reflect an exemption from taxes by age or health; however, these records, plus his absence from future records, suggest he died about 1769.

One son, James Pate, was listed on the 1769 tax list for Old Dobbs County. Records place the other sons of Charles in other areas by 1769, to be cited.

Charles purchased 301 acres of land from his brother, William Pate d. ca. 1775, in 1739, cited earlier. The land was located on a branch of Stoney Creek, a tributary of the Neuse River, in the part of Craven County that became Dobbs and, later, Wayne County. He acquired another 200 acres by grant in the same locale, 22 May 1741, *North Carolina Colonial Records,* Vol. 4, page 296. This research failed to find record of additional land acquisition by Charles in the Neuse River area. Note was made in the narration on his years in Chowan County of multiple real estate ventures in that area. He seemed to enjoy the success in real estate ventures that had apparently eluded his father.

The land-granting process in North Carolina should be of interest to researchers. The headright land was free. However, numerous officials (clerks, surveyors, agents) had to perform services and sign permits, and each received a fee. The foreword to *Abstracts of North Carolina Patents* by Margaret Hoffman, details these costs. They were sizeable, relative to the annual income of most settlers. They equated to several months of income. Settlers had to have some financial means to acquire multiple grants.

The Dobbs Deed Index Book provides record of four land conveyances by Charles. He sold land to Jonas Griffin in 1746, Book 1, page 2, and to Caleb Musgrove in 1758-1761, Book 7, page 311. Available records fail to suggest any relationship between Charles and Jonas Griffin or Caleb Musgrove. The sale to James Pate does suggest a relationship between the parties, by virtue of having a surname in common, and other records support this indicated relationship.

James conveyed 100 acres of land to Daniel Pate 21 October 1781, Wayne County Deed Book 1, pages 53-54. The deed identified the tract as "a part of a tract granted to Charles Pate 22 May 1741", located on the south side of Stoney Creek. Note that the grant to Charles on 22 May 1741 was cited earlier. The assumption is offered that part of this 200-acre grant was one of the conveyances Charles executed to James in this Dobbs Deed record. It is possible that the entire 200 acres were transferred by the two conveyances to James.

Records, to be cited, show Daniel devised 100 acres of this land to his sons in his will of 1791. Thus, these land records identify ownership of this land by four lineal generations of this Pate Family. This is the basis for the claim that James was a son of Charles d. ca. 1769. Additional support for the relationship comes from the fact that James was the only son of Charles to remain in Dobbs/Wayne County. His brothers removed to other areas, to be cited. Further, DNA testing proves that descendants of James have the same mutation at Marker 391 that is characteristic of the descendants of Charles, as previously explained.

Birth years assigned to three of the sons of Charles are arbitrary. The date for the second son was recorded. The Morgan Edwards Baptist records, identified earlier, cited the birth of Rev. Charles Pate as 1 May 1729 in Bertie County, North Carolina. This provides a birthdate to which the birthdates of his siblings can be related.

James is regarded by this research to have been the youngest son of Charles d. ca. 1769. The life span of his sons and the recorded birthdate for his brother, Rev. Charles Pate, leads to the birth year of 1735 for James.

He was absent from the 1790 U. S. Census, though his brothers were enumerated.

Further, Martha Pate, assumed to have been his widow, was identified in this census, living adjacent to his brothers. This report assigns vital dates for James, born ca. 1735 and died by 1790. He will be identified as James Pate d. ca. 1790 in this report.

Available records fail to provide any reasonable proof of any other children of Charles Pate d. ca. 1769. Traditional research failed to provide a deed that distributed his assets among heirs, a will or recorded probate record, a Bible record, or any other written document to identify his heirs. However, information has been compiled that leads to the claim of four sons for Charles, including James d. ca. 1790. Daughters should be expected, but available records fail to identify any.

This research leads to the assumption that the first-born son of Charles d. ca. 1679 was named Thoroughgood Pate, who was named to honor his father. This naming pattern was common in the colonial period. The second son was named Charles for the father. No Dobbs or Wayne County record places this son in the county of residence of his father. He first appears in records in Cumberland County, North Carolina, with his uncle, William Pate d. ca. 1775. Records prove he had an association with Charles Pate, Samuel Pate, Rice Henderson, and a number of persons from Dobbs/Wayne County. The two Pate men were his brothers. The relationship of Rice Henderson to these Pate brothers will be documented later.

A more detailed report on research involving the migration of this Thoroughgood and his brothers will be cited in the reports on each. For here, it is important to note they migrated together along with other persons from Old Dobbs County. An overview of their common origin and the fate of each will follow.

Thoroughgood departed Cumberland County and migrated to Anson County, North Carolina, with his uncle, William Pate d. ca. 1775. The brothers Charles and Samuel did likewise. The uncle settled on the west side of the Pee Dee River in Anson County, as noted earlier. His Pate nephews settled on the east side of the river, in the area that became Richmond County. Some of this area later became Scotland County in 1899.

Pate Family information deposited in the Scotland County Library reports the family descended from early Pate settlers of Wayne County. One source reported Thoroughgood Pate settled on the east side of the Pee Dee River in 1764 and was from Wayne County. This is supported by Richmond deed records that prove Pates from Wayne County continued to migrate to Richmond in the early 1800s, to be cited later. This seems to be sufficient to conclude that the Pates in Richmond County originated in Wayne County.

The relationship of Thoroughgood Pate of Richmond County to Charles Pate d. ca. 1769 of Dobbs/Wayne County has been noted. Traditional research to support these claims has also been cited, and DNA testing further confirms the claims. Descendants of this Thoroughgood Pate have the mutation at Marker 391 that is inherited by descendants of Charles Pate d. ca. 1769.

The recorded birthdate of 1 May 1729 for the second-born son of Charles d. ca. 1769 leads to the assumed birth year of 1727 for Thoroughgood. Richmond County records, to be cited, indicate he died in 1801 or 1802. He will be identified in this report as Thoroughgood Pate d. ca. 1802, a son of Charles Pate d. ca. 1769.

Baptist records provide information on Rev. Charles Pate, the son of Charles Pate d. ca. 1769. The survey by Morgan Edwards in 1772 was cited earlier. *South Carolina Baptists, 1670-1805* by Leah Townsend, provides additional information. Most of the information from both sources is more appropriate for the narrative on the son. For here, note is made that he was identified as Rev. Charles Pate in those records. He was born in Bertie County, North Carolina, 1 May 1729. Previously-cited records prove his parents lived in Bertie in 1729. He was baptized in 1760, and was ordained 7 August 1769 at Bear Creek, Dobbs County. Records show that he lived in Marion County, South Carolina, but returned to Dobbs County for ordination. One can only wonder if his father still lived when he was ordained.

Six descendants of Rev. Charles Pate are in the Pate DNA Project currently. They have the mutation at Marker 391 that is characteristic of the descendants of Charles Pate d. ca. 1769. This confirms that Rev. Charles was a son of Charles Pate d. ca. 1769.

Rev. Charles Pate may have died in Marion County after the 1790 U. S. Census was enumerated. This census is the last record on him available to this research. Two of his sons moved to Mississippi, and the writer wonders if Rev. Charles followed them and died in that state.

The 1790 U. S. Census of South Carolina recognized the old court districts of the state. Indexes report Rev. Charles Pate was in the Georgetown District. Some researchers have interpreted this to place him in or near the town of Georgetown, South Carolina. However, Georgetown District included four counties, of which Marion was one. Rev. Charles was in Marion County, Georgetown District.

He will be identified in this report as Rev. Charles Pate d. p. 1790, son of Charles Pate d. ca. 1769.

Samuel was the remaining son of Charles Pate d. 1769. He did appear in records of the Old Dobbs County area. Samuel Pate and James Pate were soldiers in the Johnston County Militia, 17 October 1755, in the Company of Simon Herring, *Colonial Soldiers of the South* by Murtie Clark. This record represents the two youngest sons of Charles Pate d. ca. 1769. Readers should recall that their uncle, John Pate d. ca. 1779, and two of their cousins, John Pate and William Pate, were in the Johnston County Militia in 1754. Further, the Dobbs Deed Index Book has one conveyance by Samuel Pate to Daniel Howell, Book 7, page 354. This was in the 1765-1769 time-frame. Note has been made that the Howell family lived on Stoney Creek and had association with the Pate Family. This record may identify the time of departure by Samuel from Wayne County.

Samuel does not appear in any records of Cumberland County found by this research. He next appears as a witness to a land sale by Rice Henderson to John Turnage, 10 September 1769 in Anson County. The witnesses were Thoroughgood Pate and Samuel Pate. Readers will note later that Thoroughgood Pate d. 1802 had a son named Samuel. Some researchers have considered these witnesses to represent Thoroughgood and his son Samuel. The birth of Samuel, the son of Thoroughgood d. 1802, was ca. 1760, with several records supporting that birth year. Some colonial laws did permit 16-year-old males to witness documents. It is unlikely that a nine-year-old boy served as a legal witness. In support of this opinion, the 1767 Tax List for Anson County reported only one male 16 years of age in the household of Thoroughgood Pate, himself. The writer concludes that the witnesses were the brothers Thoroughgood and Samuel.

Samuel moved into South Carolina with his brother Charles and Rice Henderson, returned to North Carolina, and migrated back to South Carolina over two decades. Records suggest he followed his sons to Kershaw County, South Carolina, and died there after 1810.

Samuel's birth was ca. 1732. He will be listed in this report as Samuel Pate d. ca. 1810, son of Charles Pate d. ca. 1769.

Two members of the Pate DNA Project are identified by traditional genealogy as descendants of Samuel Pate d. ca. 1810. Their DNA confirms that both carry the mutation at Marker 391 that is characteristic of descendants of Charles Pate d. ca. 1769.

This completes the report on the Dobbs County Pates. The following narrative will treat each son of Charles Pate d. ca. 1769, and their descendants, to the extent of this research. The goal is to follow the life of each son and identify three generations of descendants from each. Daughters will be recognized as records are available.

V

THOROUGHGOOD PATE
d. ca. 1802, SON OF CHARLES PATE d. ca. 1769, AND HIS DESCENDANTS

Introduction

The Pate Family of Richmond County, North Carolina, was the focus of a narrative in the *Pate Pioneers on the Pee Dee River*, published by the writer in earlier years. The paper, and its Richmond County narrative, has been popular and provided insight into this family of Thoroughgood Pate d. ca. 1802. Regardless of its popularity, ongoing research has identified errors in that paper. This report is an effort to correct known errors and improve the original narrative.

Caution is issued that assumptions, though reduced in number, must continue to be made. Further, the interpretation of some records cited here may be subject to question. Available records are simply insufficient to provide the desired definition and detail needed in some areas.

Most members of the Pate Family living in Richmond County, in the late 1700-1800 timeframe, can be identified as descendants of Thoroughgood Pate d. ca. 1802. However, research does identify Pate heads of households in the county who had origin in other lines of the family. They will be treated in other, and more appropriate, narratives in this report. They will include Willoughby Pate and his large family and Adam Pate, both of whom will be treated in detail in the report on Charles Pate d. p. 1790. The Thoroughgood J. Pate who died in the Civil War in 1863 will be treated in the narrative on "Other Pate Families of Richmond County", to follow in this chapter.

The opinions of the writer follow and are offered with apologies for any errors.

The relationship of Thoroughgood Pate d. ca. 1802 to his father is documented in the preceding report on the Pate Family in Dobbs County. Note was made that available records fail to place this son in Dobbs (or Wayne) County in the early years of his life. The earliest record of him, found by this research, was in Bladen County, North Carolina, records that pertain to the area soon to be created as Cumberland County.

The Bladen County Survey Book 1753-1754 reports a survey for a land grant for Phillip Mulky, 16 January 1754. The tract was located on the North Fork of Lower Little River. Readers will recall the presence of William Pate d. ca. 1775 and his sons John and Thomas in the Lower Little River/Cranes Creek area of Cumberland County. The survey was about one mile from William Bates, who is assumed to have been William Pate, chain bearers were Thoroughgood Pate and Charles Heard. This Thoroughgood Pate is the same as the man treated here, Thoroughgood Pate d. ca. 1802.

Records, to be cited later, prove Charles Pate d. ca. 1790, brother to Thoroughgood, was also in the Cranes Creek-Lower Little River area of Cumberland County.

Thoroughgood, and his uncle, William Pate d. ca. 1775, served on a Jury of Inquest in Cumberland County, 15 July 1774, *North Carolina Genealogical Society Journal,* Volume 1, page 26. He patented 150 acres on Cranes Creek, 3 March 1767. He had moved to Anson County, North Carolina. by 12 July 1771, where Anson County court minutes show he was a constable. Records show he settled on Joes Creek and Gum Swamp, tributaries of the Little Pee Dee River. This was in the area of Anson County that became Richmond County in 1778. Court minutes continued to identify him as a constable in 1785.

He purchased 400 acres on Joes Creek from Rice Henderson, 2 March 1769. The land was described as part of a grant to Samuel Snead in 1767, Anson Deed Book 7, page223. The Samuel Snead land is worthy of note for future reference. Rice Henderson sold another 200 acres of the Samuel Snead grant to John Turnedge 10 September 1769, Anson Deed Book 7, page 243. Witnesses for the last conveyance were Thoroughgood Pate d. ca. 1802 and Samuel Pate d. ca 1810.

Records report a close relationship of the Pate brothers -- Thoroughgood, Charles, and Samuel – with Rice Henderson. Henderson's probable brother-in-law relationship to Charles Pate will be noted in the report on Charles Pate d. p. 1790.

Thoroughgood sold the 150-acre tract granted him in Cumberland County in 1767 on 3 March 1774, Cumberland Deed Book 11, page 273. The buyer was Duncan Campbell. The deed was executed by Thoroughgood and his wife "Wine" Pate. Other records identify her correct given name as Winefred or Winnefred. Both parties signed the deed with a mark. A restriction in the deed exempted a 10-feet square graveyard from the sale. Some comments on that restriction will follow.

Thoroughgood had three sons, Samuel, Stephen, and Thoroughgood, and one daughter, Sabra. Other daughters are probable, of which more will be offered later. These seem to have been about ten years between the birth of Samuel and Stephen. The other children were born without a long interval. Further, Winnefred lived about 20 years after the death of Thoroughgood, which may indicate an age difference between them. Census records suggest she lived with her sons Stephen and Thoroughgood, not Samuel. Samuel was illiterate, signing all records with a mark, with one exception, which may have been a scribe's error. The other two sons signed with their signature. All of this is significant and may indicate two families.

The suggestion is offered that Winnefred may have been the second wife. The first wife, the mother of Samuel, was the person buried at Cranes Creek. In my opinion, Winnifred was the mother of the other children of Thoroughgood.

Family tradition reports that Winnifred was Winnifred Stewart. She was identified with this full name in *Pate, Adams, Newton* by Julia Claire Pate. Stewarts were associated with the Pate Family in Richmond County. As an example, Hardy Stewart conveyed a tract of land to Thoroughgood Pate, Jr., 4 September 1801, Richmond Deed Book F, page 178. The land was located on Joes Creek, and Winnifred Pate witnessed the deed. This research accepts the maiden surname of Stewart for Winnefred, but acknowledges that the desired proof is not available.

Thoroughgood was tried in court for treason during the Revolutionary War. The court record fails to provide details. He was among a group of men tried in the September Term of Court 1782. The jury returned a verdict of "not guilty". His support for the cause of Independence was proved by North Carolina Revolutionary War pay vouchers. He provided 1,200 pounds of beef for the army, 16 January 1781, valued at 66 Spanish milled dollars. Again, on 2 October 1782, he provided 600 pounds of beef valued at 27 Spanish milled dollars.

The first U. S. Census in 1790 was preceded by a state census in North Carolina, which was canvassed in the years of 1784-1787. The report for Richmond County is among those that survived. Two Pates were listed, Thoroughgood d. ca. 1802 and Samuel d. 1850, who will be identified later as father and son. The father had two sons under 21 years and three daughters represented on the Richmond County state census. Samuel had two young sons and one daughter represented. Records, to be cited, indicate that to be the expected family for each in 1785.

The Pates were also canvassed in Richmond County for the U. S. Census of 1790. In addition to Thoroughgood and his son Samuel d. ca. 1850, another son, Stephen d. 1839, had established his own separate household. Given the exception of Isaac Pate in 1800 and Thomas Pate and Willoughby Pate in 1820, all Pates on the Richmond County U. S. Census reports through 1830 represent Thoroughgood d. ca. 1820 and his descendants. Isaac, as noted in the preceding narrative, was from Greene County, North Carolina. Thomas and Willoughby moved to Richmond from Wayne County, to be cited.

Stephen Pate conveyed a tract of Richmond County land to John McDonald, 31 March 1797. The land was located on Joes Creek of the Little Pee Dee River and Gum Swamp. It was described as 300 acres "surveyed for Thoroughgood Pate said Stephen Pates father", on 30 March 1769, Deed Book E, page 215. Another 100 acres was in this conveyance, a tract granted to Stephen Pate, 24 April 1793. The deed was witnessed by Samuel Pate, brother to Stephen, who signed with a mark, and John Shaw.

Thoroughgood Pate, Sr., conveyed a tract of land to Thoroughgood Pate, Jr., 2 December 1802. The deed states "for and in consideration of love, good will and affection I have and do bear towards my youngest son Thoroughgood Pate, Jr. (Captain)". The deed does not state that Winnifred was his mother, though it is assumed that such was fact. The land was described as 600 acres on Joes Creek surveyed for Sam Snead 10 July 1766 and 100 acres surveyed for "Thurgood" Pate, Sr. 19 April 1786. It was noted earlier that Thoroughgood purchased the tract from Sam Snead in 1767, as he settled in Anson County. The deed was signed by Thoroughgood Pate and Winnifred Pate, both using a mark. George Wright, to be cited as a son-in-law, was a witness. The actual transfer of ownership was to be effective at the death of both parents.

The two preceding deeds are sufficient to identify Stephen Pate d. 1839 and Thoroughgood Pate d. 1836 as sons of Thoroughgood Pate d. ca. 1802. This was the last record executed by Thoroughgood Pate, Sr., found in this research. It is the source for his death date of ca. 1802. Census records indicate Winnifred lived past 1820, but her name was not found in records after this date in 1802.

This research failed to locate a record to prove Samuel was a son of Thoroughgood with the degree of definition indicated for his sons Stephen and Thoroughgood, Jr. Available records fail to provide the conveyance of land from the father to this son. However, after the death of Samuel in 1850, his heirs sold a tract of land that was part of his estate and was "known as the Thoroughgood Pate land", Richmond Deed Book K, page 206. The deed seems to prove Samuel owned land that had been associated with his father. Note needs to be made that there is no record of the above-noted conveyance of land by Thoroughgood to Stephen. The conveyance is proved by the chain of title in the deed when Stephen sold the land.

Records prove Thoroughgood conveyed land to his sons Stephen and Thoroughgood, Jr., as cited, and to his only known son-in-law, George Wright, Richmond Deed Book F, page 303. The assumption is offered that the presence of "Thoroughgood Pate" land in his estate serves to prove he did likewise for his oldest son, Samuel. Further, the presence of Samuel on Joes Creek and Gum Swamp; his appearance in records with his father, brothers, and his brother-in-law; his move to Sullivan County with his father and their joint return to Richmond County; and the use of the name Thoroughgood for one of his sons -- seem to be sufficient to confirm the father-son relationship for Thoroughgood and Samuel.

Census records indicate Thoroughgood Pate d. ca. 1802 had three daughters. In the North Carolina state census returns for Sullivan and Richmond counties and the U. S. Census for Richmond in 1790, each record reflects three daughters. The 1800 U. S. Census for Richmond County listed him with one female 10-16 years of age, in addition to his wife, suggesting the other two daughters had left the household. Available records provide identification of only one daughter, Sabra Pate, who married George Wright, 6 December 1791.

Several Wright family researchers have shared information on the family, including Pauline Skaggs and Marjorie Krueger. This information reports that George Wright married Sabra Pate. No marriage record was available, nor was proof that Sabra Pate was a daughter of Thoroughgood Pate. May Allen Form, a co-worker of the writer, shared a case from the files of the North Caroline Supreme Court that is sufficient to prove the marriage and the origin of Sabra. An abbreviated review of the genealogical information from the case is in the following paragraph. Case: *Duncan McLaurin, Administrator, vs. Samuel Wright*, December Term 1841.

Thoroughgood Pate d. 1836, son of Thoroughgood Pate d. ca. 1802 borrowed money from Samuel Wright in 1836, while ill. Pate died before the debt was repaid. The administrator of the Pate estate was a witness to the arrangements of the loan. He reported that Samuel Wright was the nephew of Thoroughgood Pate, to his personal knowledge. His testimony detailed the actions and desires of both parties as Pate attempted to borrow money in haste. Questions regarding the intent of each party arose, to which Wright responded with "Uncle, if you were dead, I would not defraud your children."

Wright family records prove Samuel Wright was a son of George and Sabra Wright. The testimony of the administrator, Duncan McLaurin, proves Samuel Wright was also a nephew of Thoroughgood Pate d. 1836, who is proved in this report to have been a son of Thoroughgood Pate d. ca. 1802. These records are sufficient to say Sabra was a sister to Thoroughgood d. 1836 and a daughter of Thoroughgood d. ca. 1802. The names of the other two daughters were not located by the writer.

Samuel Pate was born ca. 1760, probably in Cumberland County, and died in June or July, 1850, in Richmond County. He was married first, to a daughter of Darby Henegan/Sweeny, given name unknown, and second to Martha, surname unknown. More will be offered on the Henegan/Sweeny surname later.

Stephen was born ca. 1770 in Richmond County and died by February 1839 in the Weakley-Carroll County area of Tennessee. He married Honor Sweeny, another daughter of Darby Henegan/Sweeny.

Sabra was born 23 December 1775 in Richmond County and died July 1846 in Richmond County. She married George Wright, 6 December 1791.

Thoroughgood, Jr., was born ca. 1780 in Richmond County and died 27 September 1836 in the same county. He had married Mary Jane (Jannett) McColman, 22 September 1830.

The court minutes for Richmond County attest to active participation of each member of this Pate Family in community activities. This includes the father, the sons, and the known son-in-law. They were identified as constable, served on various committees, appraised estates, maintained roads, held office in the militia, served on jury duty at all levels, etc.

A reference to DNA testing on descendants of Thoroughgood Pate d. 1802 needs to be made before presenting the families of his sons. Earlier reference was made to the 9 alleles mutation at Marker 391 and the identification of descendants of Charles Pate d. ca. 1769 made possible by that mutation. Other mutations affect the family at hand and need to be noted.

An additional mutation occurred in Charles d. ca. 1769 that was not mentioned in the earlier explanation. It will be of importance only in this family line, so is only noted here. A mutation of 20 alleles occurred at Marker 570. All descendants of this Charles have the 9 alleles mutation at Marker 391. Also, all have a value of 20 alleles at Marker 570, with the exception, of great importance, of one family of descendants from Stephen d. 1839, which has a mutation value of 21 alleles. This will receive more comment at the appropriate place.

Another mutation of 9 alleles occurred at Marker 459b and was passed from Thoroughgood Pate d. ca. 1802 to his son Stephen. At the time of this writing, the other two sons are assumed to have been free of this mutation.

It was noted earlier that the writer is not an authority on DNA testing. Readers seeking more detail should access the Pate DNA Project website on the Internet. The current administrators, A. J. Pate and Joel Pate, are qualified to discuss details.

The report now moves to the children of Thoroughgood Pate d. ca. 1802.

SAMUEL PATE D. 1850,
SON OF THOROUGHGOOD PATE D. 1802

Samuel Pate was the firstborn child of Thoroughgood Pate d. ca. 1802. His will was written 7 November 1841 and proved in Richmond County Court in the July Term 1850. He was enumerated on the U. S. Census for Richmond County 29 August 1850. Obviously, his death date was not disclosed to census personnel, and he does not appear on the 1850 U. S. Census mortality schedule. This report will cite his death as in June of 1850. He was listed on the 1850 return as 90 years of age.

The age at death reflects a birth year of 1760, which is compatible with other records created in his lifetime, as follow. Note has been made that he was listed on the North Carolina state census for Richmond County 1785, and that for Sullivan County (now Tennessee) on 4 July 1787. Both returns listed him with a family that reflects two sons under 21 years and a daughter. A family of that size is compatible with his birth in 1760 and a marriage about 1780. His age on the U. S. Census for Richmond County in 1800 was between 26 and 45 years. His age on the 1810 U. S. Census was over 45 years. Both are compatible with a 1760 birth year.

Samuel married, as his first wife, a daughter of Darby Henegan/Sweeny. The assumption was made in past years that his wife at his death, Martha (Marthew) was the Henegan daughter. The writer recognizes Larry Cates for noting this error. Some records are important to justify the change noted here.

The will of Darby Henegan proves that Easter (Hester), the wife of Thomas Pate, was his granddaughter. The will of Samuel Pate d. 1850, and numerous deeds, prove the wife of Thomas Pate was a daughter of Samuel Pate d. 1850. Further, Samuel Pate was a legatee to the will of Darby Henegan. He was recognized in a list that seems to include surviving spouses of deceased daughters and living daughters: Samuel Pate, Joseph Mangram, Mary Bethea, Elizabeth Matheson, Sarah Graves, and Martha Rigdel. Other records identify the husband of Martha Ridgel as Joel Ridgel. Thus, the Henagen daughter named Martha was the wife of Joel Ridgel, not Samuel Pate.

U. S. Census reports show a progression in the age of the wife of Samuel Pate until 1820. The 1820 return listed him alone, his children out of his household, and his wife absent, assumed to have been deceased. His wife on subsequent census returns was 20-30 years younger than Samuel. The 1850 return listed their ages as 90 and 60 years.

The preceding records seem to be sufficient to say Samuel Pate d. 1850 married a daughter of Darby Henegan and she was the mother of his children. However, she was not his wife named Martha of later years. The first wife died before 1820.

The maiden surname of the second wife is unknown. She lived beyond 1870.

The Henegan surname results in confusion for researchers. Two quotes are helpful: "In 1756 James Sweeney had a son named Barney who had sons named Darby and John", History *of Marlboro*

88

County by Rev. J. A. W. Thomas; also, "James Sweeney is supposed to have been the progenitor of the present-day Henegan family. It is known they were called the Sweeney family at an early period", *History of the Old Cheraws* by Rev. Alexander Gregg. The implication of these quotes is that Sweeney became Henegan. It is the observation of the writer that the use of Sweeney still survived after Henegan appeared. Darby Henegan provided two daughters who married two Pate brothers. Descendants of the Pate Family recognized Sweeney as a given name in Georgia, Texas, and Tennessee for decades.

Records show that the man at hand used both surnames in his lifetime. His will was written with the Sweeny surname. He executed numerous deeds in his lifetime between members of this Pate Family, and each deed found in this research used the surname of Henegan.

The executors for the Darby Sweeny will were James Cole and Stephen Pate. Stephen Pate was a brother to Samuel Pate d. 1850, and both brothers were sons-in-law to Darby Henegan, to be cited. James Cole was also a son-in-law of Darby Sweeny.

Samuel acquired impressive tracts of land in the Joes Creek and Gum Swamp area, waters of the Little Pee Dee River. Several deeds refer to Pates Mill as a landmark. Note has been made that his estate sold land identified as "Thoroughgood Pate land", assumed to be acknowledgement that the land came from his father. His father-in-law was also a source for land, Richmond Deed Book C, page 101. Comments on this deed follow.

The conveyance from Darby Henegan was dated 11 May 1789 and must have been associated with the return of the Pate Family from Sullivan County, Tennessee. The tract totaled 400 acres located on Breakfast Branch of the Little Pee Dee River. It was comprised of several land grants to Darby Henegan.

Samuel executed numerous deeds in his lifetime, including Richmond Deed Book C, pages 101 and 812; Deed Book L, pages 451, 473 and 493; and others. All involved land on Joes Creek, Gum Swamp, and Breakfast Branch – waters of the Little Pee Dee River. One record identified him as Captain Samuel Pate, assumed to have been in recognition of his militia rank. Pates Mill has been noted as a landmark in this area. Most of the conveyances involved family members. His son Elias Pate and his son-in-law Thomas Pate were commonly involved. The last deed executed was in January 1850 and was a conveyance to his grandson Arthur G. Bright, Jr., Deed

Book U, page 16. The date was never filled in on the deed, but it was proved at the January Term of Court in 1850.

One of the land conveyances cited earlier was to William Clark, 4 November 1797, Richmond Deed Book C, page 812. One can only wonder if William Clark was also a family member. Specifically, could he have been the husband of Ann Pate, oldest daughter of Samuel?

Samuel wrote his will, 7 November 1841. It was proved in Richmond County in the July Term of Court 1850. The assumption is offered that he died in June 1850. The will recognized his wife, Martha (Marthew), for a dower consisting of 150 acres, the dwelling house, furniture, equipment, and slaves for her lifetime. The land was to be divided among "the heirs of my body" at her death. This research failed to find record of this division of the land in later years.

The will identified the heirs of his body to have been: Ann, Elias, Samuel, and Marthew (Martha). Also recognized were the "childring [sic] of my son Thorogood" and the "childring of my daughter Hester". He indicated that Thoroughgood and Hester were deceased, and he instructed that the division of the property among his heirs was to be "left entorily to themselves" (the heirs), and expressed the wish that they not disagree. This act seems to have eliminated the execution of court probate records. The writer has noted other estates that were divided in this manner, although they were rare. Apparently, the courts accepted this procedure.

The language of the will is sufficient to say that all his heirs, both living and deceased, were recognized. It does present obstacles for family researchers. Namely, that the children of his two deceased children are not identified. Further, the married surnames of the daughters are omitted. Since the estate was divided by family agreement, probate records were not created that would provide those details. Fortunately, other records, particularly deeds, provide the information needed to develop the history of his family.

The children of Samuel will be treated below in the order of birth, as determined by this research.

Thoroughgood was the firstborn child of Samuel Pate d. 1850. He was one of the two males in his father's household on the North Carolina state censuses for 1785 and 1787. This research assigns him a birth year of ca. 1782.

Readers need to be aware that considerable speculation is involved in the effort to recreate the life and children of this son of Samuel Pate d. 1850. Some known facts need to be recalled before speculation begins.

His given name recognizes his grandfather, Thoroughgood Pate d. ca. 1802. He married Frances Bright in Marlboro County (District), South Carolina, 20 January 1807. The bride was a sister to Arthur Godfrey Bright who married Thoroughgood's sister, Martha. They were children of Charles and Mary (Godfrey?) Bright. He had children, but the question is more about how many than their names. His widow remarried to John Brickhouse in Marlboro County, 5 July 1818. The death date for Thoroughgood is unknown, but will be cited as ca. 1810 by this research. Frances and her second husband moved to Gibson County, Tennessee, where she died after 1840.

The will of Samuel Pate gave instructions that the "childring" of his deceased son Thoroughgood would receive the legacy due their father, implying the son was survived by more than one child. However, given that the legatee was illiterate, with all the spelling errors recorded by his choice of scribes, that conclusion may be unwise. Family information in *Pate, Adams, Newton* by Julia Claire Pate, reported the husband of Frances Bright had only one daughter. Unfortunately, extant records can be interpreted both ways, as supporting the claim for one child or as supporting the claim for two children for this Thoroughgood Pate.

There seems to be no question that one daughter, from the marriage of Thoroughgood Pate and his wife Frances Bright, was fact. She was named Elizabeth Pate. This Elizabeth married John Weldon Stubbs. The marriage is reported by Julia Claire Pate in her book and by Leonardo Andrea in *Abstracts of Stubbs Estates of Marlboro County, S. C.,* page 105. Dr. Andrea provided supportive information.

Samuel, as noted, instructed that the heirs would divide his estate by private agreement. Apparently, they decided to sell the land and divide the proceeds. The sales required the signatures of the heirs on the deed of sale. Two conveyances are important for the identity of the children of the two deceased children of Samuel. They seem to account for all of his land after the 150 acres had been set aside for the widow's dower.

The first conveyance was for the sale of "all our rights and claim" in 100 acres of the estate of Samuel Pate, deceased, known as the

Thoroughgood Pate land. The deed was signed by Elias Pate, Samuel R. Pate, Martha Bright, Calvin Pate, L. G. Pate, Samuel Pate, Esther Pate, William Bailey, and Richard Chance. These signatures represent the living heirs of Samuel (Elias, Samuel R., and Martha), and the heirs of his deceased daughter, Hester, who was the deceased wife of Thomas Pate, (Calvin, L. G., Samuel, Esther, William Bailey, and Richard Chance). Two heirs of Samuel are missing -- Ann Pate, who was alive when the will was written in 1841, and the deceased son Thoroughgood. The land was sold to John W. Stubbs, the husband of the granddaughter, Elizabeth Pate. The assumption is offered that she represents, through her husband, the "childring" of the deceased son, Thoroughgood. It is important to note that no other child of the deceased son Thoroughgood is represented, or appears by name, in any of these estate records. The record was signed 22 October 1850 and recorded in Richmond Deed Book U, page 206.

Research found no additional records on the daughter Ann. She was alive and had the surname Pate, when the will was written in 1841. The assumption is offered that she preceded her father in death and without heirs.

The only known heir of the deceased son Thoroughgood and Frances (Bright) Pate was the daughter named Elizabeth, who married John Weldon Stubbs. Her husband was the grantee of the cited deed. Therefore, this deed represents the sale of estate land. All of the known surviving heirs are represented as grantors or grantees in this deed. Since no additional heirs of Thoroughgood and Frances (Bright) Pate were recognized in this record, it can be assumed none existed.

Another tract of 160 acres was sold by the heirs of the deceased daughter Hester, 2 November 1850. It was described as land from the estate of their grandfather, Samuel Pate. The deed was signed by the heirs of Hester exactly as they signed the preceding deed – Calvin, L. G., etc. There is no explanation for the absence of the other heirs of Samuel from this deed. Again, the division was by private agreement. In some manner, for reasons not reported, the children of Hester received these 160 acres of land. The sale was to Hugh Livingston. One of the witnesses to the sale was A. G. Bright, a son of Martha (Pate) Bright, one of the living heirs of old Samuel.

These deeds seem to be sufficient to identify the surviving heirs of Samuel Pate d. 1850 and limit the children of the deceased son, Thoroughgood, to a daughter, Elizabeth, who married John Weldon

Stubbs. Unfortunately, two deeds in Marlboro County, South Carolina, confuse this!

Note needs to be made that Richmond County, North Carolina, and the South Carolina counties of Marlboro and Marion were almost one community in this timeframe. Within this area, families moved frequently, marriages were common, and manyowned land on both sides of the state boundary.

Two Marlboro deeds are of interest to this report. John W. Stubbs and his wife, Elizabeth, sold 100 acres to John Odom, 5 January 1838, Marlboro Deed Book P, pages 135-136. The land was described as half of 200 acres, which was given by the Commission in Equity, in earlier years, to the said Elizabeth Stubbs and Mary Thomas, wife of John C. Thomas. The other deed was dated 19 May 1853. The Thomas family had moved to Texas (Grimes County and later Leon County). Mary Thomas was deceased, and John C. Thomas returned with power of attorney to sell the legacy of his children received from their deceased mother – William M. Thomas, Henry B. Thomas, Samuel P. Thomas, and John C. Thomas, Jr. He sold the 100 acres received by Mary in the action of the Commission in Equity to John Odom, Marlboro Deed Book S, page231.

One interpretation of the Marlboro deeds is that Elizabeth Stubbs and Mary Thomas received equal interest in 200 acres of land through action by a Court of Equity. This is assumed to mean they were sisters. Since Elizabeth Stubbs is known to have been a daughter of Thoroughgood and Frances (Bright) Pate, Mary Thomas would also be a daughter. In contrast to this opinion, Richmond County records do not identify either Mary Thomas or her husband as an heir of Thoroughgood Pate, nor do they identify Elizabeth as such. It is important to note that the land in question appears to have been Bright family land, not Pate Family land. Perhaps the land was distributed in a Bright family settlement.

Perhaps other records exist to clear the question raised here, but this research failed to find them. Leonardo Andrea was a prominent South Carolina genealogist. His opinions are certainly worthy of trust. He reviewed the at hand and wrote, "Seemingly Thoroughgood Pate became an heir to a portion of this land and at his death, the share went to his daughter, Elizabeth Pate, wife of John W. Stubbs. The widow of Thoroughgood Pate, in 1832, was the wife of John Brickhouse.", *Abstracts of Stubbs Estates of Marlboro County, S. C.*, page 108.

The distribution of the estate of Charles Bright awarded 317 acres to the heirs of Arthur Bright (married Martha Pate). The lot assigned to Frances Brickhouse (a daughter of Charles Bright, former wife of Thoroughgood Pate and now the wife of John Brickhouse) was 363 acres, Marlboro Equity Court Records 1825-1836, 11 February 1834. This research found no record of an assignment to Thoroughgood Pate. Acknowledgement is granted that the book is old, faded, and of poor script. A record could have been overlooked, but none was found when reviewed.

Records available to the writer are insufficient to claim a relationship of Mary Thomas to Thoroughgood Pate d. ca. 1810. The possibility of a relationship exists; therefore, she is reported here for future reference. Her children were identified earlier.

The children of John Weldon Stubbs and Elizabeth (Pate) Stubbs are presented as they appear in the Andrea work cited earlier:

> Derrick D. – married Esther Chance;
> Lawrence D. – married Virginia Chance;
> Campbell Easterling – married 1) Alice Hoyt, 2) Mary Catherine Mood;
> James L. – married Lucinda Pearson;
> Thoroughgood Pate – married Sally McRae;
> Martha F. – married Levander Garlington Pate;
> Mary – married Thomas Adams;
> Letitia – married W. J. McRae;
> Ann – married Thomas Jones;
> Samuel died in the Civil War, unmarried.

Ann was recognized in the will of Samuel Pate d. 1850 as a daughter. It is assumed that she was the daughter represented on the North Carolina state censuses for 1785 and 1787. She was born ca. 1783. She was alive when her father executed his will, 7 November 1841. Her absence from all records that prove her siblings leads to the assumption that she preceded her father in death, between 7 November 1841 and 1850. The absence of any heirs also suggests she died without children.

Efforts to establish a link to William Clark, who acquired land from her father in 1787, were unsuccessful.

Elias was one of the two sons listed on the North Carolina state census. His birth on the U. S. Census for Shelby County, Alabama, in 1850 reflects a birth year of 1786. The writer considers 1784 to be more probable. He died in Shelby County, Alabama, in October or November of 1853.

He married Nancy Brown, a daughter of Edmund and Nancy (Anderson) Brown of Marlboro County, South Carolina. Nancy was born ca. 1790 in Marlboro County and died in Shelby County in 1854. This research failed to find record of their marriage, but the U. S. Census for Richmond County, North Carolina, in 1810 recorded the family with one male and two females under 10 years of age. A marriage date of near 1805 is probable.

The writer recognizes Faye Vincent as a source for Brown family information.

Elias served in the Richmond County Militia in the War of 1812.

Samuel Pate conveyed 100 acres of Richmond County land to Elias, 6 February 1812, Deed Book L, page 52. The chain of title in the deed identified it as part of the land Darby Henegan conveyed to Samuel Pate, cited earlier. Elias sold this land, plus 50 acres he acquired from William Thomas, to Drury Skipper, 6 November 1832, Book O, page 357. The sale appears to mark his departure for Alabama.

Elias relocated his family to Shelby County, Alabama. He acquired Alabama land from the Federal Government, 20 September 1839. Additional land was acquired by purchase. His estate held over 230 acres of land at his death.

The estate proceedings created at his death identify his heirs and the spouses of most, Shelby County Loose Estate Records. The inventory of his personal estate was sizeable. Family members, including his brother Samuel R. Pate, bought heavily at the estate sale. The brother lived in Sumter County, Alabama, at the time. The distribution of his land noted an item of special interest; the lot assigned to his daughter, Ann Smith, reserved a one-acre burial ground.

The heirs of Elias, and their spouses, as identified in the estate records, follow (some vital dates from other sources provided):

Ann – born 1808, married James Smith, died 1854;
Elizabeth – born 1810, married Jackson Owens, died 1870;
Charlotte – born 1815, married Daniel Thomas;
Mary – born 1817, married Alexander Vick;
Rebecca – born 1820, married James Lewis Kendrick, died 31 March 1880;

George Washington – born 27 November 1824, married Martha
    J. Glean, died 22 July 1908;
Harriett – born 1827, married James H. Harper;
Robert – non-resident of Shelby County;
Samuel – non-resident of Shelby County;
James M. – born 1831, married Lindy Scarborough, died 1854.

Martha was recognized as a daughter in the will of Samuel Pate
d. 1850. She was born January 1790 in Richmond County and died
30 March 1860 in Chesterfield County, South Carolina. The dates
are reported to be from her grave marker in Stubbs Cemetery in
Marlboro County.

She married Arthur Godfrey Bright, a brother to Frances Bright,
who married her brother, Thoroughgood Pate d. ca. 1810. This
research failed to find a marriage record. However, she signed the
deed to sell the "Thoroughgood Pate land" in her father's estate, cited
earlier, as Martha Bright. She lived in the households of children from
her marriage to Arthur Bright when the U. S. Census for Chesterfield
County was enumerated in 1850 and 1860. The last land conveyance
executed by her father was the sale of other land to her son, Arthur
Godfrey Bright, Jr. The same son was witness to the sale of other land
in the Samuel Pate estate by the heirs of her sister, Hester (Pate)
Pate. She named a son Charles Pate Bright. These items seem sufficient to confirm her marriage to Arthur Godfrey Bright.

Arthur Bright was born 7 November 1788 in Currituck County,
North Carolina. He died in Marlboro County, South Carolina, 31
December 1829. He was a son of Charles and Mary (Godfrey) Bright.
Information in the estate of Charles Bright was provided in the narrative on Thoroughgood Pate d. ca. 1810 and will not be repeated
here. Arthur Bright received Lot 6, 317 acres, in the division of his
father's estate.

Arthur Godfrey and Martha (Pate) Bright had eight children,
Marlboro Estate Apartment 21, Pack 13. They were:

Charles Pate Bright – married Mary Ann Burnett; Thomas W.
    Bright – b. ca. 1815;
Drucella Ann Bright – b. ca. 1816, married George Bullard;
Rebecca Bright – b. ca. 1821, married a Davis;
Arthur Godfrey Bright – b. ca. 1825;
Easter – b. ca. 1830, married M. D. Strickland;

Elizabeth Ann Bright;
Dickson Bright.

Hester was the deceased daughter recognized in the will of Samuel Pate d. 1850. Given the spelling errors in the will, the name may have been Easter or Ester. She named a daughter Ester, and that was a common name in the community. The name was clearly Hester in the will.

Hester was born ca. 1795 and died before her father executed his will, 7 November 1841. She married Thomas Pate, a distant cousin from the Pate kin who remained in Wayne County, North Carolina. Thomas was a son of Daniel Pate d. 1791 and will be treated in more detail in the narrative on James Pate d. ca. 1790. Note needs to be made that he remarried, after the death of Hester, to Mrs. Catherine (McLaughlin) Oliver. He had six children from his first marriage and two from his second marriage. Further, Mrs. Oliver brought children from her first marriage into the household.

This area of the report will treat only the children from the marriage of Thomas and Hester. The other names will be recognized in the James Pate d. ca. 1790 narrative.

For here, it is indicated to say Thomas sold Wayne County land inherited from his father in 1811. He is absent from later Wayne County records. Thomas Pate, assumed to have been the same man, was listed on the Richmond County Tax Roll for 1812. Samuel Pate conveyed land to Thomas Pate 8 June 1816, 116 acres on Breakfast Branch of the Little Pee Dee River, Richmond Deed Book L, page 492. This was part of the land Samuel acquired from Darby Henegan in 1789.

Research failed to find a record of the marriage. The assumption is offered that they married soon after his appearance on the 1812 tax list. The first child, Maria, was born ca. 1814.

Thomas was active in land transactions, several with his father-in-law. It is of interest to note that Hester, his first wife, was deceased when Samuel wrote his will 7 November 1841. Thomas remarried 22 October 1850, the same date on which the heirs of Samuel Pate sold the first tract of estate land. He died in 1854, and his administrator was appointed at the October Term of Court 1854.

The estate records identify the heirs of his marriage to Hester as they were listed in the sales of their grandfather's land, with the exception that the daughter Easter had married Levi Ellis. They were:

Maria, wife of William Bailey; Calvin Quincy;
Jane, wife of Richard Chance; Levander Garlington;
Easter, wife of Levi Ellis and Samuel.

Comments on each follow.

Jane was born ca. 1814 and married William Bailey. They were listed on the U. S. Census for Richmond County in 1850 without children. Both were 36 years of age. No further information is available for this family.

Calvin Quincy was born 6 November 1821 and died 11 April 1915 in Kaufman County, Texas. The dates are from his grave marker in Oaklawn Cemetery, Kaufman County. He married Fannie Sabrina Morris. One researcher reported the marriage is recorded in Brooks County, Georgia. This research failed to confirm the report. The bride was a daughter of I. E. D. ("Ed") and Mary (McNeel) Morris, as proved by Jefferson County, Florida Deed Book L, page 51.

A chronological review of data in records of his early adult lifetime is of interest. One Calvin Pate, 27 years of age and born in North Carolina, was enumerated on the U. S. Census for Warren County, Georgia, in 1850. The return was dated 30 October 1850. Other records raise question that this record was for the man of this report. Available records do not identify another so-named, of the age, and from North Carolina.

Calvin signed the deeds to sell the land from his grandfather's estate in Richmond County, North Carolina, on 22 October 1850 and 2 November 1850. He executed deeds in Thomas County, Georgia, in 1851, 1857, 1858, and 1866. Most of these deeds pertain to Thomas County land that became Brooks County in 1858. Brooks County records were not reviewed in this research.

He, apparently, did not return to North Carolina for the distribution of his father's estate in 1856. The extant records identify him and note that he, and his brother Levander Garlington, resided out of North Carolina. The available records do not provide the final distribution.

The next record was the renunciation of all rights in the estate land of his father-in-law by all heirs – H. W. Morris and Angelena, his wife; Calvin Pate and Fanny S. Pate, his wife;

J. M. Pate and Mary McNeel, his wife; John Sumpter and Claud Indiana Page, his wife; Joel M. Morris. All heirs renounced their claim to the widow, Mary (McNeel) Morris, 2 December 1869.

Calvin was enumerated on the U. S. Census for Kaufman County, Texas, 17 August 1870. His brother-in-law, John Sumpter, was located near him.

Calvin and Fanny had four children as listed on U. S. Census reports and available Texas cemetery records. They were:

Mary E. – born ca. 1855 in Georgia;
Elza F. – born ca. 1857 in Georgia;
John T. – born 1860 in Georgia and died 1932;
Calvin Garland – born 9 September 1862 in Georgia, died 27 March 1946, Walker County, Texas.

The next child born to Thomas and Hester was Jane, who married Richard Chance. The couple is recorded on the U. S. Censuses for Richmond County in 1850, 1860, and 1870. They had children as follows:

Henry – born ca. 1843;
Ann – born ca. 1846;
Mary J. – born ca. 1854.

No additional information is available on Jane and her husband Richard Chance.

Levander Garlington was the next child born to Thomas and Hester. He was born 18 April 1826 and died 28 March 1883 in Sumter County, South Carolina. He married Martha F. Stubbs, a daughter of John Weldon and Elizabeth (Pate) Stubbs. The bride and groom were cousins. The groom was the son of Hester (Pate) Pate and the bride was a granddaughter of Hester's brother, Thoroughgood Pate b. ca. 1810.

Levander Garlington moved to Sumter County, South Carolina, and was reported to have been a successful merchant. His half-brother, William Henry Pate (son of the second marriage of Thomas), was also a merchant in Sumter County, South Carolina, but in later years.

The children of Levander Garlington and Martha F. (Stubbs) Pate are reported in a number of resources, including *Abstracts of* Stubbs *Estates in Marlboro, S. C.,* Leonardo Andrea. They were:

Reverend Thomas J. – a prominent Methodist Minister in South Carolina, born ca. 1852, married Alice Godbold of Marion County;

Samuel Levander – died at 20 years of age;
James Franklin – born ca. 1862, married 1) Kate Allen, 2) Mrs.
    Abbi B. McDowell, died at 52 years of age;
Lily – married Dr. Preston Pate;
Lou M. – born ca. 1864, died February 1955;
Martha – died single at 30 years of age;
Blanch – married John William Cox.

The probate records on the estate of Levander Garlington Pate are filed in Sumter Loose Estate Papers, Bundle 176, Pack 23.

Esther/Ester was the remaining daughter of Thomas and Hester. She was born September 1829. Her death date is unknown, but she was listed on the U. S. Census for Robeson County, North Carolina, in 1900. She married Levi Ellis in Robeson County 23 May 1854. This Ellis family was listed on the U. S. Censuses for Richmond County in 1860 and 1880 and Robeson County in 1900.

Levi and Esther were living adjacent to their son, John T. Ellis, in 1900. It is of interest that John T. had a daughter named Hester. The return reported that Levi and Esther had been married 46 years and she was the mother of three children, all living.

The children of Levi and Esther were:

John T. – born January 1855, married Victoria [?];
Alphremia/Marthemia – born ca. 1857;
William Henry – born ca. 1864. (Esther had a half-brother named William Henry.)

The youngest son of Thomas and Hester was Samuel. He was recognized in the deeds with which he sold his father's land in 1850. He was not recognized in the estate papers of his father, Thomas. The assumption is offered that Samuel died between 1850 and 1854.

Note needs to be made that the deeds cited earlier differentiated between the two named Samuel. The older, son of Samuel d. 1850, was Samuel R. Pate. The younger, son of Thomas and Hester, was Samuel, with no middle name or initial.

This completes the report on Hester (Pate) Pate, daughter of Samuel Pate d. 1850.

Samuel R. Pate was the youngest child of Samuel Pate d. 1850. Available records fail to identify the name represented by the middle initial. He was born ca. 1800 in Richmond County, North Carolina, and died in Sumter County, Alabama, in 1854.

He married Martha McInnis in Marlboro County, South Carolina. Her parents are unknown to the writer, but John McInnis and family migrated to Alabama with the Samuel R. Pate Family. Samuel R. identified John McInnis as a brother in his will, which is interpreted to mean they were brothers-in-law. Martha died on 9 May 1850, of pneumonia, as reported in the 1850 U. S. Census Mortality Schedule.

Samuel remarried to Mrs. Rachel J. Mayes of Greene County, Alabama, 23 April 1850, Greene County Marriage Records. The date of the marriage and that cited for the death of Martha conflict. Experienced researchers are aware that census information was not collected under oath and errors in dates are common. The death of Martha and the marriage of Samuel to Rachel seem to be fact, but the dates cited conflict. Records, to be cited later, suggest Rachel was a daughter of John and Rebecca A. Hall. The given name of her Mayes husband is unknown. This marriage seems to have been without children.

One Samuel R. Pate married Susan Fair in Early County, Georgia, 6 October 1845. Since Martha (McInnis) Pate lived until 1850, this marriage appears to represent another Samuel R. Pate.

Samuel was listed on the U. S. Censuses for Marion County, South Carolina, in 1830, and Sumter County, Alabama, in 1840 and 1850. Note was made earlier that he was a buyer at the estate of his brother, Elias, in Shelby County, 4 February 1854.

He sold Marlboro County, South Carolina, land to John Mason in 1832, Deed Book N, page 451. He and his wife signed the deed. He established a trust for his daughter, Louise A. Mitchell, wife of John Mitchell, 24 May 1845, to be administered by John McInnis, Marlboro Deed Book T, page 108. The trust, recorded in South Carolina, was to hold land in Alabama, slaves, livestock, etc. The record was recorded in Marlboro County, 24 January 1857.

Two court cases add definition to the identity of his descendants and describe some personal problem. Interpretation of the legal is not part of this report. His second wife, Rachel, attempted to recover certain property she held prior to her marriage. The case was filed in Greene County Chancery Court and was appealed to the Alabama Supreme Court, Cases Volume 189, pages 1-12, 20, 72-73. The other case was filed in Marlboro County, South Carolina Court in 1859.

The latter proves the daughter of Samuel, Louisa, returned to South Carolina after the death of her father.

A summary of the family information from the court actions follows.

Samuel was engaged in court actions with the brother-in-law of his second wife Rachel, Henry Stafford, and her mother, Rebecca A. Hall. His intent was to recover certain items possessed by Rachel before this marriage.

The Marlboro court actions prove Samuel had a daughter named Louisa, who married John A. Mitchell, and had daughters named Elizabeth and Florence. Elizabeth married Cornelius Weatherly. John Mitchell died and Louisa remarried John Mason, who died soon after Samuel R. Pate. Louisa had a son, James, from the Mason marriage. Louisa was recorded in the Marlboro U. S. Census for 1860 with three children – Martha Florence J. Mitchell, age 11 years, Jno. James Samuel Pate Mason, age 5 years, and Julia A. Mason, age 10 months.

Samuel R. Pate also had a son from the first marriage. A published roster of University of Alabama students recognizes Franklin Sweeney Pate as a student 1848-1851. He was a son of Samuel R. Pate of Sumter County, Alabama. He was a lawyer, worked in Tennessee first, and was appointed District Attorney at Starkville, Mississippi. He was born 23 January 1833 and died ca. 1885, without children.

This concludes the report on Samuel Pate d. 1850, son of Thoroughgood Pate d. ca. 1802.

STEPHEN PATE D. 1839,
SON OF THOROUGHGOOD PATE D. 1802

Stephen Pate was the second-born son of Thoroughgood Pate d. ca. 1802, though perhaps not the second-born child. Records from the North Carolina state census of 1784-1787 indicate he may have had an older sister, for whom we have no record. He was of his father's second marriage, if Winnefred (Stewart) Pate was the second wife of Thoroughgood Pate d. ca. 1802, as suggested earlier. Proof of his relationship to his father was cited earlier, Richmond County Deed Book T, page 215. The relationship is further confirmed by DNA testing.

Stephen was born ca. 1770, based on various records. He died in Carroll County, Tennessee, before 4 February 1839, when probate was initiated on his estate in Carroll County.

He married Honor Sweeny/Henegan. The confusion over the Sweeny-Henegan surname was addressed in the narration on his brother, Samuel Pate d. 1850, and will not be repeated here. Both brothers married daughters of Darby Sweeny/Henegan. The will of Darby Sweeny identified "my grandson Elisha Pate". Records, to be cited, prove this Elisha Pate was a son of Stephen and Honor (Sweeny) Pate.

The Darby Sweeny will was written 18 October 1820 and was proved in Richmond County Court, April 1821. The executors were Stephen Pate and James Cole, sons-in-law of Sweeny. The witnesses included Nathaniel Gibson, probably the father of one so- named who married a daughter of Stephen Pate.

Numerous land records place Stephen Pate in the locale of Richmond County, where his father and older brother lived, on Joes Creek and Gum Swamp, both waters of the Little Pee Dee River. The records include Richmond Deed Book C, page 101; Book Y, page 28; Book E, page 215; Book R, page 171; and others. Extant tax records identify him as taxed for 300 acres in 1792, 440 acres in 1793, 400 acres in 1795, 460 acres in 1806, and 450 acres in 1812. He was active in land conveyances with his father-in-law. He served as a witness to the transfer of land by Darby Sweeny to his brother, Samuel Pate, Deed Book C, page 101.

Note was made earlier of the frequent movement of people between the South Carolina counties of Marion and Marlboro and Richmond County, North Carolina. Stephen was recognized as a resident of Marion County, 5 December 1797, as he sold land to Matthew Milsap of Richmond County, North Carolina, Marion Deed Book B, page 52. Darby Sweeny witnessed the deed. Records, to be cited, prove a son of Stephen, Elisha, married Sarah Beckwith of Marion County.

Stephen had other kin in this area of South Carolina. The presence of two uncles, Charles Pate d. p. 1790 and Samuel Pate d. p. 1810, needs to be recognized. Both uncles resided for several years in Marion and Marlboro and the nearby North Carolina counties of Bladen and Robeson. This will be treated in more detail in the reports on the uncles. For here, it is in order to note that a son of Stephen Pate d. 1839, Daniel, served as a witness for a land conveyance executed by Charles Pate, a son of Charles Pate d. p. 1790, 16 July 1813, Robeson County Deed Book Z, page 435.

It is important to note that the various lines of the family-maintained contact as they migrated. The earlier report of members of the Richmond County family returning to Wayne County for visits appears to have been the normal style for the times. Thomas Pate and Willoughby Pate relocated from Wayne County to join Pate kin in Richmond County after 1800. Isaac Pate did likewise from Greene County, North Carolina. The sons of Samuel Pate d. 1850 returned to Richmond County from South Carolina and Alabama after the death of their father. It will be shown that a son and daughter of Stephen settled in Georgia and Alabama, and later joined their siblings in Carroll and Weakly counties of Tennessee. There is some evidence that the widow of Stephen Pate d. 1839 returned to Richmond County, North Carolina, after the death of her husband, to be cited. Thus, the association of the cousins Daniel and Charles in Robeson County was normal.

Note was made earlier of the relocation of Pate Family members in North Carolina to Obion and Gibson Counties of Tennessee. They were in the company of several kin and neighbors. The Howell and Pate Families from Old Dobbs County, and more closely associated families of Brickhouse and Randle, were among the immigrants.

Merritt Randle and Stephen Sweeny Pate, a son of Stephen Pate d. 1839, were among those who moved in the 1820s. They settled in the nearby counties of Weakley and Carroll. Merritt Randle gifted a slave to Stephen S. Pate, 8 July 1828, "who has intermarried with my daughter Becky Randle", Carroll County Deed Book C, page 112.

Other Tennessee and North Carolina land conveyances followed in rapid order. Richmond L. Pate purchased 30 acres in Carroll County from A. A. McKenzie, 14 November 1834, Deed Book C, page 420. Stephen Pate sold 140 acres in Richmond County to his grandson Nathaniel Gibson, 29 January 1835, Deed Book Y, pages 28-29. Stephen purchased 67.25 acres adjoining Richmond L. Pate in Carroll County, 12 March 1836, Deed Book C, page 419. Thomas Pate acted as agent for Stephen to sell 200 acres in Richmond County, 28 December 1836, Deed Book P, page 171. The last tract was granted to Stephen, 21 December 1822.

Stephen died intestate. The extant files that relate to the probate of his estate in Carroll County, Tennessee, appear to be incomplete. However, surviving records adequately identify the heirs-at-law of the estate. Court action of 5 July 1839 resulted in a legal advertisement in the Carroll County newspaper that identified the heirs of Stephen Pate d. 1839. They were: "John Pate, Elijah Pate, Elisha Pate, Stephen S. Pate, Duncan Pate, Richmond L. Pate, Nathaniel

Hawthorne in right of his wife Elizabeth, Eli Ely in right of his wife Hannah, and Samuel Pate, Nathaniel Pate and Honor Gibson, children of Daniel Pate Deceased, Alex Campbell in right of his wife Sally (Sarah) deceased heirs of Stephen Pate deceased."

One Carroll County record addresses the sale of land in the estate, Deed Book C, pages 348-349. It is headed "Stephen Pate and Richmond L. Pate, Administrators of Stephen Pate deceased vs. John Pate and other heirs". The other heirs were not identified.

Stephen Sweeny Pate and Richmond Love Pate purchased the interests of the other heirs in land in Richmond County, North Carolina, remaining in the estate of their father. They sold the interests, purchased and inherited, to their brother Elijah S. Pate, 16 November 1841, Book R, page 63. The heirs from whom they had purchased interests were Hannah Ely, Elisha S. Pate, Samuel D. Pate, Na. Pate, Elizabeth Hawthorne, and Samuel Pate. Two heirs of Stephen d. 1839, John Pate and Sarah (Sally) (Pate) Campbell and one heir of the deceased son, Daniel, Honor Gibson, were absent from the list of heirs. Sally preceded her father in death, but her heirs were living and should have been recognized in this record. Honor Gibson lived in Richmond County in 1841. This research has no record of John Pate after 1839.

Carroll County deeds involving the purchase of interests of other heirs include Deed Book D, pages 482 and 478. The record relates to the sale by Elizabeth Hawthorne and identifies her heirs, Lenora Jones, John Hawthorne, Joseph Hawthorne, and Nathaniel Hawthorne on 26 February 1840.

Honor (Sweeny) Pate, the widow of Stephen d. 1839, returned to North Carolina after the death of her husband. She appears to have lived with her son, Richmond L. Pate, when the U. S. Census for Carroll County was enumerated in 1840. She executed two deeds of gifts, 21 July 1841, Carroll County Deed Book E, pages 216-217. She gifted a slave woman named Bibet to her son Samuel D. Pate, "for the natural love and affection". She also gifted a slave child named Honor to her granddaughter Margaret Ann Campbell and recorded the statement, "me here unto moving", (i.e., "as the spirit moves me").

These gifts in July and the sale of remaining North Carolina land in the Stephen Pate estate in November suggest Honor joined her sons as they returned to North Carolina.

This research found no additional records on Honor.

Additional records on Stephen are available and may be of interest to descendants. Further, Barbara Clark of McKenzie, Tennessee, published two works that provide valuable information on the Pate Family in Tennessee, *Pates of Pateville* and *Search For My Self.* These resources also may be of interest to descendants of Stephen Pate d. 1839.

The children of each child of Stephen Pate d. 1839 will follow. The order of birth may be questioned.

John Pate was listed first in the list of heirs by the Carroll County Courts. This leads to the assumption that he was the firstborn and was the young male in the household of Stephen on the U. S. Census for 1790. He was born ca. 1790.

One resource reported John served in the War of 1812, *North Carolina Muster Rolls 1812-1814*, Verne Jackson. John Pate of Richmond County was reported as a soldier, with no regiment listed.

This research has no other record that can be proved to represent this man. Several items of interest will follow.

One John Pate died in Richmond County in 1863. Some researchers have suggested this was the son of Stephen who returned to Richmond County in his old age. Research, cited below, proves this John Pate was a descendant of Stephen Pate d. 1839.

It would be easy to dismiss John, the son of Stephen, without further comments, but for one Daniel Pate, of longtime interest to Pate researchers. Some background and new information from DNA testing are worthy of note. This Daniel was born in North Carolina ca. 1802 or ca. 1812, based on U. S. Census records. He died in Leon County, Texas, September 1878. He married Susannah Graham ca. 1832, probably in Wayne County, Mississippi.

Traditional genealogy, of earlier years, led to the assumption that Daniel d. 1878 was related to the Pate Family of Richmond County, North Carolina. Factors leading to that assumption include naming patterns. He had the given name of a son of Stephen d. 1839 and named five sons after males in the family of Stephen – Richmond, Daniel, Stephen, Duncan, and Ely. Two of his daughters received names of daughters of Stephen – Elizabeth and Hannah. His wife had a maiden name common to the Richmond County area. Other families are known to have migrated from Richmond County to Mississippi – Lee, Parker, McNeill, etc.

Research shared by family researchers document that Daniel d. 1878 was in Clarke County, Mississippi, tax records for 1839, and years following, until his departure in 1859. He was preceded in the tax records by a Stephen Pate in 1837. Some have suggested that this Stephen was the son of Stephen d. 1839, named Stephen Sweeny Pate. The identity of that son in Carroll County, Tennessee, in that timeframe, seems to discredit that assumption. Acknowledgement of the lack of proof for either claim is recognized. It seems more probable, to the writer, that the full name of the man in question was Stephen Daniel Pate, or Daniel Stephen, and that he made both records.

DNA testing appears to have confirmed the assumed origin of Daniel Pate d. 1878. Information shared by A. J. Pate, Pate DNA Project administrator, identifies Daniel Pate d. 1878 as a direct descendant of Stephen Pate d. 1839. A review of some DNA mutations in the Pate Family, with some interpretation, was offered earlier. Additional mutations have been observed in the Richmond County family of Thoroughgood Pate d. 1802 and his descendants. The interpretation of the results becomes more complex as additional mutations are recognized. For here, it seems sufficient to say that mutations at Markers 391, 570, and 459 identify two proven descendants of Daniel Pate d. 1878 to also be descendants of Stephen Pate d. 1839. Therefore, Daniel descends from a son of Stephen. Test results at this time are insufficient to identify that son.

The birth year for Daniel has been reported as 1802 or 1812, based on U. S. Census reports. The 1802 date appears to be in error, since the oldest son of Stephen was only 12 or 13 years of age in 1802. John was about 22 years in 1812, Elijah was 21 years, and Daniel, the son of Stephen, was 14-16 years that year. The fourth son, Stephen Sweeny Pate, was only 13 years. The assumption is offered that Daniel Pate d. 1878 was a son of one of the three oldest sons of Stephen Pate d. 1839.

John is the most probable father, in the opinion of the writer. The children of Elijah and Daniel have been identified with reasonable certainty, and this Daniel was not among them. Acknowledgement is granted that an out-of-wedlock birth is possible. However, customs of the times were for illegitimate children to carry the surname of the mother. The DNA results and the surname of Daniel Pate d. 1878 could result from an out-of- wedlock union but only from a son of Stephen Pate and a Pate female. Available records fail to provide two such candidates. However, many records fail to survive!

John was absent from available records after 1839. This research has no record of a marriage or of a family for him. Daniel Pate d.

1878 will be placed as a son of John, for organizational purposes. However, the writer believes that in fact John was the father of Daniel, legitimate or illegitimate.

Family records shared with the writer report Daniel and Susannah (Graham) Pate had children as follows:

Richmond J. – b. 29 March 1834, m. Martha Jane Smith, d. 17 July 1881;
Mary – b. ca. 1835, m. 1) Z. Z. Blacklidge, 2) Edward Gressett;
Nancy – b. ca. 1836, m. a Parker cousin;
Susannah – b. ca. 1837, m. 1) Benjamin P. Elkins, 2) T. J. Oden;
Sarah J. – b. ca. 1838, m. Elisha P. Parker;
Elizabeth – b. ca. 1840, m. W. S. Wornick;
William R. – b. ca. 1842, m. Amanda Jane Parker;
Daniel – b. ca. 1844, d. young;
Edward – b. ca. 1844 (may be same person as Daniel), d. 3 April 1926;
Meriot – b. 1855;
Duncan – b. ca. 1857;
Ely – b. ca. 1859.

Note the son named Meriot. Perhaps the given name recognized Merritt Randle, the father-in-law of Stephen Sweeny Pate.

Elijah S. (Sweeny?) Pate was the second born child of Stephen Pate d. 1839. He was born 22 July 1791 and died 24 July 1880. The dates are inscribed on his grave marker in Morrison Cemetery, Richmond County. He married Mary "Polly" Campbell. The dates on her grave marker are born 11 May 1807, died 11 October 1860.

This research did not determine the relationship between the wife of Elijah and Alexander Campbell, who married the sister of Elijah.

North Carolina death certificates are available for two children of Elijah S. and Mary (Campbell) Pate -- Stephen W. Pate and Mary (Pate) Smith. The certificate for the son reports his father was born in Richmond County, and his mother was born in Europe. The certificate for the daughter reports her father was born in McKenzie, Tennessee, and that her mother was a "foreigner". This information leads to the assumption that the wife of Elijah was among the large number of immigrants from Scotland who settled in the Richmond County area in the early 1800s.

Records available to this research do not support the claim that Elijah was born in Tennessee. He was born in Richmond County, North Carolina. Apparently, his return from Tennessee, noted earlier, confirmed the tradition handed down to his daughter, Mary. It does serve to verify that Elijah moved to Tennessee with others of his family but returned to North Carolina.

His purchase of the Richmond County land in the estate of his father from his brothers, Stephen Sweeny and Richmond Love Pate, 11 November 1841, was cited earlier.

The children of Elijah S. and Mary (Campbell) Pate were identified from family information shared by Roberto Butler, U. S. Census reports, and North Carolina death certificates. The children were:

Lorena Jane – b. ca. 1836;
Sarah A. – b. ca. 1837, m. Daniel Brown, d. 25 February 1930;
Stephen W. – b. 1838, m. Mary Jane Williamson, d. 30 December 1930;
Mary – b. 25 December 1842, m. [?] Smith, d. 1 August 1922;
Martha A. – b. ca. 1844;
Flora Ann – b. ca. 1846;
Howard – b. ca. 1849.

The third child born to Stephen Pate d. 1839 was Elizabeth Pate. She was born ca. 1794, based on limited records on hand. The death year was not determined.

Her marriage to Nathaniel Hawthorne and the children from that marriage before 20 February 1840 are proved, as she and her husband sold her interest in the estate of her father. The sale to her brothers, Stephen Sweeny and Richmond Love Pate, was noted earlier, Carroll County Deed Book D, pages 482-483.

Research on two of the daughters of Stephen Pate d. 1839, Sarah (Pate) Campbell and Elizabeth (Pate) Hawthorne, by Larry Campbell, was shared with the writer. This work reports Nathaniel and Elizabeth (Pate) Hawthorne were residents of Decatur County, Georgia, in the 1830s. Three of their children were married in Decatur County. The names of the children are the same as those appearing in the Carroll County, Tennessee, records in 1840. Apparently, the family moved from Decatur County, Georgia, to Carroll County, Tennessee, for her legacy from the estate of her father.

Their presence in Decatur County is not too surprising. Her brother, Elisha S. Pate, lived in Henry County, Alabama in the 1830s. The two counties join at the state line, separated by the Chattahoochee River.

The children named in the two records follow:

> Lenora/Lenorah Jones - m. Matthew G. Jones, 12 January 1837;
> John – appears only in the Carroll County record;
> Joseph – m. Rejinah Cork, 13 March 1845;
> Nathaniel – m. Mary Newberry, 10 December 1843.

The two marriages after 1840, and the appearance in Tennessee, suggest Nathaniel and Elizabeth returned to Georgia after settling her legacy. This research did not follow the family further.

The fourth child born to Stephen Pate d. 1839 was Daniel Pate. His birth and death dates are open for debate. This report will use 1796 for the birth year and ca. 1825 for the death year. He is proved as a son of Stephen by the records created as the estate of his father was distributed, cited earlier. These records prove he preceded his father in death.

Daniel married Elizabeth Lamb in Robeson County, North Carolina, 7 January 1812. Her parents were not identified, but several Lamb families resided in Robeson County in this timeframe.

Daniel served in the Robeson County Militia in the War of 1812.

The estate records for Stephen Pate d. 1839 identified the children of Daniel, and noted the father was deceased. The widow, and mother, Elizabeth (Lamb) Pate, was never recognized as the guardian for the children. Nor was she recognized in association with the children in later records. The assumption is offered that she also died before 1839. The children were:

> Honor – b. ca. 1813;
> Samuel – b. ca. 1815;
> Nathaniel G. – b. ca. 1819.

Honor married Nathaniel P. Gibson, as proved in the estate records cited earlier. The Gibson family lived in Richmond County, 1840-1870. Honor was without her husband in 1870. She was listed in Marlboro County, South Carolina, in 1880, without a husband.

U. S. Census reports identify her children as follows:

Stephen – b. ca. 1830;
John – b. ca. 1831;
Elizabeth – b. ca. 1832;
Nancy – b. ca. 1834;
Daniel – b. ca. 1839;
Mary – b. ca. 1840;
Frances – b. ca. 1842;
Nathaniel, Jr. – b. ca. 1843;
Hannah – b. ca. 1847, d. 30 September 1904;
Honor – b. ca. 1848.

The son named Samuel appears to be the man of that name on the U. S. Census for 1840 in Carroll County, Tennessee. He was recorded as 20-30 years of age and had a wife represented who was 15-20 years of age. This may be the family on the U. S. Census for Clarke County, Arkansas, in 1850. Samuel and his wife Julia A. were born in North Carolina and were 35 and 24 years old, respectively. They had four daughters – Elizabeth 9 years, Catherine 6 years, Martha 4 years and Louisa 3 years. The daughters were born in Tennessee. The ages and birth places suggest the correct family is in focus. The fate of Samuel after 1850 is unknown to the writer.

A South Carolina death certificate leads to the recognition and identification of the family of Nathaniel Pate. Readers should be aware that assumptions are involved in the report to follow. However, they are based on records, and the interpretation is plausible, in the opinion of the writer.

The death certificate for William F. Pate of Chesterfield County, South Carolina, reports he died 19 May 1930. His father was Nathaniel Pate, and his mother was Mary Pate. The form requested the maiden surname of the mother, and Pate was given. The birth year was not reported, but his age was 81 years. This is compatible with the U. S. Census for Chesterfield County in 1900, which listed his birth as August 1849. Both parents were born in North Carolina, as was the deceased.

Since this research has no record of another Nathaniel Pate in this area and timeframe, consideration must be given that this certificate identified the Nathaniel under review here. A review of some records follows.

Thoroughgood Pate d. 1836, the youngest son of Thoroughgood Pate d. ca. 1802, left a widow and two small sons after his death in

1836. The widow, Jennett/Jane (McColeman) Pate, was listed on the 1840 U. S. Census for Richmond County, North Carolina. Her household included her two sons, and a male and female 15/20 years each, with an under-five-year female. The 1850 return listed Jane and her two Pate sons, James Hamilton and George Thoroughgood, and three young Pate children – Mary Pate 11 years, John Pate 7 years, and William Pate 1 year. The older male and female from the 1840 return were absent in 1850.

The 1860 return listed her sons in their households. George T. Pate had John Pate, 17 years, in his household. This John is assumed to have been the seven-year-old John in his mother's household in 1850. James H. Pate had Ferdinand Pate, 11 years, in his household. Ferdinand is assumed to have been the William in his mother's household in 1850.

James H. Pate was appointed administrator of the estate of John Pate, deceased, 20 April 1863, Richmond County Loose Estate Records. The assets of the estate included $53.55 Confederate Army pay, leading to the assumption that John was a deceased Confederate soldier. The estate was settled, and a note was made on the last entry that the balance "belongs to Ferdinand Pate." This leads to the assumption that Ferdinand was the only surviving heir of the deceased John Pate.

Confederate military records provide more insight into the fate of John. He enlisted 2 July 1861, in Robeson County, in Company F, 18th North Carolina Infantry Regiment. He resided in Richmond County and was 19 years of age. John died of wounds 26 July 1862. Other Pates in this unit included Stephen Pate from Richmond County, and David, Daniel, Edward and another named Stephen from Bladen County. The Bladen County Pates were descendants of James Pate d. ca. 1790, a brother to Thoroughgood Pate d. ca. 1802.

The cited records lead to the assumption that the three young Pates in the household of Jane Pate in 1850 – Mary 11 years, John 7 years, and William 1 year – were siblings and were children of the 15/20-year-old couple in her household in 1840. The absence of Mary as an heir of the deceased John in 1863 indicates she preceded him in death. The surviving William, or Ferdinand, was the only surviving heir.

Ferdinand Pate appears on the U. S. Census for Chesterfield County in 1870, with a wife named Margaret and no children. The family can be followed on later returns, except 1910, until his death in 1930. He was listed on the 1930 return, enumerated 26 April, preceding his death 19 May. His name appears as Ferdinand Pate and William F. Pate, variously, in these records. The names of his wife and children were consistent. The records seem sufficient to confirm that his full name was William Ferdinand Pate.

The assumption is offered that the young couple enumerated in the household of Jane (McColeman) Pate in 1840 were the parents of William F. Pate, who were identified on his death certificate as Nathaniel Pate and Mary Pate. The under-five-year-old female was their daughter named Mary, born ca. 1839. The two boys who appeared on the 1850 return, John born 1843 and William born 1849, were also their sons. The couple, apparently, was engaged to assist the widowed Jane Pate in the management of her household and farming operations.

Nathaniel and Mary had departed by 1850, while the children remained with Jane. The daughter Mary had departed by 1860, when John and William Ferdinand were in the households of the sons of Jane. The fate of Mary is unknown, but she did not share in the estate of John in 1864. Her absence indicates she was deceased. William Ferdinand married Margaret [?] and moved to Chester-field County, South Carolina. His name alternated in later records between Ferdinand and William F., as it did in earlier records. The names of his wife and children give assurance that the correct person is in focus.

The U. S. Census shows William Ferdinand and Margaret had been married 30 years in 1900. She was the mother of nine children, five of whom were deceased. The surviving children were:

Whiteford Pate – b. ca. 1876;
Duncan M. Pate – b. February 1880;
Bell Pate – b. August 1881;
Lillie Pate – b. February 1887.

The 1930 return listed the son Duncan M. and the daughter Bell Hurst in the household of William F. (Ferdinand) Pate.

Records available to this research fail to identify the fate of Nathaniel and his wife Mary after 1850, and before he appeared in Carroll and Weakley counties of Tennessee in 1860. Nathaniel is assumed to have been the N. G. Pate on the 1860 U. S. Census for Weakley County. He was 41 years of age, born in North Carolina, and had no wife or children represented. William and Caroline

Gibson were in his household with two small children. Nathaniel Pate was enumerated on the 1870 U. S. Census for Carroll County, was 50 years of age, and born in North Carolina. He was listed in a household of Bowden and Farmie families, suggesting he was a boarder. His occupation was listed as "None what so ever."

Nathaniel appears to be the N. G. Pate who wrote his will in Carroll County, April 1873. It was proved in Court, May 1874. His estate was devised to James Cole and Beulah Cole, son and daughter of Richard S. Cole. The Cole and Pate Families had a long association. James Cole and Stephen Pate were the executors of the Richmond County will of Darby Sweeny in 1820. The executors were sons-in-law of Darby Sweeny.

Many questions arise from the information available on Nathaniel and his family. Unfortunately, this research failed to provide more definition. He did have descendants through his son, William Ferdinand Pate d. 1930.

Stephen Sweeny Pate was the fifth child born to Stephen Pate d. 1839. He shared the administration of his father's estate with his brother, Richmond Love Pate. Several records involving him, and the estate have been cited. The reports authored by Barbara Clark, noted earlier, treat him and the estate in detail. This report will be restricted to his vital statistics and the children of his three marriages.

Stephen Sweeny Pate was born 21 October 1799 in North Carolina and died in Carroll County, Tennessee, in 1887. His Carroll County will was written 3 May 1872 and presented for probate in January 1887. He had three marriages and children from each. The first, to Rebecca Randle, was documented as his father-in-law, Merritt Randle, gave him a slave, cited earlier. Merritt Randle also left a will in Carroll County, and the marriage was recognized in it.

The children of his marriage to Rebecca Randle were:

Richmond Love – b. ca. 1827, m.
Isabella [?]; Julia – b. ca. 1830;
Caroline – b. ca. 1832, m. Cavendish Johnson Carroll, 28
    December 1855; Stephen Sweeny – b. ca. 1836, m. 1) Mary
    E. Vanhooks, 2) Martha Jane Crowe; Jane – b. ca. 1838;
Eli Ely – b. ca. 1843, m. Ione Keating, d. 1902;
John - b. ca. 1845, m. Virginia Ferguson, d. 6 November 1872.

The children of his second marriage, to Elizabeth Huff, were:

114

Hannah E. – b. ca. 1857, m. N. H. Hull;
Darby S. – b. ca. 1858;
Mary Jane – b. ca. 1859, m. E. A. Ellsberry;
Frank Cheatham – b. ca. 1862, m. Lizzie Warner.

The children of his third marriage, to Winnie Rebecca [?], were:

Nancy Keaton – b. ca. 1867, m. Randolph L. Pate;
Winnie Huff – b. ca. 1872;
Jefferson Davis – b. ca. 1875.

Elisha S. Pate was the sixth born child of Stephen Pate d. 1839. He was born ca. 1803 in North Carolina, based on U. S. Census reports, and died after the U. S. Census for Carroll County, Tennessee, was enumerated in 1870. He was identified as Elias S. Pate on the return for 1870, E. S. Pate on the U. S. Censuses for 1840-1860, and Elisha Pate on the returns for 1820 and 1830. He was identified as Elisha Pate in the probate records of the estate of his father and the will of his grandfather, Darby Sweeny, and that of his father-in-law, Henry Beckwith – to be cited. The names of his wives give assurance that the same person is in focus in these records. The name of Elias in the 1870 U. S. Census was an error.

Elisha married, first, Sarah Beckwith, a daughter of Henry Beckwith of Marion County, South Carolina, Marion Will Book 1, page 141. Beckwith recognized his wife, Morning Beckwith, sons Hansel and Amos, and daughters Sarah Pate, Rhoda Henderson, and Martha Jane Beckwith. Sarah Pate was the wife of Elisha Pate, and Rhoda Henderson was the wife of Hopkins Henderson, Marion Estate Records 1790-1822, Rolls 44, 53, 882, 891 and 893. This Henderson family will be recognized in more detail in the narrative on Rev. Charles Pate d. p. 1790.

Elisha was in Richmond County, North Carolina, for the 1820 U. S. Census and in Henry County, Alabama, for the 1830 U. S. Census. Both records recognize him and his wife, with no children. Note was made in the narrative on his sister, Elizabeth (Pate) Hawthorne, that she and her family were located in Decatur County, Georgia, in the 1830s. The counties of Henry, Alabama, and Decatur, Georgia, were separated by the Chattahoochee River. Thus, the brother and sister were near neighbors in the early 1830s.

Records support the following assumptions. Sarah (Beckwith) Pate died in this area of Alabama or Georgia after the 1830 U. S.

Census was enumerated. Elisha joined his family in Weakley-Carroll counties, Tennessee. Since he arrived in Tennessee with a daughter, Louisa, born in Alabama ca. 1832, consideration is given that Sarah died in childbirth. Elisha remarried to Martha Ann (Parker?) in Tennessee. The first child of the second marriage was born ca. 1838.

His sister, Elizabeth, and her husband, Nathaniel Hawthorne, also traveled to Carroll County, Tennessee. Records fail to tell us if they traveled as Elisha and his daughter moved, but they were in Carroll County, Tennessee, 26 February 1840, when they sold her interest in the estate of her father, cited earlier.

Elisha had one child from his marriage to Sarah Beckwith – Louisa, b. ca. 1832 in Henry County, Alabama.

His marriage to Martha Ann (Parker?) resulted in children as follows:

James – b. ca. 1838;
William Franklin – b. ca. 1840;
Mary – b. ca. 1842;
Elizabeth – b. ca. 1848;
Nancy – b. ca. 1852;
Isabelle – b. ca. 1859;
Eugenia "Jinny" – b. ca. 1860.

The children of this marriage are based on U. S. Census reports.

Sarah Pate was the seventh-born child of Stephen Pate d. 1839. She was born ca. 1804 in Richmond County, from the best records available. She preceded her father in death, as proved by his estate records, cited earlier. She died before February 1859. Her last child was born ca. 1835. Her death likely occurred between 1835 and February 1837.

The report of the accidental death of a daughter of Stephen d. 1839, as the family moved to Tennessee, was included in family information shared with the writer in past years. The source of this information has been misplaced. Therefore, the accident is not reported as fact. However, the death of Sarah between 1835 and 1837 may relate to the accident.

Sarah Pate married Alexander Campbell of the Richmond County area. *Scattered Seed,* Myrtle Bridges, page 184, reports their marriage and provides some notes on the children of the marriage. The following is from that source:

Phillip – b. 22 November 1821, m. 1) Elinor H. [?], m. 2) Matilda
Thomkins Mullen, d. 30 May 1908;
Alexander – b. ca. 1827, m. Elizabeth Parker; Daniel – b. ca.
1832;
Margaret Ann – b. ca. 1835.

The children seem to be living in the household of their uncle,
Richmond Love Pate, when the U. S. Census for Carroll County
was enumerated. The Carroll County Court placed them under the
guardianship of Richmond L. Pate in September 1841.

Note was made earlier of the gift of a slave girl to Margaret Ann
Campbell by her grandmother, Honor (Sweeny) Pate. The act occurred
21 July 1841 and is assumed to mark the relocation of the grandmother
to North Carolina, Carroll County Deed Book E, pages 217-218.

The fate of the father, Alexander Campbell, is unknown.

Hannah Pate, a daughter, was the eighth child born to Stephen
Pate d. 1839. She was born ca. 1806 in North Carolina and died after
the U. S. Census for Weakley County, Tennessee, was enumerated
in 1860. The assumption is offered that she died in Weakley County.

She married Eli Ely. The family was enumerated on the U. S.
Census for Weakley County, Tennessee, in 1830, 1840, and 1860.
She was identified as the wife of Eli Ely in the estate records on her
father's estate. They were among the heirs who sold interests in the
estate to her brothers, Stephen Sweeny Pate and Richmond Love
Pate, 16 November 1841, Carroll County, Tennessee, Deed Book R,
page 13.

Available records do not identify the children of this couple. The
U. S. Censuses for 1830 and 1840 list a male born ca. 1825-1830, and
a female born ca. 1835, in the household of Eli Ely. This research
failed to identify their relationship to Hannah and Eli.

Samuel Duncan Pate was the ninth child born to Stephen Pate d.
1839. He was born ca. 1810 in Richmond County, North Carolina,
and died 1892 in Weakley County, Tennessee. His will was written
22 February 1881 and was recorded in Will Book 1860-1898, page
285. He was buried in Old Salem Cemetery in 1892.

Search For Myself, by Barbara Clark, provides detail on this family
and should be reviewed by the descendants of Samuel Duncan Pate.

Note was made earlier of the gift of a slave from his mother, 21
July 1841. She identified him as "my son Samuel D. Pate...for good
reason...me hereunto moving." This was interpreted as record of his

mother moving from Weakley County. The assumption was offered that she returned to North Carolina.

Samuel Duncan married Elizabeth Hayes. Their children are from *Pate Pioneers on the Pee Dee River*, a previous work of this writer. The marriages of the children are from research of Janice Case, shared in past years. The children were:

> Martha – b. ca. 1837, m. James Samuel Parker;
> John Daniel – b. ca. 1840, m. Josephine [?];
> Mary N. – b. ca. 1843, m. William Franklin Pate;
> Stephen Hays – b. ca. 1844, m. Buena Vista Allen;
> James Kelly – b. ca. 1847, m. Susan v. Turner Pate;
> Richmond Love – b. ca. 1850, m. Olivia Newton;
> Lenora Jane – b. ca. 1852, m. Edwin Wall Martin;
> Elisha Tucker – b. 15 July 1856, m. Ulysses "Eula" Martin, d.
>   12 April 1915;
> Elijah – b. 15 July 1856, d. young.
> Elijah and Elisha were twins.

Richmond Love Pate was the tenth, and last, child born to Stephen Pate d. 1839. Note was made in the narration on Stephen that U. S. Census reports list a male child in the household of Stephen in the 1810-1820 timeframe, whom available records fail to identify. The child may have been a son who died early, or one who resulted from unknown circumstances.

Richmond Love was born in North Carolina ca. 1815. He married Alto Zora Thomas, 10 March 1840, according to family information shared with the writer. He died in Carroll County, Tennessee, before the U. S. Census for 1870 was enumerated. His widow was listed without a husband, and names of the children give assurances that the correct family is in focus.

Several records, executed by Richmond Love Pate, in his personal interest and as joint administrator of his father's estate, have been cited. They will not be repeated.

The children of Richmond Love is reported as listed in *Pate Pioneers on the Pee Dee River*. That list appears to be complete. Birth dates are added from the U. S. Censuses of Weakley and Carroll counties of Tennessee. Note was made in the narrative on his sister, Sarah (Pate) Campbell, that the children in his Carroll County household in 1840 appear to be children of the deceased sister, not of Richmond Love. Further, the elderly female in his household that year is assumed to have been his mother.

The children of Richmond Love Pate were:

Alsey/Alsy – b. ca. 1841;
Henry (Franklin?) – b. ca. 1843;
Napoleon – b. ca. 1844;
Thomas Luther – b. ca. 1845;
John – b. ca. 1846;
Sarah (Lulu?) – b. ca. 1849;
Martha – b. ca. 1852;
Leander – b. ca. 1854, m. Isabella Pate;
Lenora (Tennessee) – b. 1856.

This completes the report on Stephen Pate d. 1839 and his descendants.

SABRA (PATE) WRIGHT,
DAUGHTER OF THOROUGHGOOD PATE D. 1802

Sabra Pate was the only daughter of Thoroughgood Pate d. 1802, who was identified by available records. Note was made earlier that U. S. Censuses report two additional young females in the household of her father. They could have been additional daughters, but available records fail to identify them or whether these females had a relationship to the family.

Sabra was born 25 December 1775, based on Wright family information. She wrote her Richmond County will, 15 April 1844. It was proved in court in July 1846. Her death will be listed as July 1846. She married George Wright 6 December 1791, based on Wright family information. Her marriage was confirmed when she was identified as the widow of George Wright in court records involving the probate of his estate, 17 January 1837. Records cited earlier prove the wife of George Wright was a daughter of Thoroughgood Pate d. ca. 1802.

Wright family records from several sources have advanced this project. These include Marjorie (Jones) Krueger, Pauline Skaggs, Maeallen Form, and Myrtle Bridges.

George Wright was born ca. 1770, some say in Ireland, but that has not been confirmed. He had a brother named William Wright who was also active in Richmond County records, and had children.

George died in September 1836, as proved by the probate of his Richmond County Estate, Richmond County Loose Estate Records at the North Carolina State Archives, C. R. 82.508.69.

One source reports George Wright died in North Carolina 27 September 1836 and was buried at Bethlehem Cemetery, Monroe County, Alabama. The burial site is questionable. Court records that allotted the widow's dower lands report he was a resident of, and died in, Richmond County, North Carolina. The transportation of his body to Monroe County, Alabama for burial seems unlikely. He did have a son, Daniel P. Wright, who lived in Monroe County, Alabama, and the son was buried at Bethlehem Cemetery in 1849.

George Wright was active in civil affairs, as were his Pate in-laws. He resided on Joes Creek and Gum Swamp, waters of the Little Pee Dee River, with the Pate Families. He was active in land convey-ances and executed numerous deeds in Richmond County.

His landholdings at death were large. The court identified 1,512 acres of land in his estate, to be divided among his heirs. Addition-ally, the widow was allotted 390 acres that included "the dwelling house or mansion", indicating his house was recognized as a man-sion by the standards of the time. The inventory and sale of his personal property filled six pages. Each of his heirs received shares valued at $1,194.44 each. The widow, beside her dower, also received a child's share, as she requested in a Petition to the Court.

Richmond County records provide additional information on George Wright. This report has primary interest in the children of his marriage to Sabra Pate and their fate. Additional information on George Wright will be omitted.

The legatees of George Wright are identified in the distribution of his estate, Loose Estate Records cited earlier. The heirs were: Arthur P. Wright, Duncan C. Wright, heirs of Cameron Wright, John P. Wright, Daniel P. Wright, William P. Wright, Samuel Wright, and James Wright. The assumption is offered that the middle initial of "P." recognized the Pate maiden surname of the mother.

The living heirs-at-law of George Wright petitioned the Court for a speedy partition of the land of their father, 17 January 1837. They were listed as in the distribution, except the deceased son, Cameron, was absent. The identification of the heirs in two records is cited because some Wright researchers have reported a son named George Wright. The court records did not recognize a son named George Wright. Additional information follows.

The will and estate records for Sabra (Pate) Wright provide information on the young George Wright. The will devised her personal estate to her sons James Wright and John Wright. They were sons of her marriage to George Wright and are among the heirs-at- law of George Wright, cited earlier. The land owned by Sabra was distributed among all of her sons from her marriage to George Wright. Extant deeds provide record of the sale of shares of the dower land of Sabra by two of her sons, John and Duncan, 16 January and 12 January 1850, Richmond County Deed Book N, page 29. A deed on page 307 of the same book proves the heirs of the deceased son, Cameron Wright, also received shares of the dower land, after the death of Sabra. The assumption is offered that all heirs also shared in the dower land, after the death of their mother.

An estate record on Sabra (Pate) Wright d. 1846 appears in the Richmond Loose Estates, cited earlier. This record identifies the distribution of her personal property to her sons, James Wright and John Wright, as instructed in her will. Further, the record reports that her son, George Wright, was placed under the guardianship of Henry William Harrington, 22 October 1822. Additional information is not available. The interpretation of the writer follows.

The children from her marriage to George Wright shared in the dower property Sabra received from the estate of her husband. George Wright, apparently her son, was not eligible for any legacy from the estate of her husband, George Wright. Henry William Harrington assumed guardianship of the son, 22 October 1822. The assumption is offered that this son was born outside of her marriage to George Wright. The action by Henry William Harrington may indicate he was the father of the young George Wright. No further information is available on this son of Sabra (Pate) Wright.

Caution is issued that the preceding is the opinion of the writer. Records are insufficient to prove the assumption. Readers are free to accept or reject the opinion.

Sabra must have been popular with her children. Five of her eight sons from the Wright marriage named daughters Sabra. The name continued to appear in later generations.

The vital dates available on the children of George and Sabra (Pate) Wright will follow. Their children are from a mix of court records, deed records, family information, and U.

S. Census reports. The marriage dates, when cited, are from county marriage records.

Daniel P. Wright was the first-born son. He was born ca. 1795 and died in 1849. He was buried at Bethlehem Cemetery in Monroe County, Alabama. The dates are inscribed on his grave marker. He married Ellander Godbold, 2 September 1819, in Summerville, South Carolina, as reported in family information. The bride was born ca. 1802, died in Monroe County in 1868, and was also buried in Bethlehem Cemetery. She was a daughter of Stephen and Rebecca (Grice) Godbold, and a sister to the wife of Daniel's brother, William P. Wright.

The family lived in Marion County, South Carolina, and moved to Monroe County, Alabama, soon after 1820. The writer is aware of Thompson, Lock, and Wiggins families who also relocated from this area of the Carolinas to Monroe County.

The children of Daniel P. Wright were as follows:

> Stephen – b. ca. 1820 in South Carolina;
> Samuel – b. 2 September 1822 in Alabama, m. Mary Caroline Solomon, 15 March 1846, d. 8 December 1907;
> John – b. ca. 1824, m. Eliza Ann Solomon, 15 March 1846, d. 13 July 1907;
> George – b. ca. 1825, m. Mary Frances Stokes, 8 February 1867, d. p. 1880;
> Matilda – b. ca. 1825, m. 1) [?] Williamson, 2) George M. Storey;
> Eliza – b. ca. 1828, m. Washington Nutt;
> Christopher – b. ca. 1830, m. Cynthia Johnson;
> Daniel Waide – b. ca. 1835, m. Drucilla Grimes, 4 August 1857;
> Duncan – b. ca. 1835, m. Frances Stiffenmire, 30 March 1861;
> Jefferson – b. ca. 1838, m. Sarah Jane Solomon, 2 January 1857;
> Robert – b. ca. 1841, m. Narcissa Andreas;
> Nancy – b. ca. 1843, m. Patrick Boatright;
> Elizabeth – b. ca. 1845;
> Rebecca – b. ca. 1848, m. James Thomas Langham.

Cameron Wright was probably the second born son of George and Sabra (Pate) Wright, but his birth year is not definitive. He preceded his father in death, before September 1836. His firstborn child was born ca. 1815. His birth year will be noted as ca. 1795. His brother, Daniel P. Wright, has the same birth year in this report. This is not to imply a twin birth. Each of them was born about 1795, give or take a year.

He married Lucy Ann Jones, a daughter of William Jones, Richmond County Will Book 2, pages 87-88. Lucy Ann (Jones) Wright died before 12 July 1852, when her dower land, from the estate of her deceased husband, was distributed among the heirs, Deed Book T, pages 133-135. The heirs were also identified in Richmond County Loose Estate Records dated 17 July 1837, 18 February 1838, and 1840. The heirs were:

Jane – b. ca. 1815, m. William Chance;
John G. – b. ca. 1822, m. Piety [?];
Sabra – b. ca. 1828, m. Albert Wright, 21 January 1845;
George – b. ca. 1831;
Daniel Thomas – b. ca. 1834, m. Elizabeth Smith, 22 September 1852;
James – b. ca. 1836.

William P. Wright was the third born son of George and Sabra (Pate) Wright. He was born ca. 1799 in Richmond County and died before 14 November 1846, when his widow filed for administration on her deceased husband's estate in Marion County, South Carolina, Estate Records.

He married Frances (Franky) Godbold, a daughter of Stephen G. Godbold. The bride was a sister to Ellander Godbold, who married Daniel P. Wright. The Godbold and Grice families were active in Marion County records. Frances (Godbold) Wright was born ca. 1799 and died in Marion County after the U. S. Census for 1870 was enumerated. She was listed on that return in the household of her daughter and son-in-law, Hardy and Sabra (Wright) Brantham.

The children of William and Frances are identified from family information and U. S. Census reports. The dates on the son, Darling, are from his grave marker in Richmond County. They were:

Darling – b. 6 January 1821, m. Jennett Curry McCormick, d. 31 January 1898;
Ellen – b. ca. 1825;
Stephen – b. ca. 1829, m. Mariah Leggett;
George – b. ca. 1833;
Oram – b. ca. 1836;
Mary – b. ca. 1837;
James – b. ca. 1838;
Elizabeth – b. ca. 1839;
Sabra – b. ca. 1841, m. Hardy Brantham;

William – b. ca. 1844.

Samuel Wright was the fourth born son. He was born 13 November 1802 and died in Richmond County in 1848, as proved in the division of his estate, Deed Book U, page 48. He married Ann Gibson about 1824. She died in 1866, as proved in the probate of her estate, Richmond County Loose Estates. The family lived in Richmond County.

The heirs of Samuel were identified in the division of his estate. They were:

> Elizabeth – b. ca. 1827, m. William E. O'Bryan, d. a. 1868;
> Daniel P. – b. ca. 1829, m. Caroline Jones, d 1885;
> John G. – b. ca. 1831;
> Cameron G. – b. ca. 1833, m. Eliza Jane McNeill, 17 February 1853, d. 1867;
> Sarah Ann – b. ca. 1836, m. Archibald McNeill;
> Sabra – b. ca. 1838, m. Robert Odom;
> Samuel G. – b. ca. 1841.

Arthur P. Wright was the fifth born son of George and Sabra (Pate) Wright. He was born ca. 1810 in Richmond County and died ca. 1868 in Richland Parish, Louisiana. He married Martha Purnell Turner, based on family information.

Arthur appears to have been living in the household of his father on the U. S. Census for Richmond County in 1830. He followed, or accompanied, his brother Daniel to Monroe County, Alabama, by 1840. The U. S. Census for 1850 located him and his family in Western District, Carroll Parish, Louisiana. The complete household was in Morehouse Parish in 1860. Family information reports he died in Richland Parish, where most of his children were enumerated for the 1870 U. S. Census.

Arthur sold the land received from the estate of his father, 1 May 1837, Deed Book P, page 161. The buyer was his brother, John P. Wright. Witnesses to the deed were his brothers Duncan Wright and James Wright.

The children of Arthur P. Wright is identified from U. S. Census reports. They were:

George W. – b. ca. 1837 in North Carolina;

Cameron – b. ca. 1842 in Alabama;
Andrew J. – b. ca. 1845 in Alabama;
Arthur – b. ca. 1848 in Louisiana;
Phillip – b. ca. 1851 in Louisiana;
James – b. ca. 1859 in Louisiana.

Duncan P. Wright was the sixth born son. He was born 19 December 1813 in Richmond County and died 27 November 1898 in Hinds County, Mississippi, from family information. He had four marriages and children from the first three. The brides were:

1) Permelia Goodwin ca, 1831 – she was born 15 July 1815 in Marlboro County, South Carolina and died 1 August 1869 in Hinds County, Mississippi;
2) Sally Thigpen ca. 1869;
3) Mariah Catherine Godbold 11 November 1870 – she was born 26 May 1846 in Copiah County, Mississippi and died 9 October 1883 in Hinds County;
4) Sarah Ellafar Crisler 1 March 1887 in Hinds County.

The marriage to Permelia Goodwin resulted in children as follows:

Francis "Frann" – b. ca. 1832;
Simeon – b. ca. 1836;
Sabra – b ca.1838;
L. C. (female) – b. ca. 1842, m. J. M. Jones;
Roseanna – b. ca. 1844;
Hester – b. ca. 1848;
Walter S. – b. ca.1851;
Neill – b. ca. 1853;
Robert S. – b. ca. 1862.

One child was born to the marriage to Sally Thigpen – Christopher – b. ca. 1869.

The children born to the marriage to Mariah Catherine Godbold were (dates from family information):

Hope – b. 17 September 1871;
Maggie – b. 11 September 1874;
Viola – b. 1 March 1877;

Printer – b. 21 March 1879;
Charles Walker – b. 27 May 1881.

John P. Wright was the seventh born son of George and Sabra (Pate) Wright. He was born ca. 1816 in Richmond County. His death date was not determined, but it was after 1880. He married Jennett McLeod.

John and Jennett were enumerated on the U. S. Census for Richmond County in 1850. They were not located, by this research, on the 1860 U. S. Census, but were in Lowndes County, Georgia, for the 1870 U. S. Census. The 1870 Census listed a son, Archibald, born ca. 1860 in North Carolina, and a daughter, Sabra, born ca. 1862 in Georgia. These records support that the family was in transit when the 1960 Census was enumerated, and they were not canvassed.

The children of John P. Wright, from U. S. Census reports, follows:

Daniel – b. ca. 1847;
John E. – b. ca. 1850;
Mary C. – b. ca. 1853;
Ann Ruth/twin - b. ca. 1855;
Martha/twin – b. ca. 1855;
Archibald – b. ca. 1860;
Sabra – b. ca. 1862;
Sarah – b. ca. 1864;
Sophie – b. ca. 1866;
George – b. ca. 1870.

James Cameron Wright was the eighth, and last, son born to George and Sabra (Pate) Wright. He was born 11 July 1818 in Richmond County and died 9 October 1892 in Marlboro County, South Carolina. The vital dates for this family are from grave markers. He married first to Mahalia A. Miles ca. 1850. She was born 12 October 1830 and died 10 August 1857 in Marlboro County. James Cameron married second to Jane Conner about 1862. She was born 15 February 1837 and died 8 March 1888 in Marlboro County.

The children of James Cameron are from U. S. Census reports. The children of the marriage to Mahalia Miles were:

Julia – b. ca. 1852;
Zachariah – b. ca. 1855;
Sarah – b. ca. 1857.

The children of the marriage to Jane Conner were: Edward – b. ca. 1865;

Margaret – b. ca. 1867;
Ellenora – b. ca. 1869;
James H. – b. ca. 1872;
Duncan – b. ca. 1873;
Robert – b. ca. 1875;
Jane – b. ca. 1878.

This completes the report on Sabra (Pate) Wright.

THOROUGHGOOD PATE D. 1836,
SON OF THOROUGHGOOD PATE D. 1802

Thoroughgood Pate, Jr., was identified as the youngest son of Thoroughgood Pate, Sr., as the father conveyed two tracts of land to the son 20 December 1802, Richmond Deed Book F, page 181. Comments were offered on the interpretation of this record earlier in this narrative.

One tract was identified as 500 acres of a 600-acre tract that Thoroughgood, Sr., had purchased from Rice Henderson, originally granted to Samuel Snead. This tract of land remained in the estate of Thoroughgood, Jr., as his estate was distributed among his heirs. The possession served to prove at least three lineal descendants in the family.

Thoroughgood Pate, Jr., was born ca. 1780, based on U. S. Census reports, and died 24 March 1836, as proved in the probate of his estate, Richmond Loose Estate Records. He will be identified in this report as Thoroughgood Pate d. 1836.

He married Miss Jennett (Janet) McColman, 30 September 1830, a daughter of Malcolm McColman of Cumberland County. The wedding was performed at the McColman home in Cumberland County, *Fayetteville Observer*, October 1830.

The Richmond County court minutes of June 1810 identify this son of Thoroughgood Pate d. ca. 1802 with the militia title of Colonel, and refer to activity of the Eastern Battalion of the Richmond County Militia. Numerous other records recognize him as Colonel Pate, including deeds, court minutes, and the estate proceedings after his death. It is assumed that he held that office in the North

Carolina militia. Julia Claire Pate, author of *Pate-Adams-Newton*, reports him as Colonel Pate and cites his activity as a delegate to the North Carolina Continental Convention and service in the state legislature for several terms. His service in state and local affairs seems to be well documented.

The probate of his estate resulted in some impressive personal records. His ledger for accounts due listed over 150 persons who owed untitled loans to him. The accounts varied from $0.10 to $164.44. His personal estate included an impressive array of books that include two encyclopedias, Bibles, The Psalms of David, chemistry, Life and History of George Washington, several medical books on therapeutics and diagnostics, Book of Hymns, etc.

His land holdings included 525 acres for each of his two sons and 335 acres set aside as dower land for his widow.

Silas Jones, who appears to have been a merchant, submitted bills for unpaid purchases made during the weeks preceding the death of Thoroughgood. These included a large amount of whiskey. Since alcohol was popular for the relief for pain during that time, the consumption of large quantities suggests he may have been ill for several weeks before death.

The legal debate over property used to secure a loan from Samuel Wright, executed by the administrator of the estate, was cited earlier and will not be repeated here. The value of that record for this report is the relationship proved between Samuel Wright and Thoroughgood Pate. This report avoids debate on the issues of the lawsuit.

The estate records prove the children of Thoroughgood Pate d. 1836. He had two sons – James Hamilton Pate, born September 1832, and George Thoroughgood Pate, born January 1836.

Julia Claire Pate reported that a brother of the widow, James McColman, moved into the home and managed the farm of Thoroughgood Pate d. 1836, until the sons were of age. This research suggests that her brother was not old enough for that role, initially. Records cited in the report on Nathaniel Pate d. c a. 1825, son of Stephen Pate d. 1839, suggest that Nathaniel served in that role. Her father, Malcolm McColman, was appointed guardian for the minor orphans, as reported in the estate proceedings.

A large number of extant records are available on Colonel Thoroughgood Pate. They will be of interest to descendants, but do not add to the goal of this report. The report now turns to the sons of this Thoroughgood and their children.

James Hamilton Pate was the firstborn son of Thoroughgood Pate d. 1836. He was born September 1832 and died in Scotland County (formerly Richmond County) in 1902.

Julia Claire Pate reported that he married Frances Hannah. The marriage is supported by U. S. Census reports. Peter Hannah was enumerated on the U. S. Census for Richmond County in 1850, with a daughter named Fanny, 10 years old. There is some question to the marriage. One child of James H. and Frances was located in North Carolina death records, Preston Brooks Pate. His father was identified as James H. Pate, but his mother was reported as Frances Thomson. A daughter of James H. Pate, Grace Pate, married N. Luther Covington and moved to South Carolina. Her South Carolina death certificate reported her father was James H. Pate and her mother was Fannie Hannah.

Perhaps Frances remarried to a Thomson after the death of her husband. Regardless of the confusion, the assumption is offered that her maiden name was Frances Hannah, as reported.

The children of James Hamilton Pate, and their vital dates and marriages, are from the report of Julia Claire Pate. The names were verified by U. S. Census reports and official death certificates that are available to researchers. The dates appear to be from grave markers or family records.

The children were:

George Thoroughgood – b. 17 December 1860, m. Sarah Catherine Graham, d. 14 August 1912;

Mary F. – b. 21 July 1862, m. Preston Hampton, d. 28 September 1937;

Preston Brooks – b. 12 October 1863, m. Lillie E. Pate, d. 5 November 1916;

Joseph Daniel – b. 11 September 1865, m. Annie G. Pate, d. 10 October 1910;

James Hamilton – b. 29 July 1868, d. 8 October 1878;

Annie – b. 12 July 1873, m. William Franklin Wright, d. 20 July 1933;

Nathan A. – b. 23 June 1875, d. 11 October 1935;

Robert – b. ca. 1878, d. (unknown), lived in Virginia;

Hattie – b. 20 December 1879, m. Charles Covington;

Grace – b. ca. 1881, m. N. Luther Covington, d. 15 June 1922;

James Fred – b. May 1885, m. Mertice Wilder, d. (unknown).

Lillie E. Pate, the wife of Preston Brooks Pate, was a daughter of Levander Garlington Pate, a son of the first marriage of Thomas Pate of Richmond County.

William Franklin Wright, the husband of Annie Pate, was a son of Darling Pate Wright and his wife, Jennett McCormick.

Preston Brooks Pate was a dentist, and James Fred Pate was a medical doctor, as reported in family information.

George Thoroughgood Pate was the second of the two sons of Thoroughgood Pate d. 1836. He was born 11 January 1836 and died 3 November 1917. His death is recorded in North Carolina death records, and his parents and vital records are confirmed. He married Caroline Ann Adams, a daughter of William B. Adams II. The bride was born 11 January 1840 and died 30 March 1920 in Scotland County, North Carolina.

The report by Julia Claire Pate, cited earlier, U. S. Census reports, and North Carolina death certificates identify the children of George Thoroughgood Pate. They were:

> William Thoroughgood – b. 25 January 1860, m. Hattie Gibson, d. 11 October 1922;
>
> James Franklin – b. 11 April 1864, m. Mary Gibson, d. unk;
>
> Zebulon Vance – b. 2 May 1866, m. Sally McNair, d. 17 August 1941;
>
> Artemus Ward – b. 6 June 1868, m. Mary Ann Blue, d. 11 January 1928;
>
> Charles Thomas – b. 19 May 1870, m. Mary B. Ingram, d. 15 February 1943;
>
> Annie Jane – b. 7 March 1872, m. John McGregor, d. 2 December 1948;
>
> George M. – b. 9 February 1877, m. Marie Hames, d 12 November 1944;
>
> Duncan Alpheus – b. 11 February 1882, m. Eliza Gertrude Gibson, d. 30 December 1944;
>
> Sallie Adams – b. 3 August 1883, m. none, d. 9 December 1894; one male child died in infancy.

The 1900 U. S. Census reported Mary (Adams) Pate was the mother of ten children, eight of whom were alive. The preceding list of children is in agreement with that record.

Hattie Gibson, the wife of William Thoroughgood, was a daughter of James M. and Hannah (Smith) Gibson. Mary Gibson, the wife of James Franklin, was a daughter of Robert and Elizabeth (Fletcher) Gibson. Sally McNair, the wife of Zebulon Vance, was a daughter of John F. McNair. Mary Ann Blue, the wife of Artemus Ward, was a daughter of Angus and Mary Ann (McLaurin) Blue. Mary B. Ingram, the wife of Charles Thomas, was a daughter of John B. and Mary Frances (Hanes) Ingram. Marie Hames, the wife of George M., was a daughter of Lewis and Matilda (Thompson) Hanes. Eliza Gertrude Gibson, the wife of Duncan Alpheus, was a daughter of Raiford and Helen (Lester) Gibson.

The sons, William Thoroughgood Pate and George M. Pate, were medical doctors. This completes the report on the family of Thoroughgood Pate d. 1802.

OTHER PATE FAMILIES OF RICHMOND COUNTY, NORTH CAROLINA

Comments on some unplaced Pates in Richmond County records follow.

Thoroughgood Pate d. ca. 1802 settled his family by 1767 on land that was to become Richmond County, before that area separated from Anson County in 1778. Richmond County became the ancestral home for his family, and they have been treated in the preceding narration. Recognition must be given that members of other Pate Family lines also relocated from other areas to Richmond. Most of these will be treated in more detail in other narratives in the report, but some note of their presence needs to be made here.

Thomas Pate, who married Hester, the daughter of Samuel Pate d. 1850, was of the Pate Family remaining in Wayne County. He was a son of Daniel Pate who died in 1791, in the line of James Pate d. ca. 1790. Hester, and the children of her marriage to Thomas, have been recognized in this narrative. Thomas, and the children of his second marriage, will be recognized in the narrative on James Pate d. ca. 1790. Thomas moved to Richmond County by 1812, when he was taxed for one poll, no land.

Adam Pate was younger than Thomas and closely associated with him in Richmond County records. Wayne County records prove this Adam Pate was a son of John Pate d. 1862, a son of Shadrack Pate in the line of Charles Pate d. p. 1790. Adam will be treated in detail in the narrative on Shadrack Pate d. 1837.

Willoughby Pate d. 1834 moved to Richmond County from Wayne County about 1817. He was a descendant of Charles Pate d. p. 1790, and will be discussed in detail in the narrative on his father, Shadrack Pate d. 1837. Willoughby left a large family that resided in Richmond and adjoining South Carolina counties.

A number of Pate (and Pait) descendants of David Pate in Bladen County, North Carolina, migrated to Richmond County in the mid-1800s. David was a descendant of James Pate d. ca. 1790 and will be recognized in the discussion of that family.

There were two men that the writer has assumed were both named Thoroughgood Jason Pate and were father and son. Various records indicate initials "T. J." for both men. The father was commonly known as Jason, born ca. 1777 and died post-1860 in Chesterville County, South Carolina. His narrative will be provided in detail at the end of the chapter on Samuel Pate d. ca. 1810.

Records suggest that a number of Pates were in Kershaw and Chesterfield counties of South Carolina in later years, 1840-1860, who could have been descendants of Jason or his brother, Elijah, who disappeared from records after 1817. The distance from North Kershaw and Chesterfield counties of South Carolina to Joe's Creek in Richmond, North Carolina, is only about 50 miles. The migration from Chesterville County to Richmond County would not be unusual.

Readers will recall that William Ferdinand Pate, son of Nathaniel Pate of Richmond County, migrated to Chesterfield County, South Carolina, after the Civil War.

Further information and detail on the son, commonly known as Thoroughgood, follows.

This Thoroughgood Pate appears on the U. S. Census for Richmond County in 1850, recorded as born in South Carolina about 1817. His wife, Christian McNeill, was born December 1815 in Scotland. Note needs to be made that Richmond County received a large number of immigrants from Scotland in the early 1800s. The family was also enumerated on the 1860 U. S. Census for Richmond County. The Census records identify eight children for the couple, all born in North Carolina after 1840.

Military records report he enlisted in the Confederate Army, 20 February 1862, age 42 years, which reflects a birth of 1820. He was assigned to the 46th North Carolina Infantry Regiment, which was organized at Camp Mangum, near Raleigh, North Carolina. He died 11 May 1863. He and his widow are recognized by grave markers in McNeill Cemetery in Scotland County.

A published inventory of McNeill Cemetery reports the inscription on the grave marker identified his name as Thoroughgood J. Pate, although the grave marker identifies him as only "T. J. Pate". This is the source for the middle initial assigned him in this report.

The vital dates inscribed on the grave marker for Christian (McNeill) Pate are: December 1815 -- 5 May 1893, and identified her as the wife of T. J. Pate. She was the daughter of Daniel and Sarah McNeill.

Daniel McNeill conveyed a tract of land to Christian, 11 March 1871, Richmond Deed Book 4, pages 142-144. He identified Christian as, "my daughter now wife of Thoroughgood Pate deceased" and conveyed 106 acres to her "for the natural love and affection". The land was located on the south side of Beaverdam Creek, a tributary of Gum Swamp. The McNeill Cemetery inventory identifies Daniel McNeill (1791 -- 28 July 1875) as the husband of Sarah McNeill (died 20 June 1884).

Christian conveyed 25 acres to her son-in-law William M. Caviness, 28 February 1882. It was identified as located on the west side of the Carolina Central Railway. The record locates the land as between the homes of her and Margaret Graham. Thoroughgood and Christian had a daughter named Margaret, the fate of whom is unknown.

U. S. Census reports and North Carolina death certificates identify the following children from the marriage of Thoroughgood and Christian:

Catherine Ann – b. 22 October 1843, m. William Rachels, d. 13 August 1917;

Daniel – b. ca. 1844, may have died early;

Rebecca Jane – b. ca. 1846;

Margaret – b. ca. 1848, may have died early;

Mary/Rose – b. 22 April 1849, m. [?] Chance, d. 26 August 1915;

Martha – b. ca. 1853, m. Ebb Sanders;

Sarah – b. 17 March 1857, m. William Preston Caviness, d. 25 February 1930;

Christian – b. 1861, m. Archibald Wright, d. 19 August 1921.

The fate of the son Daniel was not discovered. He appeared in the household for the 1850 U. S. Census and was absent from later records. The assumption is offered that he died before the 1860 U. S. Census was enumerated. Others have suggested this Daniel was the Confederate soldier who died in the Union prisoner of war camp, Elmira, New York, in 1865. However, that Daniel Pate appears to have been a son of John Pate of Bladen County, who will be treated in the narrative on James Pate d. ca. 1790.

This research failed to locate an estate record, after the death of Thoroughgood J. in 1863 or for his wife after her death in 1893, that would identify their heirs. However, one researcher located multiple deeds signed by their children, Catherine Ann Rachels, Mary Chance, Rebecca Pate, Ebenezer Sanders, Sarah Caviness, and Christian Wright, as they disposed of land identified as associated with their parents. This confirms the heirs from U. S. Census records, except Margaret and Daniel, whom it is assumed likely died early.

Further, death certificates are available for four of the daughters: Catherine Ann, Mary/Rose, Sarah, and Christian. All reported their parents were Thoroughgood Pate and Christian McNeill. The certificates for Mary and Sarah report the father was born in Georgia. The record for Catherine Ann reported her father was born in Richmond County, North Carolina. The form for Christian left the birthplace blank.

The daughters reported in error that their father was born in Georgia. Perhaps this error results from visits T. J. may have made to his uncles Bennett, Samuel, or Rev. William in Georgia. Records identify his arrival to Richmond County as in the 1840s. Perhaps he made trips to Georgia before settling in Richmond County.

This concludes the report on the Pate Family in Richmond County, North Carolina.

VI

Rev. CHARLES PATE

d. p. 1790, SON OF CHARLES PATE d. ca. 1769, AND DESCENDENTS

Introduction

Rev. Charles Pate and some of his descendants were covered in *Pate Pioneers on the Pee Dee River*, a work circulated by the writer in earlier years. Ongoing research results in more definition in this line of the Pate Family. This report will serve more as an addition than a correction to the earlier report.

The claim for a relationship of Rev. Charles Pate d. p. 1790 to the Pate Family of Old Dobbs County is supported in the preceding narrative on Dobbs County, in this report. Additional support and his relationship to other Dobbs County families that moved to the Pee Dee River area of the Carolinas will be noted here.

Available records fail to place Rev. Charles in Dobbs (or Wayne) County in his early life, as was the case with his brother, Thoroughgood Pate d. ca. 1802. However, a series of records from his adult years attest to his Dobbs County origin. Examples include his return to the Bear Creek Church in Dobbs County to be ordained as a minister, to be cited later. Early maps locate Bear Creek a short distance east of Stoney Creek, the ancestral homesite for the Pate Family in Dobbs/Wayne counties. One document viewed in the Crozer Manuscript Files at Furman University identified the site for the ordination ceremony as Stoney Creek. In the text, Stoney Creek was lined out, and Bear Creek was overwritten. Further, one son of Rev. Charles, Shadrack Pate, returned to the ancestral homesite to marry and live his mature life. Other examples to support the claim for his origin are available.

The association of Rev. Charles with his brothers, Thoroughgood Pate d. ca. 1802 and Samuel Pate d. p. 1810, provides support for the claim that they had a common origin, to be cited.

Charles joined his brother Thoroughgood and uncle William Pate d. ca. 1775 in the move from Dobbs County to the part of Cumberland County that became Moore County. He continued to migrate and spent most of his mature life in the Pee Dee River area of the Carolinas. The later migration of his descendants was more extensive.

Morgan Edwards recorded vital information on Rev. Charles Pate in the pre- Revolutionary War timeframe. Some documentation and background information from that report is in order. Edwards was born in Monmouthshire, Wales, 9 May 1722. He was educated at Bristol Academy and joined the Baptist faith early in life. He served churches in Wales and Ireland, and was called to the First Baptist Church in Philadelphia, 23 May 1761. His influence in the American colonies was notable. He founded Rhode Island College, the present-day Brown University.

Edwards sought to unify all Baptist churches in the American colonies. He visited each church in the colonies in person. The Beauty Spot Church, east of present-day Bennettsville, South Carolina, was on his agenda in 1772. His notes provide information of interest to this report: "began to exist as a church June 15, 1768 when it was constituted by Rev. Joshua Edwards.... had been a branch of Catfish Church.... the persons who incorporated were Charles Pate and wife, Nicholas Green and wife, and Rice Henderson and wife....no remarkable event hath happened since, except they hath chosen a man to be their minister whom nature hath made a stutterer. He is Rev. Charles Pate." The church had grown to about 40 families.

Additional information was recorded on Rev. Pate. He was a "Regular Baptist", was born 1 May 1729 in Bertie County, North Carolina (his father lived in Bertie County in 1729). He was bred a "Churchman" (Anglican) and was baptized into the Baptist faith at Catfish Creek, South Carolina, in 1760 by John Brown and was ordained, as noted earlier, by Rev. George Graham and Joshua Herring, 7 August 1769. He assumed charge of the Beauty Spot Church at his ordination.

Rev. Charles Pate married Sarah Henderson, by whom he had children named Sarah, Charles, Mary, Rebecca, Ann, Shadrack and Joel. Records, to be cited, will support the claim of an additional son, born after the visit by Edwards, Ananias Pate.

136

Three other Baptist ministers moved from Old Dobbs County to the Pee Dee River area of the Carolinas and were associated with Rev. Charles Pate. They were: Rev. Isham Peacock (1742-1830), Rev. Henry Easterling (24 May 1733-21 March 1800) and Rev. William Bennett (ca. 1717-1814). Rev. Bennett, the oldest of the four, reportedly served as a chaplain for North and South Carolina militia units in the Revolutionary War. Perhaps the others did likewise, but available records fail to document such.

The association of these men in Dobbs County is evidenced by a Wayne County deed dated 5 November 1801. John Peacock, brother to Rev. Isham Peacock, conveyed a tract of land to his son-in-law, Shadrack Pate, son of Rev. Charles Pate. The tract had been granted to William Bennett in earlier years, Wayne County Deed Book 7, page 226.

Morgan Edwards recorded his visit to the Easterling family. Easterling was baptized in Dobbs County in 1760, moved to Anson County in 1764, and was ordained by Morgan Edwards at Hitchcock Creek Church in Anson County, 28 March 1772. He married Elizabeth Bennett, who has been recorded by several researchers as a daughter of William Bennett. Edwards identified the children of Easterling as James, Elizabeth, William, Mary, Martha, Shadrack, Henry, Bennett, John, and Joel. Records prove Rev. Peacock married Martha Easterling as his first wife. The assumption is offered that she was the daughter of Rev. Easterling. His second wife was Mrs. Lydia Bennett.

Hitchcock Creek flows into the Greater Pee Dee River in the area of Anson County where Charles Pate d. p. 1790 and Rice Henderson lived in the 1760s. The uncle of Charles, Rev. William Pate d. ca. 1775, also resided in this area.

Baptist records (*South Carolina Baptists,* Leah Townsend) report that three of these ministers served the Beautyspot Church in Marlboro County, South Carolina. Rev. Pate followed the founding minister and apparently served until 1785. Rev. Easterling served Beautyspot 1785-1792, and Rev. Bennett served 1800-1804.

Rev. Easterling and Rev. Pate both named sons Shadrack and Joel. Rev. Easterling and Samuel Pate d. p. 1810 (a brother to Rev. Charles Pate) named sons Bennett, and the name continued as a given name in these families for generations. Rev. Easterling and Rev. Pate had sons born after the visit of Morgan Edwards in 1772.

Shadrack Pate, a son of Rev. Charles Pate d. p. 1790, married Dicey Peacock, a niece of Rev. Isham Peacock.

The notes compiled by Morgan Edwards in his travels were published by Mary B. Warren in 1984, *Materials Towards a History of the Baptists.* These records are also in the Crozer Manuscript Files at the Library of Furman University, South Carolina.

DNA testing has added definition to the lineage of Pate Family lines cited in earlier narratives in this report. Few descendants of Rev. Charles Pate have joined the DNA Project, resulting in fewer changes to observe. But it can be said that the mutation that separates the descendants of Charles Pate d. ca. 1769 from descendants of his brothers, John Pate d. ca. 1779 and William Pate d. ca. 1775, is present in the descendants of Rev. Charles Pate tested to date. This confirms that he was a son of Charles Pate. d. ca. 1769.

The report on Rev. Charles Pate follows.

The Morgan Edwards report cites the birthdate of Rev. Charles Pate as 1 May 1729, in Bertie County, North Carolina. It is also the source for his marriage to Sarah Henderson, but fails to provide a date. The bride is assumed, by this research, to have been a sister to Rice Henderson, a longtime companion of her husband. Records to support the sibling relationship, by their association, are numerous. Rice Henderson sold land to Thoroughgood Pate d. ca. 1802 in 20 March 1769, Richmond Deed Book 7, page 223. He and Charles Pate were officers in the Anson County militia on 19 November 1770, *Colonial Soldiers of the South,* Myrtle June Clark. Both Rice and Charles were founders of the Beauty Spot Baptist Church in 1768, cited earlier. Records, to be cited, will show their association continued in North Carolina and South Carolina in 1785 and 1790.

The last record, on Charles Pate, available to this research, is the U. S. Census for Prince George Parish, Georgetown District, South Carolina. He and Rice Henderson were enumerated. This area eventually became Marion County, South Carolina. Rice Henderson executed deeds in Marion County into the mid-1820s. One of his sons,

Hopkins Henderson, married Rhoda Beckwith in Marion County. Readers will recall that another daughter of Beckwith, Sarah, married Elisha Pate, a son of Stephen Pate d. 1839. The Henderson and Pate Families were closely associated for decades. Both had association with other Pate lines.

Charles Pate joined others of his family in the move from Old Dobbs County to Cumberland County. He acquired 60 acres of land on the Lower Little River, where others of his family settled, 11

March 1760, Deed Book 1, page 363. The land was purchased from Joseph Dunham. The deed identified the land as "the land where he now resides." Charles had resided on the land for an unknown interval before the purchase.

Readers will note that the Morgan Edwards report cited the baptism of Charles Pate at Catfish Creek Church in South Carolina in 1760. Perhaps that explains the next deed. Charles and his wife, Sarah, sold the 60 acres on Lower Little River, 20 November 1761, Deed Book 2, page 125. He was relocating to South Carolina, where he had joined the Catfish Creek Church. The sale was to William Gilman for 30 pounds, the same as his purchase price.

Cumberland County deeds document his continued presence in the area, probably by visitation, though he had moved. He witnessed a land sale by Joseph Dunham, 27 July 1762, Book 2, page 134. Also, he signed a mortgage to John Wadsworth, 12 May 1764. The association of the Wadsworth family with that of William Pate d. ca. 1775, in Cumberland County, was noted earlier. The mortgage was for $35.00. Security issued by Charles was livestock recently received from John Wadsworth, a rifle recently received from Thomas Matthews, and household furniture and plantation tools.

The presence of Charles Pate in the Anson-Richmond County area of North Carolina is indicated by the militia service of he and Rice Henderson, cited earlier, and Anson deed records. Charles Pate purchased land in Anson County, from Benjamin Thompson, 17 January 1763, Deed Book 3, page 22. The location was the southwest side of the Greater Pee Dee River. The site is more related to the location selected by his uncle, William Pate d. ca. 1775, than that of his brother on Joes Creek of the Little Pee Dee River. The stay here was brief. He and Sarah sold the tract to Thomas Wilkinson, 29 July 1763, Deed Book 3, page 95. The land was identified as the place "where Pate lives."

Charles acquired two tracts of land by grant in South Carolina, 200 acres, 3 September 1771, in the fork of Beaverdam Creek on the Pee Dee River at Paster Neck, Colonial Plats Vol. 19, page 67, and 200 acres on Three Creek, northeast side of the Pee Dee River, 17 January 1772, Colonial Plats Vol. 19, page 73.

A third tract may have been issued to him, 190 acres on the Saludy River, 18 May 1773. The name was Charles Pate, but the memorial was to Charles Patty. A Patty family from the Northern Neck of Virginia settled in South Carolina in this timeframe.

Charles was a popular given name in the Patty family. The Saluda River ran through the area they settled, the present-day counties of Chester and Newberry. This was not an area frequented by the family of Rev. Charles Pate.

This research found record of the sale of one of the grants in the Pee Dee River area. Charles and Sarah sold the 200 acres on Three Creek, northeast side of the Greater Pee Dee River, 7 December 1776, Deed Book A, page 230. The land was identified as the "Plantation whereon Charles Pate now lives." The buyer was Thomas Conner, Sr. The sale led to another move.

He was granted 100 acres on the north side of Drowning Creek in Bladen County (Robeson County today), 11 November 1779, Bladen Deed Book 19, page 471. The site was on the south side of Saddletree Swamp. A purchase from Isaac Woolf added another 100 acres to the tract, Robeson Deed Book 1, page 1. Drowning Creek, a tributary of the Little Pee Dee River, became known as the Lumber River. Witnesses to the purchase from Woolf were Rice Henderson and his oldest son, Charles Pate, Jr.

One tradition reports the name of Drowning Creek was changed to reflect the commercial use of the waterway. Logs of 100-feet length were floated south to the sawmills of South Carolina.

Two Robeson County deeds account for the sale of the two Robeson County tracts. Charles Pate, minister of Bladen County, sold the tract received by grant to his son, Charles Pate, Jr., 17 March 1785, Deed Book A, page 140. The witnesses were John Jacson (also appears as Jackson) and Joel Pate. The latter was a son of Rev. Charles Pate.

Rev. Charles returned to South Carolina after the last sale. The remaining tract in Robeson County was sold after his return. Charles Pate of Georgetown District, South Carolina, sold the remaining tract, on Saddletree Swamp, to John Harmon, 4 September 1786, Deed Book A, page 8. Charles and "Sarry" signed the deed (Sarah used a mark on all signatures), and it was proved by Charles Pate, Jr.

The 1790 U. S. Census for Georgetown District, South Carolina, listed Charles Pate and Rice Henderson. Charles had two males under 16 years of age in his household. The correct listing for his sons remaining at home should have been one under 16 and one over 16, if assumptions from this research are correct. The difference is slight and of no consequence, in the opinion of the writer. One female, in addition to his wife, may indicate a daughter remained at home.

The assumption is offered that he died after the 1790 U. S. Census was enumerated. The question is how soon after 1790. He was not canvassed for the 1800 U. S. Census, but neither was Rice Henderson. Perhaps both were missed by enumerators. Rice Henderson appears on the 1810 and 1820 U. S. Censuses and in later Marion County records. He continued to appear in land transactions in Marion County, which prove he lived into the mid-1820's. Additional information from Georgetown District is limited because courthouse fires destroyed all records.

Consideration must be given that Charles followed two of his sons to Mississippi. Joel Pate and Ananias Pate appear on Natchez District, Mississippi tax returns as early as 1810. Charles does not appear, but 20 years elapsed between his listing in the 1790 U. S. Census and the first of the Mississippi tax returns. He could have moved to Mississippi and died in that 20-year span, without leaving extant records.

The writer offers the assumption that Charles and Sarah had another son after the visit by Morgan Edwards, Ananias, born 17 January 1779. The date seems late, but is the date inscribed on his grave marker in Carroll County, Mississippi. Ananias was in the company of a Joel Pate, known to be the son of Charles and Sarah. Ananias used the given names of Joel (his older brother), Henderson (surname of his mother), and Charles (his father) as names for his sons. Records prove Ananias in the Mississippi records was born in North Carolina. His oldest brother, Charles, had a grandson named Ananias. The assumption seems sound.

Perhaps other children were born after the visit by Morgan Edwards, but available records fail to identify any.

Morgan Edwards identified Rev. Charles as a stutterer. One must wonder of the effect of that impediment on his ministry. Available records fail to evaluate his success. However, records cited earlier recognize him as a minister late into his life, an indication of some success. Further, his descendants include a number of respected ministers in later generations.

The fate of the daughters of Rev. Charles is unknown to the writer. The U. S. Census for 1790 indicated one continued to live at home. It is assumed the others were married and in their own households, or were deceased.

Leonardo Andrea was a prominent South Carolina genealogist of earlier years. His files contained several sheets on the Pate Family.

The sheet on Rev. Charles Pate notes that his children intermarried with families in the Old Cheraw District, South Carolina, and adjacent counties of North Carolina, but no names were provided. To continue with the daughters would be irresponsible speculation.

Rev. Charles and Sarah (Henderson) Pate had four sons. Three were recognized by Morgan Edwards in 1772, Charles, Shadrack, and Joel. The fourth, Ananias, was born after the Edwards visit.

Another son or daughter born after the Edwards visit is possible. Available records do not provide names for such, but a limited number of Pates existed in the Pee Dee River area, for which the origin is unknown. Perhaps DNA testing will resolve these questions in the future.

The sons of Charles Pate d. p. 1790 will be treated, individually, to the extent of this research.

CHARLES PATE D. 1825,
SON OF REV. CHARLES PATE D. P. 1790

The first son born to Rev. Charles Pate was given the name of his father, Charles. The given name also recognized his grandfather, Charles Pate d. ca. 1769. At least two generations of later descendants continued to recognize this given name.

Charles d. 1825 was born ca. 1758, based on his appearance in land records and U. S. Census reports. Two records indicate his death occurred in the year 1825. He wrote his Robeson County will, 24 August 1824, Will Book 1, pages 237-239. In 20 January 1825, he conveyed 288 acres of land to James Humphrey, Book T, page 317. The probate of his estate was completed in January 1826, when his heirs sold their legacies and departed North Carolina. The assumption is offered that he died soon after the land conveyance of January 1825.

The will identified his wife as Phebe (Pheby) Pate. Her maiden name was Humphrey as indicated by their marriage record of 1775 in Wayne County, North Carolina. He was a neighbor to several Humphrey families and interacted with them. Further, two of his children married members of the Humphrey family, to be cited. He witnessed deeds for members of the Humphrey family and they did likewise for him.

Phebe moved to Decatur County, Georgia, with her sons, John and Charles, after the death of her husband Charles. She died there ca. 1832. She inherited land from her husband "for her lifetime", that was assigned to the sons Zacheus and John at her death. The tracts were sold to James Humphrey in January 1826, Book T, pages 445 and 452. One deed was signed by Phebe and John, the other by her and Zacheus. The son John was listed on the 1825 poll tax list for Baker County, Georgia. He was in the adjoining county of Decatur by, or near, 1830. It is assumed that his mother moved with John.

The Georgia Land Lottery of 1832 placed Phebe in Decatur County. She drew Lot 55 in the 2nd District of the 4th Section of Cherokee County. She was a resident of Decatur County and registered for the Lottery as the widow of a Revolutionary War soldier. She did not claim the lot. The assumption is offered that she died before it was available, and no one in the family claimed her draw. The lot was sold at public auction, 14 February 1846. Her son Zacheus, living in Thomas County, also had a successful draw in the same Lottery, to be cited.

This research failed to find proof of Revolutionary War service for any in this family. Most of the North Carolina men served in local militia units, and record of their service failed to be recorded. Pay vouchers were honored after the War, but veterans had to file claims. This research failed to locate a voucher for Charles.

Georgia did not require proof of service for soldiers, by them or their widows, to register for the Land Lottery as veterans. Verbal claims were accepted. This does not discredit the claim by Phebe to have been the widow of a Revolutionary War soldier, but this research found no supportive proof for the claim.

Charles Pate d. p. 1790 conveyed the 100-acre land grant he received on Saddletree Swamp to his son, Charles Pate d. 1825, as cited earlier. The deed identified the parties as "Charles Pate, Senior, Minister" and Charles Pate, Jr. The witnesses were another son, Joel Pate, and Rice Henderson, a brother-in-law to Rev. Charles Pate.

Saddletree Swamp is located on maps as northwest of the town of Lumberton. Other Pates lived in this area. Note was made earlier of the association of Daniel Pate, son of Stephen Pate d. 1839, with Charles Pate d. 1825. Further, the narrative on Samuel Pate d. p. 1810, a brother to Charles Pate d. p. 1790, will report that family also resided in the Saddletree Swamp area in the late 1700's.

Charles Pate d. 1825 added to his landholdings in Saddletree Swamp and adjoining Raft Swamp by purchase and grant. He owned over 1000 acres in his active years. He sold three tracts in his old age.

He purchased 140 acres from Nathaniel Revill, 27 February 1820, Book S, page 386, and sold it back to Revill, 9 December 1820. He conveyed 100 acres to his son Zacheus Pate, 25 August 1824, Book T, page 369. This was the same day he signed his will. He conveyed the 288 acres to James Humphrey, 20 January 1825, cited earlier. The remaining land was devised to the heirs.

He was active in community affairs, as proved by the Robeson County court minutes, in the late 1700s and early 1800s. He was Commissioner of a tax district, supervised public roads, and served on jury duty at all levels.

His will, cited earlier, provides identity of his children. It is assumed that all were from his marriage to Phebe [?] and were born in Robeson County. They were:

John – born ca. 1778, married Isabelle Moore 12 August 1800, died p. 1850 in Decatur County, Georgia;

Sarah – born ca. 1782, alive when her father wrote his will, but no other information available;

Zacheus (Zachariah) – born ca. 1785, married Elizabeth Humphrey, as proved by the will of her father, died p. 31 March 1856 in Geneva County, Alabama or Holmes County, Florida;

Charles – born ca. 1790, married Lydia Pate 10 March 1821, died p. 1850, probably in Baker or Miller County, Georgia;

Elizabeth – born ca. 1794, married Alfred Best 13 February 1824, died p. 1860;

Mary – born ca. 1805, married John Humphrey 13 February 1820.

John Pate, son of Charles Pate d. 1825, married Isabelle Moore in Robeson County, as cited earlier. Her parents were not identified in this research. Robeson County was home to several Moore families in 1800. Records suggest she preceded him in death.

This research failed to find proof of his children. His family was recorded on U. S. Census reports for Robeson County in 1810 and 1820, as cited earlier. John Pate was listed on the 1825 poll tax for Baker County, Georgia. It is assumed he moved to the adjacent county of Decatur by, or near, 1830. He was enumerated in Decatur County in 1840 and 1850. A search of Decatur County deed records failed to find land records executed by John Pate.

Note needs to be made of other Pates in the Decatur County area in this timeframe. Elizabeth (Pate) Hawthorne, a daughter of Stephen Pate d. 1839, and her family, were residents of Decatur County, cited earlier. Her brother, Elisha Pate, was also in the area. Benagy Pate, a descendant of another family line from Charles Pate d. p 1790, also lived in Decatur County, to be cited. Zacheus Pate, the other son of Charles d. 1825, settled in adjoining Thomas County, as did some of his cousins from Samuel Pate d. p. 1810.

Descendants of Samuel Pate d. p. 1810 may have introduced these Pate cousins to this area of Georgia. A son of this Samuel, Samuel Pate d. p. 1840, and his son named Samuel, each drew land in the Georgia Land Lottery of 1820. They were residents of Twiggs County, Georgia in 1820. The father drew Lot 312 in the 12th District of Early County. This land was in the area that later became Decatur County. The son drew Lot 228 in the 11th District of Early County, and this land was in the area that became Baker County, and later Mitchell County. Readers will note that the later Pates settled in Decatur and Baker counties. This research failed to identify the land of the Samuels as land occupied by later Pate residents, but that is possible.

Decatur County marriage records identify three Pates who are assumed to have been among the children of John Pate d. p. 1850. The given names appear to recognize John and his mother and father. They do not appear to be from the other Pates in the Decatur area. Charles W. Pate, born ca. 1805, married Jinsey Bishop, 13 June 1833. Pheobe Pate, born ca. 1820, married Daniel Cloud, 12 March 1833. John Pate, born ca. 1825, married Margaret Ann Craigg, 25 March 1849. U. S. Census reports suggest additional daughters were probable for John. Further, the U. S. Census for adjoining Miller County, Georgia, listed a Nicholas Pate, born ca. 1825 in Georgia. He may have been another son of this John Pate.

John was 72 years of age on the 1850 U. S. Census for Decatur County. He was born in North Carolina and was a cobbler by trade His wife was absent and is assumed to have been deceased. He will be recognized in this report as John Pate d. p. 1850.

Zacheus was the next son born to Charles Pate d. 1825. He was born ca. 1785 in North Carolina and died in Geneva County, Alabama, 31 March 1856. Extant records create confusion over his given name. He appeared frequently in records as Zachariah Pate. He was recognized as Zacheus in the will of his father and in the deed executed by his father conveying land to him in 1824. Zacheus is assumed to have been his given name at birth.

The U. S. Census for Robeson County in 1810 identified him as Zachariah Pate. He was located adjacent to his father and brother John. He was Zacheus on the 1820 U. S. Census for Robeson County. He was Zachariah on the 1830 U. S. Census for Thomas County, Georgia. He was Zacheus Pate on the 1840 U. S. Census for Thomas County. His final appearance on U. S. Census reports was as Zachariah Pate in Dale County, Alabama, in 1850.

He entered military service for the War of 1812 at Lumberton, North Carolina, 23 September 1814. He was identified as Zacheus Pate and was discharged 23 March 1815, with the same name. His muster rolls are under the name of Zachariah Pate.

His military service, apparently, qualified Zacheus for two draws in the Georgia Cherokee Land Lottery of 1832. He drew Lot 86 in the 2nd Section, 22nd District, and Lot 294 in the 3rd Section, 25th District. Among the qualifications for two draws in this lottery was service in the War of 1812 that resulted in wounds or disability. Other records viewed in the research failed to identify his disability.

A deed in Thomas County is sufficient to connect both names to the same person, Deed Book D-1, page 322. The record is dated 7 September 1838 and opens with "Thomas E. Blackshear . . . of the one part to Zacheus Pate . . . of the other part . . . of the county aforesaid (Thomas County)". Several lines later, the heading is "to have and to hold to him the said Zachariah Pate his heirs and assigns". The writer offers the opinion that his name was Zacheus, but he was commonly known as Zachariah.

Zacheus married Elizabeth Humphrey. The marriage record was absent from Robeson County records reviewed in this research. However, James Humphrey wrote his Robeson County will, 30 May 1837, and it was proved in the November Term of Court 1837, Book 1, pages 310-311. He devised $1,000 to his daughter Elizabeth Pate and her children. Additional legacies were to be available at the death of his widow.

Elizabeth was born ca. 1791, based on U. S. Census reports. She survived Zacheus, though exact date of death is unknown. She was enumerated on the U. S. Census of Geneva County, Alabama, with her daughter and son-in-law, Aaron and Rachel (Pate) Davis, in 1870.

Note has been made that James Humphrey conveyed 50 acres of land to Zacheus Pate in 1816. There is no record of sale of this tract by Zacheus. However, Benjamin Pate, a son of Zacheus and Elizabeth (Humphrey) Pate, returned to Robeson County from Thomas County, Georgia, in the late 1830's. Perhaps his return was influenced by the death of his grandfather Humphrey in 1837. Benjamin married Clarissa Moore in Robeson County, 9 November 1839. Any relationship between Clarissa Moore and Isabelle Moore, who married John Pate d. p. 1850, was not determined.

Benjamin Pate sold the 50-acre tract conveyed to Zacheus by James Humphrey, as Benjamin departed Robeson County to join his parents in Alabama, 22 June 1848, Robeson Deed Book AA, page 319. The deed identified it as land conveyed to him by Zacheus Pate. These records seem to be sufficient to say Zacheus married Elizabeth, a daughter of James Humphrey, and that Benjamin Pate was a son of Zacheus and Elizabeth (Humphrey) Pate.

Zacheus lived in Robeson County, North Carolina, Thomas County, Georgia, Dale and Geneva counties, Alabama, and probably Holmes County, Florida. Note was made earlier of his presence in the eastern part of Walton County, Florida, in 1830, which may have been the same as present-day Holmes County. One son, Alexander Pate, lived in Holmes County, and records indicate Zacheus and Elizabeth lived with him in their old age.

Courthouse fires in three of the counties (Dale, Geneva and Holmes) limit land record information. However, some government land records are extant and are of value to the history of the family. The Robeson County records, cited earlier, are among those of value to this research. Others will follow. Available land records and U. S. Census reports provide the basis to identify the children of Zacheus.

U. S. Census reports list Zacheus with the potential of four sons. Three were born when he lived in Robeson County, North Carolina, and one was born when he lived in Thomas County, Georgia. Four Pate males of the correct age and birthplace are associated with him and are assumed to have been his sons: William Pate – born ca. 1811 in North Carolina; Alexander Pate – born ca. 1810 – 1815 in North Carolina; Benjamin Pate – born ca. 1820, for whom land records establish the relationship, as cited earlier; and James C. Pate – born ca. 1838 in Georgia. Other records will be cited to support the relationships.

U. S. Census reports indicate he and Elizabeth had six daughters. Available records provide assumptive identity of three. They were:

Matilda (Martila) – born ca. 1815, married John Davis in Robeson County, 21 July 1827;

Delighter (Delila) – born c. 1825, married Richard Singletary in Thomas County, 20 October 1841;

Rachel – born c. 1827, married Aaron F. Davis. Rachel's relationship to Elizabeth (Humphrey) Pate is confirmed by the 1870 Geneva County, Alabama U. S. Census. They were enumerated in adjoining homesteads.

U. S. Government land records support the claimed relationship between Zacheus Pate and his four assumed sons. Records identify three groups of men named Pate who acquired government land in the area that became Geneva County. One was Jeremiah Pate and his sons. This group had no relationship to the descendants of the Thoroughgood Pate line. It is odd that both found their way to such an isolated locale. Jeremiah Pate was from Tennessee, and came south with the army of General Andrew Jackson for the War of 1812 Battle of New Orleans. He settled in southeast Alabama. He and his sons acquired land from the U. S. Government.

Note was made earlier of Pate cousins from the line of Samuel Pate d. p. 1810, who settled in Thomas County, Georgia, with, or before, Zacheus and his sons. Two of these cousins, Samuel Pate and Joel Pate, moved to the Dale-Geneva area of Alabama, as Zacheus and his sons were relocating.

Zacheus and all four of his sons acquired land in the Geneva-Dale area. William Pate, Alexander Pate, Benjamin Pate, and James C. Pate acquired multiple tracts by purchase. Records are sufficient to say the four did not have a sibling or parental relationship to Jeremiah Pate, or to Samuel and Joel Pate of the Samuel d. p. 1810 line. Their ages, birthplaces, and locations lead to the assumption that they were sons of Zacheus and Elizabeth (Humphrey) Pate. Robeson County land records, cited earlier, are sufficient to confirm the relationship of Benjamin to Zacheus and Elizabeth, in the opinion of the writer.

Alexander Pate served in the Florida Indian War, 25 October 1838 – 24 January 1839, in a militia unit from Thomas County, Georgia. He received a pension for this service in his old age and drew bounty land for his service, to be cited. He married Terresa Deas (Dees) in Thomas County, 28 December 1837. His father, Zacheus Pate, lived in Thomas County at this time. He, like his brothers, relocated to the Dale-Geneva County area of Alabama as Zacheus moved. He and Zacheus successfully applied for bounty land warrants for their military service. The last application was filed 16 April 1855 in Coffee County, Alabama. Both resided in Holmes County, Florida. Perhaps the Coffee County facilities were used because of limitation of facilities in the recently-created Holmes County courthouse.

Zacheus listed his age as 69 years. Both noted their residence in Holmes County. The assumption is offered that the aged parents, Zacheus and Elizabeth, resided with Alexander in Holmes County. The father and son traveled to the courthouse together to execute the bounty land claims simultaneously.

Alexander and his brother, James C. Pate, executed claims for government land in Geneva County, relocated to Holmes County, Florida, and acquired additional government land by purchase. Both were taxed for land in Holmes County, 1857-1859. The 1866 Alabama state census included a question to determine the number of men who died of disease and wounds in the Civil War. This question did not appear on all forms for all Alabama counties, but was on the 1866 return for Covington County, where Alexander Pate was enumerated. He reported one member of his family died of disease. Since James C. Pate is absent from records after the War, the assumption is offered that he died of disease in the War.

Available records fail to provide additional information to support the claim that William Pate in the Dale-Geneva records was the oldest son of Zacheus and Elizabeth (Humphrey) Pate. However, the assumption is offered that William was the fourth son represented on U. S. Census reports.

Information on the families and fate of the assumed children of Zacheus and Elizabeth (Humphrey) Pate follows.

The oldest child was William Pate. He was born in Robeson County, North Carolina, ca. 1811 and died after the U. S. Census for Dale County, Alabama, was enumerated in 1880. He married Elizabeth [?], based on U. S. Census reports. She was born ca. 1808 in North Carolina and died after the U. S. Census for Dale County, Alabama, was enumerated in 1870.

This research failed to develop desired definitive information on William and his family. The loss of records in the Dale County courthouse fire was total. However, U. S. Census reports and government land records provide information of substance.

U. S. Census reports identify the birthplace of William and his wife Elizabeth as North Carolina. The oldest known child, Drucilla Pate, was also born in North Carolina. Records have been cited to show that Benjamin Pate, a brother of William, returned to North Carolina to marry Clarissa Moore near the death date (1837) of his grandfather Humphrey. The recorded birthplace of the wife and oldest child of William leads to the assumption that he joined Benjamin in the return to Robeson County, North Carolina. Drucilla was born ca. 1836.

The second child of record, a son named William R. Pate, was born ca. 1839 in Georgia. Two other children are represented on available records, Thomas I – born ca. 1846 and Martha E. – born ca. 1848 in Alabama.

Also listed on the 1860 U. S. Census for Dale County was John Godwin, 28 years old, a wife named Drucilla, 25 years old, and a year-old child, James O. Godwin. The 1870 U. S. Census for Dale County listed William Pate and his wife Elizabeth with three children in their household, J. O. – 11 years, E. H. – 8 years, and J. L. – 7 years. John and Drucilla were absent.

The 1880 U. S. Census for Dale County listed William Pate, 69 years, and Drucilla Jackson, identified as the daughter of William. Drucilla had children as follows: James O. Godwin – 21 years, Elias H. Godwin – 19 years, and Charlie Jackson – 7 years.

The preceding records lead to the assumption that Drucilla Pate was a daughter of William, married John Godwin, and had the Godwin children listed here. Her husband died, probably in the Civil War. Civil War records report one John Godwin served in the 44th Alabama Infantry Regiment and died of disease in Virginia, 31 July 1862. Drucilla married a Jackson and had a son, Charles from this marriage.

William Pate acquired three tracts of land from the U. S. Government, 1 September 1858. They totaled 120 acres and were located in Section 32, Township 3N, Range 24E.

The second child of Zacheus Pate was a son, Alexander Pate. Available information provides good definition on his family.

Alexander was born in Robeson County, North Carolina, ca. 1811-1814, based on U. S. Census reports and military pension records. He died in Holmes County, Florida, 6 December 1905, and was buried in the Pate Cemetery near the community of Esto. The death date is from his military pension records. His grave is marked with a government marker that recognized his service in the Florida Indian Wars.

He married first to Tarissa Deas (Dees), 25 December 1837, in Thomas County, Georgia, and second to Jo Ann Conley in Holmes County. He had children from both marriages. Tarissa Deas was born ca. 1818 in North Carolina and died 20 August 1876 in Holmes County. Jo Ann Conley was born ca. 1841 in Georgia and died 4 May 1906 in Holmes County.

Jo Ann, the second wife of Alexander, filed for a pension as the widow of a deceased veteran. 19 February 1906. She provided personal information of interest to family researchers. She met Alexander in 1866. He was 56 years of age, five feet, eight inches tall, had a fair complexion, black hair, black eyes, and he lived in Holmes County.

Extant records and oral traditions from descendants (Cecil Pate and others) create a colorful image of Alexander Pate.

He was well educated for his times. Letters in his script are filed in the pension and bounty land records. Material success came his way. Holmes County tax records prove he owned pleasure carriages, gold watches, over 800 acres of land, and executed interest-bearing loans to others. His household furniture tax was among the largest in Holmes County. His herds of cattle, sheep, and swine numbered 188 head in 1860.

Family traditions suggest he was active and hard-driven. They include descriptions of him riding a horse through the county at full speed, his full beard flowing in the breeze, and emitting yells that could be heard great distances.

A letter written to the Pension Commission in January 1892 described injuries he sustained in a charge on Indians in the Okefenokee Swamp in 1837. He was thrown from his horse and never recovered from the injuries received. Military records prove he served as a Corporal in Captain William's Company of Floyd's Mounted Georgia Regiment from Thomas County, Georgia.

Alexander acquired large landholdings wherever he lived. One record documents his residence in three states and is cited for this value. He purchased 250 acres of land in Thomas County, Georgia, from John Gideon, 13 November 1835, Book P, page 352. The land was not sold when he departed Thomas County, and he executed power of attorney to Ezekiel Collins to sell the land, 1 November 1840. The record states he was living in Dale County, Alabama. The land was sold by Ezekiel Collins, 16 April 1847, by the power of attorney, Deed Book F, page 273. The residence of Alexander was listed as West Florida (Holmes County was not formed until

1848). The date agrees with his appearance on the Holmes County tax list of 1848.

He purchased multiple tracts of land from the U. S. Government. Note has been made of purchases by Alexander and his brother, James C. Pate, in Geneva County, Alabama, and Holmes County, Florida. He acquired three, possibly four, bounty land grants.

Additional records are available on Alexander Pate. They are of interest to direct descendants, but do not add to the genealogy or history of this family and are omitted from this report.

A search of courthouse records in Geneva and Dale counties of Alabama and of Holmes County, Florida, fail to reveal a will, estate record, or deed to identify his heirs. Deeds indicate he disposed of land prior to death, or his heirs sold land in the aftermath of his death. The courthouse fires of 1898 and 1902 destroyed many records.

Rutherford/ Retherford family information, shared by Joel Pate, reports a daughter of Alexander not recognized earlier by this research. Reportedly, Thursey Ann Pate was born in Thomas County, Georgia, 9 June 1832, a daughter of Alexander Pate. She died in Dale County, Alabama, 30 May 1897. She married Robert C. Floyd, and the family appears on the U. S. Census for Dale County in 1850. The household has a child from the Floyd marriage, one-year old, and Mary Pate, age 9 years. They are located some 28 households from the family of Samuel Pate, a descendant of Samuel Pate d. p. 1810, recognized earlier in this report. This family is treated in the next narrative in this report.

She was widowed and married second to John Rutherford/ Retherford ca. 1857. The writer has insufficient information to support, or criticize, the claim that this lady was a daughter of Alexander Pate of this report. However, the Mary Pate in the Floyd household needs to be identified. Further, the location of the Floyd family near the Samuel Pate household is cause for concern. Samuel had a daughter named Tirzah Pate, the fate of whom is unknown. The names Tirzah and Thursey are similar. The ages of Tirzah and Thursey Ann are some six years apart, but these are ages based on U. S. Census reports and subject to error. The possibility of Thursey Ann Pate being a daughter of Alexander Pate is recognized.

The children of Alexander from his known marriages, and the children of all but one,

were recorded by Homer Pate in the 1960s. He served as family historian for many years. Cecil Pate, who succeeded Homer in this role, shared the records with the writer. The written family records were displayed in prominent mountings on the walls of the Social Hall of Sardis Church at Black, Geneva County, Alabama. The writer viewed these at the annual Pate Reunion at Sardis in 1988.

Marriage records for the children of Alexander were lost in the courthouse fires. Fortunately, Homer Pate included the spouse of each in his records. These names have been observed on U. S. Census reports, and the report by Homer Pate is confirmed, except for one child not located on U. S. Census reports, the identity of which follows later.

The marriage to Tarissa Dees resulted in seven sons and two daughters. They were:

> Elizabeth – born 25 December 1842, died 8 December 1882, never married, buried at Pate Cemetery;
> John Asbury – born ca. 1847, married Rachel Louisa Van Landingham 1871;
> Samuel – born ca. 1852, married Sarah Ann Hewitt;
> Rachel – born ca. 1855, married Henry McCrone;
> Benjamin F. – born 22 October 1853, died 13 November 1933, married Elizabeth Somerset;
> James M. – born ca. 1860, married Martha Ann Hendrick;
> William A. – born ca. 1860, married 1) Sally Campbell, 2) Mary Jean Sparkmen, 3) Mrs. Lizzie Davenport;
> Alexander Loyd 'Bud" – born ca. 1862, married Elizabeth Dyson;
> Charles – born ca. 1864, married Jennie Barnes.

The marriage to Jo Ann Conley resulted in two sons and one daughter. They were: George W. – born ca. 1877, died 23 May 1922 in Walton County, married Lizzie White; Ada (Essie) – born ca. 1880, married Will Austin;

Charles Gotha – died as an infant.

The following comments, from family information, are offered on each child of Alexander.

Elizabeth never married. She had children named Henry Pate and Missouri Pate. She and the children are listed in the household of Alexander on the U. S. Census for Geneva County, Alabama, in 1880. She was listed as a daughter of Alexander, and her children were listed as his grandchildren.

John A. Pate had nine children from his marriage to Louisa Van Landingham, four sons and five daughters. Homer Pate listed them as David H., Sally, Peter Alexander, Clayton J., Charity, Malinda, William T., Dixie, and Leila. William T. was apparently known as Carl.

Samuel and Sarah Ann (Hewitt) Pate had seven children, six sons and one daughter.

Homer Pate identified them as Will, Bass, Don, Warren, Jephtha, Benjamin, and Rosa.

Homer did not list the children of Henry and Rachel (Pate) McCrone. This research failed to locate this family on U. S. Census reports.

Benjamin F. and Elizabeth (Somerset) Pate had twelve children. Homer Pate identified them as Allen B., Clarisy D., E. Fannie, Gus H., Ida J., Kince L., Millard N., O. Pearl, Quina R., S. T., U. Vander, and Will X.

James M. and Martha Ann (Hendrick) Pate had six children, two of whom died early. The survivors were Greenie, Asbury, Hester, and Eli.

William A. Pate moved to Mississippi. Cecil Pate shared a family tradition of interest here. Caution is added, no proof, only a tradition. Alexander had a disagreement with a son, put him on train with one-way ticket to Mississippi and some "startup money". Perhaps, if true, this was William A. Pate.

William A. Pate appears on the U. S. Census of Noxubee County, Mississippi, in 1850 as a farm laborer for G. W. Campbell. He married Sallie, a daughter of Campbell, 20 July 1880, in Noxubee County. She died in twin childbirth about 2 February 1884. He remarried to Mary Jane Sparkman in Noxubee County, 10 July 1884. She must have been a widow, because the U. S. Census for 1900 listed Mary J. as his wife, Susan Shaw as his mother-in-law, and William Shaw as his brother-in-law. William remarried to Mrs. Lizzie Davenport in Noxubee County, 14 July 1918. She had Davenport children who were identified as step-children of William in 1920 and 1930.

William had living children from his second marriage that included Susan L., Lizzie S., Marie E., and William A., Jr.

Research shared by Joel Pate added detail to the report on William A. Pate.

Alexander Loyd "Bud" and Elizabeth (Dyson) Pate had six children. Homer identified them as Lula, Mollie, Ardilla, Cora, Archibald, and Alexander.

Charles and Jennie (Barnes) Pate had six children. Homer identified them as Mary, Viola, John, Comer, Maybell, Beatrice, Woodrow, and Emmett.

George and Lizzie (White) Pate had six children. Homer identified them as Cleo, Lillian, Ethel, Venera, Wynell, and Derrall.

Ade (Essie-Ada) Pate had seven children from her marriage to Will Austin. Homer listed them as Lillie, Alexander, Clifford, Lessie, Thurlie, Gaston, and Inez.

This completes the report on Alexander Pate, son of Zacheus Pate.

Martilla (or Matilda) Pate was the next child of Zacheus Pate. She remained in Robeson County, and limited information is available on her. Her given name was Martilla on her Robeson County marriage record, dated 21 July 1829. U. S. Census reports identify her as Matilda or Tilda. The assumption is offered that her correct given name was Matilda. She married John Davis, as cited.

Matilda was born ca. 1815, based on U. S. Census reports, and died after the U. S. Census for Robeson County was enumerated for 1870. Neither she nor her husband appeared on the 1880 U. S. Census. The enumerators for the 1860 and 1870 U. S. Censuses identified him as a "fisherman" and "river fisherman."

The U. S. Census reports appear to identify the children of Matilda and John. They were:

William – born ca. 1837;
Stephen – born ca. 1833;
James – born ca. 1835;
Ora J. and Calvin (twins) – born ca. 1837;
Mary – born ca. 1839;
Betsy (Elizabeth?) – born ca. 1841.

Betsy remained in the household of John and Matilda in 1870. She had a three-year-old child named Harriett Davis.

Benjamin Pate was the next child of Zacheus. He was born ca. 1820, probably in Robeson County, North Carolina, and died in Geneva County, Alabama. He married first, to Clarissa Moore in Robeson County, 9 March 1839, and second, to Mrs. Mary Anna (Corbitt) Peel (Peal) in Alabama, late in life. The second marriage was without children. Mrs. Peel was the daughter of Willis Corbitt and the widow of William Peel. She had children from her Peel marriage. Readers will note the marriage of members of the Peel family with Pate descendants of Charles Pate d. p. 1790 and James Pate d. ca. 1790 in Wayne and Richmond counties of North Carolina.

Family information shared by Patricia Ann (Hinson) Mordes reports the marriage of a descendant of Anna (Corbitt) Peel's first marriage to a descendant of Benjamin Pate's marriage to Clarissa Moore. Thomas H. Peel, a son of Anna, married Mary Elizabeth Pate, an illegitimate daughter of Benjamin's daughter, Dolly Pate. More will be offered on this item later.

The return of Benjamin Pate to Robeson County, North Carolina, from Thomas County, Georgia, has been noted. This return was near the death of his grandfather, James Humphrey. His mother and her children shared in his estate. Likewise, his marriage to Clarissa Moore and their departure for Alabama after 1848, and his acquisition of land conveyed to his father, Zacheus Pate by the grandfather Humphrey, have been noted.

Benjamin acquired land from the U. S. Government in the Geneva County area, 200 acres in Sections 8 & 9, Township 1 North, Range 25 East. This land was distributed among his legitimate heirs, by his widow and the children, and serves to identify his legitimate heirs, to be cited. He had five daughters from his marriage to Clarissa Moore. The daughters were:

> Harriett – born 19 October 1844, married David Levi Smith, died 26 March 1902 in Holmes County, Florida, Pine Hill Cemetery;
> Diana – born ca. 1847, married George Morgan, died p. 1900;
> Dolly – born 15 August 1847, married David Levi Smith after the death of her sister, Harriett, died 20 August 1925, Holmes County, Pine Hill cemetery;
> Elizabeth – born ca. 1850, married John M. McCrone, died after 1902;
> Rebecca – born 28 May 1854, married John J. Pitts, died 18 May 1903, Calhoun County, Florida.

Family tradition provides information of interest on these families. The writer recognizes Joel Pate for contributions to this information.

Harriett Pate, the oldest daughter of Benjamin and Clarissa, married David Levi Smith. They had ten children, nine living to maturity:

Henry Jefferson – born 18 December 1862, died 7 September
    1927; baby boy – born and died 1865;
Alexander – born 1 March 1867, died 23 February 1924;
Rebecca – born 15 March 1869, died 31 January 1965;
Jesse Eldridge – born 27 January 1871, died 13 July 1903;
John Benjamin – born 7 November 1873, died unk.;
James Noah – born 13 May 1876, died unk.;
William Coley – born 30 March 1881, died 22 September 1965;
Joseph Leander – born 7 October 1882, died 21 August 1971;
George Franklin – born 1 June 1889, died 24 August 1966.

Family tradition reports David Levi Smith was employed by
Alexander Pate, a brother to Benjamin Pate, for several years.

Diana/Dinnah Pate was the second born daughter of Benjamin
and Clarissa (Moore) Pate. She married George Morgan in 1860,
based on U. S. Census reports. The 1900 U.

S. Census identified her as the mother of eight children, all living.
Available records identify seven:

George A. – born ca. 1863;
Amanda – born ca. 1866;
Joseph – born ca. 1868;
Rebecca – born ca. 1872;
Elizabeth – born ca. 1874;
James – born ca. 1876;
Ira – born ca. 1882.

Diana and her husband George died after the 1900 U. S. Census
for Geneva County was enumerated.

The third daughter of Benjamin and Clarissa was Dolly Pate.
Family information reports Dolly had two children to reach maturity, who were fathered by her brother-in-law David Levi Smith.
Dolly married David Levi Smith in later years, after the death of
her sister, Harriett. They were her only reported children and had
the surname of Pate. They were: Mary Elizabeth was born ca. 1881,
married Thomas H. Peel, a son of Mary Anna (Corbitt) Peel Pate,
the second wife of Benjamin Pate; Joel T. Pate – b. 28 June 1878,
married 1) Sarah Baxley and 2) Mrs. Ida Snipes, d. 10 July 1934.

Dolly was buried with the Smith family at Pine Hill Cemetery in
Holmes County.

Elizabeth was the fourth daughter of Benjamin and Clarissa. The order of birth is based on U. S. Census reports and may be in error. She may have been born as early as 1844. Elizabeth McCrone appears in the Geneva County household of Benjamin Pate in 1880, 36 years of age, and was identified as a daughter of Benjamin. She had a 19-year-old daughter, granddaughter to Benjamin, named Caroline McCrone. Subsequent research indicates that Elizabeth Pate and John M. McCrone had a daughter, Mary Caroline McCrone, born 16 August 1861 in Geneva County, Alabama, died 18 April 1908, in Holmes County, Florida.

Elizabeth McCrone was alive when the land of her father was distributed among hislegal heirs, 15 January 1902.

The fifth daughter of Benjamin and Clarissa was Rebecca Pate. She married John G. Pitts, probably in Holmes County. She was born 28 May 1854 and died in Calhoun County, Florida, 19 May 1903. U. S. Census reports identify her children as follows:

Rufus – born ca. 1869;
Benjamin – born ca. 1870;
James – born ca. 1872;
Eliza – born ca. 1875;
Richmond – born ca. 1877;
John – born ca. 1879;
Walter – born ca. 1882;
Charles – born ca. 1886.

Several Geneva County deeds are important to the identification of the heirs of Benjamin and Clarissa, and of their spouses. They include Deed Book M, page 426, dated 15 January 1902; Book P, page 70, 1 January 1902; Book R, page 394, 1 January 1903; and Book R, page 39, 15 March 1905. These records identify the daughter Harriett as deceased, Dolly was the wife of David Levi Smith, Diana was the wife of George Morgan, Rebecca was the wife of John G. Pitts, and Elizabeth had the surname of McCrone.

Additionally, Benjamin and his second wife, Mary Ann (Corbitt) Peel Pate, conveyed land to her son, Thomas H. Peel and his wife Mary Elizabeth (Pate) Peel, Geneva Deed Book C, page 128. Also, Dolly conveyed land to her daughter Mary Elizabeth Peel, 30 January 1896, Book F, page 116.

The preceding seems sufficient to identify the legal heirs of Benjamin and Clarissa (Moore) Pate.

Family information reports that Benjamin had a mistress, Mary Woodall, and fathered a child, or children, with her. Reportedly, Benjamin and Mary had affairs that had origin in Robeson County, North Carolina. She moved to Alabama as he relocated and was near, or in adjacent households, on U. S. Census reports. She had children in her household. At least one of these, Rhoda Missouri, appears to have been a child of Benjamin Pate.

Rhoda Missouri Woodall was born 13 February 1859 in Geneva County. She married Elbert Fairchild and moved to Holmes County, Florida, where she died 15 April 1940. Her Florida Death Certificate identified her parents as Ben Pate and Polly Woodall.

The writer has no additional information on the Woodall children. This completes the report on Benjamin Pate, son of Zacheus Pate.

Delila (Delighter) Pate was the next child of Zacheus Pate. She was born 5 July 1825 and died ca. 1860. She married Richard W. Singletary in Thomas County, Georgia, 20 October 1841. Her given name on the marriage record was Delighter Pate. The U. S. Census for 1850 identified her as Delila. The assumption is offered that her correct name was Delila.

The Singletary family was active in the Robeson, Cumberland, and Bladen counties area of North Carolina and migrated to Georgia and Alabama in numbers, in the early 1800s.

Richard and Delila moved to Dale County, Alabama, before the 1850 U. S. Census was enumerated. They were listed in Dale County with two sons in 1850, Joseph – 2 years old, and Richard – 1 year.

Information published in *The History of Grady County, Georgia*, page 229, reports a short life span for Richard and Delila. The following family information is reported from that resource.

Richard W. Singletary was born 25 December 1811 and died in Thomas County, Georgia, 30 March 1857. The birth date for Delila was cited, 5 July 1825, without a death date.

She was not located on the 1860 U. S. Census. Her death will be reported as ca. 1860.

The children of the marriage follows, from family Bibles:

Amelia Elizabeth – b. 5 August 1842, d. 2 March 1843;
James Zacheus – b. 21 August 1844, d. 12 April 1848;
Joseph Benjamin – b. 5 September 1847, Dale County, Alabama,
    d. 1924, Gadsden County, Florida, buried in Slocomb,
    Geneva County, Alabama;

Richard Franklin – b. 27 May 1850, d. 17 October 1921 near
Ponce De Leon, Holmes County, Florida;
Amanda – b. 28 July 1854, married James Hinson, died 22
December 1921 in Geneva County, Alabama.

The names of the children recognized the family origin. Amelia
Elizabeth recognized her grandmother, Elizabeth (Humphrey) Pate.
James Zacheus recognized his uncle, James C. Pate, and grandfather, Zacheus Pate. Joseph Benjamin recognized a Singletary family
name, Joseph, and a brother of Delila, Benjamin Pate.

Rachel was the next child of Zacheus Pate. She was born ca. 1828,
probably in Thomas County, Georgia, and married Aaron Davis.
Record of the marriage was not located. The couple was enumerated on
the Dale County, Alabama, U. S. Censuses for 1850 and 1860, and on
those for Geneva County, 1870 and 1880. Geneva County was formed
in 1867. These U. S. Census reports provide the basis for claiming
Rachel was a daughter of Zacheus and Elizabeth (Humphrey) Pate.

Aaron and Rachel died after the 1880 U. S. Census was canvassed.

The 1860 U. S. Census for Dale County listed the household of
Aaron and Rachel with two daughters – Elizabeth 15 years and Catherine Knowles 25 years. The 1870 U. S. Census listed their household
without additional persons. Adjacent was the household of Elizabeth
Pate, 79 years, assumed to have been the widow of Zacheus Pate. Her
household included Catherine Knowles, now 30 years, and Elizabeth
Floyd. It is assumed these were the same Catherine and Elizabeth
in the household in 1860. Elizabeth also had Floyd children named
Winney, Andrew, and Mary. The 1880 U. S. Census listed the Floyd
children in the household of Aaron and Rachel Davis, with the surname of Davis and identified as the children of Aaron.

Andrew Davis was listed on the 1900 U. S. Census for Geneva
County. Among his eight children was a son named Aaron and a
daughter named Rachel, obviously in recognition of his grandpar-
ents, Aaron and Rachel (Pate) Davis. Also, in his household was
Katie Knowles, 50 years, and identified as the mother of Andrew.
Katie was reported to be the mother of one child, who was living.

This research did not pursue records to clear all of the issues
raised by these U. S. Census reports. The assumption is offered that
they support the claim that Rachel Pate was a daughter of Zacheus
and Elizabeth (Humphrey) Pate. She married Andrew Davis, and
they had children that included Catherine/Katherine who married

a Knowles and had a son Andrew. Andrew assumed the surname of his Davis grandparents. The other daughter, Elizabeth, married a Floyd and had children. Available records fail to suggest other children for Aaron and Rachel.

A Pate-Floyd marriage was also reported in the report on Alexander Pate, cited earlier. He was a son of Zacheus Pate.

The remaining child of Zacheus Pate was James C. Pate. He is assumed to have been the son born in Thomas County, Georgia, ca. 1838. Information on James is limited, but seems to be sufficient to account for his fate. Available records lead to the assumption that he did not marry and was not survived by.

Records are sufficient to establish an association between James and his older brothers, especially between him and the older brother, Alexander Pate. James S. Pate purchased land from the U. S. Government in Holmes County, Florida, 26 November 1858, and 2 April 1860. The location was Section 29 and 30, Township 7 North, Range 14 West. His brother Alexander purchased land in the same township in the same years. Further, both were listed on the Holmes County tax lists for 1858 and 1859. The taxable assets for Alexander were larger, reflecting his older age, but both were taxed for money loaned at interest.

Alexander was enumerated on the 1860 U. S. Census for Holmes County. James was absent, probably reflecting his lack of a recognized household.

This research failed to find record of James C. after the 1860 tax record. The name of James Pate appears on Confederate Army records, but individual definition is lacking. Note has been made that Alexander reported, on the Covington County, Alabama state census for 1866, of the death of a member of his family in the Civil War. The assumption is offered that James C. Pate was that family member.

This completes the report on Zacheus Pate and his. The report will return to his siblings, the remaining children of Charles Pate d. 1825.

Charles Pate was the youngest son of Charles Pate d. 1825. He was born ca. 1790, based on U. S. Census reports, and died after the U. S. Census for Baker County, Georgia, was enumerated and before his widow executed Baker County deeds, 10 February 1856. He died ca. 1855. He married Lydia Pate in Robeson County, 10 March 1821. The origin of Lydia is unknown to this research. Note was made earlier that the family of Samuel Pate d. p. 1810, a brother to Charles Pate d. p. 1790, lived in the Robeson County area. Research provides limited definition to some of his children and grandchildren. The writer is of the opinion that Lydia was a daughter of Thoroughgood Jason Pate or Elijah Pate d. p. 1817, sons of Samuel Pate d. ca. 1810, to be treated later.

Earlier narrations described the migration of Charles d. ca. 1855, his mother Phebe and his brothers, Jack d. p. 1850 and Zacheus, to Georgia. Charles was in Decatur County for the 1840 U. S. Census, Baker County for that of 1850, and some descendants were in Miller County in 1860. Miller County was formed in part from Baker County in 1856.

The will of Charles d. 1825 recognized his son Charles with a legacy of one dollar. However, the will recognized grandchildren named Sarah, Ananias. and William for sizeable legacies, including 140 acres of land. The land was identified as the plantation where his son Charles lived. The land was leased to James Humphrey. 10 January 1826, as the descendants of Charles d. 1825 departed Robeson County. The lease identified Sarah, Ananias, and William as minor children of Charles and Lydia Pate. The parents signed the lease as guardians of the minor children, Deed Book T, page 462. The lease was for a period of eleven years.

The grandchildren sold the 140-acre tract, 2 January 1847, as residents of Baker County, Georgia, to David Harrell, Robeson Deed Book 2, page 463. They were identified as Sarah Kinney, wife of Erasmus Kinney, Ananias Pate, and William Pate. The record was witnessed by Richard Pate and James Humphrey. This record provides the fate of Sarah Pate and introduces, Richard Pate, another son of Charles and Lydia (Pate) Pate.

The U. S. Census for Baker County in 1850 listed Charles and Lydia Pate with the son Ananias in their household. The son William was on the same page, as was Richard Pate. The daughter Sarah Kinney, and her Kinney family, were listed on the adjacent page. The birthplace of all but Richard Pate was North Carolina. The birthplace for Richard was recorded as "on the road"! It is assumed he was a son of Charles and Lydia and was born during the move to Georgia.

Baker County deeds support the claim for this relationship for Richard Pate. A series of deeds are recorded in Deed Book 2, page 649, page 648, page 647, and page 61, dated 10 February 1856, 19 February 1856, and 23 February 1857. Land in Lot 183, District 12, was conveyed from Richard Pate to Lydia Pate, Richard Pate to Ananias Pate, Ananias Pate to Richard Pate, and Lydia Pate to R. W. Hooks. None of these records were recorded until 9 November 1891.

Questions arise as to the interpretation of the preceding records. The writer offers the assumption that they were executed after the death of Charles Pate and involve his widow and two of their sons, Ananias Pate and Richard Pate.

The 1860 U. S. Census for Miller County listed Nicholas Pate, 35 years, born in Georgia. This research failed to associate this man with the family of Charles Pate d. ca. 1855, though Silvester Kinney was in his household. His age and birthplace suggest he may have been related to the family of John Pate d. p. 1850 in Decatur County, as noted earlier.

The preceding records seem to be sufficient to identify the children of Charles and Lydia (Pate) Pate. They were:

Sarah – born ca. 1821, married Erasmus Kinney;
Ananias – born ca. 1824, married Elizabeth [?];
William – born ca. 1825, married Sarah [?];
Richard – born ca. 1826, married Elizabeth Brooks in Decatur County, 18 March 1849.
A son named Nicholas should be considered an additional son.

This research found no records on Charles and Lydia after deeds in 1856. Ananias remained in the Miller County area, and his descendants appear on U. S. Census reports there as late as 1900. Sarah (Pate) Kinney was not located after 1850, nor was William. Richard was absent in records after 1860.

This concludes the report on Charles Pate d. ca. 1855.

Elizabeth Pate was the next child of Charles Pate d. 1825. She was born ca. 1794, based on U. S. Census reports. She married Alfred Best in Robeson County, 13 February 1824. The will of her father recognized Sion Best as living on property of the Pate estate. Any relationship between Sion Best and Alfred Best is unknown to this research. The record serves to recognize that the families may have had an association before the marriage of Elizabeth and Alfred.

Limited information is available on Elizabeth (Pate) Best. The following is from U. S. Census reports. Alfred Best was listed on the 1830 U. S. Census for Cumberland County, North Carolina. He and his wife were 30/40 years of age and had three sons and one daughter represented in the household. Betsy Best was 70 years of age on the 1860 U.

S. Census for Robeson County and had Ann Desse, 29 years, in the household. Ann C. Deas was listed on the 1870 U. S. Census for

Robeson County, with James W. Deas, 9 years and Betsy Best, 76 years, in the household. The family was adjacent to John Davis and his wife Matilda in 1870. Matilda was a sister to Elizabeth (Betsy) Best.

The preceding information indicates that Alfred and Elizabeth (Betsy) Best had. She was a widow by 1860. Ann C. Best was among the children; she married a Deas, and was a widow by 1860. Other children were not identified in this research.

Readers will note that other members of this Pate Family married into the Dees/Deas family. Alexander Pate married Tarissa Dees in Thomas County, Georgia, as cited earlier.

Mary Pate was the remaining child of Charles Pate d. 1825. She was born ca. 1805, based on available records. She married John Humphrey, 13 February 1820 in Robeson County. Note has been made earlier of the common association of the Pate and Humphrey families.

Mary was recognized in the will of her father. Her legacy was $20.00 and a share in any property that might remain at the death of her mother.

This research failed to identify the fate of Mary and her family. Households headed by one named John Humphrey appear in later U. S. Census reports of Robeson County, North Carolina, and of the Georgia counties of Thomas and Decatur. None of these men had a wife named Mary. Perhaps Mary (Pate) Humphrey died early, and her husband remarried.

No further information is available from this research on this daughter of Charles Pate d. 1825.

This concludes the report on Charles Pate d. 1825, son of Charles Pate d. p. 1790.

SHADRACK PATE D. 1837,
SON OF CHARLES PATE D. P. 1790

Note was made earlier of insufficient records to identify the fate of the daughters of Charles Pate d. p. 1790. They are omitted from this report.

The next son was Shadrack Pate. He was among the children of Rev. Charles Pate who were identified by Morgan Edwards in his visit to the South Carolina Beautyspot Church in 1772.

Shadrack was born ca. 1765, based on his appearance in records as a mature man and in U. S. Census reports. His parents lived in the Pee Dee River area of the Carolinas in that time frame. He probably died in Wayne County, North Carolina, in 1837, between the writing of his Wayne County will, 24 March 1837, and the proving of the will in the November Term of County Court in 1837. Records suggest he lived his mature life in Wayne County.

A family tradition shared with the writer in earlier years reports Shadrack had two marriages and from each. Available records fail to support this claim, and the writer considers it to be in error. Records prove Shadrack had land transactions with John Peacock, his father-in-law, as early as 1786, Deed book 3, page 446. His age seems to preclude an earlier marriage. Further, records available to this research do not support the claim for an earlier marriage.

Shadrack married Dicey Peacock of Wayne County in the early to mid-1780s. The bride was a daughter of John and Priscilla (Worrell) Peacock. Worrell family information on the Internet reports John Peacock married Priscilla Worrell in 1760. John Peacock remarried, in old age, to Elizabeth [?]. Some researchers report her surname was Bishop. The second marriage was without children.

John Peacock b. ca. 1744 wrote his Wayne County will, 31 July 1829, Will Book 1, page 78. It was proved in the November Term of Court in 1829. He identified legacies for his sons William, John, Ethelred, and daughter Penelope Bell. He provided legacies for his widow, Elizabeth, including a slave named Harry. Further, he loaned the widow certain property for her natural life. The "lent property", after her death, was to be divided between "... my children not named in the will". Thus, John did have additional children, and they were to receive legacies at the death of his widow. Daniel Howell was appointed executor of the estate. The witnesses were Lewis Pate and William Pate, a son and a grandson of Dicey (Peacock) Pate.

The additional children of John Peacock are identified in two deeds executed by the widow, Elizabeth Peacock, 8 January 1831 and 8 June 1831, Book 15, pages 215-217. She conveyed two tracts of land on the Slew/Slough Creek and Howell Branch. One of the landmarks was the "William Bennett Old Patent Corner". The acquisition of land by John Peacock from Rev. William Bennett, and the association of the Peacocks, Pates, and Rev. William Easterling with Rev. Bennett, were noted earlier in this report. Elizabeth relinquished her interests in these tracts in return for a life estate in one and assistance in the maintenance of Harry the slave devised to her by John Peacock in his will.

The children of John and Priscilla (Worrell) Peacock as identified in the will and two deeds were:

Elizabeth – born ca. 1770, married John Combs;
Dicey – born ca. 1768, married Shadrack Pate, died 1838;
Penelope – married William Bell;
Mourning – married Winfield Pope;
Ethelred – born ca. 1780, died ca. 1830;
Needham – born ca. 1785, died ca. 1850;
William – born ca. 1791, died 1853;
John – born ca. 1795, died ca. 1854.

The dates, except for Dicey, are from the research of John J. Pierce and records from the *Peacock Family Association of the South.*

Other children are possible. Their absence from these records suggest they died early and without children.

The Peacock family was among many of interest to this report who settled in the old Chowan area of North Carolina, and later found their way to the Neuse River area that appeared in Craven, Johnston, Dobbs, and Wayne counties, as the area developed, and counties were formed. A brief review of some Peacock records is of value to this report and follows.

Samuel Peacock was in Chowan Precinct as early as 15 July 1720, when he witnessed a legal document for Elizabeth Boon, wife of William Boon, Chowan Deed Book F-1, page 54. She executed power of attorney to Elias Fort. Samuel may have been on a 1716 tax list for Chowan, but the full name is not legible, only Samuel Pe-- can be read. Subsequent records show he was located in the part of Chowan that became Bertie County in 1722 and Northampton County in 1741. Other researchers report Elizabeth Boon had the maiden surname of Fort. The Boon and Fort Families came from Surry and Isle of Wight counties of Virginia.

Samuel acquired 320 acres of land on the south side of the Meherrin River, by grant, 17 April 1730. He conveyed 150 acres of the tract to William Barden, 10 July 1730, Deed Book 7, page 225. He conveyed another 100 acres of the grant to "my loving son John Peacock", 2 May 1736, Book E, page 154.

He acquired an additional 640 acres from the will of Henry Crumpton/Crampton, Land Grant Book 4, # 56. Crumpton acquired the land by grant, 1 December 1727. Crumpton identified Peacock as "Friend", a term in old records that frequently indicated a kinship. Samuel Peacock was also the executor of the will. The will recognized sons Henry and William and daughters Susannah, Elizabeth, and Jane, all with the surname of Crumpton. Each child received five shillings "and no more". All land was devised to Samuel Peacock.

Samuel Peacock and his wife Mary sold the Crumpton land to Lawrence Smith of Virginia, 5 April 1737. The wife was not recognized in other deeds executed by Samuel. Perhaps her presence in this deed indicates she had a relationship to Henry Crumpton.

The remaining land in the 320-acre grant to Samuel was sold by John Peacock and Samuel Peacock, 20 October 1742, Northampton Deed Book 1, page 44. The assumption is offered that they were the son John, who had received 100 acres of the grant in 1736, and his brother, Samuel Peacock. They were sons of the earlier Samuel and were disposing of the remainder of his land, the father being deceased.

John Peacock sold the 100-acre tract conveyed to him by his father, 22 November 1742, Northampton Deed Book 1, page 43.John and Samuel were reported on the Northampton tax list for 1742. Both disappeared from later Northamptonrecords.

Samuel received 333 acres by grant on the south side of the great Contentnea Creek in Craven County (later Dobbs), 11 November 1743. John received a warrant for 200 acres on the north side of Nahunta Swamp, 1 March 1743.

Both brothers founded large families in the Johnston/Dobbs area. *The Peacock Family Association of the South* (John J. Pierce, family historian) has detailed information on both lines. Both of the brothers had sons named John Peacock. Available records suggest John, the son of Samuel, was the father of Dicey (Peacock) Pate.

Samuel Peacock wrote his will, 30 [13?] September 1793, Johnston County Will Book 1, page 77. He identified his sons as Samuel, John, Isham, and Abraham. The son Isham was the Rev. Isham Peacock noted earlier in this report. The will identified three more men as legatees who are assumed to have been sons-in-law, Moses Lee, Simon Branch, and Charles Dickson.

This research does not have definitive proof that Shadrack Pate of Wayne County, North Carolina, was the son of Rev. Charles Pate d. p. 1790. However, the assumptive evidence is impressive. Records cited earlier prove that Rev. Charles Pate did have a son named Shadrack Pate. The given name is unusual in the Pate Family, and another so-named, of this age and timeframe, is absent from available records. The influence of Wayne County and its people on the family of Rev. Charles Pate has been noted. A Wayne County tradition shared with the writer in past years noted that old family members were aware that Shadrack Pate d. 1837 and his descendants had a different origin from the other Pate families of the county. This indicates Shadrack removed to Wayne County from another area. However, he was no stranger to the Wayne County area. Records cited earlier show his father-maintained communication with Wayne County people.

The assumption is offered that Shadrack Pate of Wayne County was a son of Charles Pate d. p. 1790. He returned to the ancestral homesite of his family, in Wayne/Dobbs County, from the Pee Dee River area of the Carolinas.

His presence in Wayne County explains his absence from records associated with his father, as were his brothers Charles Pate d. 1825 and Joel Pate d. p. 1830. He may have relocated to Wayne County in his mid-teen years. He was in the county, 1 March 1784, when he signed a petition to relocate the county courthouse, *"Old Dobbs Trail"*, May 1986. He purchased 100 acres of land on Stoney Creek from his cousin Daniel Pate, 8 May 1784, Deed Book 1, page 358. Given the birth year assigned him by this research, he was 19 years of age in 1784 and may have been married.

He acquired additional acreage on Stoney Creek. However, it is difficult, due to inadequate and confusing records, to trace and verify these additional acquisitions and subsequent dispositions.

He received a grant for 150 acres, originally assigned to his father-in-law, John Peacock, on Slough Creek, Deed Book 3, page 346. Slough Creek was a few miles north of Stoney Creek. He seems to have made his home on the Slough following this acquisition. It was also the homesite of his Peacock kin. The last tract cornered on land John Peacock had acquired from Rev. William Bennett. The association of the Pates, Bennetts, and Peacocks has been noted earlier.

Shadrack acquired additional land on the Slough by grant and purchase. This included 50 acres from William McKennie, 19 December 1786, Deed Book 3, page 388; 40 acres by land grant, 10 November 1790, Book 5, page 134; 147 acres purchased from William Alford, 15 April 1791, Book 5, page 135; 100 acres from his father-in-law, 22 December 1791, Book 5, page 176; and others.

Shadrack and Dicey (Peacock) Pate died in 1837 and 1838, respectively. Their wills, to be cited later, identify five daughters and one son. Other records verify the daughters. The following is offered to identify four additional sons.

Lewis Pate, John Pate, and Willoughby Pate witnessed documents executed by Shadrack Pate, Deed Book 7, page 226, Book 10, page 509, and Book 13, page 196. They also witnessed records for each other. These reported acts indicate a relationship between the four men. It is important to note that records have not been found to associate these three Pate men with records executed by other Pate Families in Wayne County.

The U. S. Census for Wayne County in 1790 enumerated Shadrack Pate with three males under 16 years of age in his household. The assumption is offered that the three represented, Lewis Pate born ca. 1785, John Pate born ca. 1790, and Willoughby Pate born 10 July 1790. The U. S. Census for 1800 listed one male under 10 years of age in the household of Shadrack, and the assumption is offered that this represented Silas Daniel Pate, born 25 March 1794. The U. S. Census for 1810 listed one male under 10 years in the household of Shadrack, and the assumption is offered that this represented Shadrack Pate, Jr., born 10 October 1807.

The U. S. Census for Wayne County in 1810 recorded Shadrack Pate, John Pate, Lewis Pate, and Willoughby Pate living adjacent to each other. Since available records provide no record of land acquisition by John, Lewis, or Willoughby this early, it is assumed they lived on land owned by Shadrack, their father. Shadrack conveyed land to John, 31 October 1811, Book 13, page 196. He conveyed land to Lewis, 30 January 1812, Book 13, pages 9-10. Both tracts were on, or near, the Slough and contained 75 acres. He conveyed land to Silas Daniel, but that did not occur until 1836, to be cited.

Available records do not provide proof of land ownership in Wayne County by Willoughby. He departed Wayne County, with his father-in-law, Nicholas Smith, for Richmond County, to be cited later.

Lewis Pate conveyed a tract of land to his son, Elijah Pate, in 1852, and identified it as land "which the said Lewis Pate bought of my father, Shadrack Pate", Deed Book 22, page 517. The deed is proof that Lewis was a son of Shadrack and the association of Lewis, John, and Willoughby with Shadrack, and each other, supports the claim that the three were brothers and sons of Shadrack.

Note was made in other areas of this report of the value of DNA testing to provide definition to some questions on assumed relationships. Descendants of Lewis Pate, proved to be a son of Shadrack by the deed of 1852, and Willoughby, assumed to have been a son of the same, have the same test results, which is to be expected if both men were sons of Shadrack. This is not without confusion, because all descendants of Rev. Charles Pate. d. p. 1790 and James Pate

d. ca. 1790 (brothers), tested to date, also have the same results. Hopefully, future members of the Pate DNA Project will provide a differentiating factor (mutation) to separate these lines. At this time, though DNA results from descendants of Lewis and Willoughby do not provide unquestionable proof that the two men were brothers, the test results are consistent with that assumption.

William Thompson conveyed a tract of land to Lewis Pate in 1838, Deed Book 17, pages 437-438. The land was located on the south side of the Slough and bordered on land owned by John Pate and Lewis Pate. The deed was witnessed by Shadrack Pate (Shadrack, Jr.), the son of Shadrack and Dicey, proved in their wills. The record serves to prove that John and Lewis, who acquired land from their father in 1811 and 1812, continued to own adjoining land in 1838. They continued an association with their brother, Shadrack, Jr., after the death of their father.

The will of Shadrack, written 24 March 1837 and proved 1 May 1837, identified one son, Shadrack Pate, Jr., who was the executor of the estate. Five daughters were named, but only one, Selah, was identified as a daughter. The five were Selah/Sealy/Cealy Pate, Dicey Phillips, Penelope Peel, Rebecca Wright, and Mary Roberson. He also recognized Christo Pate as a legatee, without identity. Records, to be cited, will identify Christo as his daughter-in-law Christian (Ammons) Pate, the wife of his son Silas Pate.

The will of Dicey (Peacock) Pate was written 25 April 1837 and proved in the November Term of Court. Her modest estate consisted of a few head of livestock and wearing apparel. She recognized her son Shadrack and daughters named Rebecca Whrite (Wright), Polly (Mary) Roberson, Dicey Phillips, and Sealey (Selah) Pate. The frock, apron, and handkerchief devised to Rebecca were listed apart from the other legatees, and the scribe apparently failed to recognize her relationship to Dicey. Since she was also recognized in the will of Shadrack, Rebecca is assumed to have been a daughter.

Both of these wills, in the writer's opinion, were written by the same scribe. The spelling, grammar, and sentence structure of both are far from perfect. The difference in the spelling of Rebecca's surname and failure to record her relationship is in keeping with other errors in the wills.

Penelope Peel was recognized by Shadrack, but was absent from the will of Dicey. Records, to be cited, indicate Penelope died before 1840. The assumption is offered that she died after her father, but preceded her mother in death. More will be offered on this in the narration on Penelope.

The wills of Shadrack and Dicey recognized five names who are reported here as daughters of Shadrack and Dicey (Peacock) Pate. They are: Selah (Sealy/Cealy) Pate, Mary (Polly) Roberson, Penelope Peel, Dicey Phillips, and Rebecca Wright (Whrite). Four sons are identified: John Pate, Lewis Pate, Willoughby Pate, and Shadrack Pate, Jr.

This research offers the assumption that Silas Daniel Pate was the fifth son. The following provides support for the claim.

Family traditions shared with the writer in past years reported that Silas Daniel Pate was a son of Shadrack and Dicey. This relationship also appears in print, *Debtor's Legacy,* Albert Pate, pages 65 and 107. Recognition is given that the source for Mr. Pate's claim was also oral tradition. Reportedly, Silas Daniel Pate married Christian Ammons, a daughter of Jesse Ammons, and she was known in the family by the nickname of Christo. Family researchers regard most family traditions with justifiable suspicion. In this case, records provide impressive support for Silas Daniel being a son of Shadrack and Dicey.

The will of Shadrack Pate devised the homesite and five acres to the widow Dicey Pate and the daughter Selah Pate, for their natural lives. The homesite was to descend to the son Shadrack Pate, Jr. at their deaths. Further, all other land owned by Shadrack was devised to the son Shadrack, Jr., immediately.

Note was made earlier that Shadrack retained the 100 acres on Stoney Creek, granted to him, 13 September 1785. He conveyed 40.25 acres of this tract to Silas Pate (his son!), 7 January 1836, Wayne County Deed Book 16, page 416. The bounding landowners had changed in the passing 50 years, but the description in the deed and the grant seem to relate to the same tract of land.

The will of Shadrack indicates the remaining 60 acres was devised to the son Shadrack, Jr. Shadrack Pate (Shadrack, Jr.) conveyed these 60 acres, on the north side of Stoney Creek, to Leonard H. Pate, 22 January 1840, Book 18, page 224. Leonard H. Pate was the oldest son of Silas Daniel and Christian (Ammons) Pate and was a nephew of Shadrack Pate, Jr. These 60 acres, and the 40 acres sold to his father in 1836, had the same bounding landowners.

This research offers the claim that Silas Daniel Pate was the fifth son of Shadrack and Dicey (Peacock) Pate. Other records to support the claim will appear in the narration on Silas Daniel Pate.

Readers of the earlier work circulated by the writer, *Pate Pioneers on the Pee Dee River*, may note that William Pate was listed as the fifth son in that report. The William involved was the first-born son of Lewis Pate, and was a grandson of Shadrack.

This research identified 10 children born to Shadrack and Dicey (Peacock) Pate. They will be recognized and treated in the narration to follow. The family may have included an additional daughter, who will be treated here.

Some Peele family information currently in circulation reports Penina, 25 August 1795 - 28 July 1892, the wife of John Peele, 27 May 1791 - 20 April 1879, was a daughter of Shadrack and Dicey (Peacock) Pate of Wayne County, North Carolina. John and Penina were reportedly married in Richmond County, North Carolina, 6 March 1815. Both had origin in Wayne County.

The couple departed for Indiana Territory, with his mother, shortly after marriage and made their home there until death.

The information to follow cites some records, pro and con, that affects the claimed relationship, and offers the writer's opinion on the at hand.

Shadrack Pate wrote his will, 24 March 1837. He recognized five daughters - Selah (Celia) Pate, Dicey Phillips, Penelope Peale, Rebecca Wright, and Mary Roberson. He recognized only one son, Shadrack Pate, Jr. Various records, cited elsewhere in this report, identify four more sons - Lewis, John, Willoughby, and Silas Daniel. Given the omission of four sons, it would not be a surprise to learn that he omitted a daughter who lived in Indiana. Further, the U. S. Census for Wayne County in 1810 enumerated six young females in the household of Shadrack, three under 10 years of age and three 10-16 years of age. This Census suggests he had six daughters.

His wife, Dicey (Peacock) Pate, wrote her will, 26 April 1838, and recognized the same son, Shadrack, Jr., and four daughters - Rebecca Wright, Polly (Mary) Roberson, Dicey Phillips, and Sely (Celia) Pate. Penelope Peale was omitted.

Neither recognized a daughter named Penina. In the writer's opinion, both Penina and Penelope were proper names, and neither was a nickname for the other.

The suggestion has been raised that Penelope Peale in the will of Shadrack was Penina Peele, the wife of John Peele. This seems unlikely. Penelope Peale was among four persons for whom Shadrack devised 15 head of hogs and 3 cattle, hardly an appropriate legacy for a daughter who lived in Indiana. Two daughters received legacies of cash, and that would have been more appropriate for one living in a distant and undeveloped territory.

The case is presented in the narration on Penelope (Pate) Peale, that she was omitted from the will of her mother because she was deceased. The legacies in the will of Dicey were meager in monetary value -- a frock, a handkerchief, an apron, etc. They were not items that could be distributed among descendants of a deceased heir. Further, it is important to note that other heirs were omitted from the will. The assumption is offered that Dicey recognized all of her living daughters who resided in North Carolina.

Published Peacock family information, *Birds of a Feather by* John Pierce, reports Penelope, the daughter of Dicey (Peacock) Pate, married Willis Peale. The claim is based on family tradition. There is some support for the claim. Examples can be found in naming patterns -- Willoughby Pate, a known son of Shadrack and Dicey, named a son Willis and a daughter Penelope. Five of the known siblings of Penelope named a daughter Penelope, suggesting that they were moved to memorialize their sister. Further, they recognized their siblings freely as they named children Lewis,

Willoughby, John, Celia, etc. Also of importance, none identified a daughter with the name of Penina.

An earlier researcher, Billie Faye Evans, shared with the writer from the Peele family report, *Descendants of Robert Peele I and Allied Lines,* Melinda Spiro, that Penelope Peale, daughter of Shadrack Pate, married John Peele. Miss Evans, reportedly made contact with the author and reported that there is no record to prove the relationship and marriage. The claim was based on family traditions. Current Peele family researchers report that Melinda Spiro compiled the published report from the research of Mary Spiro, now deceased.

As stated earlier, the writer does not believe Penina, the wife of John Peele, was Penelope (Pate) Peale.

Note needs to be made that the writer places no significance in the various spellings of Peele, Peale, etc. The same person appears in early records with various spellings.

Impressive records have been shared by descendants of John and Penina (Pate) Peele in this project. These include the obituary of Penina and a biographical sketch for John Peele, published in a local newspaper (Fountain City, Indiana), 23 April 1879. Both are "Genealogical Treasures". Both provide the maiden surname of

Penina as Pate, but neither identifies her parents. This suggests that the identity of Shadrack and Dicey as her parents is a "modern-day assumption".

The biographical information in the newspaper article reports John Peele had a birthright membership in the Society of Friends (Quaker). He reportedly joined the Society of Friends at 18 years of age, probably 1809. Some researchers have suggested his wife was also of the Quaker Faith by birthright. That must be questioned, if she was of the family of Shadrack Pate. Records identify this Pate Family as, originally, members of the Church of England. They joined the Baptist movement in the mid-

1700s. Shadrack was a son of a prominent Baptist minister, he had one son who was a Primitive Baptist minister, and another was identified as a "True Predestinarian Baptist" by the inscription on his grave marker. Shadrack and his sons swore to their signatures, on numerous documents. They never "affirmed" their signatures, as was the custom of Quakers. Two of his sons were justices of the peace. No record has been found to connect Shadrack or his children to the Quaker faith. Perhaps a daughter joined the Quaker faith, after she married and left home, but an association by one of the family seems unlikely.

Published records of the Contentnea Meeting House (Quaker) in Wayne County provides record of the dismissal of one John Peele for "Marrying Out of Unity" (marriage to one not of the faith) on 11 November 1815. The bride was not identified in this entry, and available records are insufficient to prove this John Peele was the man who married Penina Pate and moved to Indiana. Given that the marriage and dismissal was in 1815, the assumption is offered that the same John Peele did make both records.

Richmond County records prove that Willoughby Pate, a known son of Shadrack and Dicey, relocated from Wayne County to Richmond County in January 1815, Richmond County Deed Book I, pages 189 and 200. He purchased land from John Peele and his mother, Tabitha Peele, and from William Peele. This was as the Peele family prepared to depart Richmond County for Indiana Territory. John Peele married Penina Pate two months later, 6 March 1815. It would be easy to support the claim that Penina was a sister to Willoughby and, therefore, a daughter of Shadrack and Dicey. However, records available to the writer do not provide proof of such, and they do raise questions. There were other Wayne County Pate Families from which a female of Penina's age could have originated. Records indicate those families also had association in Richmond County.

Shadrack Pate d. 1837 had four Pate males first cousins in Wayne County -- Daniel Pate, James Pate, Isham Pate, and Elias Pate. James and Isham had females in their households in the U. S. Censuses for 1800 and 1810 who were of the age of one born in 1795, as was Penina Pate. These assumed daughters have not been identified, to the knowledge of the writer. This research has placed descendants of James in Richmond County, and it is possible that Penina had the same origin. Further, earlier in this research, note was made of Isaac Pate, a descendant of John Pate d. ca. 1779, having presence in Richmond County in 1810. Penina could have been his sister. Research is incomplete on their lines at this time.

Quaker records prove that members of the family of Isham Pate were members of the Contentnea Meeting House in Wayne County, as was one John Peele. This suggests a possible association of these families.

Penina (Pate) Peele may have been a daughter of Shadrack and Dicey. Unfortunately, no record has been found to associate her with that family. This includes the wills of Shadrack and Dicey. Further, the children of Shadrack failed to recognize Penina as they named children. It seems more probable that Penina was a daughter of James Pate or Isham Pate of Wayne County. Perhaps ongoing research will provide additional information. For the present, it seems inappropriate to assign her as a daughter of Shadrack and Dicey, without expressed cautions.

In summary, the known children of Shadrack and Dicey (Peacock) Pate were:

> Lewis – born ca. 1785, m. Elizabeth Popc, d. 1864;
>
> John – b. ca. 1790, m. 1) Elizabeth [?], 2) Mary Deans, d. 1862;
>
> Willoughby – b. 10 July 1790, m. Aseneth Smith, d. 26 July 1834;
>
> Silas Daniel – b. 25 March 1794, m. Christian Ammons, d. 12 September 1858;
>
> Selah/Celie/Sealy – b.ca. 1800, m. Josiah Gardner, d. 10 October 1882;
>
> Penelope – b. ca. 1803, m. Willis Peel, d. ca. 1838;
>
> Mary (Polly) – b. ca. 1804, m. Haywood Roberson/Robinson, d. unk.;
>
> Shadrack – b. 10 March 1807, m. 1) Penny/Penelope Howell, 2) Patricia (Ham) Smith, d. 11 October 1891;

Dicey – b. ca. 1809, m. Robert Phillips, d. p. 1860;
Rebecca – b. ca. 1812, m.[?] Wright.

Each child will be treated individually, to the extent of this research.

LEWIS PATE D. 1864,
SON OF SHADRACK PATE D. 1837

Lewis Pate was the first child born to Shadrack and Dicey (Peacock) Pate. He was born ca. 1785, based on U. S. Census reports. He married Elizabeth Pope, a daughter of Winfield and Mourning (Peacock) Pope. The two mothers (Dicey and Mourning) were sisters. This research failed to find record of the marriage, but it is proved to have occurred in Wayne County, Deed Books 12, page 461 and 17, page 150. The first child of Lewis and Elizabeth was born ca. 1808.

The probate of the Winfield Pope estate proved the relationship of Elizabeth to her father. John Peacock was the father of Dicey and Mourning, cited earlier. He was also the grandfather of Lewis Pate. Lewis and his son, William Pate, served as witnesses to the last will and testament of John Peacock, 31 July 1829.

Lewis died in 1864. His will was written 24 July 1846. It was altered by codicils on 27 August 1852 and 6 March 1858. It was presented for probate at the May Term of Court 1864. The will and information in the Wayne County Loose Estate Records provide sufficient information to identify his. Various deed records confirm the identification of some of the children.

Elizabeth, his wife, also died in 1864. Estate records, available to this research, fail to identify the order of death. The will of Lewis devised property and provisions to care for his widow. The probate of his estate failed to provide record of such actions, suggesting that Elizabeth preceded Lewis in death. Wayne County Loose Estate Records reports the sale of personal property of "Betsy" Pate, 19 July 1864 and August 1864. Betsy Pate was Elizabeth Pate, wife of Lewis. Buyers at the sale of her property included three of their surviving children.

The assumption is offered that, regardless of who died first, the terminal condition of the other was known at the first death.

In addition to the land Lewis acquired from his father, cited earlier, deed records identify additional land purchases. These include purchases from William Thompson – Wayne County Deed Book 17, page 437, Wright Langston – 19:480, Elizabeth Combs – 20:413, Rebecca Worrell – 20:414, James Forehand – 20:415, and Hardy Pope – 26:50-51.

An earlier researcher shared a family tradition of interest to this report. Reportedly, Lewis made his original homesite on land acquired from his father, on the Slough. He later acquired land nearer to Stoney Creek and moved his homesite to that location. The present-day community of Patetown developed around the second homesite of Lewis Pate.

The children of Lewis and Elizabeth (Pope) Pate follow. Important information from his will and probate proceedings will be cited as the appropriate child is recognized. Some birth dates appear to be out of order because they are a mix of approximations and grave marker inscriptions. The children were:

> William – b. ca. 1808, d. ca. 1830, m. Lucretia Herring;
> Letty – b. ca. 1810, d. p. May 1864;
> Stephen – b. 1818, d. 1893, m. 1) Winifred Howell, 2) Patsy
> (Martha) Copeland, 3) Martha (Patsy) Howell;
> Willoughby – b. ca. 1817, d. 1875, m. Nancy Peacock;
> Bryant/Binum – b. ca. 1819, d. p. 1870;
> Cenith (Sini) – b. ca. 1820, d. a. 1870, m. 1) Calvin Pate, 2) John
> Strickland; Penelope – b. ca. 1825, d. p. 1860, m. Needham
> Peacock;
> Elizabeth – b. ca. 1827, d. p. 1860;
> Elijah Bryant – b. ca. 1829, d. 15 July 1862, m. Sarah "Sally"
> Forehand.

Each child will be treated to the scope of this report.

William Pate was the first child born to Lewis and Elizabeth (Pope) Pate. Readers will recall that Lewis and William were witnesses to the will of John Peacock. The will of Lewis, written 24 August 1846, recognized William as deceased. A shotgun was devised to William Pate, son of William Pate, deceased. The full name of the grandson was William Robert Pate. It is of interest that the second born son of Lewis also named a son William Robert Pate.

William Pate was the direct ancestor of Billie Faye Evans, a well-known Pate researcher of past years. The research of Miss Evans provided many details for thisreport.

Lewis Pate served as administrator of the estate of his son, William.

William married Lucretia Herring, a daughter of Jacob Herring. The will of Jacob Herring, filed in August 1839, recognized Lucretia as his daughter. She had married George W. Cherry after the death of William Pate. The Herring will recognized "my grandson W. R. Pate and his mother Cressy Cherry." The Wayne County Loose Estate Records include a court order to George W. Cherry of Duplin County to appear in Wayne County and renew his bond as the guardian for William R. Pate on 16 January 1846.

Family tradition shared by Miss Evans reports that Lucretia had a daughter, Alice, born soon after the death of William Pate. The daughter died early in life. Lucretia (Herring) Pate also had from her marriage to George WilliamCherry.

William Robert Pate married Mary Ann Winder of Duplin County. He lived adjacent to, or near, his mother and step-father, and named a son George William Pate. The name, apparently, recognized his step-father. The children, and vital dates, follow, from the research of Miss Evans:

John Lewis – b. 24 March 1854, d. 17 February 1923, m. Barbara Allan Kornagay;

Winnefred Ann – b. 12 December 1855, d. 27 November 1873, m. 1) Bright Gardner, 2) Levi Brock;

George William – b. 10 February 1879, d. 17 December 1924, m. Latha Jane Whitman;

James Thomas – b. 25 April 1860, d. 2 September 1927, m. Mary E. Brock;

Sceanie – b. ca. 1861, d. 1891, m. Harold Brock;

Stephen B. – b. 15 April 1862, d. 15 October 1935, m. 1) Rack E. Cherry, 2) Susan Lou (Cherry) Hill;

Samuel A. – b. ca. 1866, d. ca. 1910;

Piercy Lucretia – b. 26 September 1867, d. 22 August 1922, m. Elias Brock;

Benjamin Franklin – b. 10 April 1869, d. 8 January 1944, m. Mary B. Anderson;

Augustus – b. 15 March 1870, d. 16 June 1944, m. Prudence "Mitty" Rogers;

Robert Bryant – b. 24 February 1879, d. 24 November 1938, m. Georgia J. [?].

The second child born to Lewis and Elizabeth was recognized in the will of Lewis as Letty. No surname was identified. The will devised her one "bed and stead" and furniture she already possessed. Additionally, she received seven acres of land, on which her house was located. The land was part of the tract Lewis purchased from William Thompson, 7 April 1838.

The assumption is offered that Letty was married and living on the land she inherited. Apparently, Letty was a nickname, and it was not found in other records associated with the Pate Family. Land record searches failed to provide a lead to her married surname.

The 1830 U. S. Census reports a daughter born about 1810 in the household of Lewis. This appears to have represented Letty. The will leaves no doubt that she was alive when the will was written in 1846. Neither of the codicils added in 1852 and 1858 reassigned her legacy of land to another heir, suggesting she was alive on those dates. It is assumed she survived her parents.

This research failed to develop additional information on Letty Pate.

Stephen was the third child born to Lewis and Elizabeth. His father recognized him as "Stephen Pate my oldest son" in his will. Note needs to be made that he was the oldest living son in 1846, when the will was written. His deceased brother, William Pate, preceded Stephen in birth. Lewis, through his will, devised the land Stephen lived on to him and noted this tract had been purchased from Wright Langston. Stephen received additional tracts, which were identified as the remaining land purchased from William Thompson and a field known as the Pond Branch Field.

Stephen's name resulted in some confusion, in the time he lived and for modern-day researchers. He was identified in early records as his father recognized him, Stephen Pate. He was identified in later years, after the 1850s, as Stephen L. Pate. The middle initial was used consistently in his older years. Some researchers have assumed the L. represented Lewis and was part of his birth name. Records suggest he acquired the middle initial after birth.

The confusion resulted from another man named Stephen Pate in Wayne County in the 1800s. The two men had a similar birth year. The other Stephen Pate descended from the line of James Pate d. ca. 1790, married Elizabeth Best, and died in the Confederate Army in 1862. The extant voters list for three elections in Wayne County, held in 1849, 1850, and 1851, list both men. The son of Lewis was identified as "Stephen Pate of Lewis" on all three voters lists. The assumption is offered that if either man had a middle name or initial, the identification given the son of Lewis would have been unnecessary. The son of Lewis was recognized as Stephen L. Pate in most later records.

This Stephen Pate will be recognized as Stephen Lewis Pate in this report, with the caution that the middle name is assumed to have been acquired sometime after birth.

Stephen L. Pate was born in 1818 and died in 1893. The dates are from his grave marker in Pate Cemetery and published in the County Cemetery Book. His second wife, Martha (Patsy) Copeland, and son, Jefferson Davis Pate, are buried with him.

He had three wives. The first had the given name of Winnifred and the couple executed deeds as husband and wife. One was to Stephen Howell in 1843, Wayne County Deed Book 19, page 214. No marriage record was found in this research. One family tradition reports Winnifred had the maiden surname of Jernigan. There is support for the claim in records. Lydia Jernigan died in 1797, leaving a son named Arthur Jernigan. This son had a wife named Winnifred, and the couple would have been of age to have a daughter named for her mother. This research failed to find identity of a daughter sonamed.

Records available to this research suggest the maiden surname of the first wife of Stephen was Forehand/Howell. Elizabeth Howell, widow of Archilus Howell, died in 1821. Her will recognized two granddaughters named Winnifred Howell. They were daughters of her sons Needham Howell and John Howell. Another son was named Stephen Howell, probably the man to whom Stephen and Winnifred Pate conveyed land in 1843, cited earlier. Stephen had other land transactions with the Howell family. This research failed to document any transactions between him and the Jerniganfamily.

The assumption is offered that Winnifred Howell married Stephen L. Pate, as his first wife. The burial site for the first wife was not identified.

Stephen married secondly to Martha "Patsy" Copeland, about 1860. The bride was a daughter of Robert and Wealthy (Aycock) Copeland, Deed Book 19, page 519. The couple conveyed land to her brother, Dempsy Copeland, Deed Book 33, page 281. Stephen and Patsy Copeland were buried in Pate Cemetery.

The third wife was Martha "Patsy" Howell, daughter of John and Nancy Howell, proved by her death certificate. They were married 6 October 1885. She was born September 1852 and died 28 November

1936. She was buried in the Howell Cemetery with her son Dempsey/Dock Pate and her daughter Nicey (Pate) Howell.

Stephen died intestate and left no estate to probate. His children are identified by other records executed during his lifetime and after his death. He conveyed numerous tracts of land to his children and third wife. These include: to John L. Pate – Wayne County Deed Book 27, page 668, 1867; to his wife Patsy Pate – 56:567; to Jefferson Davis Pate – 57:374, 1887; Jefferson Davis, Zilphia and Wm. R. Pate to Probate Pate, et al – 58:394, 1886; Jeff. D., Mary K., Martha and S. S. Pate to Wm. R. Pate 69:372, 1898; and Patsy Pate to Jeff. D. Pate – 71:13, 1895.

He also conveyed to several persons of other surnames. A conveyance to Memorial Baptist Church, for a church site, was made in 1885, Book 54, page 171.

Wayne County marriage records identify the following children of Stephen and the appropriate wife: John L. Pate, Elizabeth Pate, Martha/Patsy Pate, Jefferson Davis Pate, Senia/Aseneath Pate, Greely Pate, Nicey Pate, and Mary K. Pate.

North Carolina death certificates prove the following as children and the appropriate wife: Stephen Sanford Pate, Rachel Florence Pate, William Robert Pate, Nancy Pate, and Dock/Dempsey Pate.

Deeds, cited earlier, prove the relationship of Probate/Provitt to his siblings.

The combined sources identify 14 children for Stephen Lewis Pate. U. S. Census reports confirm each as living in his household, or that of his widow after his death. They were identified as his children when that relationship was recorded.

Note needs to be made that the fifteenth child, Linden or Lydia, appeared only on the 1850 U. S. Census. She apparently died early in life. Perhaps she died when her mother, Winnifred, died.

The children of Stephen Lewis Pate and his first wife, Winnifred Howell, were:

> John Lewis – b. 6 July 1842, d. 4 November 1923, m. Jack Ann Howell, daughter of Fort and Sina (Sasser) Howell;
> Linden – b. ca. 1846, listed on the 1850 U. S. Census; Elizabeth – b. ca. 1848, d. 17 June 1897, m. Enoch Mitchell;
> Martha – b. ca. 1850, d. unk., m. Wiley Barnett 9 July 1878, son of Joshua and Nancy Barnett;
> Ceneth – b. ca. 1851, d. unk., m. Elijah Lane, 22 September 1870.

The children of Stephen Lewis Pate and his second wife, Martha "Patsy" Copeland, were:

>Jefferson Davis – b. 1 June 1861, d. 5 June 1932, m. 1) Zilphia Pate, 20 September 1881 – daughter of Charles and Belinda Pate, 2) Mary L. (Maddie) [?], 3) Cary N. Howell, 29 March 1903, daughter of Taylor and Frances Howell;
>
>Mary K. – b. ca. 1863, d. unk., m. Cullen Watson, February 1885, at the home of Stephen Pate, groom was son of Solomon and Harriett Watson;
>
>William Robert – b. 11 May 1865, d. 1 November 1936, m, Martha Ann Cocker;
>
>Provitt/Probate – b. ca. 1870, d. unk., m. Fannie Holland, 18 October 1893;
>
>Greely – b. ca. 1872, d. 9 March 1949, m. Jacob Whaley, 1 September 1895;
>
>Stephen Sanford – b. 25 August 1874, d. 28 June 1952, m. Emma F. Brown, daughter of Jessie and Patsy (Pate) Brown;
>
>Rachel Florence – b. ca. 1979, d. 11 February 1919, m. George Whaley.

The children of Stephen Lewis Pate and his third wife, Martha "Patsy" Howell, were:

>Nicey – b. 1 September 1886, d. 22 September 1934, m. William Franklin Howell, son of William and Diannah (Crumpler) Howell;
>
>Dempsey/Dock – b. ca. 1891, d. 7 January 1934;
>
>Nancy M. – b. 3 December 1891, d. 8 August 1975, m. Thomas Joseph Talton.

Willoughby Pate was the fourth child born to Lewis and Elizabeth. He received the given name of a brother of Lewis. He was born ca. 1817 and died 17 August 1876. The death date is reported in the probate of his estate, Wayne County Loose Estate Records. Willoughby died intestate. The estate records recognize his widow and all of the surviving children of his marriage.

Willoughby married Nancy Peacock in the early 1840s. Available marriage records fail to provide the date of the marriage. The bride was a daughter of William Peacock, a son of John Peacock. The grandmother of Willoughby and this William Peacock were siblings.

Nancy (Peacock) Pate was born ca. 1815 and died in 1895. Her will was presented for probate at the July Term of Court in 1895. The heirs in her will were the same as the heirs recognized in the probate of Willoughby's estate. The same children were listed in their households on U. S. Census reports.

Lewis Pate devised two tracts of land to Willoughby. One was described as the west part of the Old Field Place. The east part of this tract was devised to Willoughby's sister, Elizabeth Pate, for her lifetime. The east part was to descend to Willoughby upon the death of Elizabeth. The other tract was one-third of the Piney Woods tract bought from Hardy Pope.

The probate of the estates of Willoughby and Nancy identify four heirs, sons named Weddell (Weddie), Mark, and Martin, and one daughter named Aseneath. U. S. Census reports identify two additional children, a son named Zadack born ca. 1849, and a daughter named Isabelle born ca. 1854. Zadack and Isabelle are absent from later records, apparently died early in life.

Vital information on the children who lived to maturity follows:

Weddell/Weddie – b. ca. 1844, d. December 1895;
Mark (twin) – b. 12 March 1845, d. 26 April 1905, m. Marsala/ Ursula Combs;
Martin (twin) – b. 12 March 1845, d. 8 November 1904, m. Elizabeth Forehand;
Missouri – b. ca. 1852, d. ca. 1892, m. Jordan Holland.

Brief notes on the children follow.

Weddell appears to have been handicapped. He had lived with his parents, and the probate of his mother's estate recognized him as then living in a mental institution. He inherited 23 acres of land in the division of his father's property. This resulted in the probate of his estate. The probate records recognized the land as from the division of his father's estate. The heirs of Weddell were his brothers Mark and Martin and the heirs of his sister Missouri Holland. The heirs of Missouri were Nettie, wife of Major Howell, and Eva, wife of Duffy Chase. Weddell died intestate, December 1895.

The other sons of Willoughby and Nancy were Mark and Martin. The U. S. Census for 1850 identified them as twins. North Carolina death certificates are available on each. They provide vital dates in this report and proof of their parents.

Missouri was recognized as the wife of Burden Holland in the estate records for Willoughby, 17 August 1876. She preceded her mother in death. The will of Nancy recognized the daughters of Missouri, deceased, for legacies. The daughters were Ina Permette (Nettie) Howell and Eva M. Holland. Eva married Duffy Chase after her mother wrote her will, 10 January 1894, and before the death of Weddell in December 1895.

The fifth child of Lewis and Elizabeth was Bryant/Binum Pate. The proper given name appears to have been Bryant. The nicknames of Binum and Bynum appear in some official records. The assumption is offered that the name recognized Bryant Handley Pate, a cousin of Lewis who enjoyed social prominence in the generation of Lewis. The namesake descended from James Pate d. ca. 1790.

Bryant, the son of Lewis, was born ca. 1830 and died after the U. S. Census for 1870 was enumerated. He did not marry.

The will of Lewis devised furniture and two tracts of land to his son Bryant. One tract was identified as "one field none [known] by the name of the Old Rie [Rye] Field joining the widow Garner". The widow Garner appeared to have been the sister of Lewis Pate, Celias Pate, who married Joseph Gardner. The other tract was from the Piney Woods land Lewis had bought from Hardy Pope, cited earlier.

A codicil was added to the will, 6 March 1858. Lewis added a bay mare to the legacy for the son Bryant. The legacy for Bryant was placed in a trust with the son Elijah as trustee. Further, note was made that Bryant was unmarried and that if he died without children, the legacy was to descend to Elijah.

The probate of the estate of Lewis, Loose Estate Records, reported that Lewis sold the "Rye Field" tract, devised to Bryant, before his death. Further, Elijah died in the Confederate Army. The Court appointed the brother Willoughby to replace Elijah as trustee for Bryant. Bryant was described as "very poor" and lacked the means to feed and care for his mare, assumed to be the bay mare left to him by Lewis. Willoughby was ordered to care for the mare.

The U. S. Census for 1870 listed Bryant as a pauper, living in the county "Poor House". The records suggest Bryant died after 1870, without children.

The sixth child of Lewis and Elizabeth Pate was the daughter named Cenith. She was frequently recognized by the nickname of Seni and Sena. The given name was popular in Wayne County in that timeframe and may have been a corruption of the Biblical name of Aseneath. Willoughby Pate, the brother of Lewis (not the son) married Aseneath Smith of Wayne County. The name of Cenith appeared in later generations of the Pate Family.

Available records suggest Cenith was born ca. 1820 and died before the U. S. Census for 1870 was enumerated.

Lewis recognized her as "Seny" in his will. He devised her four acres of land, "which I have leased to her husband Calvin Pate", and furniture she had received. The name of her husband leads to more confusion.

Two men named Calvin Pate lived in Wayne County in these years of concern. They had similar birth years. One was a son of Samuel Pate d. 1870, a descendant of James Pate d. ca. 1790. He married Pernicia Pate, a daughter of Silas and Christian (Ammons) Pate. This Silas d. 1858 was a brother to Lewis d. 1864, the father of this Cenith Pate. The family will be treated in more detail later in the narrative on Silas.

The other Calvin was the first husband of Cenith, the daughter of Lewis. He was a son of John Pate, to be proved in the narrative on John Pate d. 1862, to follow in this report. This John Pate and Lewis Pate d. 1864 were brothers and sons of Shadrack Pate d. 1837. Comments on the marriage of Cenith and Calvin are in order here.

This research failed to find record of the marriage of Calvin and Cenith. The proof is in the will of her father. Lewis said his daughter Cenith was the wife of Calvin Pate. The other Calvin was married to Pernicia Pate before Lewis wrote his will in 1846. The U. S. Censuses for 1850 and 1860 listed Cenith in the household of her father, without a husband or child. The 1850 U. S. Census for Johnston County, North Carolina, adjoining Wayne County, listed Calvin in the household of Everitt Waddell, Sr., without a wife or child. The household was adjacent to Mary (Pate) Peacock, the sister of Calvin.

The preceding records lead to the assumption that Cenith Pate married Calvin Pate in the 1840s. The marriage did not last. Available records do not tell us how the marriage was dissolved, whether by divorce, annulment, etc. Her presence in the household of her father without a husband, and his presence adjacent to his sister, seems to be sufficient for the claim that the marriage was short-lived.

Cenith Pate was a buyer at the estate sale of her brother, Elijah Pate, in 1862 and at the estate sale of her mother, Elizabeth (Betsy) (Pope) Pate, in 1864. She purchased items from the estate of her mother, 19 July 1864. Wayne County marriage records report the marriage of Sena Pate and John Strickland, 30 August 1864. The second estate sale for her mother's property was held 17 October 1864. Sena did not buy, but John Strickland did buy items.

No further records were found on Cenith or John Strickland, including U. S. Census reports for 1870 and 1880. The assumption is offered that Cenith was the Sena Pate who married John Strickland. She had no from either marriage. She was near the end of her childbearing years when she married John Strickland.

Readers are cautioned that assumptions are involved in the report on this daughter of Lewis Pate.

The seventh child born to Lewis and Elizabeth was a daughter named Penelope Pate. She was frequently identified by the nickname of Penny. Note needs to be made of the popularity of this given name in the family. Dicey (Peacock) Pate had a sister so-named, and she named a daughter Penelope. Lewis Pate, the father of the Penelope treated here, had two brothers, John and Willoughby, who named daughters Penelope. One of his sisters, Mary, also named a daughter Penelope. Shadrack Pate, the brother to Lewis, John, Willoughby, and Mary, married Penelope Howell as his first wife, to becited.

Penelope, the daughter of Lewis, was born ca. 1815 and died after 1860. She married Needham Peacock as his second wife, as reported in Peacock family information. The marriage is not included in Wayne County marriage records available to this research, but other records seem to confirm the marriage.

Her father identified her as Penelope, no surname listed, in his will in 1846. He devised her furniture that she had in her possession and four acres of land on which her "old house stands." The four acres was part of the tract Lewis bought from Hardy Pope, cited earlier. The U. S. Census for 1850 listed Needham Peacock and Penny adjacent to the household of Lewis Pate. This Census listed a daughter from Needham's first marriage, Letha – 45 years of age, and a daughter from his marriage to Penelope – Sarah, 9 years old. Needham was about 30 years older than Penelope.

The name of Needham's first wife is unknown to this research. Peacock family information reports he was born ca. 1785 and died in 1852. Penelope (Penny) was living in the household of her married daughter, Sally (Sarah) and son-in-law James Pilkington, when the U. S. Census for 1860 was enumerated.

The fate of Penelope (Pate) Peacock after the 1860 U. S. Census is unknown to this research.

Elizabeth was the eighth child born to Lewis and Elizabeth. She was born ca. 1827, and records suggest she died after 1860. The assumption is offered that she did not marry.

The will of her father recognized her as Betsy, with no surname given. He devised to her furniture, already in her possession, and a tract of land. The land was identified as "half of my Old Place Field during her natural life." Note was made in the narrative on her brother Willoughby that he received the other half of this field. Further, the half devised to Elizabeth was to descend to Willoughby at the death of Elizabeth. The records seem to predict that Elizabeth would precede Willoughby in death, and she would be without children.

The Loose Estate Records on the estate of Elijah Bryant Pate, the remaining son of Lewis and Elizabeth, reported Elijah Bryant had agreed to pay Elizabeth Pate annual payment of $10.00 per year, on 17 March 1855, for her maintenance. The agreement was for 10 annual payments.

The preceding records indicate the family did not anticipate Elizabeth would have a long life or a marriage. She was listed in the household on the U. S. Censuses for 1850 and 1860. Her fate after 1860 is unknown to this research.

Elijah Bryant Pate was the ninth, and last, child born to Lewis and Elizabeth. He was born ca. 1829 and died in the Confederate Army at Richmond, Virginia, 15 July 1862. He married Sarah/Sallie Forehand, 7 March 1852, Wayne County marriage records. The bride was a daughter of Bryant and Elizabeth (Peacock) Forehand. She was born ca. 1833 and died soon after her husband. The Loose Estate Records created in the probate of Elijah's estate included a payment of $75.00 on 26 April 1864 to William Crumpler for a coffin for Sarah Pate.

Sarah Forehand had two sisters who married kinsmen of Elijah. Alice Forehand married Hyman Pate, a son of Shadrack Pate d. 1891, brother to Lewis Pate d. Elizabeth Forehand married Martin Pate, a son of Willoughby Pate, and a brother to Elijah.

Elijah enlisted in the Confederate Army, 11 October 1861, Company I, 35th North Carolina Infantry Regiment. He was promoted to corporal, 15 May 1862. He died of wounds, 15 July 1862, at Richmond, Virginia. The Regiment participated in the Seven Days Battle in Virginia, preceding his death.

Records suggest Elijah farmed with his father. Lewis conveyed six acres of land to Elijah in 1852, Wayne County Deed Book 22, page

517. This was the year of Elijah's marriage and appeared to have been his homesite. The land was from the tract Lewis acquired from his father, Shadrack Pate d. 1837. The will of Lewis conveyed all of his land, not devised to other children, to Elijah after the death of Elizabeth, the widow ofLewis.

The Loose Estate Records on Elijah describe his heirs dividing land on the south side of the Slough and Old Field Branch, known as Old Field Place. This was land that originated in the ownership of John Peacock, father-in-law of Shadrack Pate d. 1837. It passed in lineal descent to descendants of Shadrack's sons, John, Lewis, and Shadrack d. 1871. This land is among the items that prove John Pate d. 1862 was the son of Shadrack Pate. It establishes the sibling relationship of John Pate d. 1862 and Lewis Pate d. 1864.

The children of Elijah were also heirs in the division of the land of their uncle, L. B. Forehand, as proved by the Loose Estate Records.

Elijah wrote his will 19 January 1862. It was presented for probate at the August Term of Court 1863. Witnesses to the will were Henry Pate and James Pilkington. Pilkington had married Sarah Peacock, daughter of Needham and Penelope (Pate) Peacock, cited earlier. The will recognized the children born at that date: daughters Louvania, Lavinie, and Henrietta and son Lewis Bryant.

The third daughter, Elijah Ann, was born 9 July 1862. Her birth preceded Elijah's death by six days. The four heirs and their spouses were identified in the Loose Estate Records, when the landd of Elijah and of their uncle, L. B. Forehand, were divided.

The children of Elijah Bryant and Sarah (Forehand) Pate were:

Louvina/LaVina – b. ca. 1854, d. unk., m. J. W. Talton; Henrietta – b. ca. 1857, d. unk., m. Rommelus S. Best;

Lewis Bryant – b. 15 August 1858, d. 28 February 1940, m. 1) D. Smithy Sasser, 2) Sarah Catherine Howard;

Elijah Ann – b. 9 July 1862, d. 18 May 1937, m. John Stephen Warrell.

This completes the report on the family of Lewis Pate d. 1864, son of Shadrack Pate d. 1837.

JOHN PATE D. 1862,
SON OF SHADRACK PATE D. 1837

John Pate d. 1862 is the next child of Shadrack and Dicey (Peacock) Pate. Researchers must work through a maze of confusion to organize the family of this son. There were two Pate men in early Wayne County with the given name of John. They were of similar ages and were located, initially, in the Stoney Creek area. It is difficult to assign records to the correct John Pate.

One of these men appears in records as John Pate, John A. Pate (the A was probably an H), and John H. Pate. This man is a descendant of James Pate d. ca. 1790. He will be treated in more detail in the narrative on that line of the family. An overview, to differentiate him from the son of Shadrack Pate d. 1837 named John Pate, is in order here. James Pate (not James d. ca. 1790) conveyed land located in the Stoney Creek area to him in 1814. He married Lydia Cox, conveyed the land back to James Pate, and moved to land owned by the Cox family, south of the Neuse River. He died ca. 1833. Records suggest he was survived by his widow and no living.

The son of Shadrack d. 1837 named John Pate was introduced in the narrative on Shadrack. The basis for recognizing him as a son of Shadrack was cited there. Some note needs to be made regarding the land involved in the process. The land that Shadrack conveyed to his sons, Lewis and John, was identified by landmarks that included "south side of the Slough" and "Old Field Branch". The two tracts were adjacent. These landmarks appear in the division of land in the estates of grandchildren of Lewis and John. As an example, they are present in the estate records for the sons of Lewis named Elijah Bryant Pate and Willoughby Pate, cited earlier, and for the sons of John, who will be identified here. The lineal descent of these lands is valid support for the claim that Lewis and John were brothers.

John Pate, the son of Shadrack d. 1837, was born ca. 1785 and died in 1862. His will was written 22 January 1859 and presented for probate at the May Term of Court 1862. He will be identified in this report as John Pate d. 1862.

Additional confusion appears when the wife, or wives, of John are considered. One earlier researcher reported that this son of Shadrack married Martha J. Verrell of Franklin County, North Carolina. She died in 1823, and he remarried to Nancy Williams, the widow of John Williams of Franklin County. The first marriage was proved by a newspaper article (unidentified). The second marriage was reported from a marital agreement recorded in Franklin County, Deed Book 23, page 170.

The details provided in that report (dates, names, etc.) are impressive. However, questions arise when other records are considered by the writer.

One John Pate was enumerated on the U. S. Census for Franklin County, North Carolina, in 1830. Additionally, two men named John Pate and John H. Pate were enumerated in Wayne County. Further, Nancy Pate, apparently the widow of John Pate, was enumerated on the U. S. Census of Franklin County in 1850. She lived in the household of her married daughter, Nancy Whellus.

John Pate, the son of Shadrack, continued to be listed on the U. S. Censuses for Wayne County, 1840 to 1860. He was enumerated in 1850 with his wife Mary and five children from the second marriage.

The writer does not question that the John Pate noted above had married Michele J. Verrell and Nancy Williams. However, the assumption is offered that this John was not the son of Shadrack Pate d. 1837. Additional information follows.

The oldest son of John d. 1862, Adam Pate, lived in Richmond County, North Carolina, with kin from Thoroughgood Pate d. ca. 1802, in his early adult life. He returned to Wayne County, after the death of his wife and near the time of his father's death. He married Catherine Pate in Wayne County in February 1868. The marriage book during this time recorded the parents of the bride and groom. This record identified the mother of Adam as Elizabeth Pate and the father as John Pate. Records will be cited to prove Adam was a son of John Pate d. 1862. It is important to note that the mother's name was Elizabeth, not Martha or Nancy.

George Duncan Pate, a son of the second marriage of John, lived until 26 May 1920. His North Carolina death certificate identified his father as John Pate and his mother as Mary Deans. Other records support that John Pate and Mary (Deans) Pate were his parents, of which more will be written later.

It is the opinion of the writer that the two preceding records correctly identify the wives of John Pate d. 1862. Available records do not disclose if Pate was the maiden surname of Elizabeth. The parents of the bride in that marriage, Catherine Pate, were Daniel Pate and Sarah Pate. The assumption is offered that the mothers of the bride and groom were identified by their married surnames.

The U. S. Censuses for Wayne County in 1850 and 1860 add support for the claim that John married Mary Deans as his second wife. The 1850 U. S. Census listed the household of John, his wife Mary, and identified the five children from the second marriage. Mary was absent from later records. The assumption is offered that she died after the return for 1850 was enumerated and before John wrote his will, 22 January 1859. She was not recognized in the will.

John was the only person in his household in 1860. He was located two households from his sister, Dicey (Pate) Phillips. Two of his immature children were living in the household of 76-year-old Charlotte Deans, assumed to have been their grandmother. Charlotte Deans appears on U. S. Census reports without a husband represented, as far back as 1830. It is assumed that she was the mother of Mary (Deans) Pate. It is of interest that one Anderson Deans, of similar age to Mary, appears in Wayne County records. The youngest son of John and Mary was named Anderson Pate. The son may have been named to recognize a Deans kinsman.

In addition to the 75 acres of land that John acquired from his father, 31 October 1813, Wayne County Deed Book 13, page 196, he purchased 133 acres from Elijah and Charles Crooms, 2 October 1826, Book 13, page 203. The second tract was also on the south side of the Slough and had boundary lines in common with the tract his brother, Lewis Pate, purchased from William Thompson in 1838, Book 17, page 437.

John devised legacies through his will to his four sons, named Jackson (John Jackson), Richard (Richard Washington), George (George Duncan), and Anderson. Additionally, his daughter Penny (Penelope), and his granddaughter Bashaby (Bathsheba) Peacock were identified. He acknowledged that other heirs existed, with the instructions that all of his property and notes remaining after the legacies were honored, would be divided between "my four named sons, my daughter Penny and my granddaughter Bashaby Peacock." Other records support the claims that John had other children.

The daughter and granddaughter each received $400 in cash or notes. The son Anderson received the "home place" tract of land. Jackson received one-third of the tract known as the "old place", identified as the land between Shade Pate (brother to John) and T. H. Sasser. The remaining land in the "old place" was to be equally divided between George and Richard.

Anderson died early, before his brother Adam sold his interest in Anderson's estate to their brother Richard, 26 January 1863, Wayne County Deed Book 27, page 292. His estate was still in probate, 31 August 1867, when the land division among his heirs was made. The land he received from his father was divided among his living siblings and half-siblings. The heirs of his deceased half-sister, Mary (Pate) Peacock, received one share. The heirs identified by the court were: Adam Pate, Calvin Pate, the heirs of Polly (Mary) Peacock – Penny (Penelope) Mitchell, James D. Peacock and Jesse Peacock; Penny (Penelope) Scott; George (Duncan) Pate and (John) Jackson Pate. The latter two were not fully named in the will, as noted. The brother Richard Washington Pate died soon after he purchased Adam's interest in Anderson's estate and before the land division was made.

The will of John Pate d. 1862 and the estate record of Anderson are sufficient to prove the heirs of John Pate d. 1862.

The children of John from his marriage to Elizabeth [?] were:

Adam – b. ca. 1815, d. p. 1880, m. 1) Mary McGill, 2) Catherine Pate;

Calvin – b. ca. 1819, d. p. 1900, m. 1) Cintha Pate, 2) Rhody [?], 3) Mrs. Drusilla Davis; Mary – b. ca. 1820, d. p. 1850, m. Peter Peacock.

U. S. Census reports show another daughter was born to this marriage 1815-1820, who must have died early.

The children from his marriage to Mary Deans were:

John Jackson – b. 15 September 1837, d. 23 February 1901, m. 1) Pernicia Scott, 2) Elizabeth Ferrell;

George Duncan – b. ca. 1840, d. 26 May 1920; Richard Washington – b. ca. 1842, d. ca. August 1867;

Anderson – b. ca. 1844, d. ca. 26 January 1863;

Penelope – b. 30 February 1845, d. 14 May 1936, m. Joseph A. Scott.

Selected information on the children of John Pate d. 1862 follows.

Adam Pate was the first child of John Pate and Elizabeth. As noted earlier, his marriage record in Wayne County identified the given name of John's first wife. Adam was one of four Pate men from

Wayne County who joined the descendants of Thoroughgood Pate d. ca. 1802 in Richmond County, North Carolina, in the early 1800s. Two were descendants of James Pate d. ca. 1790 -- Thomas Pate d. 1854 and Thoroughgood J. Pate d. 1863. They will be treated in more detail in the narrative on that line of the family. Some detail on Thomas is offered in the report on Thoroughgood Pate d. ca. 1802.

The other two, Adam and Willoughby Pate d. 1834, were descendants of Shadrack d. 1837 and are recognized here. Willoughby Pate was a brother to John Pate d. 1862. He was an uncle to this Adam Pate, in the opinion of the writer. Willoughby will be treated as the next child of Shadrack d. 1837. Records prove he relocated to Richmond County with his father-in-law, Nicholas Smith, in 1815, to be cited.

Available records do not provide a date for the relocation of Adam, or note if the move by his uncle influenced his relocation. He was listed as 15/20 years of age in the Richmond County U. S. Census for 1830, and his wife was 20/30 years. Other U. S. Census reports suggest she was ten to twelve years his senior. The returns for Richmond County in 1850 and Wayne County in 1870 and 1880 suggest Adam may have been born nearer to 1810, than the 1815 year suggested in this report.

Adam was closely associated with Thoroughgood Pate d. 1854 and the children of Willoughby Pate d. 1834. He was a witness to deeds executed by Thomas, and they owned adjacent tracts of land, as proved by the probate of the estate of Thomas. He purchased land from, and sold land to, some of the sons of Willoughby Pate.

Nathaniel P. Gibson conveyed land to the trustees of the Methodist Episcopal Church South, for a church site, on 22 November 1847, Richmond County Deed Book N, page 189. The trustees included two sons of Willoughby (Nicholas and Lewis) and Adam Pate. Note was made earlier that Honor Pate, a daughter of Daniel Pate d. 1825, married Nathaniel Gibson.

Caution is issued that earlier researchers questioned that Adam Pate in Richmond County was the same man of that name in Wayne County. This research found no records of Adam Pate in Wayne County in the timeframe of his appearance in Richmond County. Likewise, no record was found of his presence in Richmond after he returned to Wayne County. His signature on records in both counties was made by a mark. It is the opinion of the writer that the same man made the records in both counties, and he was a son of John Pate d. 1862.

Adam acquired land in Richmond County by grant and purchase, Book Q, page 144, Q:303, and S:92. He sold three tracts of land to Calvin Pate, a son of Thomas Pate d. 1854, as he departed Richmond County, 24 October 1859, Deed Book X, page 478.

He married Mary McGill, a daughter of Allan McGill, before the U. S. Census for 1830 was enumerated. The marriage is proved as the McGill heirs sold the family land, 10 October 1831, Deed Book N, page 437. No children resulted from this marriage. Mary died after the U. S. Census for 1850 was enumerated. She did not sign the deed of sale as Adam departed Richmond County. She was some 10-12 years older than Adam, based on U. S. Census reports.

Adam was not enumerated on the U. S. Census for 1860. He married Catherine Pate in Wayne County in February 1868. The Wayne County marriage book for 1867-1872 identified the parents of each bride and groom. Adam was a son of John Pate and Elizabeth Pate, as reported earlier. Catherine was a daughter of Daniel Pate and Sarah Pate. Daniel was a son of James Pate d. 1826, in the line of James Pate d. ca. 1790. They will be treated in the narrative on that line of the family.

In the opinion of the writer, Catherine Pate was a sister to Thoroughgood J. Pate d. 1863, one of the four men who immigrated to Richmond County in the early 1800s.

Adam and Catherine were enumerated on the U. S. Census for Wayne County in 1870. They had two children in the household, James T. Pate – 10 years old and Mary A. Pate – 8 years. The children were born some six to eight years before Adam and Catherine were married. This research failed to develop additional information on James T. Pate. However, Mary A. Pate married Dennis Davis in Wayne County, 21 August 1884. The marriage record identified her parents as A. Pate and C. Pate. The assumption is offered that the initials represented Adam and Catherine. Further, both children are assumed to have been the children of Adam and Catherine, born before the 1868 marriage.

Adam received Lot 2 in the division of the estate of Anderson Pate. The lot was 37 acres. He sold his interest in his brother's estate to the brother Robert Washington Pate, 26 January 1863, Wayne County Deed Book 27, page 292. Apparently, the early death of Robert Washington prevented the actual transfer of this interest. He sold the lot to Robert Combs, 26 July 1869, Book 29, page 162.

Catherine did not sign the conveyance of 1863, as she and Adam were not married. After their marriage, Adam and Catherine signed the record of 1869 with marks.

Adam was enumerated in the adjoining county of Lenoir in 1880. Catherine was absent. It is assumed she died before 1880. This research failed to find records on Adam after 1880. His death is reported here as p. 1880.

Calvin Pate was the next child born to John and Elizabeth. He was another Wayne County Pate man for whom the given name results in confusion for researchers. Two men, so named, had similar birth years and intermarried with the same families.

One Calvin was a son of Samuel Pate d. 1870, in the line of James Pate d. ca. 1790. His family will be treated in more detail in the narrative on that line. For here, it is necessary to differentiate between the two. This Calvin married Pernicia Pate, a daughter of Silas and Christian (Ammons) Pate. This Silas d. 1858 was a son of Shadrack d. 1837 and a brother of the man treated here, John Pate d. 1862. Silas recognized the daughter in his will of 1858 as "Pernicy Pate". His widow, Christian (Ammons) Pate, recognized her as "my daughter Pernicia, wife of Calvin Pate", and appointed her sons–in-law, Calvin Pate and Dewitt Clinton Pate, as executors of her will.

The U. S. Census for 1850 enumerated the household of this Calvin and Pernicia as adjoining the household of Silas and Christian. They appear on U. S. Census reports as husband and wife through 1880. The name of the wife is sufficient to differentiate this Calvin from the son of John Pate d. 1862, also named Calvin.

Calvin, the son of John, was born ca. 1817. He died after the U. S. Census for 1900 was enumerated and before his widow died in 1905. He had three marriages. The first was to Cenith/Seny Pate, a daughter of Lewis Pate d. 1864. Lewis recognized this daughter as the wife of Calvin Pate in his will of 24 July 1846. Cenith was in the household of her father, without children, for the U. S. Census of 1850. Calvin was in the adjoining county of Johnston in the household of Everitt Weddell, adjacent to his sister and brother-in- law, Peter and Mary (Pate) Peacock. It is accepted that the marriage occurred since Lewis had recognized it in his will. Apparently, it was dissolved in some manner. Available records do not recognize any children from this marriage.

Calvin was enumerated on the 1870 and 1880 Censuses with a wife named Rhody. He married Drusilla Davis in Wayne County, 13 November 1887. U. S. Census reports suggest that the bride was the widow of William Davis. Calvin and Drusilla were listed on the 1900 U. S. Census for Wayne County. The return reported she was without children.

Calvin preceded Drusilla in death. Wayne County Loose Estate Records report Caleb Grant was appointed administrator of her estate, 21 February 1905. The file did not contain additional information.

The estate record for Anderson Pate recognized Calvin as a brother and heir. He received Lot 4 in the division of the land of Anderson. This lot bounded on Robert Combs and the heirs of Elijah Pate, a son of Lewis Pate. This research failed to find record of the disposition of this land. The U. S. Census for 1900 identified Calvin as a homeowner. Perhaps the home was the estate probated when Drusilla died.

Available records fail to identify from any of Calvin's three marriages.

Mary was the next child of John and Elizabeth. She was born ca. 1823 and died after the U. S. Census for 1850 was enumerated. She married Peter Peacock in the 1840s, a son of Jacob Peacock b. 1778, according to Peacock family information. Peter was born ca. 1819 and died after 1880. He married Sally Bass, 5 April 1853, in Wayne County, after the death of Mary.

Mary had three children from her Peacock marriage: Bathsheba/Bashaby – b. ca. 1844, d. unk., m. James Caswell Mitchell; James D. – b. ca. 1846, d. unk.;

Jesse – b. ca. 1850, d. unk.

The daughter, Bathsheba, was recognized in the will of John. Her legacy was $400. She and her brothers were recognized in the division of the land of Anderson Pate. They drew Lot 1, 35 acres, in the division. The lot adjoined land owned by Robert Combs.

U. S. Census reports indicate another daughter was born to John and Elizabeth, who must have died early.

John Jackson Pate was the first child born to John and his second wife, Mary Deans. He was born 15 September 1837, died 23 February 1901, according to his grave marker in Perkins Cemetery. His son, Ulysses S. Pate, was buried with him. Jackson married 1) Pernecia Scott, 2) Elizabeth Ferrell. The marriages are based on death certificates for his two children, one resulting from each marriage. Jackson survived both wives.

He married Pernicia Scott in the mid-1860s and had of Winnie (Winnifred?) – b. ca. 1867, d. 20 April 1930. Winnie married D. L. Lancaster. The parents of Pernicia were not identified in this research. A cursory review of Scott records did not confirm a relationship between Pernicia Scott and Joseph A. Scott, who married Penelope Pate, the sister of Jackson. Jackson purchased the lot inherited by Penelope from the estate of Anderson Pate, Wayne County Deed Book 28, page 119. Pernicia apparently died soon after the birth of Winnie.

He married Elizabeth Ferrall (Farrell) before the U. S. Census was enumerated in 1870. They had of one child, Ulysses S. Pate – b. 5 August 1871, d. 19 August 1917, married Elizabeth (Betsy) Pate, a daughter of Mark and Arsula (Combs) Pate. Betsy was born 11 March 1876, d. 22 April 1951. Mark Pate was a grandson of Lewis Pate, brother to John Pate d. 1862.

Jackson wrote his will 14 February 1898. His son Ulysses was the executor. The probate of his estate reports he had conveyed land in Carteret and Craven Counties to his brother, George D. Pate. Several tracts were devised to the son and daughter. Among them was a tract known as Lot 4 from the division of land of Major Farrell and Lot 3 from the same source. Major was a given name, not a title. U. S. Census reports identify a daughter named Elizabeth in the household of Major Farrell in 1850. The assumption is offered that she was the second wife of Jackson Pate, and a daughter of Major Farrell/Ferrell. The lot of land recognized here was her legacy, or part of her legacy, from her father's estate.

John Jackson appeared in records most commonly as Jackson Pate. He served as a justice of the peace in the 1870s, and was active in real estate in Wayne, Craven, and Carteret counties. He served in Company F, 1st Light Artillery Regiment, in the Civil War.

George Duncan Pate was the second born child of John and Mary (Deans) Pate. He was born ca. 1840 and died 26 May 1920 at St. Luke's Hospital, New Bern, North Carolina. He was buried at Slocum Creek Cemetery, Carteret County, North Carolina, according to his North Carolina death certificate.

This research failed to find record of a marriage for George. However, he was enumerated on the U. S. Census for 1870 in Craven County with a wife represented, Sarah. The 1880 U. S. Census listed him alone, no other person in the household. He was identified as married, not single or widowed. The 1900 U. S. Census listed him as widowed. Available records fail to identify any for George. The assumption is offered that he married Sarah [?]. She preceded him in death, and he had nochildren.

Research confirms that George and his brother, John Jackson Pate, owned land in Carteret County. His death certificate identified his residence as South River, a coastal community of Carteret County.

George received Lot 6 in the division of the land of his brother, Anderson, Wayne Loose Estate Records. This lot adjoined the land he received from the will of his father in 1862. He sold part of the tract to Mark Pate, a son of Willoughby Pate d. 1876, in 1871, Wayne County Deed Book 31, page 332. The remainder of both tracts was sold to his brother, Jackson Pate, in 1874, Book 36, page 126. These acts seem to mark his relocation to the New Bern area.

The third child born to John and Mary (Deans) Pate was another son, Richard Washington Pate. He was born ca. 1842, based on U. S. Census reports and Confederate Army records. He enlisted in Company F, 1st North Carolina Light Artillery Regiment, 2 July 1862, as 20 years of age. This is compatible with his age on U. S. Censuses for 1850 and 1860. He died after 26 January 1863, when he purchased the interests of Adam Pate in the estate of their brother, Anderson. He was deceased when the estate of Anderson was divided in August 1867. Available records fail to provide record of a marriage for Richard.

His presence, and that of his sister Penelope, in the household of 76-year-old Charlotte Deans in 1860 is the basis for assuming she was his grandmother, mother of Mary (Deans) Pate.

Richard was recognized as a son of John in the will probated in 1862. He was a buyer at the estate sale of his father, 12 June 1862. Note appears in the Loose Estate Records of his father that W. G. Howell was paid 22 November 1867 for the division (survey?) of the land of Anderson Pate and Richard Pate, deceased. This research failed to find record of the division of the land of Richard.

The assumption is offered that he died in the Civil War. The unit in which he served was in heavy combat, including Gettysburg Battlefield.

The fourth child, and last son of John and Mary (Deans) Pate, was Anderson Pate. He was born ca. 1844, based on U. S. Census reports. He died by 26 January 1863, only a few months after the death of his father. The date is that of the record by which his brother Richard purchased the interests of Adam Pate in Anderson's estate. The assumption is offered that he had no marriage or.

Anderson was recognized as a son of John in the will of John. The probate of his estate also proves he was a son of John Pate d. 1862 and recognizes his brothers and sisters, as noted earlier.

Anderson was of prime age to have served in the Confederate Army. Records available to this research do not identify any military service. This, and his death soon after his father, leads to the consideration of his health. He may have been handicapped. John devised the home place to him.

One child of John and Mary (Deans) Pate remains for recognition, a daughter, Penelope Pate. She was born 30 February 1845 and died in Duplin County, North Carolina, 12 May 1936, as proved by her North Carolina death certificate. She and many of her family were buried in the Mt. Olive Cemetery in Duplin County.

Penelope (Penny) married Joseph A. Scott, 29 January 1866, in Wayne County. Joseph was born 20 August 1842 and died 29 August 1933, from his death certificate. He was a son of Council and Anne Marie (Pate) Scott. Anne Marie was a daughter of Joseph Pate d. 1847, a descendant of James Pate d. ca. 1790.

Joseph and Penelope moved to Duplin County, North Carolina, and raised their children in the Mt. Olive Community. Their children are proved by death certificates (some of the dates are inconsistent) and U. S. Census reports. They were:

> Richard Bryant – b. 4 June 1863 [?], d. 8 September 1939, m.
>   Barbara Whitman;
> Kizzy – b. 23 August 1870, d. ca. 1880, m. Council Scott;
> Shadrack - b. ca. 1875, d. unk.;
> Ernest J. – b. 23 September 1872, d. January 1948;
> Fred – b. 4 September 1878, d. 12 November 1960;
> Arnold Jackson – b. 4 February 1875, d. 12 June 1927, m.
>   Winnie [?];
> Daisy – b. 9 February 1882, d. 19 September 1969, m. Charles
>   Walton Holmes.

John Pate d. 1862 devised $400 to his daughter, Penny Pate, in his will. She, as Penny Scott, drew Lot 5 in the division of the land of her brother, Anderson Pate, in 1867. The lot was 35 acres. She and her husband, J. A. Scott, sold the 35 acres to her brother, John Jackson Pate, apparently as they relocated to Duplin County, Wayne County Deed Book 28, page 119.

The children of Kizzy were enumerated in the household of Joseph and Penelope in the 1880 U. S. Census. The assumption is offered that Kizzy was deceased at that time. Gurney Scott, a son of Kizzy, died 18 September 1974. His death certificate identified his parents, Council and Kizzy (Scott) Scott. The relationship of this Council

Scott to Joseph A. Scott was not determined. Note has been made that Joseph was a son of an older Council Scott.

The U. S. Census for 1900 identified Penelope as the mother of nine children, six of whom were alive in 1900. Kizzy was one of the deceased children. The other two were not identified in this research.

This completes the report on John Pate d. 1862, a son of Shadrack and Dicey (Peacock) Pate. The report continues with the next child of Shadrack and Dicey, Willoughby Pate.

WILLOUGHBY PATE D. 1834,
SON OF SHADRACK PATE D. 1837

Willoughby Pate was the third child born to Shadrack and Dicey (Peacock) Pate. He was born 10 July 1790, apparently in Wayne County, and died in Richmond County, North Carolina, 26 July 1834. The dates are from a transcript of his family Bible record housed in the Andrea Collection at the South Caroliniana Library, University of South Carolina.

The Bible record was reprinted as a transcript of the original. Later holders made one major, and erroneous, entry to the record. The claim was recorded that this Willoughby Pate was a son of the original Thoroughgood Pate, who settled in Anson and Richmond Counties of North Carolina, identified as Thoroughgood Pate d. ca. 1802 in this report. That claim has been proved to be in error by traditional research and DNA testing, cited earlier in this report.

Sufficient records have been cited to support the claim that Willoughby was a son of Shadrack and Dicey. Otherwise, the Willoughby Pate Family Bible appears to be correct. The marriage cited for him and the children assigned to him are confirmed by traditional research.

Willoughby married Aseneth Smith in Wayne County, the daughter of Nicholas and Elizabeth Smith. Aseneth was born 28 July 1788 and died in Richmond County, 5 December 1855. They had 12 children who lived to maturity.

Nicholas Smith reportedly moved his family from Wayne County to Richmond County in 1815. His three sons-in-law, with their wives, relocated in the same timeframe – Willoughby Pate, Joshua Fletcher, and Daniel Evans. Nicholas Smith died 6 February 1828. His will was probated in Richmond County, 1 April 1828, Will Book 1, pages 203-5.

His wife died 26 February 1831.

A family tradition reported to the writer makes the claim that Aseneth was the second wife of Willoughby. Reportedly, Aseneth was the mother of Smithy, born 15 September 1816, and the children born after her. The children born earlier are reported to have been of the first marriage. No record was found in this research to support this claim. The following observations are important.

The marriage date for Willoughby and Aseneth was recorded in the family Bible record. Unfortunately, time and wear has rendered the date illegible. The transcript viewed in this research recorded the marriage date as (blank)(blank)18(blank). It seems important that an additional marriage was not recognized, and should have been, if one existed. All children born to Willoughby were identified, and they were listed after the marriage of Willoughby and Aseneth was recorded, including those born before Smithy. Further, this Bible record became the family Bible record of the son, Willis Pate, who made no effort to record an earlier marriage of his father.

This report will recognize one marriage for Willoughby Pate, to Aseneth Smith. All children were of this marriage, in the opinion of the writer.

The basis for identifying Willoughby as a son of Shadrack Pate d. 1837 was cited in the narration on his father. Some review of that family information is in order here. The U. S. Census for Wayne County in 1810 enumerated Willoughby with a wife represented. He was listed as adjacent to his father and brothers Lewis and John. Since deed records do not recognize any of the brothers as landowners, it is assumed they lived on land owned by their father. Reference was made earlier that Willoughby and his two brothers served as witnesses for deeds executed by Shadrack Pate, before Willoughby departed Wayne County, Book 7, page 226, 10:509, and 13:196.

The sale, by Shadrack Pate, in Book 10, page 509, was witnessed by Willoughby Pate and Joshua Fletcher. Both were sons-in-law of Nicholas Smith and the date, 6 January 1816, seems to mark the departure of Willoughby from Wayne County. Perhaps this record represents the sale, by Shadrack Pate d. 1837, of the land on which Willoughby lived. The sale price, $99.00, was similar to the price Willoughby paid for 135 acres in Richmond County, $100.00. Records prove each of the other sons of Shadrack acquired land from their father. Perhaps this was his legacy from his father.

Willoughby acquired two tracts of land in Richmond County ten days after he witnessed the Wayne County sale by Shadrack, 16 January 1815, Richmond Deed Book I, pages 189 and 200. Both deeds identify him as "of Wayne County". The witnesses to both records were Thoroughgood Pate and George Wright, a son and son-in-law of Thoroughgood Pate d. ca. 1802.

The first tract was 135 acres acquired from John Peel and his mother, Tabitha. The second was 6 acres acquired from William Peel, a brother to John Peel. Both tracts were located on Panther Creek. This waterway meandered in Richmond County and Marlboro County, South Carolina. It was part of the water system formed around the Little Pee Dee River, a landmark for the homesite of most of the Richmond County Pates.

More information is offered on the Peel/Peele family members in the narration on Penina Pate, presented earlier, as the children of Shadrack Pate were identified. John and William were brothers and sons of Tabitha, the widow of Isaac "Passco" Peele. Their relationship to Willis Peale, the husband of Penelope Pate, sister to Willoughby, was not determined.

Willoughby acquired additional land in Richmond County. He purchased 135 acres from William Bundy in September 1817, on Panther Creek, Book L, page 66. One of his daughters married John L. Bundy. He purchased 135 acres from Daniel Evans (another son-in-law of Nicholas Smith), 31 December 1832, Book O, page 74, and he purchased a tract from Archibald McGee, 9 December 1826, Book N, page 33.

He was identified as a son-in-law in the will of Nicholas Smith, cited earlier, and was recognized with the notation that he had already "received a comfortable portion" of the Smith estate. The "comfortable portion" was not identified.

The family Bible record reports his death date as 26 July 1834. The only extant record created in the probate of his estate was the petition for dower rights filed by the widow in the July Session of Richmond Court in 1837. The record recognized his death, but the month and year of death were never recorded. The death date from the Bible record will be accepted in this report.

The dower petition identified Aseneth (Smith) Pate by her nickname, Senath. She reported her husband died possessed of 400-500 acres of land located on both sides of Panther Creek. She reported her husband was survived by the following "heirs and heiresses":

Carrington Pate, Benagy Pate, Sally Pate now married to Wesley Covington, Smithy Pate alias Gibson, Polly now married to John Bundy, and minors as follows – Lewis, Penny, Lany, Nicholas, Travis, Harris, and Willis. Currington Pate, Smithy Gibson,

Benagy Pate, Wesley Covington and Sarah Covington, and John Bundy and Mary Bundy signed the court notice of the dower petition. G. A. Nichols signed as guardian for the minor heirs.

Aseneth sold 135 acres of her dower land to her son Nicholas, 27 December 1844, Book S, page 175. The remaining 135 acres were sold to her son Willis and daughter Penelope Pate, 20 August 1850, Book U, page 131. The last deed included land, furniture, and livestock. The deed also included the restriction that Willis and Penelope would provide care sufficient to maintain her lifestyle for the remainder of her life, Book U, page 131. She died 5 December 1855.

The children of Willoughby and Aseneth are identified in the Richmond County estate record and the family Bible record. Some vital dates appear in the Bible record and are used here. Julia Claire Pate, a descendant of Willoughby, published *Pate-Adams-Newton* in 1958, a valuable contribution to Pate Family history. The work provides details, vital dates, and marriages for most of the children of Willoughby. The related families of Adams, McCall, Newton, and Covington were treated to some extent. Miss Pate prepared her report from family traditions and vital information. This research confirmed most of the claims by traditional research. Some additions resulted. The error in her identification of the father of Willoughby has been cited earlier.

The children of Willoughby and Aseneth (Smith) Pate were:

Currington – b. November 1810, d. 25 January 1847, m. Rachel
    Covington;
Benagy – b. 9 November 1813, d. p. 1880, m. Elizabeth Parker;
Sarah – b. 30 December 1814, d. p. 1880, m. Wesley Coving-
    ton; Smithy – b. 15 April 1816, d. 22 September 1885, m.
    Pleasant Newton;
Mary – b. 1817, d. p. 1870, m. John L. Bundy;
Lewis – b. 1819, m. Sarah McKinnon;
Penelope – b. 3 November 1820, d. October 1859, m. Thomas
    W. Huckabee;
Nicholas – b. 16 May 1822, d. 10 September 1867, m. Eliza
    Smith;

Julaney – b. 15 March 1824, d. p. 1900, m. Daniel Skipper;

Harris – b. 17 October 1825, d. 9 May 1904, m. 1) Margaret Adams, 2) Mary Odom, 3) Sarah Jane Odom;

Travis – b. 16 March 1827, d. 10 August 1894, m. Angeline Adams;

Willis – b. 26 July 1829, d. 30 December 1888, m. Norvilla Rachel Newton.

A brief account will be offered on each child.

Currington was the first child born to Willoughby and Aseneth. His wife, Rachel (Covington) Pate was the daughter of Samuel and Lucy (Pankey) Covington. She was born ca. 1813 and died before the U. S. Census for 1860 was enumerated. The family made their home in Marlboro County, South Carolina.

Note was made earlier of a tradition that reported Aseneth was the second wife of Willoughby. Julia Claire Pate recognized this tradition with the report that Currington was a half-brother to Travis. As noted earlier, the writer considers the tradition to be without merit. It is recognized here only because Currington was reported to have been a son of the first marriage.

The children of Currington and Rachel (Covington) Pate were:

William Alfred – b. ca. 1832, d. 1865 (Confederate Army), m. Caroline Usher, daughter of John P. and Mary (Newton) Usher;

Sarah – b. ca. 1834, d. unk., moved to Texas and Arkansas, m. [?] Johnson; Willoughby – b. ca. 1836, d. ca. 1860;

Elizabeth – b. ca. 1840, d. unk., m. John C. Usher, brother to Caroline Usher;

Noah – b. ca. 1843, d. (Confederate Army), m. Mary Jane Covington, 28 July 1859, daughter of Wiley and Rebecca Covington, moved to Holmes County, Mississippi, with her parents before the U. S. Census for 1860 was enumerated;

Mary Jane – b. ca. 1847, d. unk., m. Daniel F. Stubbs.

Benagy was the second child of Willoughby and Aseneth (Smith) Pate. His wife, Elizabeth (Parker) Pate, was a daughter of Moses Parker and his second wife, Nancy Parker. Elizabeth was unmarried when the land of her father was divided among his heirs, 11 December 1834, Marlboro County Estate Records. She was married to Benagy by 14 December 1835, when he sold 30 acres of her inheritance to Alex. Graham, Richmond Deed Book O, page 385. The deed described the land as "now belonging to the heirs of Moses Parker". She was recognized as Elizabeth Pate in the Marlboro will of her mother, Nancy Parker, 3 January 1853.

Moses Parker was an impressive character in the Pee Dee River area of the Carolinas. He was active as a patriot in the Revolutionary War, amassed over 4,200 acres of land on both sides of the state line in Richmond and Marlboro counties, and fathered 19 children from his two marriages.

The name of Benagy has been of interest to researchers, including the writer. Most have assumed it was some corruption of Benjamin. It probably was, originally. However, the name was not unusual in the Wayne County area. It has been observed in several families, including Howell, Peacock, and Worrell. These families had a relationship with the Pate Family. The assumption is offered that his given name recognized a Benagy in an earlier generation of one of these three families.

Benagy sold two additional tracts of land in Richmond County to Joshua Fletcher. The buyer was probably the son-in-law of Nicholas Smith, who was also an uncle to Benagy. The sales may mark the departure of Benagy from the Pee Dee River area, to Georgia. The tracts were 199 acres and 30 acres. Deeds were executed 15 July 1837, Richmond Deed Book P, pages 393 and 399. Benagy was enumerated on the U. S. Census for Marlboro County in 1840, adjacent to his brother-in-law, Lewis Parker. However, he had a son born in Georgia about 1839, based on U. S. Census reports. His presence in Marlboro in 1840 may mark a visit back to Carolina.

Benagy and Elizabeth relocated to Decatur County, Georgia. Readers will recall that descendants of Charles Pate d. 1825 relocated to Decatur and Baker counties of Georgia in the 1820s. Descendants of Stephen Pate d. 1839 were in Decatur and Henry counties, Alabama, in the same timeframe. Further, descendants of Samuel Pate d. p. 1810 lived in these areas of Georgia and Alabama.

The children of Benagy and Elizabeth are identified by family records of Joan Pate (whose husband was a descendant of Benagy), by U. S. Census records, Confederate military records, and a North Carolina death certificate.

Henry Harrison Pate was the firstborn child. He appeared as Harris Pate in most records, suggesting he was named to recognize his uncle, Harris Pate, a brother of Benagy. Since his full given name was Henry Harrison, consideration must be given that his uncle was more properly Henry Harrison Pate. The names Harris and Harrison as given or middle names among the Thoroughgood Pate descendants occurs multiple times.

This unmarried son of Benagy was born in Georgia ca. 1839 and died 16 January 1862 at the Confederate Hospital in Richmond, Virginia.

The second child was William Nelson Pate, born 22 September 1843 and died in Montgomery County, Texas, 9 May 1906, (dates according to his grave marker). He married Clarkie Lucy McDaniel in Jackson County, Florida, 27 September 1865 and moved to Texas. He was survived by heirs.

The third child born to Benagy and Elizabeth was Sennie Ann. Note is made that Sennie may have been a nickname for Aseneth. She was born in October 1843, from the 1900 U. S. Census for Dale County, Alabama. She died after the 1920 enumeration. She married Edward H. Woodham in Decatur County, 8 April 1867. The family moved to Dale County, Alabama.

The fourth child was Marinda Pate. U. S. Census reports indicate she was born ca. October 1850, in Georgia. She and her father returned to the Pee Dee River area of the Carolinas. Marinda married Murcock Brown in Marlboro County in 1879. Her death certificate reported that she died in Scotland County, North Carolina, in 1928.

Benagy returned to Marlboro County by 1880, as a widower. He was enumerated in the household of his sister, Smithy (Pate) Gibson and was identified as her brother. The death date for Benagy is unknown.

The 1860 U. S. Census for Decatur County, Georgia, listed Benagy and Elizabeth with a male named William, eight years of age. He apparently died early. Other records identify only four children. Henry Harrison died in the Civil War. William Nelson moved to Texas. Sennie Ann moved to Dale County, Alabama, with her husband and children. Marinda returned to the Carolinas with her father.

The death certificate for Marinda (Pate) Brown listed her birthplace as Tennessee. As noted, this conflicts with U. S. Census reports. Note was made earlier of the relocation of Stephen Pate d. 1839 and his family to Carroll County, Tennessee. Note was also made that one son of this Stephen, Elisha Pate, lived in the Decatur

County, Georgia, area before joining his family in Carroll County, Tennessee. Perhaps the reported Tennessee birthplace for Marinda reflects a trip to Tennessee by her parents.

The third child of Willoughby and Aseneth, Sarah, married Wesley Covington. He was a brother to Rachel Covington who married Currington Pate. As noted earlier, the Covington siblings were of Samuel and Lucy (Panky) Covington.

Wesley and Sarah lived in Marlboro County when the U. S. Census for 1850 was enumerated. They were canvassed in Richmond County, North Carolina, in 1860, 1870, and 1880. The death year for each is reported here as after 1880. The birthplace of their children, reported on U. S. Census reports, reflect repeated moves across the state line.

Their children, as recorded on U. S. Census reports, were:

Mary – b. ca. 1835 SC;
Henry – b. ca. 1837 SC;
Smithy – b. ca. 1839 NC;
Lucy – b. ca. 1841 NC;
Caroline – b. ca. 1843 NC;
Samuel – b. ca. 1845 SC;
Sarah M. – b. ca. 1847 SC;
Aseneth (Celia) – b. ca. 1850 SC;
Martha – b. ca. 1853 NC;
Ada – b. ca. 1859 NC.

The fourth child born to Willoughby and Aseneth was Smithy. The assumption is offered that the given name reflected the maiden name of her mother, Smith. She was identified as Smithy Gibson in the court records that set off the dower lands in the estate of her father, cited earlier. This indicates she married a Gibson as her first marriage.

The report by Julia Claire Pate reports Smithy married Pleasant Newton. This was confirmed by U. S. Census records. She was the wife of Pleasant Newton, a son of James Newton, Jr., when the U. S. Census for Marlboro in 1850 was enumerated. She had no from either marriage.

Reportedly, her sister Penelope lived with Pleasant and Smithy when she met her future husband, Captain Thomas W. Huckabee. The Newtons provided care for her orphaned infant, after the early death of Penelope.

Mary Pate was the fifth child born to Willoughby and Aseneth. She married John L. Bundy about 1837. The family was enumerated in Marlboro County in 1840 and 1850. They moved to Pike County, Alabama, before 1854, when the son Elijah was born. John L. Bundy purchased 120 acres of land from the U. S. Government, 6 November 1858, identified as Sections 20 and 29, Township 8, Range 21. This was in the Spring Hill Community of Pike County.

Their children, identified by U. S. Census reports, were:

> Sarah A. – b. ca. 1837;
> William B. – b. ca. 1839;
> Laura Jane – b. ca. 1841;
> Willis – b. ca. 1842;
> John L. – b. ca. 1844;
> Henry – b. ca. 1846;
> Sherrod/Sherwood – b. ca. 1848;
> Nicholas Parker – b. ca. 1850;
> Elijah – b. ca. 1854;
> Mary A. – b. ca. 1858;
> Celia B. – b. ca. 1861.
> Elijah, Mary A., and Celia B. were born in Alabama. The others were born in South Carolina.

Lewis Pate was the sixth child born to Willoughby and Aseneth. Julia Claire Pate reported that he died in Elizabethtown, North Carolina, as he returned home from the Confederate Army at the end of the Civil War. U. S. Censuses enumerated him in Richmond County in 1850 and 1860.

The children of Lewis and Sarah (McKinnon) Pate were identified in the report of Julia Claire Pate. U. S. Census reports and death certificates confirm the relationship. The children were:

> Eldridge – b. ca. 1841, d. (Confederate Army);
> John Alexander – b. ca. 1842, d. 13 December 1921, Cumberland County;
> Simeon K. – b. 9 July 1845, d. 13 April 1930, m. Anna J. Quick;
> Catherine "Kate" – b. ca. 1846, d. 17 August 1911, Cumberland County, m. Henry McLeod;
> Lewis L. – b. March 1853, d 11 February 1915, Robeson County, m. 1) Nancy J. Quick, 2) Maggie Odom;
> Samuel Hiram – b. 30 August 1856, d. 4 January 1901, m. 1) Leta Hayes, 2) Mary "Mollie" Giles.

North Carolina death certificates area are available for John Alexander, Simeon K., Catherine, and Lewis L.

The seventh child born to Willoughby and Aseneth was Penelope. She lived with her married sister, Smithy (Pate) Newton, when she met and married Captain Thomas W. Huckabee, as reported by Julia Claire Pate. Her orphaned 10-month-old daughter was in the care of Pleasant and Smithy (Pate) Newton on the U. S. Census for Marlboro in 1860. Penelope, apparently, died in childbirth.

The daughter, named Penelope, married Tally Huckabee at maturity. She died 7 April 1932. Her death certificate confirms her parents.

Thomas W. Huckabee married Mrs. Frances Covington, the widow of Noah Covington, after the death of his wife, Penelope.

The eighth child born to Willoughby and Aseneth was Nicholas. He received the given name of his maternal grandfather, Nicholas Smith. He married Eliza Smith, who was a daughter of Richard "Dickey" Smith, a brother to Aseneth. Eliza was born 1 July 1822 and died 8 November 1890. She married William "Billy" Jones after the death of Nicholas and had from both marriages.

The children of Nicholas and Eliza were:

William M. – b. 22 May 1851, d. 4 January 1880, m. Emily
    Smith Adams;
Mary Jane – b. 6 December 1852, m. Richard Tobias Webster;
Eliza Ann "Liddie" – b. November 1856, m. James S. Jernigan;
    Julia Ann – b. 15 July 1859, d. 13 September 1862;
James Henry – b. 17 September 1860, d. 27 December 1916, m.
    RomellaUsher;
Eddie F. – b. 16 April 1861, d. 1893, m. David McCall;
Martha "Mackie" – b. 15 April 1864, m. John McCall.

North Carolina death certificates are recorded for Eliza and James Henry.

The ninth child born to Willoughby and Aseneth was Julaney. She married Daniel B. Skipper, a son of Josiah Skipper, as proved by Richmond County Loose Estate Records for Josiah Skipper.

Julaney and Daniel had three children:

Harris (Harry) – b. September 1847, d. 13 April 1925, m. 1)
    unk., 2) Elizabeth Thomas;

Mary F. – b. 20 February 1848, d. 28 January 1924, m. Robert
    H. Farmer;
Eli – b. 5 May 1857, d. 13 December 1927, m. Hattie McNeill.

North Carolina death certificates confirm the parents and vital
dates for these children.

Harris was the tenth child of Willoughby and Aseneth. His given
name appears in the family Bible record and Richmond County
estate records for his father, as the heirs were identified. Note has
been made of the son of Benagy Pate who appeared as Harris, but
had the proper name of Henry Harrison. Further, Julaney (Pate)
Skipper had a son identified with the given names of Harris, Harrison, and Harry. Perhaps this son of Willoughby had the proper name
of Harrison. Caution is issued that this was not proved. He appears
as Harris in all records available to this research.

Harris married 1) Margaret Adams, a daughter of John P. and
Julia (Newton) Adams. The bride was born 25 April 1831 and died
20 July 1868. He married 2) Mary Odom, a daughter of Philip and
Mary Odom of Marlboro County. She was born 18 December 1842
and died 6 March 1882. He married 3) Mrs. Sarah Jane (Odom)
Parham, a sister to Mary Odom, who was born 23 February 1833
and died 6 August 1911. The dates are from grave markers. Harris
had from the first and second marriages.

The children of Harris and Margaret (Adams) Pate were:

Julia Mary – b. ca. 1852, d. p. 1910, m. Peter L. Newton, who
    remarried in 1887;
Peter L. - b. ca. 1854, d. p. 1910, m. Martha Jane Covington;
M. J. – b. ca. 1860;
Henrietta – b. ca. 1861, d. unk., m. Elijah Gibson;
Claudius "Claude" Beatty – b. 7 June 1865, d. 22 June 1939,
    m. Lillie Hubbard;
Alice – b. ca. 1866.

The children of Harris and Mary (Odom) Pate were:

Henry Thomas – b. 27 February 1870, d. 22 April 1956, m.
    Sallie [?];
Willie J. – b. ca. 1871, d. unk., m. Francis Moore, daughter of
    A. Y. Moore;

Thomas – b. 6 October 1871, d. 21 June 1882;
Edward C. – b. September 1873, d. unk., m. Daisey E. [?];
Sallie – b. 30 October 1880, d. 21 June 1882.

The vital dates are from the death certificate of Henry Thomas Pate and grave markers.

Records indicate that Peter L. Pate married Martha Jane Covington, who was a daughter of Wesley and Sarah (Pate) Covington. This Sarah was a sister to Harris.

Travis Pate was the eleventh child born to Willoughby and Aseneth. He was born 16 March 1827 and died 10 August 1894. He was buried at Hebron Church in Marlboro County. He married Angeline Ann Adams, a daughter of John P. and Julia (Newton) Adams. The bride was born 1 June 1825 and died after 1880.

Travis and Angeline had one son and one daughter. They are identified in the report of Julia Claire Pate and are confirmed by U. S. Census reports. They were:

John Adams Pate – b. 10 November 1849, d. 30 August 1919, m. Jennie McCall, daughter of John L. and Nancy (Sinclair) McCall;

Emily Adams Pate – b. 16 March 1854, d. 24 April 1900, m. 1) William Pate, son of Nicholas Pate, b. 22 May 1851, d. 4 January 1888, 2) William Thomas Jones, 27 February 1889. Emily had from both marriages.

John Adams Pate was the direct ancestor of General Randolph McCall Pate, who served as the twenty-first Commandant of the United States Marine Corps from 1956 to 1959. He was also the direct ancestor of Julia Claire Pate, author of *Newton, Pate, Adams*. She provided additional details on most of the descendants of Willoughby and Aseneth (Smith) Pate, not cited here. Further, she provided details on the Adams, Covington, and Newton families.

The twelfth child born to Willoughby and Aseneth was Willis Pate. Willis was born 26 July 1829 and died in 1888. He married Nouvella Rachel Newton, a daughter of Daniel C. Newton, 28 December 1851. The bride was born 28 December 1834 and died 7 March 1912. Both were buried at Newtonville Cemetery in Marlboro County, South Carolina.

The children of Willis d. 1888 and Rachel were identified by Julia Claire Pate, which was confirmed by U. S. Census reports. Their was:

Horatio C. – b. 7 February 1853, d. 24 February 1905, m.Ida Shirley, 23 September 1875;

Robert Thomas – b. 18 October 1854, d. 8 July 1944, m. Lucy Ann Hubbard;

Daniel William – b. 10 June 1856, d. 22 June 1928, m. Aggie Nora Hubbard, 21 December 1871;

James Henry – b. 11 March 1859, d. 9 May 1860;

William Walter – b. 19 July 1862, d. 16 November 1921, m. Willie [?]. The father-in-law of William Walter Pate is listed in his household on the U. S. Census for 1900 and 1910, but the surname is illegible to the writer.

John Porter – b. 1 August 1864, d. 15 August 1889.

South Carolina death certificates are recorded for sons Daniel William and William Walter, which confirm the reported information.

This completes the report on Willoughby Pate. The report returns to the children of Shadrack and Dicey (Peacock) Pate.

SILAS DANIEL PATE D. 1858, SON OF SHADRACK PATE D. 1837

Silas Daniel was the fourth child born to Shadrack and Dicey (Peacock) Pate. He was born 25 April 1794 and died 12 September 1858, as recorded on his grave marker in Pelt-Pate Cemetery in Wayne County. The inscription also identified him as "a true Predestinarian Baptist", as reported in a published inventory of the cemetery.

The narration on his father provided the basis for the claim that Silas was a son of Shadrack and Dicey. That information will not be repeated here; however, some other records cited here will also support that claim. They include Deed Book 36, page 339. Tracts of land described in these deeds associate sons of Silas with land that appears to have been holdings of Shadrack d. 1837.

Silas married Christian Ammons, a daughter of Jesse and Cynthia (Jernigan) Ammons. The marriage was acknowledged in the will of Jesse Ammons. He devised a slave to "my daughter Christian and her husband Daniel Pate". The identity of Silas as Daniel Pate raises questions. All other records, available to this research, identify him as Silas Pate, without a middle name or initial. Silas was the only Pate of record in Wayne County, in this timeframe, with a wife named Christian. Further, Shadrack Pate d. 1837 recognized Christian as a legatee in his will by her nickname, Christo Pate. Other researchers have reviewed this item and come to the conclusion that Silas had the middle name of Daniel. The writer agrees with the assumption.

Christian (Ammons) Pate was born ca. 1796, based on U. S. Census reports. She died between December 1872, when her will was written, and 7 June 1873, when it was presented for probate.

Silas wrote his will 4 September 1858, and it was presented for probate in November 1858. He recognized his wife and six children as heirs. The widow, Christian Pate, received a horse and buggy, considerable livestock, and furniture. The son, James H. Pate, received one bed and furniture. He had received land earlier, to be cited. The daughters Leathia (Talithia) Pate, Pernicia H. Pate, and Eliza V. Howell, received $150.00 each. The son, Leonard H. Pate, received 40 acres of land on the south side of Stoney Creek, adjoining his own land and the land of Exum Howell. This tract appears to have been the tract Silas Daniel acquired from his father, Shadrack Pate, in 1836, cited earlier. The sons James A. Pate and Silas Pate were to share in the horse and buggy, after the death of the widow, Christian (Ammons) Pate.

He identified his sons Leonard H. Pate and Silas Pate as executors of his will. Leonard H. renounced his right to qualify as co-executor in court, November 1858. Perhaps Leonard H. was ill. His Loose Estate Records report he died in 1858, and his widow was appointed to administer his estate at the December Term of Court.

Silas D. C. Pate was appointed to serve as sole executor for his father's estate. He had been identified only as Silas Pate in the will of his father.

Christian (Ammons) Pate wrote her will in December 1872, the date being omitted. It was presented for probate, 7 June 1873. She recognized three daughters, as follows. Leathia (Talithia) was the wife of DeWitt Clinton Pate and received one-third of the estate. The daughter Pernicia was the wife of Calvin Pate and received one-third of the estate. The daughter Eliza V. Howell (married Stephen Howell) was deceased, and her daughter Ursula, wife of Henry Tilton, and son, Arrington Howell, received the remaining one-third of the estate. The executors of her will were her sons-in-law, Calvin Pate and DeWitt Clinton Pate.

The sons were not recognized. Records, to be cited, prove Leonard H. and James A. were deceased. Leonard was survived by heirs. The son, Silas D. C. Pate, resided in Arkansas, of which more will be offered.

The children of Silas Daniel and Christian (Ammons) Pate will follow, with the available vital information:

Leonard H. – b. ca. 1816, d. 1858, m. Mary [?];
Talithia /Leathia – b. ca. 1819, d. p. 1880, m. DeWitt Clinton Pate;
Pernicia H. – b. ca. 1825, d. p. 1880, m. Calvin Pate;
Eliza V. – b. ca. 1825, d. ca. December 1872, m. Stephen Howell;
James A. – b. ca. 1830, d. 21 July 1862 (Confederate Army);
Silas D. C. – b. 8 April 1834, d. 11 February 1895, m. Mary Borden, 6 June 1872.

Limited information on each child follows.

Leonard H. Pate was the first child born to Silas and Christian. He was born ca. 1816, based on U. S. Census reports. He died between the November Term of Wayne County Court, when he renounced his right to serve as co-executor of his father's will, and the December Term of Court, when his widow was appointed administratrix of his estate.

This research failed to identify the parents of his wife, Mary (Polly). The death certificate for their son, Amos, recognized his father, Leonard Pate. The mother's maiden name and parents were reported as unknown. The death certificate for their daughter, Amy Jane, reported the mother had the maiden surname of Pate. If correct, she could have been the daughter of several families in the line of James Pate d. ca. 1790. The married surname of the mother, while not requested, was commonly reported in these certificates. The birth years for their children indicate they were married before 1845. Mary was enumerated in the household of her daughter, Amy Jane (Imogene) and her husband, Jerry Deans, in 1880. Her death is reported here, after 1880.

The Loose Estate Records of Wayne County report Leonard H. Pate owned 300 acres of land at his death. His widow Mary received 88 acres as her dower. Deeds recorded in Book 39, page 431 and

47/340, in addition to deeds cited earlier, account for the distribution of the land among his heirs.

The heirs of Leonard and Mary are identified in the Loose Estate Records. They were Asa Pate, Debbie Pate, Amos Pate, and Amy Jane (Imogene) Pate. It is of interest that Debbie A., clearly identified as a daughter of Leonard H. in the estate record, was absent from his household on all U. S. Census reports.

Asa was born ca. 1845 and died 2 April 1865 in a Union Army prison at Elmira, NY, as reported in Confederate military records. He enlisted in Company F, 1st Light Artillery Regiment, 5 February 1864. Records of the Elmira prison report that a large number of Confederate prisoners died there in a smallpox epidemic in the Spring of 1865. Asa was recognized as a son of Leonard in the early estate records, but was absent when distribution was made in 1866, indicating his death in the intervening months.

The assumption is offered that Asa never married and died without children.

Debbie A. is reported as the next heir in the estate proceedings. She received her distribution from the estate, $658.14, in 1866. She was absent from the proceedings in 1873, when Amos and Amy Jane (with her husband Jerry Deans) attempted to recover estate assets from Shadrack Pate (an uncle to Leonard H.) and his son, Henry Pate. The fate of Debbie A. is unknown to the writer.

Amos was born ca. 1847. His death is recorded in his North Carolina death certificate, 29 April 1915. He married Louise Howell, a daughter of Exum and Martha Howell. Deed records show Exum Howell was an adjacent landowner to the Leonard H. Pate Family. Louise was a sister to Penelope Howell, who married Silas D. Pate, a son of DeWitt Clinton and Talithia (Pate) Pate. Talithia was a sister to Leonard H. Pate.

Amy Jane appeared with the given name of Imogene in some records. Apparently, this was a corruption of Amy Jane. She was born 1 August 1851 and died 10 April 1921, as reported in her North Carolina death certificate. She married Jerry Deans, 10 February 1876. She was a widow living in the household of Buck Deans on the U. S. Census for 1910. She was identified as his step-mother. As noted earlier, the death certificate identified her mother as Polly Pate.

Talithia (Leathia) N. Pate was the second child of Silas and Christian (Ammons) Pate. She was born ca. 1820, based on U. S. Census reports. She and her husband were enumerated in Wayne County on the U. S. Census for 1880, but were absent in 1900. One researcher reported her death date as 4 September 1891. She appears in records with various spellings for her given name – Lithia, Leafy, Lethia and Talithia. Talithia seems to have been the proper name. Her father recognized her with the middle initial in his will, Leathey N. Pate.

Talithia married DeWitt Clinton Pate, a son of Bryan/Bryant Handley Pate. This Pate Family descended from James Pate d. ca. 1790. The groom will be treated in more detail in the narration of that line.

Silas recognized her as his daughter in his will and devised her $150.00. Christian recognized her as "oldest daughter Leathum, wife of Clinton Pate" and devised her one- third of the estate of Christian. The sons-in-law, Clinton Pate and Calvin Pate, were the executors of Christian's will.

DeWitt Clinton Pate and his wife, Talithia, died intestate. Further, Wayne County Loose Estate Records do not provide probate records of the estate of either. A series of deeds executed late in life indicate they disposed of their land and personal property before death. These include records in Deed Book 25, page 91, 29/328, 37/191, and 36/339.

U. S. Censuses for 1850 to 1870 identify the children of DeWitt Clinton and Talithia. Other records confirm most of them, to be cited. The children were:

> William H. (Henry?) – b. 8 August 1838, d. 15 January 1915,
> m. Mary (Polly) Langston, 6 May 1858;
> Richard J. – b. ca. 1838, d. 6 May 1862 (Confederate Army at
> Gordonsville, Virginia);
> DeWitt Clinton – b. ca. 1843, d. 31 May 1862 (Confederate Army
> at Seven Pines, Virginia);
> Christian Melvina – b. 18 November 1844, d. 5 October 1895,
> m. Thomas J. Pate, 31 August 1863;
> Henry Franklin – b. 12 February 1847, d. 26 October 1915, m.
> 1) Harriett Howell, 2) Henrietta Sherrod, 3) Obelia Davis;
> Silas Dewitt – b. ca. 1849, d 1927, m. 1) Penelope Howell 14
> January 1875, 2) Pernicia Edmundson;
> Lathia Ann – b. ca. 1855, d. unk., m. William C. B. Tilton, 7
> January 1880;
> John B. – b. ca. 1858, d. 1867;
> Daniel Wiler – b. ca. 1861, d. unk.

The deeds cited earlier confirm William H., Henry Franklin, Silas D., and Lathia were children of DeWitt Clinton and Talithia. Confederate military records confirm the same relationship for Richard J. and DeWitt Clinton and provide their death dates. Grave markers in Wayne County provide many of the vital dates cited here.

Silas D. has an informative estate record. Henry Franklin has a death certificate that also adds detail for this report. Most of the marriages are recorded in Wayne County marriage records.

Confederate military records report Richard J. died of disease, and DeWitt Clinton was killed in action.

Thomas J. Pate, the husband of Melvina Pate, was a son of Shadrack Pate d. 1854. This Shadrack was a son of Isham Pate, in the line of James Pate d. ca. 1790, and will be treated in detail in the narrative on that line.

The son, Henry Franklin Pate, married first to Harriett Forehand, the widow of a deceased Confederate soldier. She was a daughter of Cullen and Lucinda (Crumpler) Howell.

Their children were:

Deems Henry Pate, 1868 - 1946;
Absillia Pate, 1872 - 1906;
Charlie Franklin Pate,1874 - 1940;
Daniel Floyd Pate, 1878 - 1954;
Horatio Thomas Pate, 1880 - 1960.

He married second wife Henrietta Sherrod on 24 December 1889; they had no children. Then he married Obelia Davis, 6 November 1896, and they had three children:

Byron Leslie Pate, 1891 - 1980;
Letha Essie Pate, 1892 - 1926;
James Brantley Pate, b. 24 June 1902, d. 17 November 1973, Wayne County, North Carolina, wife Eva Scott.

Silas D. Pate married first to Penelope Howell, a daughter of Exum and Martha Howell.

The bride was a sister to Louisa Howell, who married Amos Pate, a son of Leonard H. Pate. He married second to Pernicia Edmundson, a daughter of William and Louisa (Exum) Edmundson.

217

This research failed to develop information on the two youngest sons of DeWitt Clinton and Talithia (Pate) Pate, John B. Pate and Daniel Wiler Pate. Both were present in the household of DeWitt and Talithia on U. S. Census reports.

Pernicia H. Pate was the third child born to Silas and Christian. The name represented by her middle initial is unknown to the writer. She was born ca. 1825, based on U. S. Census reports, and died after 1893, as proved by land records, to be cited. She married Calvin Pate about 1840, a son of Samuel Pate d. 1870 and his first wife. The family of the groom descended from the line of James Pate d. ca. 1790, and will be treated in more detail in the narrative on that line.

As noted earlier, Silas recognized her as a daughter in his will, and devised her $150.00. Christian, her mother, recognized her as a daughter and the wife of Calvin Pate. She devised her one-third of her estate, with a restriction. Half of the third part was to be equally divided between two daughters of Pernicia – Evaline, the wife of George Crumpler, and Sally (Sarah), the wife of John J. Tilton. The two appear to be the only surviving daughters of Pernicia.

The narration on John Pate d. 1855 recognized the confusion created for family researchers by two men named Calvin Pate in Wayne County. One was the son of John Pate d. 1855, and the other was the man treated here, the son of Samuel Pate d. 1870. For here, it is sufficient to note that the other Calvin Pate d. p. 1900 had three wives, in contrast to the man treated here. Calvin d. p. 1893 and Pernicia appear as husband and wife on all U. S. Census reports for 1850 to 1880. They executed numerous land transactions as husband and wife – Deed Book 43, page 38, 44:106, 48:276, 49:482, and 65:585. The last was the sale of a lot of land in 1893, assumed to be their last landholding, which apparently was disposed of in anticipation of death. Subsequent research into the Calvin Pate who married Pernicia indicates that her maiden name was Hooks. This is borne out in the name given their son, Troy Hooks Pate, 1852 – 1918.

No will or estate record was found for either in this research. They appear to have disposed of all property before death.

The children of Calvin and Perncia are identified from U. S. Census reports. Some are verified by other records. The son, Monroe/Maniford, was party, with Calvin and Pernicia, to the deed recorded in Book 57, page 647. The deed in Book 57, page 647, involved Jane Pate, the wife of their son, Troy Hooks Pate. The North Carolina death certificate for Troy Hooks Pate identified his parents as Calvin and Pernicia. The marriage record for Sarah Pate and John J. Tilton identified her parents as Calvin and Pernicia. The marriage record for the son Sherrod Pate and Charity Daniel identified his father as Calvin; the mother's name was absent. The will of Christian identified Evaline Crumpler as her granddaughter.

The children of Calvin and Pernicia were:

Evaline – b. ca. 1842, d. p. 1900, m. George Crumpler;
James A. – b. ca. 1844, d. 23 June 1862 (ConfederateArmy);
Sherrod – b. ca. 1847, d. p. 1880, m. Charity Daniel;
Sarah – b. ca. 1849, d. 4 January 1916, m. John J. Tilton;
Troy Hooks – b. ca. 1852, d. 8 February 1918, m. Jane Pate, 23 June 1871;
Lamar Monroe – b. ca. 1860, d. unk.;
Almedia – b. ca. 1869, d. unk.

Additional comments on the children follow.

The son born ca. 1860 appeared in records with multiple names. He was identified on the U. S. Census for 1860 as Lamar M. Pate, as Marilie on the 1870 Census, and as Monroe on the 1880 Census. The 1880 Census recognized him as a son of Calvin. He is assumed to have been the Moniford Pate who was a co-signer of the deed with Calvin and Pernicia in 1884, Wayne County Deed Book 51, page 447. This research failed to provide additional information on him.

Almedia was in the household of Calvin for the U. S. Census in 1870, one year old. She is assumed to have been a daughter of Calvin and Pernicia.

The son, James A. Pate, is assumed to have been the man of that name who died of disease, 23 June 1862, in the Confederate Army, stationed at Raleigh, North Carolina. It is of interest that his uncle of the same name, died in the Confederate Army near Richmond, Virginia, 21 July 1862.

James A., the uncle, was party to a group of deeds that are valuable to this research, Deed Book 26, page 145, 26:598, and 31:236. Silas, the father, conveyed 65 acres of land to his son, James A. Pate, 17 August 1858, acknowledging the father-son relationship. Silas reserved a life estate in the land for himself and his wife, Christian. James A. conveyed the land to his brother, Silas D. C. Pate, 95 September 1860. The life estate for Christian was recognized. Silas D. C. Pate and his wife, Mary, conveyed land to a Mr. Weil, after the death of Christian. The deeds reflect the relationship of Silas, Christian, James A., and Silas D. C. and his wife Mary.

Charity Daniel, who married Sherrod, was a daughter of William and Elizabeth Daniel.

Jane Pate, who married Troy Hooks Pate 23 June 1871, was a daughter of Bryan H. Pate and Sarah Pate, descendants of James Pate d. ca. 1790.

Eliza V. Pate was the fourth child born to Silas and Christian. She was born ca. 1828, based on U. S. Census reports. She died after the U. S. Census for 1870 was enumerated. She married Stephen Howell in the mid-1840s. The groom was a son of John Howell, who died in 1838, and a brother to Winnifred Howell, who married Stephen L. Pate d. 1893.

The will of Silas recognized Eliza V. Howell as his daughter and devised $150.00 to her. The will of Christian recognized her daughter, Eliza V. Howell, as deceased in 1872. Her third part of Christian's estate was devised to her two children. They were Ursula, wife of Henry Tilton, and Arrington Howell. Ursula was born ca. 1848, married Henry Tilton, and died before the 1870 U. S. Census was enumerated. Arrington Howell was born 31 August 1855 and died 3 July 1927, as recorded in his North Carolina death certificate. U. S. Census reports identify his wife with the given name of Charlotte, but her maiden name was not identified in this research.

Stephen Howell married Smithy Pate, after the death of Eliza. Smithy was a daughter of Shadrack Pate d. 1891 and his first wife, Penelope Howell. This Shadrack was a brother to Silas Pate, treated here. More will be offered on this family in the narration on Shadrack, to follow.

James A. Pate was the next child born to Silas and Christian. He died in the service of the Confederate Army, 21 July 1862, as noted earlier. The assumption is offered that he was unmarried and died without children.

Silas D. C. Pate was the last-born child to Silas and Christian. His grave marker in Reiff Chapel Cemetery, Washington County, Arkansas, provides dates for his birth and death – 8 April 1834 – 11 February 1895. He married Mary Borden in Wayne County, 6 June 1852.

The names represented by the initials D. C. are unknown. Perhaps they represent the name of his brother-in-law DeWitt Clinton Pate. His sister, Talithia N. Pate appears to have married DeWitt Clinton Pate shortly before Silas D. C. was born. The initials appear in most records throughout his life, but were omitted from the wills of his father and mother. Note has been made that he served as executor of his father's will, which identified him without the initials. The records created in the probate of the estate recognized him as Silas D. C. Pate.

Deeds have been cited to prove the relationship of Silas D. C. Pate to his brother James A. Pate and to their parents. The life estate held by the parents in a tract of land that passed from the father to James A., and later to Silas D. C., was noted.

Silas D. C. and Mary (Borden) Pate departed Wayne County after the death of his father. They were enumerated on the U. S. Census for Lafayette County, Arkansas, in 1860. The U. S. Censuses for Washington County, Arkansas, listed them in 1870 and 1880. The inventory of Reiff Chapel Cemetery, Washington County, lists his grave marker. The name was D. C. Pate. The dates have been noted earlier.

U. S. Census reports listed Silas D. C. and Mary with three children. The name for the oldest daughter in 1860 is almost illegible. It appears to be Jemdisay, born ca. 1855 in North Carolina. This is probably the daughter recognized as E. L. in 1870. Andrew J. was born ca. 1859 in North Carolina. Arabelle S. was born ca. 1874 in Texas. No further information on these children is available.

This completes the report on Silas Pate d. 1858, son of Shadrack and Dicey (Peacock) Pate. The report returns to the remaining children of Shadrack and Dicey.

Celia/Selah Pate was the fifth child born to Shadrack and Dicey. She was born ca. 1800, based on U. S. Census reports. She died 11 October 1882, as recorded in the family Bible record of her brother, Shadrack Pate d. 1891. She married Josiah Gardner after 1840, when she was enumerated in her household on the U. S. Census as Celia Pate, and before 20 November 1844, when she and Josiah conveyed the land she inherited from her father to her brother, Shadrack Pate. The deed recognized them as husband and wife.

Her given name appears in records with various spellings – Celia, Selah, Sealy, etc. Celia appears to have been the proper spelling.

Celia remained at home with her parents until they died. Her father, Shadrack Pate d. 1837, devised the home place (house and five acres of land) to his widow Dicey and their daughter Selah. They were to hold the property for their lifetimes, when it would descend to the youngest son, Shadrack Pate d. 1891. Dicey died in 1838. Celia appears to have been in possession of the property when the U. S. Census for 1840 was enumerated.

Celia married Josiah Gardner about 1844. He was several years her senior and was a widower. The newly-married couple conveyed the home place to her brother, Shadrack, 20 November 1844, Book 19, page 412. The deed acknowledged the origin of the property and her relationship to her brother.

The Gardner Cemetery inventory provides records of interest to this research. Josiah Gardner was born 1781 and died 1865. He was buried beside his first wife, Polly Bell, 1785 -- 1825. An adjoining marker, reportedly, is partially legible, with only the name Celia legible. The assumption is offered that this is the gravesite for Celia (Pate) Gardner. Her death date, 11 October 1882, was recorded in the family Bible record of her brother Shadrack.

Celia was enumerated in the household of her nephew, Howell Pate (son of her brother Shadrack), on the U. S. Census for 1880.

Celia died without children. Josiah Gardner wrote his will in June of 1865. It was presented for probate in November 1865. He acknowledged one son, William T. Gardner and his widow, Celia Gardner.

This completes the report for Celia (Pate) Gardner, daughter of Shadrack Pate d. 1837.

Penelope Pate was the sixth child born to Shadrack and Dicey (Peacock) Pate. She was born ca. 1803, based on various records. The assumption is offered that she died in 1837/1838, after her father wrote his will 24 March 1837 and before her mother wrote her will 20 April 1838. She was recognized in the will of her father, but was omitted from the will of her mother. The will of her mother disposed of personal items, wearing apparel, and livestock. All of the other daughters were recognized. The writer assumes that her absence indicates she was deceased.

Recognition has been given that Peele family information reports that Penelope, the daughter of Shadrack and Dicey, married John Peele and migrated to Indiana Territory in 1815. That claim was recognized, with some detail, as the children of Shadrack were introduced in this report.

Birds of a Feather, a work by John Pierce of the Peacock Family Association, recognizes the marriage of Shadrack Pate and Dicey Peacock. Their daughter Penelope is reported to have married Willis Peele. No proof was cited, but some support for the marriage exists.

Again, details on these issues were presented earlier. For here it is sufficient to say that current research is insufficient to prove the claim in the Peele report or the claim in the Peacock report. The writer does not believe that Penelope Pate, the daughter of Shadrack Pate d. 1837, was Penina Pate who married John Peele, as reported in the Peele report. It seems more probable that Penelope, the daughter of Shadrack and Dicey, married Willis Peale. Willoughby Pate, a brother to Penelope, treated earlier in this report, named a son Willis Pate and a daughter Penelope Pate. Further, five of the siblings of Penelope named a daughter Penelope. None named a daughter Penina. The naming process seems to recognize Penelope as their sister. Readers are urged to review the information presented earlier in the narration on Shadrack.

Given the preceding information, the assumption is offered that Penelope Pate was born ca. 1803, married Willis Peele, and died 1837/1838. A number of men named Willis Peale appear in Wayne County records. Unfortunately, available records fail to identify one with a wife named Penelope. One, of similar age to Penelope Pate, married Elizabeth Johnson. This research was unable to establish their marriage date. It is possible that he married Penelope first and, after her death, married the Johnsonlady.

This completes the report on Penelope, daughter of Shadrack Pate c. 1837.

Mary Pate was the seventh child born to Shadrack and Dicey (Peacock) Pate. Available records fail to provide the definition desired for a report on Mary and her family. Some background information follows.

She was recognized in the will of her father as Mary Roberson. Her mother recognized her with the common nickname for Mary – Polly Roberson. The assumption is offered that Mary was the wife of a Roberson. The only clue to the identity of her husband is the purchase of items at the estate sale of the personal property of her father by Haywood Roberson on 1 May 1837, Wayne County Loose Estate Records.

Haywood Roberson was listed on the U. S. Census for Wayne County in 1830, with what appears to be a young family. His wife and two sons under five years of age were represented. He was enumerated on the 1840 U. S. Census as Haywood Robinson. He was Haywood Roberson in 1850 and Haywood Robinson in 1860. His wife on the 1850 U. S. Census had the given name of Mary. She was identified with the nickname of Polly in 1860.

The spelling of Robinson seems to have been in common use in the later years and will be used in this report.

A daughter named Elizabeth appeared on the U. S. Censuses for 1850 and 1860, born ca. 1838. She married Feraby Grant, 21 May

1869. The marriage record identified her father as Haywood Robinson. The name of her mother was omitted.

The assumption is offered that Mary Pate, the daughter of Shadrack and Dicey, married Haywood Robinson. She was born ca. 1804, and died after the U. S. Census for 1860 was enumerated and before the Census for 1870 was canvassed. Census reports indicate the following were of this marriage. Two males born 1825-1830 do not appear in later records, but are assumed to have been sons. Those who did appear, by name, in later records were:

Jessee – b. ca. 1834; Henry – b. ca. 1836;
Elizabeth – b. ca. 1838, d. unk., m. Feraby Grant, 25 May 1869;
William – b. ca. 1842;
Penelope – b. ca. 1844.

Note needs to be made that Mary had a sister named Penelope. Perhaps she was the namesake of her daughter, Penelope.

This concludes the report on Mary (Pate) Robinson.

Shadrack was the eighth child born to Shadrack and Dicey. The North Carolina death certificate for his daughter Susan identified her father as E. S. Pate. Other records viewed in this research identify him as Shadrack Pate or Shade Pate, with the variant spellings cited for his given name. He was born 10 March 1807 and died 11 October 1891, as recorded in his family Bible record.

He married Penelope Howell, a daughter of Henry and Bethany Howell. They had nine children, who were recorded in the family Bible record. Penelope was born 6 May 1813 and died 11 July 1869. Shadrack was married second to Patience Smith, 27 June 1872. Patience was born 12 December 1826 and died 19 November 1891. The second marriage was without children.

Shadrack was a minister of the Gospel. His obituary appeared in *Zion's Landmark*, a newsletter for the Primitive Baptist faith, Vol. 25, January 1892, page 99. Highlights from the obituary follow. Shadrack joined the Primitive Baptist faith in May 1828, at 21 years of age. He began preaching soon after and served the church at Nahunta, Wayne County, until he died in 1891. His marriage to Penny Howell was recognized, and the birth of nine children was acknowledged. Patience Smith was recognized as his wife when he died. His service to the faith, until his death, was recognized in detail.

His father, Shadrack Pate d. 1837, identified this Shadrack as a son in his will, cited earlier. The homesite and five acres of land were devised to the widow Dicey and daughter Celia for their lifetimes. The homesite was to descend to Shadrack upon their deaths. The widow died in 1838, and Celia married Josiah Gardner soon after. Gardner and his new wife conveyed her interests in the homesite to her brother, Shadrack, 20 November 1844, Wayne County Deed Book 19, page 412. Shadrack also inherited "all other land" owned by his father in 1837.

Records indicate that Shadrack continued to reside on the family homesite until his death. He appears to have sold the "other land" to his nephews Leonard H. Pate, Elijah Pate, and Willoughby Pate.

The family Bible record maintained by Shadrack d. 1891 was published in *Old Dobbs Trails,* April/June 1995, pages 9 and 10.

The children of Shadrack and Penelope are from his Bible Record. Cemetery records, death certificates on some of his children, loose estate records, marriage records, and U.

S. Census reports provide additional information.

The children were:

Mary Ann – b. 11 December 1829, d. 25 September 1908, m. Thomas Whitman Wells;

Henry – b. 8 April 1832, d. 31 October 1882 (grave marker inscribed 3 October 1881), m. Mrs. Elizabeth (Brown) Smith, 31 December 1873;

Hyman – b. 30 August 1834, d. 1912, m. Alice Forehand;

Sarah – b. 30 August 1837, d. 25 December 1904, m. Jeremiah Strickland;

Stanley – b. 20 June 1840, d. 30 October 1862 (Confederate Army);

Smithy – b. 24 June 1843, d. 18 October 1882, m. Stephen Howell;

Imogene – b. 7 January 1846, d. 1903;

Susan – b. 30 November 1848, d. 29 July 1932, m. Goodhue Duran Pate;

Hassell – b. 5 April 1852, d. 23 December 1923.

Limited information on each child follows.

Mary Ann Pate was the first child born to Shadrack and Penelope. She married Thomas Whitman Wells in Wayne County, 27 August 1855. Apparently, the family moved between 1870 and 1880, as they were enumerated on the 1880 U. S. Census in Johnston County. Both were buried at Patetown Cemetery in Wayne County, where her brother Henry Pate is listed as adjacent to them on the cemetery inventory.

The children of Mary Ann (Pate) Wells are identified on U. S. Censuses for 1860 to 1880. The U. S. Census of 1880 is of value. The oldest child, John H., was listed adjacent to his parents. All other children resided at home and were identified as sons and daughters of Thomas and Mary Ann. Further, North Carolina death certificates for the sons John, Henry, and Shadrack Wells identify them as children of Tom Wells and Mary (Polly) Pate. These records provide other information of value to this report.

The children were:

> John Hays – b. 22 February 1858, d. 9 February 1926, m. Winnie Elizabeth Brown;
> Henry – b. 23 June 1860, d. 13 August 1928, m. Bethany Ann Mitchell;
> Polly Ann – b. 9 February 1861, d. 27 August 1933, m. Asa Batten;
> Katura "Kittie" – b. August 1865, d. 9 April 1943;
> Rebecca – b. ca. 1866; Louis Wilson – b. 1870;
> Shadrach W. "Shade" – b. 5 January 1879, d. 29 December 1946.

This concludes the report on Mary Ann (Pate) Wells.

The second child born to Shadrack and Penelope was Henry Pate. His birth and death dates were cited earlier. Note needs to be made that the death date inscribed on his grave marker in Patetown Cemetery is reported to be 3 October 1881. The other date, 31 October 1882, is from his father's Bible record. This report will recognize the record from the family Bible record. Henry was buried adjacent to his sister Mary Ann (Pate) Wells and her husband.

Henry was listed in the household of his father on the U. S. Censuses for 1850 to 1870 as unmarried. He married Elizabeth (Brown) Smith, 31 December 1873. Family information reports the bride was the widow of George Smith. One George Smith was a Confederate Soldier, who served in the 61st North Carolina Infantry Regiment.

The U. S. Census for Wayne County in 1880 listed Henry and Elizabeth with two children from her Smith marriage, Robert – born ca. 1877 and Joseph – born ca. 1879. Both had the surname of Pate in this record. Later records recognized them with the Smith surname.

U. S. Census reports identify three children as of the marriage of Henry and Elizabeth. They were:

Emma – born ca. 1875, d. 2 June 1934, m. Richard Butts;
Henry Marshall – born ca. 1877, d. unk., m. Bettie Butts;
John W. – b. 1878.

The death certificate for Emma (Pate) Butts provides the name of her husband, names of her parents, and needed dates. The death certificate for Norman Henry Pate, a son of Henry Marshall Pate, provides some of the information listed here.

Elizabeth was listed on the U. S. Census for 1900 in the household of Henry Marshall Pate and his family. They were only five households from Joseph Smith, a son from her first marriage.

This concludes the report on Henry Pate d. 1882.

The third child born to Shadrack and Penelope was Hyman Pate. His birth date, 30 August 1834, was recorded in his father's Bible record. His death year of 1912 is from the Loose Estate Records created as his estate was probated. He married Alice Forehand, sister to Sarah Forehand who married Elijah Pate and sister to Elizabeth Forehand who married Martin Pate, as reported by tradition. U. S. Census reports indicate the Forehand sisters were daughters of Bryant and Elizabeth (Peacock) Forehand. Their mother Elizabeth was buried near Hyman and Alice in the Forehand Cemetery, Pikeville, Wayne County, North Carolina. The dates on her grave marker are 1819 – 10 January 1891.

The dates inscribed on the marker for Alice are 1836 -- 1903, as reported in the cemetery inventory.

Hyman was proved to be a son of Shadrack d. 1891 in the Bible record, cited earlier. The children of Hyman and Alice are proved in the Loose Estate Records compiled in the probate of his estate and confirmed by U. S. Census reports. Additionally, North Carolina death certificates for John Pate, Nellie (Pate) Helms, Bethania "Betsy" (Pate) Pate, Laura (Smith) Pate, and two children of DeWitt Starling Pate – John Pate and Mollie (Pate) Carter – add information of value to this research. The U. S. Census for 1900 reports Alice was the mother of eight children, five of whom were alive. The records listed confirm that number of living children in 1900. This research failed to identify one of the deceased children.

The children were:

Bethania "Betsy" L. - b. November 1860, d. 9 February 1940, m. Bryant H. Pate;

DeWitt Starling – b. 11 February 1863, d. 22 July 1898, m. Elizabeth Forehand;

William B. – b. ca. 1865, d. ca. 1880;

John S. (Spicer?) – b. 13 April 1869, d. 5 February 1945, m. Ellen Simpson;

Penelope "Nellie" – b. November 1872, d. 1 September 1938, m. Frederick F. Helms;

Stephen H. – b. 6 November 1875, d. 19 August 1952, m. Laura Smith;

Mary Alice – b. ca. 1879, d. unk., m. Joshua Aycock.

There was a Henrietta Pate in the household of Hyman on the 1870 U. S. Census. The writer believes she was the daughter of Elijah Pate, so named. Elijah was a son of Lewis Pate and was deceased in 1870. Henrietta was not among the heirs of Hyman identified in the probate of his estate.

Additional information on the children follows.

Bryant H. Pate, the husband of Bethania "Betsy", was a son of Major Isham and Elizabeth (Howell) Pate. He was a descendant of James Pate d. ca. 1790, and will be treated in more detail in the narration on that line. Betsy was buried in the Forehand Cemetery, near her parents.

DeWitt Starling Pate preceded his parents in death. His share of his father's estate was divided between his two children – John H. Pate and Mollie (Pate) Carter. Death certificates on each identify their parents as DeWitt and Elizabeth (Forehand) Pate.

William B. appears on the U. S. Census for 1870, five years old. He was absent from the household in 1880. Further, he was not among the heirs recognized when Hyman's estate was divided.

The death certificate for John S. Pate identified his parents, Hyman and Elizabeth (Forehand) Pate, and his spouse, Ellen Simpson.

Penelope "Nellie" died in Raleigh, Wake County, North Carolina, 1 September 1938. Her husband, Frederick Helms, was buried in Forehand Cemetery with her parents. Perhaps Nellie was also buried there in an unmarked grave. The dates inscribed on his marker were 1876 -- 1936.

The death certificate for Stephen H. Pate identified his parents, Hyman and Alice, and his wife, Laura Smith.

Mary Alice, the youngest child of Hyman and Alice, married Joshua Aycock. The marriage and her parents are proved in the death certificate of her daughter Minnie (Aycock) Newman.

The fourth child born to Shadrack and Penelope was Sarah Pate. Sarah married Jeremiah "Jerry" Strickland, 21 February 1856. The groom was born 29 July 1835 and died 15 June 1899, as inscribed on his grave marker in the Patetown Cemetery, where both were buried.

The children of this marriage appear to be identified in U. S. Census reports, cemetery records, and death certificates of some of the children. Nine of the children appear in this Strickland family household on the U. S. Census for 1880. All are identified as sons or daughters of the family. A tenth child was listed on the U. S. Census for 1870, seven years of age, who was absent in 1880. An additional daughter Mary was born 18 December 1883. Her death certificate identified her parents as Jerry Strickland and Sallie (Sarah) Pate. Her husband was Giles Smith.

The children were:

Frances "Fanny" – b. ca. 1859, d. unk., m. 1) Isham Atkinson, 25 March 1874, 2) Festus Bartlett, 11 April 1886;
Daniel – b. 18 January 1861, d. 17 September 1930, m. Annie Baker, 19 January 1913;
Nathan – b. ca. 1863, d. ca. 1880, did not marry;
Abraham – b. 25 July 1865, d. 11 January 1946, m. Colonia "Lana" Williams, 25 February 1891;
Dorsey – b. 27 December 1867, d. 31 January 1950, m. Winnie Howell, 19 October1889;
Melvina – b. ca. 1869, d. ca. 1910, did not marry;
Alonza L. – b. 1 October 1873, d. 30 May 1967, m. Hettic Bell Sauls, 30 May 1899;
Octavia – b. March 1876, d. 19 July 1930, m. Joseph John Smith, 22 January 1899;
Margaret L. – b. 30 September 1878, d. 24 May 1946, m. J. Rom Best, 1 January 1913;
Charles Robert – b. 6 January 1880, d. 9 May 1949, m. Sarah Tilton, 9 January 1901;
Mary – b. 15 December 1883, d. 9 July 1956, m. Giles Smith, 28 February 1903.

Some of the dates cited are in conflict. Most are conflicts in approximate U. S. Census reports and reported data in the records cited.

North Carolina death certificates add detail in this report on Octavius (Octavia) (Strickland) Smith, Mary (Strickland) Smith, Abram/ Abraham Strickland, Dorsey Strickland, Alonzo L. Strickland, Calonia (Williams) Strickland, and Winnie (Howell) Strickland. Published cemetery records for Patetown, Saulstown, and Strickland cemeteries provide some dates cited.

Winnie (Howell) Strickland was a daughter of Stephen Howell and his second wife, Smithy (Pate) Howell. Smithy (Pate) Howell was a sister to Sarah (Pate) Strickland. Calonia (Williams) Strickland was a daughter of Phenius and Acye (Carr) Williams.

The fifth child born to Shadrack and Penelope was Starling Pate. Military records report that Starling enlisted in Company F, 1st Light Artillery Regiment, 2 July 1861, at 21 years of age. He died of disease at Wilmington, North Carolina, 31 October 1862. The assumption is offered that he never married and died without children.

The sixth child born to Shadrack and Penelope was Smithy Pate. Smithy married Stephen Howell as his second wife. The groom was born ca. 1822, based on U. S. Census reports, and died in 1892, as proved by his Loose Estate Records. He was a son of John Howell, who died in 1838, and his wife, Nancy Howell. Stephen was a brother to Winnefred Howell, who married Stephen L. Pate (son of Lewis Pate), as proved by the Loose Estate Records on John Howell.

Stephen Howell first married Eliza V. Pate, a daughter of Silas Pate d. 1858. They had two children, Mary S. (Ursula) Howell, who married Henry Tilton, and Arrington M. Howell. These children were recognized as heirs of Stephen in the settlement of his estate. They were treated in more detail in the narration on Silas Pate d. 1858.

The children of Smithy and Stephen Howell were identified in the probate of his estate, Wayne County Loose Estate Records. U. S. Census reports confirm them. North Carolina death certificates for Archillus Patrick Howell, Louvinia (Roberts) Howell, Winnefred (Howell) Strickland, Stephen Strickland, and Myrtle (Roberts) Strickland add detail to this report.

The children were:

Archillus Patrick – b. 31 February 1867, d. 30 October 1939, m. Louvinia E. Roberts;

Isabella "Bella" – b. ca. 1868, d. (before her father), m. Joseph Forehand;

Penelope "Penny" – b. ca. 1870, d. (before her father), m. John
  Thigpen;
Winnefred – b. 26 February 1873, d. 15 July 1944, m. Dorsey
  Strickland;
Frances "Fannie" – b. ca. 1878, d. p. 1891;
Stephen – b. 1880, d. 7 January 1963, m. Myrtle Roberts;
Smithy – b. ca. 1882, d. p. 1891.

Louvenia E. Roberts and Myrtle Roberts were daughters of Eleanea and Abigail (Lewis) Roberts.

Dorsey Strickland was a son of Jeremiah and Sarah (Pate) Strickland, treated earlier.

Imogene Pate was the seventh child born to Shadrack and Penelope
(Howell) Pate. She resided in the household of her parents for the U. S.
Censuses of 1850 to 1870. She resided with her brother Hassell in 1880
and was identified as his sister. The U. S. Census for 1900 listed her
in the household of Hassell and identified her as his unmarried sister.
Smithy Howell, their niece, was also in the household. The niece was
the 17-year-old daughter of the marriage of their sister, Smithy Pate,
to Stephen Howell. Both parents of the niece were deceased by 1900.

Available records lead to the assumption that Imogene did not
marry and died without children.

The eighth child born to Shadrack and Penelope was Susan Pate.
Susan married Goodhue Duran Pate, 19 September 1874. The groom
was a son of Thoroughgood and Priscilla (Lancaster) Pate, descendants of James Pate d. ca. 1790.

Goodhue Duran Pate, b. 22 June 1845, d. 11 June 1915, Wayne
County, North Carolina. He married Susan Pate, b. 30 November
1845, d. 29 July 1932, Wayne County, North Carolina. This marriage
is indexed in *North Carolina Marriages, 1741-2011*, Female Index,
Number 1874-20, page 5. They had two children:

Martha Pate, b. 14 September 1875, d. 20 October 1949, m.
  Joseph Forehand, 24 February 1897;
Levi Duran Pate, b. 10 December 1879, d. 17 November 1959,
  m. Mary Pollard.

Susan was also the Administratrix, and only surviving sibling of
the estate of her brother, Hassell Pate, when his estate was probated
1915 to 1918.

North Carolina death certificates are available for Susan and Goodhue Duran and for both of their children who reached maturity. These provide needed details for this report and confirm the relationships represented here.

The U. S. Census for 1900 reported Susan was the mother of four children, two of whom were alive. This research failed to identify the deceased children. The assumption is offered that they died early in life and without children.

Joseph Forehand was born January 1874 and died before the U. S. Census for 1910 was enumerated. His wife and two children were enumerated, with Susan's parents, in the household of Susan's brother, Hassell Pate.

Hassell Pate was the ninth and last child of Shadrack and Penelope (Howell) Pate. His birth and death dates were recorded in the Bible record compiled by his father – 5 April 1852 -- 22 December 1914.

Hassell was identified as single in records that would report his marital status. He was associated with his father in various deed and court records, but never with a wife. His sister, Susan (Pate) Pate, was the Administratrix of his estate, Loose Estate Records.

Hassel Pate died unmarried and without children.

This completes the report on Shadrack Pate, son of Shadrack and Dicey (Peacock) Pate. The report now returns to the remaining children of Shadrack and Dicey. Three daughters remain to be identified.

Dicey (Pate) Phillips was the ninth child born to Shadrack and Dicey. Shadrack recognized her in his will for a legacy of five shillings. He did not identify her relationship, but Dicey did recognize her as a daughter in her will. Dicey instructed that her "waring cloths" were to be equally divided between her daughters "Polly Robinson and Dicey Phillips".

Dicey married Robert Phillips ca. 1830. The marriage is recognized when their daughter Mary married William Ham, 3 September 1869. Mary, the bride, was identified as a daughter of Robert Phillips and Dicey Phillips.

Dicey Phillips was enumerated on the U. S. Census for Wayne County in 1840, without a husband represented. It is assumed that she was a widow. She had two daughters reported in the household. The 1850 U. S. Census identified Dicey, 44 years of age, and her daughters Nancy, 18 years, and Mary, 16 years. She was living adjacent to her brothers, Shadrack and Lewis, and sister Celia Pate in 1840. She continued to live as a neighbor to her family in 1850 and 1860. She was absent from the U. S. Census reports after 1860.

The assumption is offered that Dicey Pate married Robert Phillips ca. 1830. They had two daughters, born ca. 1832 and ca. 1834. Robert died before, or soon after, her parents died. Neither her father nor her mother recognized her husband in their wills. Dicey died after the U. S. Census for 1860 was enumerated.

The daughters were:

Nancy – b. ca. 1832;
Mary – b. ca. 1834, d. unk., m. 1) Harry Daniels, 2) William Ham 13 May 1869.

Note needs to be made that the given name of her first husband is from the research of Billie Evans. Dicey married William Ham as Dicey Daniels.

This concludes the available information on this Dicey Pate.

The tenth and last child born to Shadrack and Dicey was Rebecca Pate. She was identified as Rebecca Wright in the will of her father. She and her sisters, Penelope Peal and Mary Roberson, and sister-in-law Christo (Christian) Pate received 15 head of hogs and three cattle. She was identified in the will of her mother as Rebecca Whrite and received wearing apparel, a frock, an apron, and a handkerchief.

This research failed to develop additional information on Rebecca. There was only one Wright on the U. S. Census for Wayne County in 1830, John Wright. He was on the enumerations for 1840 and 1850. His wife in 1830 was of the age of this daughter of Shadrack and Dicey. However, his wife in 1850 was named Eliza O. Wright. Perhaps he married Rebecca Pate, she died early, and he married to Eliza O. [?]. Readers are cautioned that available records fail to support this thought.

This completes the report on Shadrack Pate d. 1837, son of Charles Pate d. p. 1790. The report now returns to the other sons of this Rev. Charles Pate. Two remain for recognition, Joel Pate d. p. 1830 and Ananias Pate d. 1859.

JOEL PATE D. P. 1830,
SON OF CHARLES PATE D. P. 1790

Joel Pate was the third son and seventh child born to Charles Pate d. p. 1790 and his wife, Sarah (Henderson) Pate. He was identified as a son of Rev. Charles Pate by Morgan Edwards in 1772, as the latter inventoried the Baptist churches in the American colonies, cited earlier.

Joel was born ca. 1770, based on U. S. Census reports, probably in Marlboro County, South Carolina. However, a birth across the state line in North Carolina cannot be ruled out. The last record on him, found by this research, was his enumeration on the U. S. Census for Jefferson County, Mississippi in 1830. His death is reported here as after 1830.

The information available on Joel Pate is less than that for the other sons of Rev. Charles Pate d. p. 1790. This includes the brother, Ananias Pate, who accompanied Joel in the move to Mississippi. Some records on Ananias document the association of Joel and Ananias and will appear in this report on Joel, as they add to the history of Joel.

Joel served as a witness to the conveyance of land from his father to his brother, Charles Pate, Jr., 17 March 1785, Deed Book A, p.148. The U. S. Census for Georgetown District, South Carolina, in 1790 enumerated two young males in the household of Rev. Charles Pate. These are assumed to have been Joel and Ananias. This research failed to find record of either brother in later records of North Carolina. As noted earlier, research also failed to find additional records on the father, Rev. Charles Pate.

The assumption is offered that Joel served as a namesake for Joel Pate d. 1871, a cousin and a descendant of Samuel Pate d. p. 1810, to be introduced later. Likewise, Ananias served as a namesake for Ananias Pate d. p. 1880, a son of his nephew Charles Pate d. ca. 1855.

Available records fail to provide a date for the move of the brothers Joel and Ananias to Mississippi. Both were there when they appeared on the official tax list for Adams County in 1810.

Records lead to the assumption that James Dunlap joined the brothers in the relocation. He may have been a brother to Sarah (Dunlap) Pate, the wife of Ananias Pate. Several Dunlap families were enumerated on the Lancaster County, South Carolina, U. S. Census for 1790. Ananias Pate employed, later, an overseer from

Lancaster County, to be cited. One Oliver Dunlap was enumerated in Georgetown District in 1800, of which more will be offered later. James Dunlap was also on the 1810 Adams County tax list.

The assumption is offered that Joel and Ananias married before the relocation. The 1816 state census for Adams County listed the households of James Dunlap, Joel Pate, and Ananias Pate. The return for Joel reported Joel, his wife, and two young children, a boy and a girl. The household for Ananias reported him and his wife, with two sons. Records prove Ananias had no daughters born in 1816. Both owned slaves.

Other records on Ananias need to be recognized. They serve to identify the origin of the Pate brothers. *Carroll County, Mississippi Pioneers,* p. 197, by Betty Weltsline, reports that Ananias Pate was born 17 June 1779 in North Carolina. *The Shute Family of Piedmont Carolina* by J. Ray Shute, reports that Sylvester Shute traveled from Lancaster County, South Carolina, to Carroll County, Mississippi, to become the plantation overseer for Ananias Pate in 1805. Reference was made earlier of the association of the Pate and Dunlap families with Lancaster County, South Carolina.

The Pate brothers continued in Adams County when the U. S. Census for 1820 was enumerated. Joel was listed without children in his household. He and his wife were over 45 years of age. Available records fail to identify the fate of the son and daughter represented on the earlier U. S. Census. The brothers separated after 1820, moving to different counties.

The wife of Joel apparently died after the U. S. Census for 1820 was enumerated. He remarried to Mary Curtis, 19 September 1826, in Jefferson County. He appears on the U. S. Census for Jefferson County in 1830. The household included a young male 15/20 and a wife 20/30 year. This research found no additional records on Joel. The assumption is offered that he died after the 1830 U. S. Census was enumerated.

Several young Pates appear in records of Adams, Jefferson, Claiborne, and Wilkinson counties of this area of Mississippi. It is difficult to relate them to Joel Pate because another Pate Family had appeared in the area. John Pattie died in Adams County, 23 July 1829. His will identified him as from Kentucky. His heirs were his brothers and sisters, who were not identified by name or location.

One Ann Pate married R. F. Colman in Adams County, 10 April 1809. Coleman wrote his will 11 August 1818. The heirs were his wife Nancy Coleman (Ann?) and children Richard A. Coleman, Indiana Coleman, William D. Coleman, Elvira (Coleman) Temple, and an unborn child. The relationship of Ann/Nancy (Pate) Coleman to Joel, if any, is unknown.

No additional information is available on Joel Pate.

ANANIAS PATE D. 1859,
SON OF CHARLES PATE D. P. 1790

Ananias Pate was the last child born to Rev. Charles and Sarah (Henderson) Pate. The vital dates inscribed on his gravemarker in Rose Hill Cemetery, Carroll County, Mississippi, are 17 June 1779 North Carolina – 19 July 1859. The writer believes he was born a few years earlier than 1779, and U. S. Census reports support the belief. The Mississippi state census for 1820 reported he was over 45 years of age, reflecting a birth year before 1775. The U. S. Census for 1840 reported he was 69/70 years of age, reflecting a birth 1770-1780. The inscribed dates will be used in this report, but readers are advised that the birth year was probably near 1775.

His birthplace is recorded as North Carolina in multiple Mississippi records. This research has placed the residence of his parents in South Carolina, at the time of the visit by Morgan Edwards, where Rev. Charles served churches. However, Rev. Charles also owned land in Robeson County, North Carolina. He conveyed the last of the North Carolina land to his oldest son, Charles Pate, Jr., 17 March 1785, Deed Book A, page 140. This was after the birth of Ananias.

Records and facts have been cited to support the claim that Ananias was a son of Rev. Charles Pate, born after the visit by Morgan Edwards. Additional support is found in the names given to his children. The firstborn son was named Joel Henderson Pate. The name apparently recognized the brother of Ananias, Joel Pate, and the maiden surname of his mother, Sarah (Henderson) Pate. His second son was named James Dunlap Pate. The assumption has been offered that James Dunlap was a brother-in-law who joined the Pate brothers in the relocation to Mississippi.

The third son was named Jefferson Charles Pate. The middle name recognized the father of Ananias, Rev. Charles Pate. His only daughter was named Ann Jane Pate. Ann was one of the names Morgan Edwards recorded for the daughters of Rev. Charles Pate, sisters of Ananias.

The names of his children recognized the families of Ananias and his wife.

Ananias and Joel were located in Adams County until after 1820. Ananias was in Claiborne County for the 1830 U. S. Census and Wilkinson County for the 1840 Census. Records from the U. S. Government Land Office show he acquired 320 acres of landfrom the government, 1 August 1821, in Jefferson County. These counties are all located in the Natchez, Mississippi, area. *Reminiscences of Preachers and Churches in Mississippi,*

B. F. Maguire, reports Ananias removed from Whitetown in Wilkinson County in 1842 or 1843 to Carroll County. He settled on Coila Creek and established a large plantation. He was instrumental in establishing the first Christian church in Carroll County, Bethel Church, now called New Hope Christian Church, according to the cited manuscript. Ananias enjoyed material success. Apparently, he prospered in the boom in cotton. He wrote his will June 1856, and it was presented for probate 1 August 1859. His assets included 81 slaves, and his oldest son owned 17 more. The U. S. Census for 1860 identified over 100 slaves owned by his heirs. His will disposed of items associated with wealth – money, carriages, furniture, etc. One report credited him with owning several thousand acres of land. The size of his plantation was not determined, but the Carroll County Deed Index Book lists over 80 deeds executed by Ananias and his family.

The role of Sylvester Shute as overseer of the Pate Plantation has been noted. Shute family information, shared by Mrs. Louise (Jones) Tilghman, reports Shute acquired the Pate Plantation, after the death of Ananias and his sons.

His children are identified in his will, Carroll County Will Book A, page 184, with vital information from grave markers at Rose Hill Cemetery, Carroll County:

Joel Henderson – b. ca. 1814 in Adams County, Mississippi, d. 16 July 1850, m. 1) Sarah Sharkey, 2) Margaret S. Conner;

James Dunlap – b. ca. 1817, d. 17 July 1851 (1861?), m. Eleanor E. Conner;

Jefferson Charles – b. ca. 1826, d. 19 March 1859, m. Eliza Frances [?];

Ann Jane – b. ca. 1832, d. unk., m. Augustus O. Winn, 27 August 1850.

Brief comments are offered on the family of each child.

Joel Henderson Pate was the first child born to Ananias Pate. He married Sarah Sharkey, 10 December 1836, in Clairborne County, Mississippi. The bride was a daughter of Allen N. Sharkey. Allen Sharkey preceded the Pates in the relocation from the Natchez area to Carroll County. He died 14 September 1841 in Carroll County, and his son-in-law Joel Henderson Pate was the executor of his estate. Sarah died 13 January 1846, and Joel remarried to Margaret S. Conner, 25 April 1848. Margaret (Conner) Pate remarried to D. A. Jones, 2 October 1852, after the death of Joel Henderson Pate.

Joel had children from both marriages.

The children of Joel Henderson and Sarah (Sharkey) Pate were:

> Allen Sharkey – b. ca. 1837, d. unk., m. 1) Sarah M. Terrell, 20 January 1859, 2) Arabella Bean, 12 November 1874;
>
> Charles – b. ca. 1840, d. unk., m. Mary E. Pate, 1 November 1859;
>
> James Henderson – b. 5 July 1842, d. 27 June 1862 (Confederate Army).

Joel Henderson Pate had of one daughter from his marriage to Margaret Conner:

> Annie Jane – b. ca. 1850, d. 7 July 1850.

The son, Charles Pate, married Mary A. (or Mary E.) Pate, a first cousin, and daughter of James Dunlap Pate. Family tradition reports that Mary was employed by her Uncle Joel for domestic service when she and Charles decided to marry.

Many of the family were buried at Rose Hill Cemetery, Gravel Hill, Carroll County, Mississippi.

James Dunlap Pate was the second born child of Ananias Pate d. 1859. He married Eleanor Ellen Conner in Wilkinson County, Mississippi, 10 January 1839. *The Carroll County Pioneer Book* by Betty Wiltshire reported his death as 17 July 1851. He was enumerated on the U. S. Censuses for 1860 and 1870. Apparently, the year of 1851 was in error. Perhaps 1871 was the correct year. The cause of his death was reported as a gunshot wound inflicted by James Wesley Conner. Any relationship between James Wesley Conner and Eleanor (Conner) Pate is unknown to the writer.

The children of James Dunlap Pate is identified in U. S. Census reports. They compare favorably with the children assigned to him by Ms. Wiltshire in her *Carroll County Pioneer Book*. They were:

Sarah Jane – b. 1839, d. 14 July 1846, Wilkinson County;
Joel L. C. – b. ca. 1841, d. May 1880, m. Ella A. Lane, 1 November 1859;
Mary E. – b. ca. 1842, d. unk., m. Charles A. Pate, 1 November 1859;
William A. – b. ca. 1843, d. (Confederate Army?);
Sarah A.– b. ca. 1845, d. unk., m. J. A. McKinley, 3 November 1872; Margaret N. – b. ca. 1847, d. unk.;
Olivia- b. ca. 1849, d. unk.;
James Dunlap, Jr. – b. ca. 1854, d. unk., m. Laura W. Kittrell [?].

The last child was identified in the U. S. Census for Carroll County in 1860 as J. D. Pate, Jr., six years old, and in the household of James D. Pate and E. E. Pate. He was identified as Jeff Pate on the 1870 U. S. Census, again in the household of James and Ella Pate. A marriage for Jeff Pate and Laura W. Kittrell is recorded in Mississippi marriages, posted on Ancestry on the Internet. The assumption is offered that these records represent the youngest son of James Dunlap Pate. Recognition is given that he was identified as "Junior" in the household of James Dunlap Pate. Perhaps Jeff was a nickname acquired in later years.

Jefferson Charles Pate was the third child and last son born to Ananias and Sarah (Dunlap) Pate. He married Eliza Frances Smith, 22 February 1848, in Carroll County. The bride was born 21 November 1829 and died 17 September 1881.

The Carroll County Pioneer Book by Ms. Wiltshire and U. S. Census reports identify the children of Jefferson Charles and Eliza Frances (Smith) Pate. They were:

Sarah Frances – b. ca. 1849;
George A. – b. ca. 1854, d. unk., m. 1) Maggie McGrath, 24 December 1874, 2) Josie A. Pate, 8 December 1884;
Bloom – b. ca. 1858;
Anna – b. unk., d. young.

This research failed to identify the parents of Josie A. Pate, who married George A. Pate, as his second wife, 8 December 1884. Researchers of the Pate Family of colonial Southampton County of Virginia have identified descendants of this family in this area of Mississippi. DNA testing proves they are from a different line of ancient people from the subject of this report.

The last child born to Ananias and Sarah was Ann Jane Pate. She married Augustus O. Winn, 27 August 1850. The groom was born ca. 1822 and died 4 May 1858.

The Carroll County Pioneer Book reports the couple had one son, Oliver Winn. The son is not recognized in the U. S. Censuses of 1860 and 1870, with his mother. The will of Augustus O. Winn was recorded in Carroll County Will Book A, page 163. Winn recognized his wife and two nephews, but no son. The assumption is offered that the son, if he existed, preceded his father in death.

Ann J. Winn was enumerated in the household of her brother, James Dunlap Pate, in 1870. She was in the household of her nephew, Joel L. C. Pate, in 1880 and was identified as his aunt.

This ends the report on Ananias Pate d. 1859, son of Charles Pate d. p. 1790.

Further, this ends the report on Charles Pate d. p. 1790 and his descendants. Note was made earlier of the lack of information, in available records, to provide a report on the daughters of Charles d. p. 1790 – Sarah, Mary, Rebecca, and Ann.

The report will move to Samuel Pate d. p. 1810, the next son of Charles Pate d. ca. 1769.

VII

SAMUEL PATE

d. ca. 1810, SON OF CHARLES PATE d. ca. 1769

Introduction

The two preceding chapters in this report treat two sons of Charles Pate d. ca. 1769. Some assumptions and speculation are present in these narrations. However, for the most part, available records are sufficient to permit a definitive report on each. The mix of available records includes some wills, estate records, land records that place successive generations on family property, grave markers, church records, marriage records, census records, etc. The assumptions offered are based on official records, not speculation. The final reports are a credible account of these lines of the Thoroughgood Pate Family, in the opinion of the writer.

Unfortunately, the report on this son of Charles Pate d. ca. 1769 falls short of the definition provided on his older brothers. This research failed to locate a will, estate record, grave marker, or land record that established family lineage on Samuel or any of his children or grandchildren. There are some extant marriage records on a few of his grandchildren.

The family is reported based on the writer's interpretation of associations, locations, migrations, a few deeds, land grants, U. S. Census reports, etc., with limited DNA testing.

Several descendants of Samuel d. ca. 1810 have joined the Pate DNA Project. These include descendants of his sons Bennett, Samuel, and Rev. William. The results do not reveal any definitive mutations, as have been found in some lines of this family. However, the results compare favorably with the results for descendants of the siblings of Samuel – Thoroughgood Pate d. ca. 1802, Charles Pate d. p. 1790, and James Pate d. ca. 1790. The

241

results support the claim that the four were brothers and sons of Charles Pate d. c. 1769.

This research has followed records on the line of this Samuel for some 30 years. One of his fifth-generation descendants was the great-grandmother of the writer, Caroline "Callie" (Pate) Mitchem Cawthon – 1861 -- 1944. Her relationship to Samuel, as with most of his assumed descendants, cannot be proved in the desired fashion. However, the time has arrived that the meager file of available records, and the associations to which they lead, should be recorded. The years of research and personal knowledge of this family justify the report. It is presented with confidence that the results are plausible.

Samuel Pate was the third son born to Charles Pate d. ca. 1769. The birth year, ca. 1732, is arbitrary, based on records that prove the second son was born 1 May 1729. Records cited earlier prove the family lived in the Chowan/Bertie counties area in North Carolina at the time. His given name is a departure from names common to the Thoroughgood Pate Family. One Samuel Pate, of the family from Southampton County, Virginia, was in this area of North Carolina, as noted earlier, and may have served as a namesake for this son of Charles d. ca. 1769. Note needs to be made that DNA testing proves the families were not related, though they share the same surname. Also, of importance, the name is Biblical, and the family produced a number of Baptist ministers.

The death year of Samuel is also arbitrary. He was enumerated on the U. S. Census for Kershaw County, South Carolina, in 1800. His sons Bennett, Jason, and William were near neighbors. He was absent from the U. S. Census for Kershaw in 1810. His son Elijah was enumerated and had an elderly male living in his household, who is assumed to have been his father. Acknowledgement is granted that this research has no record of Samuel after the 1800 return. His death will be listed as ca. 1810.

Samuel grew to maturity in the Stoney Creek area of present-day Wayne County, North Carolina. The area was in Craven County when the elder Charles Pate relocated his family to the Stoney Creek area in the late 1730s. The progression of county names for the area – Craven, Johnston, Dobbs, Wayne – has been noted earlier and will not be repeated here.

The earliest appearance in records for Samuel is his appearance on the muster roll of the Johnston County Militia, 7 October 1755. He and his brother James were members of the militia company commanded by Captain Simon Herring. His brother James was the only son of Charles d. ca. 1769, who remained in the Wayne County area, as did Simon Herring. Herring was listed on the 1769 tax list for Dobbs County, and a will for one of his name was probated in Wayne County 1817/1819. The county names changed as the area progressed. The continued presence of Simon Herring and this James Pate in the locale seems to support the claim that Samuel was of the Stoney Creek Pate Family.

Samuel sold a tract of land between April 1765 and April 1, 1769, as recorded in the extant Dobbs Deed Index. The survival of this record book from the courthouse fires has been documented earlier. The sale was recorded on page 354, suggesting the sale occurred near to the 1769 date. Available records fail to identify his acquisition of the land. The conveyance of land from his father to his brother James is documented in this Index, but no conveyance to Samuel was found.

Samuel sold the land to Daniel Howell. Daniel Howell appears in records of Wayne County, including the 1786 tax list for the county. Also listed in the district with Daniel Howell in 1786 was Daniel Pate, a nephew of Samuel. Daniel Howell died in 1803, as proved by the probate of his will. He owned land at his death that adjoined Stoney Creek, the old Pate homesite. Further, James Pate was guardian for the minor heirs of Daniel Howell. Acknowledgement is granted that available records do not prove that the same Daniel Howell made all of these records, though the assumption is offered that he did. The records support the claim that this Samuel Pate was of the Pate Family in old Dobbs/Wayne County.

Records cited earlier prove the two older brothers, Thoroughgood Pate d. ca. 1802 and Charles Pate d. p. 1790, moved from the Dobbs/Wayne County area to the part of Cumberland County that became Moore County. They moved farther south to the part of Anson County that became Richmond and, later, Scotland County. Samuel joined them in Anson County. His presence is proved as Rice Henderson sold a tract of land to John Turnedge, 10 September 1769, Anson County Deed Book 7, page 243. The witnesses to the conveyance were Thoroughgood Pate and Samuel Pate, brothers.

The brother-in-law relationship of Rice Henderson and Rev. Charles Pate d. p. 1790 was suggested earlier. The three men, Charles Pate, Rice Henderson, and Samuel Pate moved to South Carolina in a similar timeframe. Further, the presence of Rice Henderson and Charles Pate in the Beauty Spot area of South Carolina has been noted. Rev.

Charles Pate was minister of the Beauty Spot Baptist Church. The relationship of these three men to Rev. Henry Easterling and Rev. William Bennett has been noted earlier. Easterling and Bennett succeeded Rev. Charles Pate as minister for the Beauty Spot Church.

The preceding associations are important as note is made that Samuel Pate received a South Carolina land grant, 8 July 1774. The land was 200 acres, surveyed for Samuel Pate, 5 May 1773, on a branch of Three Creeks. The tract adjoined neighbors John Hawthorne and John Ward. Note was made earlier, in the narrative on Charles Pate d. p. 1790, that John Hawthorne gave the land for the Beauty Spot Church site and was a founding member of the Church. Rev. Charles Pate and Rice Henderson were also among the founding members.

Charles Pate also received land by grant on Three Creeks that adjoined John Ward. These records prove the brothers Charles and Samuel received land grants in close proximity. Three Creeks is a tributary of the Greater Pee Dee River in the Beauty Spot area of present-day Marlboro County.

The brothers, Samuel and Charles, relocated to the area of Bladen County, North Carolina {that became Robeson County in 1786) as early as 30 January 1779, Robeson County Deed Book T, page 138. The new home was in the Raft Swamp-Saddletree Swamp area, northeast of present-day Lumberton. Samuel received a land grant for 200 acres on the northeast side of Raft Swamp. Adjoining neighbors were Jesse Oliphant and Chambers Humphrey, who were also neighbors of the Charles Pate Family, as cited earlier.

There is suggestion that Bennett Pate, to be introduced as a son of Samuel, was seated on this land when the U. S. Census for 1790 was enumerated.

Samuel relocated again, to the Mill Branch in Bladen County, southeast of Raft Swamp. The date is unclear. This tract was originally surveyed for Benjamin Willis, 22 September 1784. The surveyor was Return Strong, who was involved in other records on the Samuel Pate Family, to be cited. Willis sold his rights to the grant to Samuel Pate, 26 September 1792. Samuel may have entered the land earlier, because the U. S. Census for 1790 enumerated him in Bladen County, not Robeson. Further, John Rowland sold a Bladen County tract to Solomon Kersey, 20 March 1785. The deed was witnessed by Lydia Rowland and Samuel Pate, Bladen Deed Book 1, page 299.

Samuel acquired another tract of Bladen-Robeson land, 100 acres on Cow Pen Prong Swamp, Robeson Deed Book M, page 184. The location was not identified on available maps. This research failed to find record of his acquisition of the tract, but the deed reports the sale by Samuel to Nathan Horn, 30 September 1785. The record identified Samuel Pate as a resident of Craven County, South Carolina (Beauty Spot Area), suggesting he had returned to South Carolina temporarily. The tract of land had been granted originally to Joseph Oates, 9 November 1764.

William Perritt was a witness to the conveyance to Nathan Horn. The deed apparently was not recorded until 1802, when Samuel had removed to Kershaw County, South Carolina. William Perritt proved the signature of Samuel Pate.

The tract acquired in the Benjamin Willis grant included a grist mill and all other improvements on both sides of Mill Branch. Samuel recorded this record in the Bladen County Deed book, 16 July 1795, Book 7, page 104. It is interesting that a North Carolina land grant for 100 acres on Gapway Swamp was issued to Bennett Pate the same day. Available records fail to provide the conveyance of these tracts by Samuel or Bennett. Later deeds, to be cited, refer to land adjacent to the plantation where Bennett Pate lived in Gapway Swamp.

Gapway Swamp was south of Mill Branch and located on both sides of the state line. Both waterways are identified on modern-day maps of Columbus County. Columbus County was formed from Bladen County in 1808.

Samuel, and perhaps all of his family, departed the Bladen-Robeson County area after the 1795 date cited earlier. They were enumerated on the U. S. Census for Kershaw County, South Carolina, in 1800. Return Strong, the surveyor for the Willis Grant purchased by Samuel Pate, sold a tract of land to Nicholas Gautier, 16 May 1798, Bladen Deed Book 7, page 150. The land was described as located on the north side of Gapway Swamp, near the plantation where Bennett Pate formally lived. These records suggest this Pate Family relocated between 1795 and 1798.

There was confusion in locating this Pate Family in Kershaw County, South Carolina, on the 1800 U. S. Census. The enumerator had misspelled the surname. Samuel was identified as Samuel "Paile". The surname of his sons Bennett, William, and Jason was spelled "Paiste". All were located on the same page, marked by numbers 415 and 157. The surname was spelled correctly on the 1810 U. S. Census. Bennett continued to be present, but Jason and William were absent, of which more will be offered later. The names of Elijah Pate, Allen Pate, and Samuel Pate appeared. Samuel and Elijah were the two remaining sons of old Samuel d. ca. 1810. Allen was a son of the younger Samuel, of which more will be offered later. The elder Samuel does not appear by name in records available to this research after the 1800 U. S. Census. He is assumed to have been the extra old male in the household of Elijah on the 1810 U. S. Census, of which there is no proof. He could have died any time after 1800. His death is listed here as about 1810.

The 1810 U. S. Census for Kershaw County provides vocational activity that involved the Pate Family. A census of manufacturing activity for the county appears at the end of the enumeration. Over 400 looms were active in the manufacture of cotton cloth. They produced over 73,000 yards of finished material that had a value of 50 cents per yard. Members of the Pate Family participated in the weaving industry. Two units that involved Pates were identified – 'Cleber and Pate' and 'Pate and Pate'. The name of Cleber is probably a corruption of Cliborn and probably represents William Cliborn and a Pate, probably Bennett Pate. These men were neighbors in Robeson County, North Carolina, and Kershaw County, South Carolina, and were enumerated in adjacent Kershaw County households in 1810. 'Pate and Pate' may have recognized the two sons of Samuel d. ca. 1810, who remained in the county – Elijah and Samuel. Each unit had two looms. 'Cleber and Pate' produced 200 yards of cloth, and 'Pate and Pate' produced 100 yards.

Comments on the Pate and Cliborn family association are in order. Cliborn appears in various spellings – Clayborn, Clyborne, Cleborn, etc. Rice Henderson, brother-in-law of Rev. Charles Pate, conveyed a tract of land to John Clayborn, 18 December 1779, Bladen Deed Book 19, page 439. The land was located in the Saddletree Swamp area that became Robeson County. Saddletree has been identified as the home site of the Charles Pate and Samuel Pate Families. John Clyborn and William Clyborn were enumerated in adjacent households on the 1790 U. S. Census of Robeson County. William Cliborn owned land adjacent to members of the Charles Pate Family in Robeson County, cited earlier. He and Bennett Pate were enumerated on the U. S. Census for 1790 as near neighbors.

Bennett Pate and William Cliborn were close neighbors on the U. S. Census for Kershaw County, South Carolina, in 1800. They were in adjacent households on the 1810 U. S. Census. Note has been made that the Pate and Cliborn families were jointly involved in commercial weaving by 1810. Then, it is not surprising that Levi Pate, to be introduced, married Sarah Cliborn, a daughter of William Cliborn, to be cited.

Note was made earlier of the absence of traditional records to prove the children of Samuel Pate d. ca. 1810. This research found no record to identify his daughters. U. S.

Census reports suggest he had at least two daughters, possibly three. An attempt to identify any of these would be speculation and is avoided. This research identified five sons by a mix of records, which will be cited – Bennett, Samuel, Elijah, William, and Jason. The U. S. Census reports indicate all five lived near, or adjacent to, Samuel d. ca. 1810 in Kershaw County. Records cited earlier report on association between Samuel and Bennett, the oldest son, in Bladen and Robeson counties, North Carolina.

The U. S. Census for 1790 listed the household of Bennett Pate in Robeson County, with two mature males and two females. The assumption is offered that the listing represents Bennett and a married brother and their wives. The 1790 U. S. Census of the household of their father, Samuel Pate d. ca. 1810, accounted for only three sons. The assumption is offered that the other two, Bennett and Samuel or Elijah, were in the household of Bennett. Thus, all five sons were represented on the 1790 Census.

Valuable support for the claim that three of these men were sons of Samuel is found in DNA testing. Descendants of Bennett, Samuel, and William are in the Pate DNA Project. The results support the claim that these three men had a common ancestor. Other supportive information will be cited as the report progresses.

The association of Samuel d. ca. 1810 and his brother, Rev. Charles Pate, with Rice Henderson, Rev. Henry Easterling, and Rev. William Bennett has been noted. Note was made in the narrative on Rev. Charles Pate that his children and the children of Rev. Easterling shared given names. Note has been made that Shadrack Pate d. 1837 acquired Wayne County land from Rev. William Bennett. The assumption is offered that William Bennett served as namesake for the first son born to Samuel Pate, Bennett Pate.

Bennett was born ca. 1755 in the Stoney Creek area of present-day Wayne County, North Carolina. He died after the U. S.

Census for 1830 was enumerated, in Thomas County, Georgia. His death is listed as p. 1830.

The association of Bennett and Samuel d. ca. 1810 in Robeson and Bladen counties of North Carolina has been noted. They relocated to Kershaw, South Carolina. between 1795 and 1798, as cited earlier.

The second-born son of Samuel d. ca. 1810 was named for his father, Samuel. The younger Samuel was born ca. 1760, before the family departed the Stoney Creek area of Wayne County. The last record made by him, found by this research, was a Bibb County, Alabama, court record dated 21 October 1833, to be cited. He died after 1833.

Samuel was named for his father and appears on the 1810 U. S. Census of Kershaw County, living adjacent to his brothers Elijah and Bennett. This research failed to find an earlier record made by him.

Samuel d. p. 1833 migrated to Georgia with his three sons, and later to Alabama with his son Allen. His brothers Bennett and William also moved to Georgia.

Elijah was the third son born to Samuel d. ca. 1810. He was born ca. 1765, probably in the Stoney Creek area of present-day Wayne County, North Carolina. The Dobbs County land sale, cited earlier, indicates Samuel moved his family between 1765 and 1769. The move was probably nearer to the later year, supporting the claim that Elijah was born before the relocation.

His first appearance in records by name is the U. S. Census for Kershaw County in 1810. The assumption has been offered that his father was represented in Elijah's household in 1810. His death year is unknown to this research. He was absent from all records examined after he sold land in Kershaw County in 1817, to be cited. He will be reported here as died after 1817.

William was the fourth son born to Samuel d. ca. 1810. He was born ca. 1774, probably in South Carolina. He died in what was then Dooly County, Georgia, in 1841. He moved to Georgia after appearing on the U. S. Census for Kershaw County in 1800, with his father and brothers Bennett and Jason.

Jason was the fifth son born to Samuel d. ca. 1810, whose full name is believed by the writer to be Thoroughgood Jason Pate (also known as T. J.). He was born ca. 1777, probably in South Carolina. He appeared in deed records of Lancaster County, South Carolina, in the 1790s. This research failed to find records on Jason after his appearance on the U. S. Census for Kershaw County in 1800, until his appearance on the U. S. Census in 1860 for Chesterville County, South Carolina. His death will be listed here as died p. 1860.

Detailed reports will follow on each of his sons.

Comments need to be presented on Levi Pate of Kershaw County before treating the assumed sons of Samuel Pate d.ca. 1810.

The earliest record on Levi Pate, found in this research, is his purchase of 130 acres of land in Kershaw County, 25 November 1818, Deed Book K, page 239. The grantor was his father-in-law, William Cliborn, Sr. William Cliborn, Jr., was a witness to the deed. The land was located on Little Lynches Creek in Kershaw County.

Levi was the only Pate enumerated on the U. S. Census for Kershaw County in 1820. The patriarch of the family, Samuel Pate d. ca. 1810, was deceased. His sons Bennett, Samuel, and William were located in Georgia. The fate of Elijah and Jason is questionable, of which more will be said later. Suffice it to say, for here, that Elijah and Jason are absent from available records of Kershaw and the adjoining counties of South Carolina.

The origin of Levi Pate has been an unresolved for a number of researchers, including the writer. Preston Newman and Eleazar Scarborough shared detailed research with the writer in past decades. Harold Rad Pate has added detail for later generations. Preston Newman published his work, in typescript format, in 1993. There was a plurality of agreement, at that time, that Levi was a grandson of Samuel Pate d. ca. 1810, through Elijah or Bennett.

DNA testing is a valuable new tool for genealogy, which has given us a new term "genetic genealogy". Unlike traditional genealogy, genetic genealogy is conclusive in establishing family bloodlines. The male Y-chromosome provides definition to some unresolved questions of past years. Persons tested are placed into haplogroups by genetic characteristics. For the practical use of modern genealogy, persons from different haplogroups have no blood relationship. The three different major Pate Family lines in the Pate DNA Project are identified by their unique haplogroups.

The Pate DNA Project has sufficient data to identify all descendants of Throughgood Pate d. 1713 as Haplogroup I-M223. Nine descendants of Levi Pate have joined the Project and tested in Haplogroup R-M269. Descendants of three sons of Samuel d. ca. 1810, Bennett, Samuel, and William, have tested in Haplogroup I-M223. The results leave no question that Levi Pate did not have a paternal relationship to Samuel Pate d. ca. 1810.

The term "non-paternal event" has been used to describe this situation. Newly-found information, in this case DNA testing, proves a person previously accepted as of a given man may not be genetically related to that person. Circumstances resulting in this error include, but are not limited to, step-sons who adopted the surname of the step-father, children left as orphans in the frontier society who adopted the surname of a befriending family, marital infidelity, formal adoption, etc.

Family tradition shared with the writer in past years made the claim that Levi Pate was not associated with the Pate Family on the Kershaw U. S. Censuses of 1800 and 1810. The failure of Levi to have a genetic likeness to the family of Samuel Pate d. ca. 1810 could be interpreted as support for that claim. This would suggest that Levi entered the Kershaw locale after the departure of the I2b1 Pates from the county. Available records do not support that claim. The association of William Cliborn with Samuel and his son Bennett in Bladen and Robeson, North Carolina, and in Kershaw South Carolina define a long-term relationship of the families. The marriage of Levi Pate to a daughter of William Cliborn seems to have evolved from that association. The records support the assumption that Levi was among the Pates of Kershaw 1800-1810.

Two Pate Families on the 1800 Kershaw U. S. Census had a young male the age of Levi, Samuel d. ca. 1810 and his son Bennett. Further, available records lead to the claim that Bennett had only two sons, Samuel born ca. 1800 and Joel born ca. 1805. Census reports list three potential sons. The assumption is offered that Levi was the 10/16- year-old male in the household of Bennett in 1800 and the 16/26-year-old male in the same household in 1810. Further, the claim is offered that Bennett was the Pate associated with William Cliborn on the manufacturing census of weaving firms in Kershaw County in 1810, cited earlier.

A young male was not represented in the household of Bennett Pate on the U. S. Census for 1790. The enumeration date for that return was 2 August 1790. A child born after that date, in 1790, would not appear on the return. U. S. Census reports reflect a birth year of 1790 for Levi Pate.

Given the preceding information, the writer offers the assumption that Levi Pate came to Kershaw County with the family of Bennett Pate. His presence with the Pate Family resulted from causes unknown, with marriage and adoption among the options. He remained in Kershaw County as the Pate Families moved to

250

other areas. He and his descendants carry the Pate surname and are recognized by this report.

Levi Pate was born ca. 1790 in North Carolina. The birthplace appears on U. S. Census reports and is recorded in family information from Eleazar Scarborough. He married, first, to Sarah (Sallie) Cliborn, a daughter of William Cliborn, as recorded in family information. He died 23 April 1873, as reported by Harold Rad Pate. Sarah (Cliborn) Pate was born ca. 1768 and died 5 August 1864.

Levi married, secondly, Gatsey Robinson, 10 January 1865, according to their marriage contract, Deed Book W, pages 255-256. Her South Carolina death certificate reports she was a daughter of Frank Robinson. The writer questions this information. Gatsey, nine years of age, was enumerated in the household of Isaiah and Sarah Robinson on the U. S. Census for Kershaw County in 1850. The household had 12 children, Gatsey and 6-year- old Levi Robinson being the youngest. This research was unable to locate a Frank Robinson of the age to have been the father of Gatsey. South Carolina death certificates are available for Gatsey and Levi Robinson. Levi was a son of Isaiah and Sarah (Deason) Robinson. The assumption is offered that Gatsey was a sister to Levi Robinson and a daughter of Isaiah and Sarah (Deason) Robinson.

Gatsey (Robinson) Pate died 26 April 1916.

The children of the marriage of Levi Pate and Sarah Cliborn is reported here as they are listed in the manuscript by Preston Newman. They are correct in the opinion of the writer. Some vital dates have been added from the research of Harold Rad Pate. Mr. Newman recognized one unnamed daughter born 1810-1815. The other children were:

James – b. ca. 1815, d. ca. 1855, m. Harriett Railey;
Rebecca – b. ca. 1818, d. 2 August 1848, m. Ervin Railey (he remarried to her sister, Sarah, after the death of Rebecca);
Henry – b. ca. 1820, d. 31 August 1875, m. 1) Elizabeth V. Peebles, 22 December 1847, 2) Emma Peebles, a sister to Elizabeth;
Levi, Jr. – b. ca. 1822, d. 13 July 1864 (Confederate Army in Virginia), m. Dorcas Hough;
Sarah – b. ca. 1826, d. 16 September 1856, Pike County, Alabama, m. Ervin Railey (see Rebecca above);
Chapman – b. 22 February 1826, d. 26 January 1891, Lee County, South Carolina, m. Nancy Segars, 6 June 1850.

Some additional comments on these children follow.

Harriett Railey and Ervin Railey were children of William and Mourning Railey. Ervin moved to Pike County, Alabama, reportedly after his marriage to Sarah Pate. He then married Mary A. P. Williams, 18 September 1856, after the death of Sarah, perhaps in childbirth. However, there is some confusion as to the marriage of Ervin Railey to Sarah Pate, as noted here. Marriage records in Barbour County, Alabama (which adjoins Pike County), listed the marriage of Sarah Ann Pate to Nathaniel G. Raeley, 30 December 1845.

James and Harriett (Railey) Pate moved to Yalobusha County, Mississippi. They were enumerated there on the U. S. Census for 1850. They returned to Kershaw before he died about 1855. Harriett and her children were enumerated in the household of her father in 1870. Descendants of James and Harriett returned to Mississippi, and later moved to Texas.

Henry had from both marriages. Some researchers have assigned him the middle name of Anderson. The writer believes that middle name represented his son named Henry Anderson Pate.

Dorcas Hough was a daughter of Moses Hough.

Chapman Pate married Nancy Segars, a daughter of John and Dicey (Hayes) Segars. The bride was born ca. 1836 and died 1919 in Lee County, according to her death certificate.

One son resulted from the marriage of Levi Pate to his second wife, Gatsey Robinson, in the opinion of the writer. Some researchers have assigned other children to their marriage. The opinion is offered that they were not children of Levi, at least during the time of his marriage to Gatsey.

The son was Jesse Pate, born 1867 and died 5 April 1916. The dates are from his South Carolina death certificate. He married Henrietta Mingo, a daughter of Augustus and Jincey (Miller) Mingo, per her death certificate. The bride was born in 1871 and died 21 October 1916 of typhoid fever. Jesse had died five months earlier of lobar pneumonia.

Available records indicate that Gatsey (Robinson) Pate had outside her marriage to Levi Pate. The U. S. Census for Kershaw County in 1870 listed Levi Pate with his 28-year old- wife, Gatsey. Note has been made that they were married in 1865. The household included children as follows: Susan Pate – 10 years old, Frances Pate – 8 years old, and Jesse Pate – 4 years old. The assumption is offered that Susan and Frances were children born before her marriage to Levi. Their father is unknown. The U. S. Census for 1880 enumerated Gatsey in the household of Henry T. Pate, a son of James and Harriett (Railey) Pate. Also in the household was Jesse Pate – 13 years and William Pate – 1 year. The wife of Henry T. Pate was Susan Pate – 21 years of age.

The relationship of Gatsey, Jesse, and William to the head of the household provides the information needed to interpret this puzzle. The writer claims Susan, the wife of Henry T., was the 10-year-old daughter in the household of Levi Pate in 1870. The 1880 U. S. Census identified Gatsey as the mother-in-law of Henry T. Pate. He had married Susan, the 10-year-old daughter of Gatsey on the 1870 U. S. Census. Jesse and William were brothers-in-law of Henry T., because they were half-brothers of Jesse. All three, Susan, Jesse, and William, had different fathers. Levi Pate was the father of Jesse. Available records fail to identify the fathers of the others.

This ends the report on Levi Pate.

The report moves to the five assumed sons of Samuel Pate d. ca. 1810.

BENNETT PATE D. P. 1830, SON OF SAMUEL PATE D. CA. 1810

Bennett Pate was born ca. 1755, based on his appearance in records and his age on U. S. Census reports. It is assumed he was born before his father departed Old Dobbs County, North Carolina. He died in Thomas County, Georgia, after the U. S. Census for 1830 was enumerated. His wife had the given name of Elizabeth, but her surname is unknown. North Carolina land grant records place Bennett on a tract of land in Gapway Swamp that adjoins the widow Summerset. Citation for this land grant was presentedearlier.

The association of Bennett with the family of his uncle Charles Pate d. p. 1790 was noted earlier, as was his presence on the U. S. Census for Robeson County as a neighbor to the family of his uncle. Records were cited to support the claim that Bennett removed from North Carolina to Kershaw County, South Carolina in the 1765-1782 timeframe. He with his father and some siblings were enumerated in Kershaw County on the U. S. Census for 1800. Their surname was misspelled as Paile and Paiste.

U. S. Census reports associate the Pate Family in Kershaw County with the weaving industry. Further, the association of Bennett Pate and William Cliborn in Robeson County continued in Kershaw. The narration on Levi Pate, presented earlier, makes the case for Levi Pate being a boy adopted, in some fashion, by Bennett Pate.

Bennett departed Kershaw County for the Montgomery/Emanuel counties area of Georgia after the 1810 U. S. Census was enumerated.

Montgomery County, Georgia, by Dorsey and Derden, recognized that a large number of early settlers came to Montgomery from Robeson County, North Carolina, and the upper part of South Carolina (Kershaw County area) in the 1800-1815 timeframe. These included Bennett Pate and his family. Montgomery County jury records report Bennett Pate and Greenberry Akridge were jurors, 13 July 1816. Greenberry Akridge will be introduced later. For here, it is important to note the association and recognize that the oldest daughter of Akridge married the oldest son of Bennett Pate. The families migrated through Georgia and Alabama together for several decades.

The U. S. Census for 1820 enumerated Bennett Pate in Emanuel County, Georgia, an adjoining county to Montgomery. Research failed to provide record of land ownership by Bennett in Kershaw, Montgomery, or Emanuel counties. He acquired land in Georgia in the Georgia land lottery of 1820.

Bennett Pate, of the 395th District of Emanuel County, drew Lot 378 in the 9th District of Irwin County. The lot was 490 acres. The land was surveyed for Bennett, 4 May 1820. The surveyor's notes reported the land was on low ground and contained "bay galls and ponds". Today the lot is in Cook County. It also appeared in Lowndes and Berrien counties over the years, as county lines were revised.

No record was found of the sale of this lot in any of the named counties. The frequent boundary changes and courthouse fires in Berrien and Lowndes counties may account for the absence of this record.

Records suggest the family made their home in Thomas County.

Bennett Pate died without a will or estate record. As with so many in the Samuel Pate d. ca. 1810 line, there is no available record to identify his heirs or.

Note was made earlier that U. S. Census reports support the claim that Bennett was the father of two sons, Samuel Pate b. ca. 1800, South Carolina, and Joel Pate b. ca. 1805, South Carolina. This research found no records to suggest additional sons. Levi Pate, treated earlier, was raised in the household, but was not a blood relative, proof cited earlier.

The daughters are more confusing. The U. S. Censuses for 1800 ("Benet Paile") amd 1810 ("Bennet Pate") enumerated his household with net count of six younger females. These two census enumerations suggest that they were daughters of Bennett Pate. Some may have been adopted, as was Levi Pate, and some may have died before maturity. This research found records to identify three of them:

Mary b. ca. 1805, South Carolina; Fereby b. 1800-10, South Carolina; Nancy b. ca. 1815, South Carolina.

Support for the claim that these five were children of Bennett Pate follows. Cutts family records shared by Ella Bea Johnson report that William Porter Cutts married Mary Pate in Thomas County, Georgia, ca. 1822. This research failed to find marriage records recorded in Thomas County that early. The U. S. Census for Thomas County in 1830 enumerated William P. Cutts, Bennett Pate, Samuel Pate, and Joel Pate in adjacent households. Cutts and the two Pate brothers migrated to the same area of Alabama, and later Florida after the death of Bennett. The last record found by this research on this Samuel Pate was his sale of Walton County, Florida, land to Wm. C. King, 14 December 1867. King was related to the Cutts family by marriage. Joel Pate named sons Bennett and Joel, Samuel Pate named a son Joel, and Cutts named a son Joel. The association and common names support the claim that Joel Pate, Samuel Pate, and Mary (Pate) Cutts were siblings and children of Bennett Pate.

Fereby Pate married Samuel Miller in Montgomery County, Georgia, 4 November 1819. Bennett was the only Pate of record in Montgomery or Emanuel County, and was of the age to have been her father. Fereby/Phereby had the given name of the wife of Charles Pate d. 1825, a first cousin of Bennett. Note has been made that Charles and Bennett were near neighbors on Raft Swamp in Robeson County, North Carolina. The assumption is offered that Fereby (Pate) Miller was a daughter of Bennett Pate.

The Samuel Miller family was enumerated on the U. S. Census for Montgomery County in 1840. The family was reported with two daughters under 5 years of age and one son 5-10 years of age. This research failed to find additional records on this family.

Nancy Pate married Job Elbert Wilder Smith in Thomas County, 4 February 1834. This Smith household had an elderly female in the U. S. Census for Lowndes County, Georgia, in 1840. She continued to be present in the household in 1850 and was identified as Elizabeth Pate, 85 years old and born in North Carolina. After searching all

Pate households in the Georgia area of concern, it is assumed that this Elizabeth Pate was the widow of Bennett and the mother-in-law of Job E. W. Smith. If so, she was the wife represented in the household of Bennett on the Robeson County, North Carolina, U. S. Census for 1790, and all subsequent Census reports.

In review, this research assigns five children to Bennett Pate. Perhaps other daughters existed, and available records fail to identify them. The children were:

> Samuel, b. ca. 1800, d. p. 1867, Walton County, Florida, m. Tirzah Akridge;
>
> Joel, b. ca. 1805, d. 30 January 1871, Washington County, Florida, m. Elizabeth Sloan, 11 November 1837, Thomas County, Georgia;
>
> Mary, b. ca. 1805, d. 5 January 1879, Walton County, Florida, m. William Porter Cutts ca. 1822, Thomas County;
>
> Fereby, b. ca. 1800-1810, d. unk., m. Samuel Miller, 4 November 1819, Montgomery County, Georgia;
>
> Nancy, b. ca. 1815, d. p. 1880, Echols County, Georgia, buried Hebron Cemetery, Hamilton County, Florida, m. Job Elbert Wilder Smith, 4 February 1834, Thomas County, Georgia.

Each child of Bennett will be treated to the extent of this research.

SAMUEL PATE, D. P. 1867,
SON OF BENNETT PATE D. P. 1830

Samuel Pate appears to have been the oldest child of Bennett Pate d. p. 1830. He was born ca. 1800, when his father lived in Kershaw, South Carolina. He died in Walton County, Georgia, after he sold his last landholding, 14 December 1867, Deed Book 5, page 300. He married Tirzah Akridge, as proved by the Louisiana death certificate of their son, Samuel Pate d. 1920.

Assumptive evidence, supported by records, identifies Tirzah as the oldest child of William Greenberry and Prudence (Parker) Akridge. There are various spellings of the Akridge surname. The research of Hugh Akridge, Neil Akridge, and Ermine Branch traces the Akridge family back to William Akridge who married Eliza Simmons 3 July 1722 at All Hollows Parish, Anne Arundel, Maryland. Their son, Abel Akridge, ca. 1738-1785, was a Revolutionary War soldier in South

Carolina. His son, William Greenbery Akridge, was in Montgomery County, Georgia, as early as 1807, as proved by land records.

Prudence Parker may have been a daughter of Hardy Parker of early Jefferson County, Georgia. Greenberry and Prudence named a son Hardy Akridge. Another Hardy Parker, assumed to have been her brother, was a near neighbor of the Pate and Akridge families in Emanuel County and Thomas County, Georgia.

Samuel Pate and William Greenberry Akridge drew lots of land in Houston County, Georgia, in the land lottery of 1821. Both were residents of Emanuel County. Both sold these lots and moved to Thomas County with Bennett Pate and his family.

The Akridge family moved on to Baker and Mitchell counties of Georgia and was a neighbor to the Pate descendants of Charles Pate d. p. 1790, identified earlier as being residents of Baker and Mitchell.

Two of Tirzah's brothers, James Akridge and Hardy Akridge, moved to Dale County, Alabama, with the Pate brothers, Samuel and Joel. Tirzah had a brother named Hansford who served as namesake for her youngest son, Hansford Pate. Hansford Akridge named a son Samuel Akridge.

Samuel was a resident of Thomas County, 26 January 1830, when he acquired Lot 278, 8th District, Book D-1, page 169. He was a resident of Lowndes County when he sold this tract, 18 November 1836. Other deeds identify him as a resident of Thomas County Deed Book, D-1, page 365, 6 December 1838; D-1, page 391, 25 December 1838; C, page 91, 16 February 1839. The record in Deed Book C, page 213, 1 February 1840, identified him as a "former resident of Thomas County, Georgia, but now a resident of Dale County, Alabama".

District 8 of Thomas County became Colquitt County in 1856.

One deed, recorded in Lowndes County dated 7 October 1838, was witnessed by Job Smith, his brother-in-law, Book W, page 375. Job and Nancy (Pate) Smith lived in Lowndes County before moving to Hamilton County, Florida.

Samuel enlisted in the Thomas County militia 15 July 1836 for service in the Florida Indian Wars. His application for bounty land, for this service, was filed 31 March 1855 in Dale County, Alabama. He served in the company commanded by Captain Crawford Tucker and saw action in the Battle of Brush Creek. He was discharged at Little River, Lowndes County, 15 August 1836.

He moved his family to Dale County, Alabama, before 1 February 1840, as proved by the deed cited earlier. He acquired five tracts of land from the federal government in Dale County between 1841 and 1852. The courthouse fire in Dale County in the early 1800s limits the available Dale County records.

Samuel moved to Coffee County, Alabama, before 1855, when he and his son Nathaniel were enumerated on the Alabama state census in Coffee County. He and his wife Tirzah sold one of the Dale County land tracts from Coffee County, 30 March 1848, Deed Book B, page 230. One of the witnesses was their son, Samuel Pate, Jr.

The U. S. Agricultural Census for 1850 provides insight into the lifestyle of Samuel and his family. He owned 80 acres of improved land and 240 acres of unimproved land. The value of his farm was $960.00. He had 2 horses, 2 milk cows, 2 oxen, and 20 swine. The farm provided 400 bushels of corn, 50 bushels of oats, 800 pounds of rice, 3 bales of cotton, and 400 bushels of sweet potatoes.

The U. S. Census for 1860 enumerated the family in Walton County, Florida. His son Nathaniel was listed as head of the household. Tirzah was absent, apparently deceased. His married son Isaiah was in the household, as was the unmarried son, Hansford.

The last record on Samuel, found by this research, was his sale of the Walton County land, 14 December 1867, to William C. King, cited earlier. The legal description on this land located the tract on the east side of the Yellow River, in present-day Okaloosa County, Florida. Okaloosa was formed from Walton County in 1910. The records of the acquisition of the tract would have been burned in the Walton County courthouse fire in 1885.

Samuel and his family suffered dire effects from the Civil War. The family was divided in allegiance to the two sides, as were many in the Walton County area. The son Joel died in 1872 from wounds suffered in the War. The son Samuel served in the Confederate Army in a Louisiana unit and claimed permanent eye damage from that service.

Nathaniel died at home of wounds suffered in combat. Isaiah served in a Confederate cavalry unit, but family members report his religious beliefs were in conflict with the cause. Matthew served in the Union Army. Several of his nephews, sons of his brother Joel Pate, served in the Union Army, to be cited.

Matthew applied for a pension for his Union Army service after the War. He reported his father's family Bible record was the only source for proof of his birth year, but it was destroyed by a Confederate cavalry unit during the War. Records prove a unit of Mississippi cavalry patrolled the West Florida and South Alabama area seeking deserters. Family accounts report they pillaged and destroyed homes of residents who were unfriendly to their cause. Perhaps the Pate Family Bible was destroyed in one of these acts.

Various records lead to the assumption that Samuel and Tirzah had nine children who reached maturity. They were:

Joel – b. ca. 1824, d. 1872, m. Mary Ann Kemp; unknown daughter – b. 1820-1825;

Samuel – b. 8 January 1827, d. 18 November 1920, m. Lucinda Hanchey;

Nathaniel – b. ca. 1827, d. 4 April 1863, m. Rebecca J. Cravey;

Malatha – b. ca. 1831, d. 20 January 1874, m. 1) Wingate Flowers ca. 1847, 2) Lott Flowers, 12 September 1870;

Isaiah – b. 18 February 1833, d. 12 January 1924, m. Alcey/Elsie Bray;

Tirzah – b. ca. 1838, d. p. 1850, m. 1) (?) Milbrey, b. 11 September 1839, d. 1 February 1916, 2) Wright Flowers;

Matthew – b. 4 July 1841, d. 22 November 1923, m. Rebecca Franklin;

Hansford – b. 3 July 1846, d. 21 November 1919, m. Mercy Smith.

Each child will be treated to the extent of this research.

JOEL PATE D. 1872,
SON OF SAMUEL PATE D. P. 1867

Joel was the first child born to Samuel and Tirzah. He was born ca. 1824 and died 1872 in Baldwin County, Alabama. He married Mary Ann Kemp, probably in Dale County, Alabama.

His full name may have been Samuel Joel Pate. The Alabama death certificate for his youngest son, Lawrence Pate, identified the father of Lawrence as Samuel Joel Pate and his mother as Mary Ann Kemp. This is the only record found by this research of the full name. Question as to the name is raised because the deaths of the father and grandfather of Joel were near in years. This report will use the name of Joel, but does recognize that the full name may have been Samuel Joel. That would recognize the father and grandfather.

The death certificate for the son Henry Tillis Pate confirms the parents as Joel Pate and Mary Ann Kemp.

Mary Ann Kemp was born ca. 1830 and died after the U. S. Census for 1880 was enumerated. Her parents were not proved by this research. However, Henry Kemp of Dale County may have been her father. Joel and Mary Ann named a son Henry Tillis Pate. Uriah Kemp, of age to have been her brother, was enumerated in the household of Joel and Mary Ann in 1860.

The family was enumerated in Dale County in 1850 and 1860, Baldwin County in 1870, and Mary Ann was a widow in Baldwin County in 1880. She resided in the Baldwin County community of Whistler when she applied for a Confederate widow's pension, 12 May 1897.

Joel served in Company A, 32nd Alabama Infantry Regiment, in the Confederate Army. The unit saw combat in several areas. Mary Ann reported he died of wounds received in the Civil War.

The children of Joel and Mary are from the U. S. Censuses for 1850 to 1880. The Alabama death certificates of Henry and Laurence confirm their relationship to Joel and Mary Ann. Both of these sons were enumerated in the household of Mary Ann in 1880 and were identified as her sons. Further, Luraney Frank was in the household and was identified as her daughter. The husband of Luraney, Henry Frank, was identified as her son-in-law. Given the proof that these three were children of Joel and Mary Ann, the assumption is offered that the other children in their household 1850 to 1880 were also their children.

The children were:

Joel B. – b. ca. 1844, may have died in the Civil War;
Nathaniel – b. ca. 1847;
William A. – b. ca. 1848, Dale County, Alabama;
Samuel Joel – b. ca. 1850;
Sarah A. M. – b. ca. 1855, Dale County, Alabama;
Luraney – b. ca. 1857, m. Henry Frank;
Mary A. M. – b. ca. 1857;
Rebecca G. – b. ca. 1858;
Henry Gillis(?) Tillis – b. 1 July 1859, d. 9 February 1935, m. Julia Baker, 23 December 1886, Escambia County, Florida;
Lawrence H. – b. 22 March 1871, d. 16 November 1936, m. Virginia Thomas, b. 22 November 1870, d. 28 October 1950.

This completes the report on Joel Pate d. 1872, son of Samuel Pate d. p. 1867.

SAMUEL PATE D. 1920,
SON OF SAMUEL PATE D. P. 1867

Samuel Pate was the second child of record born to Samuel and Tirzah. He was born 8 January 1827 and died 18 November 1920 in Beauregard Parish, Louisiana. He was buried at Dry Creek Cemetery. The information is from his death certificate. He married Lucinda Hanchey, as proved by the death certificate of their son, Charles Forrestial Pate.

The Hanchey name was also spelled Hinchey. Lucinda appeared in the Pike County, Alabama, household of William Hinchey on the U. S. Census for 1850. Pike County adjoined Dale County. The assumption is offered that she was a daughter of William and Frances Hinchey and became the wife of Samuel Pate. The marriage, if recorded in Dale County, was lost in the courthouse fire in the early 1880s.

Samuel served as a witness to the land sale by his parents in Coffee County, 30 March 1848, Deed Book B, page 230. He was identified as Samuel Pate, Jr. He acquired 40 acres of land in Dale County from the U. S. Government, 1 January 1852, Township 5, Range 23, Section 28. Available records fail to provide record of his sale of this land, probably the result of the Dale County courthouse fire. He was identified as Samuel Pate, Jr., in records of the purchase.

His oldest child was born ca. 1861 in Florida, suggesting he moved to that state as his parents and siblings moved. This research failed to find him on Florida U. S. Census for 1860.

His application for a Confederate veteran's pension, filed 10 May 1909, reported he had lived in Calcasieu Parish, Louisiana, for 48 years. This reflects his residence as Louisiana in 1861. He enlisted in Company A, Louisiana Crescent Regiment of the Confederate Army, 20 October 1863.

His Louisiana death certificate identified the maiden name of his mother as Tirzah Akridge (Acrage/Ackridge/etc.).

U. S. Census reports identify Samuel and Lucinda with two sons and one daughter. The 1900 U. S. Census for Calcasieu Parish reported Lucinda was the mother of three children, two of whom were alive. Obituaries from the *Lake Charles Press* and Louisiana death certificates for Samuel Pate, Charles Forrestial Pate, Charles Pate, Villula V. Pate, and Albin Pate provide information on the children of Samuel and Lucinda.

The children were:

Charles Forrestial – b. ca. 1861, d. 11 May 1922, m. Villula V.
  Smith, daughter of Allen and Marjorie (Holliday) Smith;
William Albin – b. ca. 1865, d. 1 December 1922, m. Estelle
  Edwards;
Leola A. – b. ca. 1870, d. ca. 1900.

This completes the report on Samuel Pate d. 1920, son of Samuel
Pate d. p. 1867.

NATHANIEL PATE,
SON OF SAMUEL PATE D. P. 1867

Nathaniel was the third child of record born to Samuel and Tirzah.
He was born in 1829. His Confederate military records report he died
4 October 1863. The family record compiled by his son, Isaiah Samuel
Pate, reports he died 30 March 1863. The military date will be used
in this report. He died at home from disease contracted in service.

He married Rebecca Jane Cravey, 18 December 1849, as recorded
in the records of Isaiah Samuel Pate. She was born 3 November 1830
and died 6 July 1877. Rebecca applied for compensation due families
of deceased Confederate soldiers as the widow of Nathaniel Pate, 17
June 1863. This research failed to identify the parents of Rebecca.

Nathaniel and Rebecca were enumerated on the U. S. Census
for Coffee County, Alabama, in 1850. He and his father were enumerated in Coffee County on the Alabama state census for 1855.
Nathaniel acquired land from Ransom Hughes, 26 September 1853,
in Coffee County, Deed Book B, page 329. All of the Samuel Pate
Family was in Walton County, Florida, when the U. S. Census for
1860 was enumerated.

Nathaniel and his brother, Isaiah, enlisted in Company D, 3rd Battalion Florida Cavalry, 4 October 1862. Both served as teamsters.
Nathaniel became ill and returned home to recuperate. He died at
home, 4 April 1863. Earlier family reports list the cause of his death
as wounds suffered in combat. The muster roll of the 3rd Battalion
reports he died at home of disease.

Family information reports Rebecca returned to her family home,
then located in Crenshaw County, with the children. She died 6
July 1877.

U. S. Census reports identify the children of Nathaniel and Rebecca. More importantly, the oldest son, Isaiah Samuel Pate, recorded extensive family information in a notebook that survived. Ella Bea Johnson shared a copy with the writer in past years.

The children of Nathaniel and Rebecca were:

> Isaiah Samuel – b. 28 March 1852, d. 9 May 1938, m. Nancy
> Catherine Goodwin;
> Jacob H. – b. 10 September 1853;
> I. A. (male) – b. 21 December 1855, d. ca. 1860;
> Susannah E. – b. 6 December 1856;
> James N. – b. 10 January 1860, d. 11 November 1943, Riesel,
> McLennan County, Texas;
> Minerva M. – b. 26 January 1862.

Martha Pate, 17 years of age, enumerated in the household on the 1870 U. S. Census, probably domestic help and perhaps a descendant of Zacheus/Zachariah Pate, treated earlier.

Family information reports Isaiah Samuel and James N. maintained communication and visited between Alabama and Texas in later life.

This completes the report on Nathaniel Pate, son of Samuel Pate d. p. 1867.

MALATHA (PATE) FLOWERS, DAUGHTER OF SAMUAEL PATE D. P. 1867

Malatha (Nalatha) was the fourth child of record born to Samuel and Tirzah. She was born ca. 1831 in Thomas County, Georgia, and died 20 January 1874 in Pike County, Alabama. She married 1) Wingate Flowers of Pike County, Alabama, ca. 1847. He was born 25 March 1825 and died 13 September 1861. She married 2) Lott Flowers, 12 September 1870, in Pike County.

Wingate and Lott Flowers were brothers, sons of Luke and Dorothy (Risen) Flowers, based on Smith family records shared by Ella Bea Johnson. They were also brothers to Wright Flowers who married Milbrey Pate, a sister of Malatha.

Malatha was buried at Union Springs Primitive Baptist Church in Pike County, with others of the Flowers family.

The Smith, Flowers, and Pate families were related by multiple marriages. Wingate and Malatha had a daughter named Elizabeth who married Cornelius Smith. They had a son named James Robert Smith. Isaiah Samuel Pate, a son of Nathaniel Pate, who was a brother to Malatha, married Nancy Goodwin and had a daughter named Maggie Pate. James Robert Smith married Maggie Pate.

Further, Hansford Pate, youngest brother to Malatha, married Mary (Mollie) Smith, who was a sister to Cornelius Smith.

The children of Malatha is identified by U. S. Census reports, cemetery records, death certificates, and Smith family records. Most marriages are from Pike County records.

The children were:

Elizabeth – b. 4 December 1849, d. 7 September 1934, m. Cornelius Smith, 13 April 1867;

Susannah – b. 2 December 1850, d. 7 November 1900, m. Malcom H. Whittington, 2 February 1872;

Dorothy – b. ca. 1853, d. unk., m. John A. Ward, 18 June 1874;

Tirzah – b. June 1854, d. 1 December 1940, Coffee County, m. Jefferson Asa Fuller, 28 February 1871;

Rebecca – b. ca. 1856, d. p. 1860;

Orpha – b. 10 June 1858, d. 6 January 1922, m. 1) Mitchell Maughon, 2 April 1891, 2) J. Nelson Huston;

Abel – b. 12 December 1859, d. 7 January 1930, m. Mary Ellen Dismukes, 10 February 1881.

This completes the report on Malatha (Pate) Flowers, daughter of Samuel Pate d. p. 1867.

ISAIAH PATE,
SON OF SAMUEL PATE D. P. 1867

Isaiah Pate was the fifth child of record born to Samuel and Tirzah. He was born 18 February 1833 in Thomas County, Georgia and died 12 January 1924 in Bluff Springs, Escambia County, Florida, at the home of his son James Floyd Pate. He was buried at Old Sullivan Cemetery, Perdido, Alabama. The dates are from his Florida death certificate.

He married Alcey/Elsie Bray ca. 1854. The U. S. Census for Escambia County in 1900 reported they had been married 46 years. The marriage record was probably lost in the Coffee County, Alabama, courthouse fire.

Alcey/Elsie Bray was born ca. 1838 in Henry County Alabama, and died before 1920, when Isaiah was listed as a widower on the U. S. Census for Escambia County, Alabama. She was a daughter of Littleberry and Elzenia (Johnson) Bray. Littleberry Bray was born ca. 1801 in Washington County, Georgia, and died in Santa Rosa County, Florida, in 1885.

Isaiah failed to create the records needed to develop the history and genealogy of his family. He apparently never owned land or a home site. Fortunately, two of his granddaughters had personal knowledge of his life and shared needed details with the writer, Bessie Mae (Presley) Ernest and Lillie James (Pate) McCall. Mrs. McCall prepared a notarized record of her memories for this research. Additional information on his came from Rev. Frank Page, Jean Stewart, and Henrietta Sanks.

Isaiah applied for homestead land in Santa Rosa County, Florida, 13 May 1869, but never completed the requirements for the Homestead Act. He appeared on the Santa Rosa County tax lists for 1872 and 1876. He moved to Baldwin County, Alabama, before 1880 and was employed by the Alger-Sullivan Lumber Company. His death certificate identified him as a sawyer. The lumber company was large and provided houses, schools, and commissaries for the employees. The death certificate for Isaiah identified the undertaker as Alger-Sullivan Lumber Company.

Note has been made that Isaiah enlisted in the Confederate Army with his brother, Nathaniel Pate. Family information reports he was not a strong supporter of either cause in the War. The military records prove that he continued with the unit until 30 June 1864. There is doubt that he remained with the unit until the end of the War, as he never applied for a pension as a Confederate veteran. His financial status has been described as "desperate" in old age. It appears he would have applied for support if he had been eligible.

He was of the Primitive Baptist faith and was an active supporter of his church. One of his sons, Isaiah Samuel Pate, was a minister in that faith.

The children of Isaiah and Elsie were identified from U. S. Census reports and the knowledge of Mrs. Ernest and Mrs. McCall. The U. S. Censuses for 1900 and 1910 reported Elsie was the mother of twelve children, eight of whom were alive. Two of the deceased children are identified on early U. S. Census reports, and two are unknown to the writer.

The known children were:

Matilda (Tilly) – b. 11 January 1856, d. 25 February 1938, m.
Matthew Wright Stokes;
Mary – b. ca. 1857, died early;
William Irvin – b. January 1859, d. 3 August 1920, m. Georgia
Duer, Baldwin County, 23 February 1880;
Caroline "Callie" – b. 17 July 1861, d. 19 July 1944, m. 1) Abra-
ham Mitchem, 2) John Cawthon;
Isaiah Samuel – b. June 1864, d. 29 November 1938, m. Sarah
Ellen Bray; Margaret – b. ca. 1866, died early;
Joel - b. 15 March 1870, d. 29 July 1957, m. Henrietta Sanks;
James Floyd – b. 10 September 1870 [?], d. 7 September 1949,
m. 1) Georgia Littles, 2) Minerva Lee Gray, 3) Mrs. Pearlie
Lee (Savage) Foster;
Elizabeth 'Bessie" – b. 26 November 1872, d. 10 May 1916, m.
Charles E. Presley; Elsie Ellen – b. 1 December 1877, d.
16 December 1932, m. William T. Ardis.

Additional notes: Death certificates are available for most of the
children, and most dates are from them. Sarah Ellen (Sarah A. in
some records) Bray was a daughter of William Wilburn Bray, a
brother to Elsie (Bray) Pate.

Caroline "Callie" Pate was the great-grandmother of the writer,
and he has knowledge of the Isaiah Pate Family. The death certificate for Grandma Callie reports her father as Joel Pate. This is
in error, to the knowledge of the writer, Lillie James McCall, and
Bessie Mae Ernest. Joel Pate was her brother, and Isaiah Pate was
her father. Carolina had no from her second marriage.

This ends the report on Isaiah Pate, son of Samuel Pate d. p. 1867.

TIRZAH PATE,
DAUGHTER OF SAMUEL PATE D. P. 1867

Tirzah was the sixth child of record born to Samuel and Tirzah.
Researchers have debated the existence of this daughter. Some
report her as the same as Malatha, who was a different daughter of
Samuel and Tirzah, in the opinion of the writer.

The U. S. Census for 1840 listed the household of Samuel with
three daughters who were born after 1830. The assumption is offered

SAMUEL PATE

that these were Malatha, who was married ca. 1847, and appeared in her Flowers household in 1850, and Tirzah and Milbrey, who were identified in the household of Samuel on the 1850 U. S. Census. Tirzah was 12 years, and Milbrey was 10 years on the 1850 Census. Family records prove Milbrey was born 11 September 1839.

Available records fail to provide later information on Tirzah. Note has been made that Malatha had a daughter named Tirzah Flowers, born in June 1854. Perhaps this daughter was named to recognize her sister, Tirzah, who likely died in the early1850s.

This completes the report on Tirzah Pate, daughter of Samuel Pate d. p. 1867.

MILBREY (PATE) FLOWERS,
DAUGHTER OF SAMUEL PATE D. P. 1867

Milbrey was the seventh child of record born to Samuel and Tirzah. She was born 11 September 1839 and died 1 February 1916 in Mobile County, Alabama, based on family records. She married Wright Flowers of Pike County, Alabama. The groom, as noted earlier, was a brother to Lott and Wingate Flowers, who were husbands of her sister, Maletha (Pate) Flowers.

Wright Flowers was enumerated in the Pike County household of his father, Luke Flowers, on the U. S. Census for 1850. Milbrey was in the Dale County household of her father. They were enumerated, as husband and wife, in Pike County in 1860 and 1870. They relocated to Escambia County, Florida, by 1880. This research failed to locate them on the U. S. Census for 1900. Milbrey was in the Baldwin County, Alabama, household of her son, Samuel Flowers, as a widow, in 1910.

The 1910 U. S. Census reported Milbrey was the mother of 14 children, 12 of whom were alive. U. S. Census reports and family records from Gerald Mancill identify them and provide some dates and marriages. Death certificates confirm nine as of Wright and Milbrey and confirm some reported marriages. Caution is issued that the last daughter was not proved in U. S. Census reports or death certificates.

The children of Wright and Milbrey (Pate) Flowers were:

Eli – b. 15 April 1858, d. 30 November 1938;
Lucretia – b. 16 November 1859, d. unk., m. 1) John W. Dubose,
2) John S. [?];

267

Orville – b. 31 March 1861, d. 13 March 1933, Escambia, Florida, m. Ardilla Coleman;

Wright – b. 1 February 1862, d. 11 September 1937, Baldwin, Alabama, m. Frances Lenox Coleman;

Gilpin – b. 16 January 1865, d. January 1927, Baldwin, Alabama;

Leona – b. 16 March 1866, d. 16 October 1950, Escambia, Florida, m. William Jesse Agerton;

Amanda Serepy – b. 30 August 1867;

Susan – b. 2 July 1870, d. 8 December 1956, m. Obediah Wilson;

Annie Missouri – b. 19 November 1972, d. 1 May 1957, Baldwin, Alabama, m. John T. Wilson;

Samuel – b. 19 November 1874, d. 11 January 1952, Baldwin, Alabama, m. 1) Mary Frances Joiner, 2) Mary Jane Kirksey;

Sterling – b. 15 February 1877, d. 1 December 1957, Escambia, Florida, m. Annie Joiner;

Daisy – b. 4 May 1878;

Milbrey – b. 1 June 1881, d. unk., m. Ransom Mitchell;

Lavania – b. 23 February 1883, d. unk., m. Theodore Coleman (Charles Richard Coleman?).

This completes the report on Milbrey (Pate) Flowers, daughter of Samuel Pate d. p. 1867.

MATTHEW PATE D. 1921,
SON OF SAMUEL PATE D. P. 1867,

Matthew Pate was the eighth child of record born to Samuel and Tirzah. He was born 4 July 1841 in Dale County, Alabama, and died 22 November 1921 in Santa Rosa County, Florida. The birthdate is from his Civil War pension application, and the death date is from his Florida death certificate. He was buried at Red Oak Cemetery, Santa Rosa County.

He married Mrs. Rebecca (Franklin) Snoden, the widow of James Snoden, who died in service with Matthew Pate. Rebecca was a daughter of Wyatt Franklin of Santa Rosa County, Deed Book X, page 474.

Note was made earlier that Matthew reported the record of his birth was destroyed by a Confederate cavalry unit and the possibility that his father's house was destroyed in the act. He entered the Union Army, 23 March 1864, and was discharged 17 November 1865. In his old age, he drew a pension for his service.

He acquired homestead land from the U. S. Government, W1/2 SW¼ Section 18, Township 4, Range 25, 6 April 1898. This appears to be the land he and Rebecca conveyed to Ernest Snoden, 22 August 1899, Book O, page 292.

The pension records document that he was blind in one eye. Family information reports he was very talented in "calling turkeys" on hunting expeditions. His call was so real that one hunter thought he was a turkey and shot him.

His pension application reports he and Rebecca were separated as of 24 April 1924. The separation date is unknown, but the U. S. Census for 1910 enumerated him as a boarder with brothers of Rebecca. The U. S. Census for 1920 listed him in the household of James Barnhill, who was a son-in-law of Hansford Pate, brother to Matthew.

The pension application dated 24 April 1915 reported he had no living or deceased child. Welthy A. Pate, 14 years old, appeared in his household on the 1880 U. S. Census. She was born before he and Rebecca married, if the age is correct. Perhaps she and Ernest Snoden, to whom he and Rebecca conveyed land, were children of her marriage to James Snoden.

Family information reports that Matthew had a daughter, Samantha, who never married. This research was unable to confirm this claim.

This completes the report on Matthew Pate, son of Samuel Pate d. p. 1867.

HANSFORD PATE,
SON OF SAMUEL PATE D. P. 1867

Hansford Pate was the ninth child of record and the last born to Samuel and Tirzah. He was born 3 July 1846 and died 21 November 1919. Burial was at Bryan Chapel, Okaloosa County, Florida. He married Mary "Mollie" Smith, a daughter of Cornelius Smith. The intermarriage of the Pate and Smith families was treated earlier. She was born 12 July 1840 and died 15 November 1925, as reported in her Florida death certificate.

The death certificate for Hansford reports he was a son of J. H. Pate. Ella Bea Johnson interviewed descendants of Hansford Pate who had knowledge that he was a son of "Grandpa Sam" Pate. Further, this research earlier reported that his mother was Tirzah (Akridge) Pate, and that she had a brother named Hansford Akridge, for whom her youngest son was named.

Hansford and Mary had three children, as proved by U. S. Census reports and confirmed by Ella Bea Johnson. They were:

Susan Justice – b. 11 December 1871, d. 4 May 1966, m. James Lexture Barnhill;

Charles Wilson – b. 4 January 1875, d. 7 July 1948, m. 1) Amanda Cornelius Hart, 2) Margaret Steele;

Mary Ella – b. 4 June 1881, d. 25 February 1954, m. William Asbury Stewart.

This completes the report on Samuel Pate d. p. 1867 and his children. The report returns to the other children of Bennett Pate d. p. 1830.

JOEL PATE D. P. 1871,
SON OF BENNETT PATE D. P. 1830

Joel Pate was the second son born to Bennett Pate d. p. 1830. He was born ca. 1805,

when his father resided in Kershaw County, South Carolina. He died in Washington County, Florida, 30 January 1871 and was buried in an unmarked gravesite at Bethel Primitive Church Cemetery, based on family information. He married Elizabeth Sloan in Thomas County, Georgia, 18 November 1828. The bride was born ca. 1809 in Georgia and died after 1 June 1880 in Washington County, Florida.

This research failed to identify the parents of Elizabeth. However, William Sloan and John Slone were enumerated three households from Bennett Pate and his two sons, Samuel and Joel, and his son-in-law William Porter Cutts, on the U. S. Census for Thomas County in 1830. William Slone was enumerated in Irwin County, Georgia, in 1820. Part of the original Irwin County became Thomas County in 1825. These locations and the selection of the given name of John for the first son of Joel and Elizabeth lead to the assumption that she was a daughter of John Slone.

Researchers will find record of a land acquisition in Coffee County, Alabama, by Joel Pate, Jr. This was not the son of Joel and

Elizabeth, as he was not of age for this action. It was an acquisition by the nephew of Joel, son of his brother, Samuel Pate d. p. 1867.

Some researchers have identified Joel Pate d. 1871, the son of Bennett Pate d. p. 1830, with the full name of Joel Bennett Pate. This research found no record of a middle name for this Joel. Further, he named a son Joel Pate, and no record on that son recognized a middle name. In fact, the grave marker on the son at Bethel Cemetery in Washington County, identified him as Joel Pate, Jr. The records indicate that neither Joel, the father, nor Joel, the son, had a middle name, in the opinion of the writer.

Joel was a prominent Primitive Baptist minister in the Thomas County area of Georgia in the 1830s, as was his brother-in-law Job E. W. Smith. Both appear in the minutes of the church at Sardis, located in present-day Colquitt County. Rev. Pate preached from I Timothy, chapter 16, on 24 January 1835 and from Revelation, chapter 22, verse 17, on 21 February 1835. He and his brother-in-law spoke to the church in May 1835.

He acquired two tracts of land in Thomas County, Deed Book A1, page 477, 21 January 1831, and Deed Book B, page 135, 23 February 1833.

Joel moved to Dale County, Alabama, with his brother Samuel, at the start of the year 1840, cited earlier. He represented the Mt. Pleasant Primitive Baptist Church at a convention in Coffee County in 1845. He was appointed the first moderator for the Clay Bank Primitive Baptist Association, founded in 1846, *History of Geneva County, Alabama,*

J. J. Collins. He apparently relocated to Coffee County at this time.

Coffee County suffered loss of official records in courthouse fires and repeated floods of the Pea River. Three records involving Joel are among the extant records and are important to this report.

James Newton of Coffee County sold a tract of land to John Sawyer of the same county, 13 February 1849, Book P, page 301. Joel Pate witnessed the conveyance. The record serves to identify his residence on that date. Joel and Elizabeth sold 40 acres, NW1/4 NE1/4, Section 19, Township 5, Range 22, to the same John Sawyer, 22 September 1849. Joel and his family were enumerated on the U. S. Census for Washington County, Florida, 25 October 1850, marking their relocation to Washington County.

The third Coffee County record was dated Washington County, Florida, 5 May 1851, and was the sale of 40 acres in Coffee County,

Alabama, by John Pate. The sale was to John Sawyer of Coffee County. The deed was signed by John Pate and witnessed by Joel Pate, William A. F. Potter, James Nichols, and Stephen I. Locke, J. P. The record was recorded in Coffee County, 10 August 1853.

The writer identifies with the parties in the last deed as follows: John Sawyer, the grantee, had purchased the land of Joel Pate as the later removed from Coffee County. John Pate, the grantor, was the oldest son of Joel and Elizabeth. Joel Pate witnessed the conveyance by his son. William R. F. Pattee was a brother-in-law to John Pate and son-in-law of Joel. This record will receive further consideration in the narration on the son, John Pate.

Joel continued in the service of his church. He was identified as a minister on the Washington County U. S. Census for 1850 and the U. S. Census for Calhoun County, Florida, in 1860. He and James Moseley acted in conference to ordain James Stephens, First Lord's Day of May 1859, Calhoun Deed Book A, page 11.

Joel served in a Thomas County, Georgia, militia unit in the Florida Indian Wars, as did his brother, Samuel. Military records report his unit "saw action". Elizabeth applied for bounty land as the widow of a veteran of the Indian Wars, 10 March 1876. The application reports he served in Picken's Company of the Georgia militia in 1836. Two of the sons-in-law, W. Lumpkin Raley and Gadi Yates, attested to the validity of the claim.

This research failed to find record of the distribution of land to her. Her application appears to have been valid.

The children of Joel and Elizabeth were identified by U. S. Census reports, family records shared by Max Yates, cemetery markers, and military records. The U. S. Censuses for 1850 and 1860 named the children. Other records cited here confirm the relationship of these children to Joel and Elizabeth.

The children of Joel and Elizabeth were:

> John – b. ca. 1829, d. p. May 1851;
> Nancy Jane – b. 18 September 1831, d. 7 February 1897, m. William Rufus Franklin Potter;
> Bennett – b. 12 September 1833, d. 21 June 1864, m. Amy Yates;
> Susan – b. 19 December 1835, d. 15 May 1892, m. Gadi Yates;
> David – b. 22 June 1838, d. p. 1 June 1880, m. Elizabeth Carver;
> Lucinda – b. November 1840, d. ca. 30 December 1865, m. Levi Yates;

Elizabeth – b. July 1843, d. 12 November 1886, m. Levi Yates,
after death of her sister Lucinda;
Rudolph – b. 3 July 1846, d. 28 June 1864;
Joel – b. 10 April 1848, d. 8 January 1910.

Each child will be treated to the extent of this research.

JOHN PATE D. CA. 1851,
SON OF JOEL PATE D. 1871

John Pate was the first child born to Joel and Elizabeth. Note has
been made that his grandfather Sloan may have been the source for
his given name. He was born ca. 1829 in Thomas County, Georgia,
and disappeared from records available to the research, after the
deed executed in Washington County, Florida, 5 May 1851, and
recorded in Coffee County, Alabama, 10 August 1853, cited earlier.
Acknowledgement is granted that no record of his death has been
found, but it is assumed to have occurred near to the date of this
deed. He could have been among the many pioneers who sought
their fate in Western lands.

NANCY JANE (PATE) POTTER,
DAUGHTER OF JOEL PATE D. 1871

Nancy Jane was the second child born to Joel and Elizabeth. She
was born 18 September 1831 in Thomas County, Georgia, and died
7 February 1897, in Washington County, as reported in family
information. She married William Rufus Franklin Potter, as proved
in family information and in the Florida death certificatez of their
sons, Alexander W. Potter and Angus Potter.

This research located the family on the U. S. Census in 1860,
failed to locate the family in 1870, and Nancy Jane was enumerated
as a widow on the Washington County U. S. Census for 1880.

Records provide conflicting information on the time of death
for her husband. Military records report that one William Potter
enlisted in Apalachicola, Florida, in Company K, 6th Florida Infantry
Regiment. He died in the Battle of Chickamauga, Tennessee. It is
assumed this was the husband of Nancy Jane Pate. He served in
the same company and regiment as did her brothers David Pate and
Bennett Pate. Note needs to be made that the household of Nancy

Jane in 1880, included three children born after the Civil War. The birth year for these children may suggest her husband survived the War and died ca. 1875.

As noted, two of the children were identified by Florida death certificates. One of these was Angus Potter, and his death certificate identified his birth year as 1871. Both children's parents were identified as William Potter and Nancy Jane (Pate) Potter. Available records are insufficient to clearly resolve the question of the year of death for William Rufus Franklin Potter.

However, records prove both Pate brothers were mustered out of service soon after enlisting. Perhaps the brother-in-law, William Potter, left the army in the Battle of Chickamauga and was assumed to have been killed by the authorities.

The death certificates report both sons were buried at Potter Cemetery, Vernon, Florida. The inventory of this cemetery reports a number of unmarked grave sites. Perhaps William and Nancy Jane were buried in unmarked graves.

The children of William and Nancy Jane were identified from U. S. Census reports and the Florida death certificates cited. Note needs to be made that a long interval occurred between the birth of Alexander, born 1860, and the next child, Bennett, born 1867. Perhaps another child was born in this interval.

The children identified in this research were:

> John – b. ca. 1856; Walter – b. ca. 1857;
> Alexander W. – b. ca. 1860, d. 25 September 1929, m. Mary Gaines;
> Beaulah – b. ca. 1867;
> Angus – b. ca. 1871, d. 17 November 1943, buried Potter Cemetery;
> Virginia – b. ca. 1873.

BENNETT PATE D. 1864,
SON OF JOEL PATE D. 1871

Bennett Pate was the third child born to Joel and Elizabeth. He was born ca. 1833 in Thomas County, Georgia, and died 21 June 1864 in Washington County, Florida, as reported in family records. His last child, Amy Jane (Pate) Swindle, was born 8 July 1864, as reported in her Florida death certificate. He married Amy Yates, 22

February 1856. The bride was a daughter of James A. and Malinda Real Youngblood Yates, as reported by family information.

James Yates and his wife Malinda had three children who married four children of Joel and Elizabeth. Amy Yates married Bennett Pate, Gadi Yates married Susan Pate, Levi Yates married Lucinda Pate, and, after her death, he married her sister Elizabeth Pate. These will be treated in more detail as the report progresses.

Bennett Pate d. 1864 enlisted in Company K, 6th Florida Infantry Regiment, 8 March 1862. One military record reports he was mustered out of service 14 June 1864.

Another record reports he deserted in June 1862. This research was unable to resolve the conflict in records. The death date of 21 June 1864 seems to be correct.

Note needs to be made that his brother David Pate and brother-in-law William R. F. Potter also served in Company K, 6th Florida Infantry Regiment. David was mustered out 1 July 1862 and records, to be cited, prove he enlisted in the Union Army. William Potter reportedly was killed in action 19 September 1863, but that is questionable, as noted earlier.

Amy (Yates) Pate married Wilson Lumpkin Raley, after the death of Bennett. Note has been made that he and another son-in-law, Gadi Yates, witnessed the bounty land application filed by Elizabeth (Sloan) Pate after the death of Joel. Amy was buried at Bethel Cemetery with other of her Yates family. The grave marker dates are 25 March 1841 -- 23 November 1875. Her second marriage was without children.

The children of Bennett and Amy were:

James Levi – b. 5 November 1857, d. 21 November 1893, m. Olivia Wilcox, daughter of Mark and Dorcas (Gipson) Wilcox, as proved by her death certificate;

Angus M. – b. 27 March 1859, d. unk., m. Susan Wilcox, sister to Olivia;

Nancy Elizabeth – b. 13 January 1862, d. 14 March 1958, m. George Wesley Parish;

Amy Jane – b. 8 July 1864, d. 1948, m. James William Swindle, buried Bethel Cemetery.

This ends the report on Bennett Pate d. 1864, son of Joel Pate d. 1871.

SUSAN (PATE) YATES,
DAUGHTER OF JOEL PATE D. 1871

Susan was the fourth child born to Joel and Elizabeth. She was born 19 December 1835 in Thomas County, Georgia, and died 15 May 1892 in Washington County, Florida. She and her husband were buried at Bethel Cemetery in Washington County. She married Gadi Yates about 1853. As noted earlier, the groom was a son of James A. and Malinda Youngblood Real Yates. Gadi married 2) Nancy Sellers, about 1893, no resulted.

The children of Susan and Gadi are identified by U. S. Census reports, grave markers and Florida death certificates. Eight of the children continued to live in the household of Gadi and Susan when the U. S. Census for 1880 was enumerated. This Census identified the relationship of all in the household to its head. All eight were children of Gadi. Two of the others are among persons for whom Florida death certificates are recorded. One child, Sarah Ann, was not confirmed as by records. She was not located after the 1870 U. S. Census was enumerated, when she was six years of age.

The children of Gadi and Susan (Pate) Yates were:

James – b. 17 August 1854, d. 31 January 1919, m. Martha Palmira/Palmyra;

John – b. 2 March 1857, d. 8 March 1892, m. Mary Olive May;

Lewis – b. 25 March 1861, d. 21 November 1938, m. Catherine [?];

Sarah Ann – b. ca. 1864;

Malinda – b. ca. 1866, d. 1 April 1873;

Elizabeth – b. ca. 1870;

Amy – b. ca. 1872;

Joseph – b. ca. 1874;

Bennett – b. ca. 1877, d. unk., m. Minnie Lee Bush, 5 August 1905;

Eliza A. – b. ca. 1881.

This ends the report on Susan (Pate) Yates, daughter of Joel Pate d. 1871.

DAVID PATE D. P. 1880,
SON OF JOEL PATE D. 1871

David was the fifth child born to Joel and Elizabeth. He was born 22 June 1830 in Thomas County, Georgia, and died after 1 June 1880, probably in Walton County, Florida. He married Elizabeth Carvey.

David enlisted in Company K, 6th Florida Infantry Regiment of the Confederate Army, 8 March 1862. Note has been made that he and his brother Bennett and brother-in-law William R. F. Potter joined the same unit. David was mustered out of service 1 July 1862. Available records do not provide a reason for his discharge. He enlisted in Company C, 1st Florida Cavalry Regiment of the Union Army, 3 August 1864, at Ft. Barrancas, Florida. His brothers Joel and Rudolph joined the same unit. He and Joel served until the end of the War. Rudolph died of disease in service, to be documented.

The children of David and Elizabeth are identified by U. S. Census reports and Florida death certificates. They were:

Elizabeth – b. ca. 1859;
John – b. ca. 1861, d. 1942 Walton County, m. Sarah Simmons, Walton County, 12 January 1887;
Rudolph – b. ca. 1864, d. unk., m. Nancy Courtney, 22 October 1893, Walton County.

This ends the report on David Pate d. p. 1880, son of Joel Pate d. 1871.

LUCINDA (PATE) YATES,
DAUGHTER OF JOEL PATE D. 1871

Lucinda (Pate) Yates was the sixth child born to Joel and Elizabeth. She was born November 1840, probably in Alabama, though records are not clear that Joel had moved from Thomas County, Georgia, by that date. She had died before 30 December 1865, when her widowed husband remarried to her sister, Elizabeth Pate. She married Levi Yates, another son of James A. and Malinda Youngblood (Real) Yates, as cited earlier.

Levi and Lucinda Yates were enumerated on the U. S. Census for Washington County in 1860. A 10-month-old female was in the household, Mary L. Yates. Mary does not appear on later records of this family. The assumption is offered that the mother and child (Lucinda and Mary) died soon after 1860. It is assumed that no living children resulted from the marriage of Lucinda Pate and Levi Yates.

ELIZABETH (PATE) YATES,
DAUGHTER OF JOEL PATE D. 1871

Elizabeth was the seventh child born to Joel and Elizabeth. She was born 1 July 1843 in Alabama and died 12 January 1886 in Washington County, Florida, based on family records. She married Levi Yates 30 December 1865, the widowed husband of her sister, Malinda.

This research did not develop personal information on this family. The children of Elizabeth and Levi are from the records of Max Yates, grave markers and Florida death certificates. The children are confirmed by U. S. Census reports. There was:

> Effie Jane – b. 7 September 1866, d. 11 June 1948;
> Thomas Wilson – b. 1 April 1869, d. 25 January 1953;
> Lucinda – b. 22 February 1871, d. 6 May 1889;
> Alexander D. – b. 15 October 1873, d. 20 February 1953;
> James Henry Davison – b. 5 June 1876, d. 1 June 1880;
> Nancy Elizabeth – b. 23 February 1878, d. 22 December 1952;
> William Call – b. 25 June 1881, d. 16 August 1972;
> Daniel McKinnon – b. 13 January 1886, d. 10 December 1955.

This ends the report on Elizabeth (Pate) Yates, daughter of Joel Pate d. 1871.

RUDOLPH PATE D. 1864,
SON OF JOEL PATE D. 1871

Rudolph Pate was the eighth child born to Joel and Elizabeth. He was born 3 July 1846 in Alabama and died of malaria, 28 June 1864, in the military hospital at Ft. Barrancas, Florida. He was buried at Ft. Barrancas.

He enlisted in Company C, 1st Florida Cavalry Regiment of the Union Army, 15 February 1864. Note has been made that he served in this unit with his brothers David Pate and Joel Pate and a cousin Matthew Pate.

The assumption is offered that he never married and died without children. Two of his brothers used the given name of Rudolph for sons.

JOEL PATE D. 1910,
SON OF JOEL PATE D. 1871.

Joel Pate was the ninth child born to Joel and Elizabeth. He was born 10 June 1848 in Alabama and died 8 January 1910. He was buried at Bethel Cemetery, Caryville, Florida. His grave marker identified him as Joel Pate, Jr. As was the case of his father, he was not represented with a middle name or initial. He married Sarah Hewitt, a daughter of Marion Hewitt.

The marriage occurred ca. 1868. The 1900 U. S. Census reports the couple had been married 32 years, indicating 1868. He and Sarah appear as husband and wife on the U.

S. Census for Washington County in 1870. They were in the household of his parents, Joel and Elizabeth. Holmes County, Florida court records report Joel filed for divorce from Sarah, 27 July 1908. The divorce was granted 5 October 1908. Sarah was enumerated in the household of her brother Andrew Hewitt on the U. S. Census for 1910 as a widow.

Various records report Joel was active in farming and logging operations throughout his life.

The U. S. Censuses for 1900 and 1910 report Sarah was the mother of two children, one of whom was alive. Available records fail to identify the name of the deceased child. The living child was a son, Rudolph Pate b. 26 May 1885, d. 19 May 1934. He married Ollie [?]. The dates are from his Florida death certificate. He was buried at Bethel Cemetery, Caryville, Florida.

This ends the report on Joel Pate d. 1871 and his family.

The report returns to the children of Bennett Pate d. p. 1830. Three known daughters need to be recognized.

Note was made earlier that U. S. Censuses for 1800 to 1820 enumerate nine young females in the household of Bennett Pate d. p. 1830. Any or all could have been daughters. Some could have died early, and some could have been adopted children, just as was Levi Pate, treated earlier. DNA testing will be cited to prove that Bennett's brother, Rev. William Pate, also had children in his household who were not genetically related to that Pate Family.

Available records provide good assumptive evidence to identify two daughters of Bennett and sufficient evidence to support the claim for a third. Narration on these follows.

MARY (PATE) CUTTS,
DAUGHTER OF BENNETT PATE D. P. 1830

The writer acknowledges Cutts family information from Ella Bea Johnson and Robert Bryan. The family information reported that William Porter Cutts married Mary Pate ca. 1822 in Thomas County, Georgia. The assumption is offered that the bride was a daughter of Bennett Pate d. p. 1830. The assumption is supported by the absence of another Pate in the Thomas County area, of the proper age to have been her father. Further, the U. S. Census for 1830 enumerated Bennett Pate, his sons Samuel Pate and Joel Pate, and William P. Cutts in adjacent households. William P. Cutts and Mary named sons Samuel, Joel, and Zachariah. Zachariah Pate, treated earlier, was a cousin to Samuel Pate and Joel Pate, and moved from Thomas County to Alabama as the other Pates and Cutts Families relocated. William and Mary also named a daughter Milbra, as did Samuel Pate d. p. 1867 and Mary's sister, Nancy (Pate) Smith. The latter will be cited later.

Joel Pate purchased Thomas County land from William Cutts, 23 February 1833, Deed Book B, page 135.

William P. Cutts and Mary were enumerated on the U. S. Census for Walton County, Florida, adjacent to the Samuel Pate d. p. 1867 family in 1860. This Samuel Pate sold his last tract of land in Walton County to William C, King, 14 December 1867, Deed Book 5, page 300. William C. King was the father–in-law of Milbra (Cutts) King, a daughter of William and Mary (Pate) Cutts,

The records seem to be sufficient to support the assumption that Mary (Pate) Cutts was a daughter of Bennett Pate d. p. 1830.

Mary was born ca. 1805 in South Carolina and died 5 January 1879 in Walton County. She was buried at Old Dorcas Cemetery in the area of Walton County that became Okaloosa County.

The children of William Porter and Mary Susan (Pate) Cutts is reported as received from Ella Bea Johnson. They were:

Arcadia – b. ca. 1823, d. 4 June 1890, buried Old Dorcas Cemetery, m. Thomas Burk;

Micajah – b. ca. 1824, d. 4 September 1862 (Confederate Army), m. Elizabeth Hailey; Olive – b. ca. 1826, d. p. 1860;

William Porter – b. 9 May 1829, d. 20 May 1907, buried Oakwood Cemetery;

Montgomery -- m. Sarah A. Heath (1834 - 1915);

Milbra – b. 4 January 1831, d. 24 June 1917, buried Gum Creek
Cemetery, Walton County, m. Michel King (1827 - 1902);
Joel – b. ca. 1832, d. (Confederate Army), m. Cordelia [?];
Susan – b. ca. 1832, m. Charles Benjamin Cutts;
Hezekiah – b. ca. 1838, d. ca. 1885, m. Eliza Jane Clary;
Samuel – b . ca. 1839, d. 1863 (Confederate Army);
Zachariah – b. 21 February 1840, d. 5 December 1914, Coving-
ton County, Alabama, m. 1) Adaline [?], 2) Rhoda West;
Mary – b. ca. 1844, m. (?) Milton.

The writer has no additional information on Mary (Pate) Cutts.

FEREBY (PATE) MILLER,
DAUGHTER OF BENNETT PATE D. P. 1830

Fereby Pate was born ca. 1800-1810, based on the U. S. Census for
1830. This research has no record of her death.

Fereby Pate married Samuel Miller in Montgomery County, Georgia, 4 November 1819, Book 1811-1850, page 31. Bennett Pate d. p.
1830 lived in Montgomery and Emanuel counties of Georgia 1817 to
1821. Court records and jury records of both counties associate Bennett as a neighbor to Miller families. The two counties were adjacent.

Bennett Pate was the only male Pate of record and of age to have
been the father of Fereby Pate. Fereby had the given name of the
wife of Charles Pate d. 1825, a cousin of Bennett Pate. The cousins
had lived as close neighbors in Robeson County, North Carolina.
The assumption is offered that Bennett named a daughter for the
wife of his cousin, Fereby.

The Miller family appeared on the U. S. Census for Montgomery
County in 1830. The household included two males and four females
under 10 years of age.

This research was unable to locate additional information on
this family.

NANCY (PATE) SMITH,
DAUGHTER OF BENNETT PATE D. P. 1830

There is no proof that Nancy Pate was a daughter of Bennett Pate
d. p. 1830. However, as was the case for Nancy (Pate) Cutts being a
daughter of Bennett, the claim has strong support in records.

Nancy was born ca. 1815 in South Carolina, based on U. S. Census reports. Bennett Pate lived in Kershaw County, South Carolina, in 1815. She died after 1880 in Echols County, Georgia, and was buried at Hebron Cemetery in Hamilton County, Florida. She married Job Elbert Wilder Smith in Thomas County, Georgia, 4 February 1834. The groom was a Primitive Baptist pastor, and records of the Sardis Church in present-day Colquitt County, Georgia, report that he and Joel Pate d. 1871 preached at that church in 1836. They were brothers-in-law.

The U. S. Census for Lowndes County, Georgia, in 1840 enumerated the household of Rev. Smith. An elderly female, 60-70 years of age, was listed in the household. The assumption is offered that she was the widow of Bennett Pate d. p. 1830 and the mother of Nancy (Pate) Smith, wife of Rev. Smith. The U. S. Census for Lowndes County in 1850 again listed the elderly female and identified her as Elizabeth Pate, 85 years of age and born in North Carolina. The age and birthplace are compatible for the widow of Bennett.

A biographical sketch on Rev. Job E. W. Smith appears in *Pioneers of Wiregrass Georgia*, Folks Huxford, Vol IV, p. 267. Some excerpts are of value to this report.

Job E. W. Smith was the son of Job Smith, Revolutionary soldier from North Carolina. He was born 10 December 1801 in Washington County, Georgia, and died 2 December 1880 in Echols County, Georgia. He was buried at Hebron Church Cemetery in Hamilton County, Florida, a church he had founded in his early years.

Job E. W. Smith married 1) Lucretia – surname unknown. She died from complications of childbirth. Secondly to Susan Graddy of Thomas County, who died 2 December 1832, and third to Nancy Pate.

Nancy and Job lived in Lowndes County until the winter of 1853/54. They moved to Hamilton County, Florida, near the town of Jennings. They were members of the Bethel Church at Jennings and transferred to Hebron Church in Hamilton County, where he became the first pastor. He served 1859 to 1867. The U. S. Census shows they were in Chatham County, Georgia, in 1870, listed as farmers. They were in Echols County, Georgia, in 1880, and he was a miller. The inventory of the Hebron Cemetery included his grave marker and that of several of his children and grandchildren. The biographical sketch reports that Nancy was also buried at Hebron.

U. S. Census reports do not list any children from the marriage of Nancy and Job. However, the biographical sketch identified three children from the first marriage, four from his second marriage, and three from his marriage to Nancy.

The children from his marriage to Nancy (Pate) Smith were:

Sarah – b. 13 November 1837, d. unk, m. Phillip Hiers, 14 September 1854;

Milbrey – b. August 1842, d. unk., m. William Bland;

Uriah – b. 26 February 1845, d. unk., m. 1) Eliza McCall, 2) Catherine Hiers.

The name Milbrey needs to be noted. Samuel Pate d. p. 1867 named a daughter Milbra, Mary (Pate) Cutts named a daughter Milbra, and Nancy named a daughter Milbry. This research considers the three parents to have been siblings.

This completes the report on Bennett Pate d. p. 1830 and his family. The report will treat the second son of Samuel Pate d. ca. 1810 next.

SAMUEL PATE D. P. 1833,
SON OF SAMUEL PATE D, CA, 1810

Samuel was born ca. 1760 in North Carolina, according to U. S. Census reports. He died after 1833, when he sought to recover a debt in Bibb County, Alabama court, 21 October 1833, Court Minutes 1826-1836. This research has no record to identify his wife.

Readers are cautioned that extant records on this family are insufficient to provide a definitive report. This narration will cite available records and offer the writer's interpretation. Information from the research of Richard Fowler and Leah Wakefield are acknowledged.

The assumption has been offered that Samuel d. 1833 and his wife were the unnamed couple in the Robeson County, North Carolina, household of Bennett Pate d. p. 1830, on the U. S. Census for 1790. Acknowledgment is granted that, given the birth years cited here for Samuel and his children, the assumption may be in error. This research found no additional records on this Samuel until he was enumerated on the Kershaw, South Carolina, U. S. Census for 1810. He was listed with his brothers Bennett and Elijah and his son Allen. He was probably engaged in the weaving industry of Kershaw County with his brother Elijah, and they were the company of 'Pate and Pate' recorded in the industrial census.

The U. S. Census for Kershaw County in 1810 is the only one this research can report as representing this Samuel Pate. That record leads to the assumption that his included three sons and no daughters. The sons are identified here because the records on them, though few in number, are of value in interpreting the life of their father. Caution is issued that this research has no record to prove the sons of Samuel Pate d. p. 1833. The fact that three young Pates appear in Twiggs County, Georgia, with this Samuel influences their assignment as sons of Samuel.

The sons were:

> Abimilech – b. ca. 1785, North Carolina, d. ca. 1837, Butler County, Alabama;
> Allen – b. ca. 1790, North Carolina, d. p. 1850, Bibb County, Alabama;
> Samuel – b. ca. 1795, North Carolina, d. ca. 1848 or 1849. Probably an adopted son, to be cited in more detail later.

Samuel d. p. 1833 appeared on the 1810 U. S. Census with a male 16/26 years in his household, who was Samuel, Jr. Allen, 16/26 years, was living adjacent to Samuel, Sr. Abimilech is assumed to have moved to Georgia before this Census enumeration.

The family moved to Twiggs County, Georgia. All U. S. Census reports for Twiggs County before 1830 were lost. Additionally, a courthouse fire, 7 February 1901, destroyed all records. Fortunately, some state tax records, militia records, and land grants provide needed information.

Abimilech Pate was a private, 3rd Regiment, Wimberly's Georgia Militia, War of 1812. Part of a detachment to the frontier of Twiggs County, Georgia, "for the protection of the inhabitants and for the erection of a fort called Telfair, by Brig. General Blackshear, from the 9th of August to the 13th of September, 1813." He also served as an ensign in Twiggs County militia. His name is spelled Ebemilech in somerecords.

Abimilech served in Col. Wemberley's Regiment of the Georgia militia in the War of 1812. It is interesting to note that Charles Pate d. 1837, who later moved to Tuscaloosa County, Alabama, served in the same unit. Charles was a resident of Morgan County, Georgia, at the time of the War. Camp Hope, located between Marion in Twiggs County and Madison in Morgan County, was the assembly point for the unit. This Charles Pate is thought to have been a descendant of William Pate d. 1775.

The association in the militia of two from different lines of the Thoroughgood Pate Family serves to show distant descendants-maintained contact in the frontier area.

Twiggs County tax records for 1818 identify Allen Pate and Abimilech Pate as land owners in Land District 27, Lots 31 and 46. They were near neighbors on Big Sandy Creek.

The Georgia land lottery of 1810 identified two named Samuel Pate, from Twiggs County, as fortunate drawers of land in the newly-formed Early County. They were Samuel Pate, Sr., a Revolutionary War soldier, who drew Lot 312 in District 15, which became Decatur County, and Samuel, Jr., who drew Lot 228 in District 11, which became Mitchell County. Both disposed of their land.

Narration on Charles Pate d. p. 1790 documents his descendants as settlers in Decatur and Baker (precursor to Miller) counties in the mid-1820s. A search of deeds failed to produce proof that the two Samuels sold the land to other Pate kinspersons, but the possibility is present.

The tax records of 1818 and lottery records of 1820 are interpreted as recognizing Samuel d. p. 1833 and his three sons, Abimilech, Allen, and Samuel.

The identification of Samuel as a Revolutionary soldier is the only record found by this research of his Revolutionary War service. Note was made earlier that Fereby, the widow of Charles Pate d. 1825, drew a tract of land in the land lottery, as the widow of a Revolutionary soldier. Georgia did not require proof of service for this recognition, just a verbal statement. Most men from North Carolina served in militia units, not in the Continental Army Line, and these records had a poor survival rate.

U. S. Census reports enumerate Abimilech in Butler County and Allen in Bibb County in 1830. The younger Samuel remained in Twiggs County for a few years, apparently until his death after 1840.

Available records fail to identify the year Samuel d. p. 1833 and his son Allen departed Twiggs County. Allen was in Bibb County when his daughter Elizabeth married, 22 December 1825. Samuel was not enumerated on either U. S. Census in 1830. Samuel purchased 40 acres of Bibb County land from Charles Cottingham, 14 August 1831, Deed Book A, page 31. He continued to have presence in Bibb County, 21 October 1833, when he sued George McDaniel over a promissory note. The court ruled in Samuel's favor, Court Minutes 1826-1836.

Researchers might question the identity of the Samuel Pate in Bibb County. U. S. Censuses for 1830 and 1840 continue to enumerate a Samuel of the age of the son of Samuel Pate d. p. 1833, in Twiggs County. The assumption is offered that the Samuel in Bibb County records was Samuel Pate d. p. 1833.

Bibb County adjoined Shelby County. Both counties were formed in 1818 from Montgomery County. Readers will recall that Elias Pate, a son of Samuel Pate who died in Richmond County, North Carolina, in 1850, married Nancy Brown. Nancy Brown was proved to be a daughter of Edmund Brown who died in Marlboro County, South Carolina, 1821, cited earlier. Elias Pate and some of the other Brown descendants moved to Shelby County, Alabama, in the late 1820s or early 1830s. Samuel Pate arrived in Bibb County in the same timeframe. Consideration must be given that Samuel and Elias traveled from Georgia at the same time.

One researcher has reported that Mary, the wife of Samuel Pate's son Allen, was also a Brown. She was not one of the heirs of Edmund Brown identified in *South Carolina Baptists*, Townsend. Nancy, the wife of Elias, was an heir of Edmund Brown.

No record was found on Samuel Pate d. p. after 1833. A review of each son of Samuel Pate d. p. 1833 follows.

ABIMILECH PATE,
SON OF SAMUEL PATE D. P. 1833

Abimilech was the oldest son of Samuel d. p. 1833. He was born ca. 1780 in North Carolina or South Carolina and died in Butler County, Alabama, ca. 1837. He married Susannah Brimley, as reported by the research of Richard Fowler. Brimley families were near neighbors to the Pate Families in Kershaw County, South Carolina, 1800-1810.

Richard Fowler was a diligent family researcher. He compiled records on the family of Abimilech from family records, U. S. Census reports, and records from the Sweetwater Church of Butler County. The following information was shared with the writer in the early 1990s.

The children of Abimilech were:

Elijah – b. ca. 1818 Alabama, d. unk., m. Elizabeth (Clement?);
Amy P. "Emma" – b. ca. 1821, Alabama, d. p. 1880, Milan County, Texas, m. James Hardcastle;

Matilda Amanda – b. 22 December 1823, d. 6 January 1863, Milam County, Texas, m. Alexander Fowler;

Nancy – b. ca. 1825, Alabama, d. p. 1855, m. Joseph Lofton;

Susan – b. ca. 1827, d. p. 1880, m. Eli Hardcastle;

Joe (Joel?) – b. ca. 1829, Alabama, d. unk., m. 1) Rebecca Fisher, 2) Sallie Whittle;

Elizabeth – b. ca. 1833, Alabama, d. unk., m. George Worcester;

Sarah – b. ca. 1834, Alabama, d. unk., m. Samuel Smith.

Elijah was reported to have joined the California Gold Rush. The others eventually settled in various areas of Texas.

The writer has no additional information on Abimilech Pate.

ALLEN PATE,
SON OF SAMUEL PATE D. P. 1833

Allen Pate was born ca. 1785 in North Carolina or South Carolina, based on U. S. Census reports. He died after the U. S. Census for Bibb County, Alabama. was enumerated in 1850, apparently dying in Bibb County. He married Mary [?], who was born in South Carolina ca. 1788, based on U. S. Census reports. She died after the Bibb County U. S. Census for 1860 was enumerated. She was listed in the household of her son, Stephen Pate, in 1860. Note was made earlier that she may have had the maiden name of Brown, but this research failed to confirm that claim.

Twiggs County, Georgia, tax and land records made by Allen have been cited. He was enumerated on the U. S. Censuses for Bibb County in 1830, 1840, and 1850. He acquired 80 acres of land from the U. S. Government, 27 July 1840, the east half of the northwest quarter, Section 30, Township 23, Range 13.

This research failed to locate a will, estate record, or deed to prove the children of Allen Pate. Bibb County marriage records report eight marriages for Pate males and females in a timeframe to have been children of Allen Pate. Allen Pate was party to the license process for two of them. Most of the others lived in close proximity to Allen after marriage. They reported birthplaces of South Carolina, Georgia, and Alabama, where Allen lived when they were born. The assumption is offered that the eight were children of Allen and Mary. A possible ninth child will be recognized later.

The assumed children of Allen and Mary were:

Elizabeth – b. ca. 1808, South Carolina, d. unk., m. Spencer
Rea/Ray, 22 December 1825;
Sarah – b. ca. 1812, Georgia, d. unk, m. Erasmus Hubbard, 27
October 1833;
Charles – b. ca. 1815, Georgia, d. unk, m. Eliza Nix, 4 January 1833;
Stephen – b. ca. 1818, Georgia, d. unk, m. Elizabeth Martin, 24
January 1837;
Anna – b. ca. 1820, Georgia, d. unk, m. Stephen Scott, 5 Sep-
tember 1837;
Alfred Jackson – b. ca. 1822, Georgia, d. unk, m. Angeline Scott,
20 July 1842;
Milly – b. ca. 1825, Alabama, d. unk, m. Charles Rea/Ray, 1
September 1841;
James C. – b. ca. 1830, Alabama, d. unk, m. Mahala Gammon,
3 January 1856.

Allen and Mary may have been the parents of Mary Pate, who
married John Martin in Shelby County, Alabama, 17 August 1845.
The relationship of the Pates in Bibb and Shelby counties has been
noted earlier. This Mary was born ca. 1824 in Alabama.

Elias Pate of Shelby County had a daughter named Mary, cited
earlier. She married Alexander Vick, as reported by the estate
records of her father. Note that Stephen Pate, son of Allen, married
Elizabeth Martin, with the consent of John Martin. The records
suggest that Mary Pate, who married John Martin in Shelby County,
may have been the ninth child of Allen and Mary.

This ends the report on Allen Pate, son of Samuel Pate d. p. 1833.
One son of Samuel remains for review.

SAMUEL PATE D. P. 1848,
ADOPTED SON OF SAMUEL PATE D. P. 1833

This is the Samuel Pate that earlier researchers identified as a
son of Rev. William Pate. John Ben Pate identified him as such in
American Geneology [sic] *of the Pate Family*. The assumption is
offered that he had a relationship to the nephew of Rev. William
Pate, Samuel Pate d. p. 1833. This research has no record of an
association between this Samuel and Rev. William.

He was born ca. 1790 and died in Twiggs County, Georgia,
in 1848 or 1849. He had two marriages and children from each.

Neither has been identified, but the second wife had the given name of Elizabeth.

The following is a recap of information offered earlier in this report. There is no available record to prove the children of Samuel Pate d. p. 1833. He had an association with three Pate males in Kershaw County, South Carolina, and Twiggs County, Georgia. Allen and Samuel d. p. 1833 were named in Kershaw. The extant Twiggs County records locate Abimilech and Allen as near neighbors on Big Sandy Creek in Twiggs County. Tax records place Samuel, the elder, on Big Sandy Creek. Georgia land lottery records identify Samuel, Sr. and Samuel, Jr. (the latter being the adopted Samuel of this report), of Jefferson District in Twiggs County, receiving land in the 1820 lottery.

Originally, these records led to the assumption that Abimilech, Allen, and Samuel were sons of the elder Samuel, with Rev. William as their uncle.

DNA testing added another factor to this relationship. Samuel d. 1848 had children from two marriages. Descendants from one son of each marriage have joined the Pate DNA Project, Joseph S. Pate of the first and Elijah Pate of the second. Neither are in the Thoroughgood Pate Haplogroup I-M223. They tested as Haplogroup R-M269.

This leads to the opinion that, like Levi Pate and Maxie Pate mentioned earlier in this narrative, Samuel was an adopted son. Actually, the question of his relationship to Rev. William or Samuel is not of genealogical significance in that he was not a genetic Pate.

The children are listed here because they had the Pate surname and future researchers may have interest in this origin.

The children of the first marriage are reported in tradition. They were:

> Joseph S. – b. 1815, d. ca. 1868, Woodville, Texas;
> Dock – b. ca. 1818;
> Kate – b. ca. 1821, d. unk, m. [?] Jernigan;
> Stephen Swinny – b. ca. 1 July 1823, d. (Confederate Army), m.
> Margaret McKinnon;
> Tillman – b. ca. 1825.

Joseph and Stephen are confirmed by U. S. Census reports.
The children of the marriage to Elizabeth [?] were:

William Thomas – b. ca. 1839, d. unk, m. Mary Ann Rains;
Isaac – b. ca. 1841, d. (Confederate Army, Gettysburg, Pennsylvania);
Martha – b. ca. 1843;
Elijah – b. ca. 1844, d. 1905, m. 1) Miss McElraw, 2) Martha Bull; Nancy Rebecca – b. ca. 1846;
Benjamin F. – b. ca. 1848.

Joseph of the first marriage and William Thomas of the second are known to have moved to Texas.

The report returns to the remaining sons of Samuel Pate d. ca. 1810.

REV. WILLIAM PATE,
SON OF SAMUEL PATE D. CA. 1810

Researchers, over the years, have identified this son of Samuel Pate d. ca. 1810 as "Reverend William Pate of Georgia". He was born ca. 1773 in North Carolina or South Carolina. The migration of his father between those states has been described. His death year is controversial. John Ben Pate, author of *American Geneology* [sic] *of the Pate Family*, reported he died near Warwick, Georgia (originally Pulaski County, now Turner County) in 1837. The same writer reported in *The History of Turner County* that he died in the pulpit after preaching in 1841. Since he was enumerated on the 1840 U. S. Census for Dooly County, Georgia, the 1841 death year will be recognized in this report.

Earlier researchers have compiled a mass of confusion on the history of this family. Regardless of the well-intended actions, erroneous assumptions have resulted in the recording of errors that have frustrated researchers for decades.

The following statements in this paragraph are examples of the errors perpetuated about this family. These early erroneous reports identified Rev. William as a son of Jacob and Zilla (Broach) Pate of Virginia, who was born about 1750 in Virginia, migrated to North Carolina, served in the Continental Army in the Revolutionary War, migrated to Georgia where he had a brother in Washington County, and other issues to be cited later. All incorrect.

The writer prepared a documented narrative that corrected these errors in 1996. The following paragraphs are based on that narrative, and they provide an accurate record for this family.

Rev. William was born ca. 1773, as he had not reached his teen years of life when the last major battle of the Revolutionary War was fought. Thus, could not have been a Revolutionary War soldier. At least two men named William Pate from North Carolina did serve in that war. One, from Cumberland County, died at the Valley Forge Encampment in 1778. The other served under Captain Fenner with a North Carolina Regiment in the Continental Army. He was on the muster rolls at White Plains, New York, in 1778. He returned to Jones County, North Carolina, after the War and died there in 1812.

It is worthy to note that Jacob and Zilla (Broach) Pate had several daughters, but nomale child has ever been identified in records available to this research. Rev. William was not their son.

This report has assigned Rev. William as a son of Samuel Pate d. ca. 1810, as noted earlier. Available records fail to prove the children of Samuel, as reported earlier. The identity of his children is an assumption supported by records. Most were cited earlier.

A few remarks follow. Rev. William appears on the 1800 U. S. Census for Kershaw County, South Carolina, with his father and brothers, Bennett and Jason. His brothers Elijah and Samuel were in Kershaw in 1810. These given names and others, identified as common for the Thoroughgood Pate line earlier in this report, appear repeatedly in the children and grandchildren of Rev. William. These include Samuel, Elijah, Bennett, Phoeby, Stephen, Swinney, and others.

The given name of Phoeby/Fereby is of interest. Tradition reports that Rev. William married first to a Miss Weathersby. They had one daughter named Phoeby. The wife died, and the daughter was left with her maternal kin, as William moved from the area.

The U. S. Census for 1790 listed Weathersby families only in Barnwell County, South Carolina. It was not a large family. The U. S. Census for 1800 enumerated Isham Weathersby and Shadrack Weathersby in Bladen County, North Carolina, and others of that surname continued to be present in Barnwell County, South Carolina. Readers should recall that Samuel Pate d. ca. 1810, father of Rev. William, lived in Bladen and Robeson counties of North Carolina until about 1795. Contact between Rev. William and a Miss Weathersby could be expected.

Charles Pate d. 1825, a nephew of Samuel Pate d. ca. 1810 and a cousin to Rev. William, was a near neighbor to this Samuel and his family in Robeson and Bladen counties. His wife was Phoeby

(Humphrey) Pate. Perhaps she served as a namesake for the reported daughter of Rev. William named Phoeby.

This research failed to locate an official record to identify the children of Rev. William -- a will, deed, estate record, etc. The family tradition, criticized earlier, does appear to provide a list that includes the children of Rev. William. However, contradictions appear in the list, which includes names other records prove were not children of Rev. William. Regardless of the errors, gratitude is expressed for the efforts in preparing the list. No other source for the children has been found in this research.

DNA testing has confirmed that two of the sons have DNA results to be expected for descendants of Samuel Pate d. ca. 1810, Elijah Bennett Pate (1815-1899) and James David Pate (1817-1865). One son previously identified in traditional genealogy, Samuel Pate (1786-1848), is proved by DNA testing to not be a Pate descendant. More will be offered on this later. This Samuel, like Levi Pate, presented earlier in this narration, was a "non-paternal event". Another child, Maxie Pate (1846-1870), was recognized in traditional genealogy as an adopted child, and DNA testing has confirmed this status as a non-genetic Pate.

The other children identified in the tradition – Elizabeth, Nancy, Mary, and Sarah – appear to have been children of Rev. William. They were associated with him and each other as near neighbors, and their ages appear to be correct for his children.

The tradition reports Rev. William had a second marriage, wife not identified, and that Samuel and Elizabeth were children of that marriage. Elizabeth is acceptable as his daughter, but this research does not consider that Samuel was a son, adopted or otherwise, of Rev. William.

This Samuel is the man reported earlier in this narrative as a son of Samuel Pate d. p. 1833. He also was proved to not to be a genetic Pate by DNA testing. He must have been an adopted son of Samuel. Records cited in the report on Samuel d. p. 1833 identify a male of his age in the Kershaw, South Carolina, household of the elder Samuel. Both moved from Kershaw to Twiggs County, Georgia, with the two young Pate males, Abimilech and Allen. This research has no record of a young Pate male named Samuel in the Pulaski/ Dooly counties area where Rev. William lived. The writer believes the Samuel identified in this tradition as a son of Rev. William was the adopted son of Samuel d. p. 1833.

Actually, the association is of no significance to Pate genealogists. Y-DNA testing proves this Samuel was not a genetic Pate.

Elizabeth was probably a daughter of the reported second marriage of Rev. William. The time between her birth and that of the first child of the third marriage was over ten years.

Rev. William married Tempty (Temperance?) Parkerson as his third wife. She was born 30 August 1782 and died 9 August 1865. She was buried at Friendship Baptist Church in Pulaski County with her daughter Mary (Pate) Holt. The grave marker identified her as Tempty Parkerson Pate, wife of Rev. William Pate. She was a daughter of Jacob Parkerson, a Revolutionary War soldier from Virginia. Ruby (Pate) Bodkin reports the relationship is proved in Pulaski County estate records.

Rev. William departed Kershaw County, South Carolina, after the U. S. Census for 1800 was enumerated, and before 1810. He was on the payroll of a detachment of Pulaski County militia stationed at Fort Lawrence, Georgia, 8 September 1814 to 3 November 1814. Fort Lawrence was located on the west side of the Flint River in present-day Taylor County. It was established to protect the old Federal Road through Indian Territory in western Georgia. He was paid $8 per month, *Georgia Military Affairs 1814- 1819.*

The militia record is among the records used to determine the true birth year of Rev. William. Men over 45 years were exempt from military service during this time. Thus, he was under 45 years in 1814, thus born after 1769. This and U. S. Census reports lead to the assumed birth year of ca. 1773.

Earlier researchers have credited Rev. William and his brother Elijah Pate for the large number of Pate/Patty records in early Greene and Hancock counties of Georgia. The Elijah "Patty" who drew Early County land in the land lottery of 1820 has been identified as being the brother Elijah Pate. Members of the actual Patty family made these records, in the opinion of the writer. Records fail to identify any relationship between the Pate Family of this report and the Patty family.

The writer has followed the Patty family from the Northern Neck of Virginia, in the 1600s, to Newberry and Fairfield Counties of South Carolina. The given names of Charles, Elijah, and William are common to the family. Elijah and William Patty were in early Greene County records and eventually moved to Cherokee County, Alabama.

John Ben Pate authored *The History of Turner County, Georgia.* He reported an event of 13 November 1833 that is of interest to this report. An impressive astronomical event filled the night sky with a fiery display of falling stars. The local population interpreted the display as a Providential Act and sought the assurance of Rev. William. Scripture was read, and hymns were sung. As the gathering grew hungry, the sons of Rev. William, Elijah and James, were put to work digging potatoes and cutting firewood. His wife, "Aunt Tempty", and daughters, Polly Holt, Sarah Johnson, Betsy Story, and Nancy Blanchard, were active in the kitchen.

The story is impressive for this report in that John Ben Pate identified what is believed to have been the genetic offspring of the second and third marriages of Rev. William. Further, the daughters were correctly identified with their married surnames. Maxie and Samuel were not his sons and were not recognized.

The children of Rev. William's first and second marriages follow:

Phoebe – b. of the first marriage in North Carolina and left with her maternal kin (Weathersby ?);
Elizabeth – b. of the second marriage, ca. 1795, d. 1872, m. Samuel Story, 20 August 1815.

The children of the third marriage to Tempty Parkerson were:

Mary – b. 16 December 1812, d. 26 May 1878, m. James Holt, 12 January 1832;
Nancy – b. 8 January 1813, d. 1912, m. Reuben Blanchard;
Elijah Bennett – b. 15 April 1815, d. 1899, m. Mary Smith;
James David – b. 24 January 1817, d. 28 August 1865, m. Jane Moore, 12 January 1840;
Sarah – b. 1819, d. 1899, m. David Johnson.

The dates are from grave markers, Pulaski County marriage records, biographical sketches in *Pioneers of Wiregrass Georgia,* Folks Huxford, and *Historical and Genealogical Collections of Dooly County* by Watts Powell.

The adopted son, Maxie Pate, was born ca. 1807 and died in 1872 in Wilcox County, Georgia. He married Catherine Holt, reported to have been a sister to James Holt who married Nancy Pate. U. S. Census reports identify 18 children born to this marriage. The records of Ruby Pate Bodkin identify the same number, though they differ in some of the given names. They were:

William – b. ca. 1835,
Elizabeth – b. ca. 1836,
James D. – b. ca. 1837,
Sarah A. – b. ca. 1838,
Elijah – b. ca. 1839,
Lucinda – b. ca. 1840,
Samuel W.– b. ca. 1842,
John A. – b. ca. 1843,
Joseph E. – b. ca. 1845,
Tempty – b. ca. 1846,
Edmond J. – b. ca. 1848,
Jonathan P.– b. ca. 1849,
Mary – b. ca. 1851,
Nancy – b. ca. 1852,
Rebecca – b. ca. 1854,
Maxie – b. ca. 1856,
Jason (Manasseh) – b. ca. 1858,
Jincy/Cornelia – b. ca. 1859.

A brief review on each child of Rev. William follows.

ELIZABETH (PATE) STORY,
DAUGHTER OF REV. WILLIAM PATE

Elizabeth (Pate) Story was born 15 April 1795 and died 4 August 1872. The dates are from family records. She married Samuel Story in Pulaski County, 20 August 1815.

There is confusion with the children of this marriage. U. S. Census reports identify fourteen children fathered by Samuel Story. Family tradition reports that nine of these were born out of wedlock to Samuel and Anna Brown. U. S. Census reports enumerate Anna Brown living two households from Samuel and Elizabeth in 1850 and 1860. Anna Brown was living in the household of Alice (Story) Hall in 1870. Alice has been identified among the children of Samuel Story and Anna Brown. The returns for 1850 and 1860 enumerated several of these children in the Story household and that of Anna Brown. Those in the Brown household in 1850 had the Story surname. Those in the Brown household in 1860 had the Brown surname.

All of the children married with the surname of Story, not Brown.

The writer does not have available resources to prove that the children assigned to Samuel Story came from two different mothers. The children will be listed in order of birth based on available information, and the following paragraph will identify those reported to have been from his relationship to Anna Brown.

The children were:

> Richard – b. ca. 1816, m. Sarah Willis;
> Nancy – b. ca. 1818, m. Edwin Taylor;
> James – b. ca. 1821, m. Mary Kerce;
> Mary Ann – b. ca. 1824, m. [?] Davis;
> Caroline – b. ca. 1826, m. Phillip Pitkins/Pittman;
> Alexander – b. ca. 1828, m. Narcissus Watson;
> Jincy – b. ca. 1830, m. John B. Royal;
> Frederick – b. ca. 1832, m. Martha Watson;
> Alice – b. ca. 1833, m. Warren W. Hall;
> Warren Lumpkin – b. ca. 1834, m. Henrietta Jenkins;
> Samuel – b. ca. 1836, m. Martha Jane Stewart;
> William Jackson – b. ca. 1838, m. Adaline Royal;
> Llewellin – b. ca. 1840, m. 1) Ida Handley, 2) Mary Emma
>   McRae;
> Alfred – b. ca. 1841, m. Pinky Goff.

Information shared with the writer in earlier years identified the following as children of Anna Brown: Richard, Alexander, William Jackson, Jincy, Frederick, Warren Lumpkin, Alice, Samuel, and Llewellin.

Assuming the information is correct, the others were children of Elizabeth (Pate) Story. Readers are cautioned that this is from unproven sources.

MARY (PATE) HOLT,
DAUGHTER OF REV. WILLIAM PATE

Mary (Pate) Holt was born 16 December 1812 and died 26 May 1878, as inscribed onher grave marker at Friendship Baptist Church in Pulaski County. She and her husband were buried near her mother, Tempty (Parkerson) Pate. She married James Holt 12 January 1832 in Pulaski County. He was born 16 November 1812 and died 16 May 1877.

The children of James and Mary are from family tradition and have been confirmed by U.

S. Census reports, marriage records, and *Historical Collections of Dooly County*, Watts Powell. The family appears on U. S. Census reports for Dooly and Wilcox Counties.

The children were:

Nancy E. – b. 25 December 1835, d. unk, m. Hardy Triplet, 1 December 1853;

Sarah C. – b. ca. 1834, d. unk, m. [?] Faircloth;

Tempty C. – b. 10 March 1836;

Mary J. – b. 11 October 1838, d. unk, m. James Warren;

Fereby Ann – b. 4 May 1840, d. ca. 10 December 1866, m. William H. Gammage;

Elizabeth – b. 15 February 1842, d. unk, m. William H. Gammage, after death of sister Fereby Ann;

Pinky A. (Winey) – b. 30 October 1845, d. unk, m. George Gammage;

James Freeman – b. 6 October 1850;

William Lovett – b. 10 March 1852, d. unk, m. 1) Ellen Finlayson, 2) Eugenia Finlayson, sister to Ellen;

Elijah Thomas – b. 20 March 1855;

Bennett W,- b. 5 February 1857, d. unk, m. Mary Queen Faircloth.

A biographical sketch in *Pioneers of Wiregrass Georgia* by Folks Huxford, assigned James and Mary a son named Greenberry Holt. Greenberry Holt is absent from records on James and Mary available to this research. He does appear on the U. S. Census for 1850 in the Dooly County household of Sarah Holt, apparently a widow. Greenberry is probably a son of this Sarah Holt, not James and Mary (Pate) Holt.

This ends the report on Mary (Pate) Holt.

NANCY (PATE) BLANCHARD, DAUGHTER OF REV. WILLIAM PATE

Nancy (Pate) Blanchard was born 8 January 1823 and died 1912, based on a biographical sketch in *Pioneers of Wiregrass Georgia*, Folks Huxford, vol. 9. She married Reuben Blanchard 28 February

1834 in Pulaski County. The groom was born 20 October 1810 in
Pulaski County and died in St. Johns County, Florida, between
1862 and 1864.

Reuben Blanchard served in the Georgia militia in the Creek
Indian War in 1836. He received a bounty land grant in 1855 to
land in Orange County, Florida, for this service. The family moved
to Florida for a few years. They relocated from Orange County to St.
Johns County after 1860, when they were enumerated on the U. S.
Census for Orange County. Reuben died in St. Johns County, and
his widow and children returned to Georgia.

The children of Reuben and Nancy (Pate) Blanchard were:

> Mary Ann – b. ca. 1835, d. unk, m. 1) Isaac Marchant, 10 Jan-
> uary 1850, 2) Andrew J. McDaniel, 16 February 1865;
> William Green - b. ca. 1837, d. 1864 (Confederate Army, at
> Fredericksburg, Maryland), m. Nancy Eldridge;
> Nancy Jane – b. ca. 1844, d. unk, m. 1) Wesley Summers (Sim-
> mons?), 2) Steward Summers, 29 February 1866;
> Elizabeth – b. ca. 1846, d. unk, m. Jordan Rigdon;
> Elijah Daniel – b. ca. 1847, d. 9 November 1929, m. 1) Mary
> Newborn, 2) Mittie Ida Cannon Jones, 24 July 1907;
> Diantha – b. ca. 1853, d. unk, m. Elijah Rigdon;
> Sylvania – b. ca. 1855, d. 20 April 1937, m. Micajah Roberts.

No other information is available on this family.

ELIJAH BENNETT PATE,
SON OF REV. WILLIAM PATE

Elijah Bennett Pate had the given names of his uncles, Elijah
Pate and Bennett Pate. He was born 15 April 1825 and died
13 November 1899 in Crisp County, Georgia. He, his wife, and
three of his children have grave markers at Zion Hope Cemetery
in Crisp County. He married Mary Smith 15 February 1842 in
Dooly County. The bride was a daughter of Jonathan and Nancy
Smith.

The children of Elijah and Mary (Smith) Pate are identified by
U. S. Census reports, family tradition, marriage records, grave
markers, and the *History and Genealogy of Dooly County* by Watts
Powell. The children were:

William Allen – b. ca. 1843, d. 1863 (Confedate Army, at Gettysburg, Pennsylvania);

James Daniel – b. 15 April 1845, d. 22 January 1917, buried Zion Hope Church, Crisp County, m. Rachel Whiddon, 11 May 1865, Irwin County;

John S. – b. 27 June 1847, d. unk, m. Jennie Clements, 27 June 1872, Dooly County;

Samuel Bennett – b. 25 December 1849, d. 9 May 1895, Zion Hope Cemetery, m. Elizabeth Clements, 16 January 1870, Irwin County;

Mary Jane – b. ca. 1851, d. unk, m. William C. Cone, 7 July 1883, Dooly County;

Joseph L. – b. 4 April 1854, d. 24 September 1881, Zion Hope Cemetery, m. Jane Davis, 30 November 1876, Dooly County;

Elijah A. E. – b. 9 September 1857, d. unk, m. Sallie Clements, 20 February 1876, Dooly County;

Elizabeth – b. ca. 1861, d. unk, m. [?] Owens;

Sarah Ann – b. January 1862, d. unk, m. Joseph C. Hamilton, 3 January 1884, Dooly County.

This completes the report on Elijah Bennett Pate, son of Rev. William Pate.

JAMES DAVID PATE,
SON OF REV. WILLIAM PATE

James David Pate was born 29 January 1817 and died 28 August 1865 in Wilcox County. He, his wife, and two of his sons were buried at Oklahoma Church Cemetery in Wilcox County. He married Jane "Jincy" Moore in Pulaski County 21 January 1841. The bride was born 12 October 1823 and died 28 April 1917. The dates are from grave markers and marriage records.

James David was conscripted into the Confederate Army late in the War. He returned home after the War. He died of typhoid fever 28 August 1865. Civil War letters between Jane and her husband are posted on the Wilcox County Genweb page and provide personal history on this family.

The children of James David and Jane are from U. S. Census reports, grave markers, marriage records, and the Dooly County book by Watts Powell. These recognize ten children. The Civil War letters refer to fourteen children, but do not name them. Ten children seem to be correct. They were:

William Bennett – b. 2 October 1842, d. 10 December 1915, m. Catherine (Rainey) Chandler, 28 May 1868;

Elijah Thomas – b. 24 January 1845, d. 24 February 1941, m. [?] Henrietta [?]);

John Thomas – b. 22 January 1847, d. 24 February 1924;

Mary Jane – b. 17 November 1848, d. unk., m. George Gammage, 11 January 1866;

Nancy – b. 14 May 1851, d. unk, m. John Clements, 25 November 1877;

Sarah – b. 20 April 1854, d. unk., m. Thomas Gibbs, 27 December 1874;

Elizabeth – b. 29 February 1856, d. unk., m. L. D. Taylor, 8 June 1874;

Narcissus – b. 2 August 1858, d. unk;

James Hanson – b. ca. 1862, d. unk, m. Alice Bass, 10 January 1884;

Benjamin Samuel – b. 13 April 1864, d. unk, m. Nancy E. Pitts, 28 July 1881.

SARAH (PATE) JOHNSON, DAUGHTER OF REV. WILLIAM PATE

Sarah was the last child born to Rev. William and Tempty (Parkerson) Pate. She was born 15 May 1819 and died 12 November 1899 in Clinch County, Georgia. She was buried at Ramah Primitive Baptist Church in Clinch County. She married David D. Johnson.

Pioneers of Wiregrass Georgia by Folks Huxford, has a biographical sketch on this family. They moved from Pulaski County to Clinch County in 1855. They settled on Suwannoochee Creek near the Echols County line.

David Johnson enlisted in Company G, 14th Georgia Infantry Regiment of the Confederate Army, 9 July 1861. He died of wounds in the military hospital in Richmond, Virginia, 26 July 1864.

Sarah lived on the home place with her bachelor son William for many years. She was enumerated in the household of her daughter, Nancy (Johnson) Griffis, in Clinch County in 1880. She reportedly died in the house of her daughter Mary (Johnson) Chancey, 12 November 1899.

The children of Sarah (Pate) Johnson were:

Tempty C. – b. 30 June 1842, d. unk, m. Guilford Harnage;
William A. P.– b. 21 January 1844, d. 1914;
Nancy E. – b. 15 December 1845, d. 13 June 1934, buried Ramah Cemetery, Clinch County, m. Dixon Griffis;
Mary C. "Polly" – b. 30 March 1847, d. unk, m. Shelton B. Chancey.

Shelton B. Chauncey was buried in Chauncey Cemetery in Clinch County. The dates are from his grave marker. Mary (Pate) Chauncey was probably buried at the same, without a legible grave marker.

This completes the report on Rev. William Pate and his family. The report will now focus on the next son of Samuel Pate d. ca. 1810, Elijah Pate d. p. 1817.

ELIJAH PATE D. P. 1817,
SON OF SAMUEL PATE D. CA. 1810

Elijah Pate was the third son born to Samuel Pate d. ca. 1810. The brother of Elijah, Rev. William Pate, was born ca. 1773 and was the fourth born son of Samuel. Rev. William preceded Elijah in this report because he was reported to have had an association with the adopted son of Samuel Pate d. p. 1833. It seemed best to have the two brothers in successive narratives.

Elijah was born ca. 1765, probably in North Carolina. He died after 10 October 1817, the date of the last record found on him. His wife had the given name of Milly. Her surname is unknown to the writer.

Elijah was enumerated on the U. S. Census for Kershaw County in 1810. He was in an adjacent household to his brothers Bennett and Samuel. The assumption has been offered that the elderly male in his household was his father, Samuel Pate d. ca. 1810. He is also assumed to be one of the Pates in the weaving firm of 'Pate and Pate', listed on the Kershaw industrial census in 1810.

Elijah was the only member of the family to acquire land in Kershaw County. Perhaps it should be said that he was the only member to record land transactions in Kershaw. Some landowners never recorded deeds in the frontier areas. He purchased 200 acres on

Hanging Rock Creek, 13 February 1813, from Joseph Clark, Book G, p. 232. He also acquired 100 acres on Rutledge Branch of Hanging Rock Creek. Record of his acquisition of the 100 acres was not found, but he and wife Milly sold the 100 acres, 26 October 1817, Book H, page 265. He and Milly sold the 200-acre tract to Samuel West, 10 October 1817, Book H, page 270.

Elijah had three young males in his household in 1810.

This research found no additional records on Elijah Pate. Note has been made that earlier researchers assumed he was the Elijah Patty in records of Greene, Hancock, and Early counties of Georgia. That man was from the Patty family of Newberry and Union counties, South Carolina, in the opinion of the writer, and moved on to Cherokee County, Alabama, before 1850.

THOROUGHGOOD JASON PATE D. P. 1860, SON OF SAMUEL PATE D. CA. 1810

Thoroughgood Jason Pate was the fifth and last son born to Samuel Pate d. ca. 1810. He was born ca. 1777, in North Carolina or South Carolina and died after 1860 in Chesterfield County, South Carolina. His wife had the given name of Elizabeth. Her surname was not identified.

The given name of Thoroughgood is an assumption. Background details follow. Jason Pate appears in Lancaster County, South Carolina, in 1797 and 1798 and on the 1800 U.

S. Census for Kershaw County, South Carolina. This research found no additional records for him until 1860, when the U. S. Census for Chesterfield County, South Carolina, enumerated T. J. Pate, 83 years of age in the household of James R. Knight, 26 years old, and his wife, Mary, 30 years old.

The assumption is offered that this elderly T. J. Pate was the Jason Pate on the earlier censuses, identified as a son of Samuel Pate d. ca. 1810. He was living with persons in the generation of his grandchildren.

Jason Pate d. p. 1860 purchased 50 acres in Lancaster County, South Carolina, from James McVey, 6 January 1797, Book D, page 184. The land was identified as the former homesite of Dicey Fuller and bordered on Margaret Bishop and Benjamin Hale. Jason and his wife Elizabeth sold the land 26 July 1798 to Benjamin Johnston, Book D, page 185. This deed described the land as part of the original grant to Henry Massey. Massey conveyed the tract to Margaret Bishop, who sold it to Benjamin Hale. It is not clear if Dicey Fuller purchased the land from Benjamin Hale or lived on it as a renter. Further, it is unclear how James McVey acquired the authority to sell the tract to Jason Pate.

Perhaps the preceding deeds hold a clue to the maiden name of Elizabeth, wife of Jason Pate.

Jason was enumerated adjacent to his Pate brothers, Bennett, William, and Samuel, on the Kershaw U. S. Census for 1800. The surname was misspelled as Paiste, as noted earlier; in the Census, he was recorded as 16-26 years of age, born 1774-1784. One child was in the household, a female under 10 years of age.

The next record on him available to this research is the 1860 U. S. Census for Chesterfield County, as discussed above.

The identity of the daughter is unknown. The writer has suggested she may be the Lydia Pate who married Charles Pate d. ca. 1855 in Robeson County, 10 March 1821. This Lydia died in Baker County, Georgia, after 1856. Her age on the 1800 U. S. Census is a bit old for this person, but Census ages tend to be inconsistent, as noted above.

Caution is given that the writer is working with assumptions based on a limited number of records. Readers may accept or reject the conclusions.

This ends the report on Samuel Pate d. ca. 1810.

VIII

JAMES PATE d. ca. 1790,
SON OF CHARLES PATE d. ca. 1769

*This chapter was not completed before the death
of Jim Peacock. Joel Pate was requested to take
this task, which he graciously accepted.*

Note by Joel Pate

Writing the concluding chapter for Jim Peacock's book on Thoroughgood Pate is an honor and a unique challenge. Jim had a different writing style. We differ in syntax and person or voice. For example, Jim referred to himself in the third person, using the terms "this writer" or "the writer" multiple times in his manuscript. I use first person pronouns, e.g., "I", "my", and "mine". I also tend to revert to Latin and Latin abbreviations more so than did Jim. Jim's approach to family history or genealogy was, no doubt, influenced by his medical and scientific background; my approach is tempered by my legal, law enforcement, and criminal investigative background.

Given all of these differences, Jim and I were of one mind on many key issues. We strongly advocate the idea that genealogy, like faith, is best when shared. We shared a strong belief in avoiding unproved data or at least noting it as unproven. We both carefully note opinions and assumptions. I prefer conclusions rather than assumptions. We also share the desire to properly cite or credit the source or reference we quote.

One unique thing that Jim and I share, and few know about, is the fact that we both, as undergraduate students at Florida State University, met the wonderful women who would become our loving and devoted wives and who would walk with us, for decades, on our life journeys. This chapter is dedicated to Margaret Linda Hoadley Peacock and Linda Anson Pate.

In compiling the data for this chapter, I turned to published or previously published genealogical material and private correspondence retained in my papers. First among the resources I used are the writings of Jim Peacock in the *Pate Pioneers*, a quarterly newsletter published in the 1980s and 1990s by Clovis Byars Herring; Jim's monograph series, *Pate Pioneers on the Pee Dee River;* Jim's genealogical papers stored in the Alumni and Special Collection of the Robert Draughton Brown Library at Auburn University, Auburn, Alabama; and notes from a paper Jim delivered at the September 12-14, 2008 Pate Genealogical Convocation in Colonial Williamsburg, Virginia. I also used the writings of several other Pate surname researchers. These are Linda Harmon, Lynn Lancaster, Jinks Pate-Lee, Samuel Thedford Pait, Sr, A. J. Pate, William S. "Chip" Pate, Carol Ann Moore Robinson, Joseph Harris Scarborough, Randy Santee, and Audrey Parker Young.

In researching and writing family history, it is important that the researcher have a sound understanding of the where as well as who. A basic grasp of place names and evolution of political subdivisions (i.e., states, territories, districts, and counties) is critical. In researching the Pate surname in North Carolina, it becomes clear that a major wellspring of Pate families is Wayne County, especially near Goldsboro and a small stream known as Stoney Creek.

The brief pedigree of Wayne County is: Johnston County was formed in 1746, Dobbs County was formed from Johnston in 1758, and Wayne County from Dobbs in 1779. In 1791, Dobbs County was divided into Glascow and Lenoir counties and ceased to exist as a county. Jim's references to "old Dobbs County" make sense when you understand the shifting, shrinking, and even extinction or disappearance of North Carolina counties.

One of the primary tools used in genealogical research is the decennial federal census prescribed by the Constitution of the United States. Beginning in 1790, the federal census is taken every ten years, in the decade year, and released as a public access document 74 year after it was taken.

Pate families in the North Carolina 1790 census, alphabetic by name of head of household:

Name	County	Page	District
Benet Pate	Roberson	049	Fayette
Charles Pate	Roberson	050	Fayette
Daniel Pate	Wayne	150	New Bern
Elias Pate	Wayne	150	New Bern
Isaac Pate	Beaufort	125	New Bern
Isun Pate	Wayne	150	New Bern
James Pate	Wayne	150	New Bern
James Pate	Orange	094	Orange
John Pate	Orange	093	Chatham
John N. Pate	Orange	097	St Thomas
John Pate, Jr	Dobbs	136	New Bern
John Pate, Sr	Dobbs	136	New Bern
Joseph Pate	Dobbs	135	New Bern
Martha Pate	Wayne	150	New Bern
Phillip Pate	Jones	144	New Bern
Richard Pate	Jones	144	New Bern
Samuel Pate	Bladen	187	Fayette
Samuel Pate	Richmond	047	Wilmington
Sarah Pate	Dobbs	136	New Bern
Shadrack Pate	Wayne	150	New Bern
Steohen Pate	Dobbs	461	New Bern
Stephen Pate	Richmond	046	Fayette
Thomas Pate	Orange	095	Hillsborough
Thoroughgood Pate	Richmond	047	Fayette
Traverse Pate	Johnston	142	New Bern
William Pate	Jones	144	New Bern
William Pate, Jr	Dobbs	136	New Bern
William Pate, Sr	Dobbs	136	New Bern

Enumerators of the 1790 census were to include the following categories in the census: name of head of household, number of free white males of sixteen years and older, number of free white males under sixteen years, number of free white females, number of all other free persons, number of slaves, and sometimes town or district of residence. There were 28 Pate households enumerated in this census.

There were six Pate households enumerated in Wayne County. In order of listing, they were:

Head of house: **James Pate**
Free White males under 16: 3
Free White males 16 and over: 1
Free White females: 4
Slaves: 1
Household total: 9

Head of house: **Isum Pate**
Free White males under 16: 0
Free White males 16 and over: 1
Free White females: 2
Slaves: 13
Household total: 16

Head of house: **Elias Pate**
Free White males under 16: 0
Free White males 16 and over: 1
Free White females: 0
Slaves: 0
Household total: 1

Head of house: **Daniel Pate**
Free White males under 16: 2
Free White males 16 and over: 1
Free White females: 2
Slaves: 0
Household total: 5

Head of house: **Martha Pate**
Free White males under 16: 0
Free White males 16 and over: 0

Free White females: 1
Slaves: 0
Household total: 1

Head of house: **Shaderack Pate**
Free White males under 16: 3
Free White males16 and over: 1
Free White females: 1
Slaves: 0
Household total: 5

In my opinion the Martha Pate and Shaderack Pate enumerated in the 1790 census of Wayne County, are not children of James Pate. Shaderack Pate enumerated in the 1790 census was perhaps a sibling or cousin of James Pate.

Some researchers suggest that this Martha Pate was the wife of James Pate. I do not concur. This Martha Pate was obviously an adult (age 16 or older) and recognized as a head of household in the census. There was, however, an adult female in the James Pate household. This unidentified female was, no doubt, the wife of James Pate.

Most researchers hold that James Pate died in 1790. Perhaps that is accurate, but the fact that he was enumerated in the 1790 census causes some confusion. It is possible that he was enumerated and then died in the same year.

The earliest record of James Pate that I found was a 1754 military record, where he is listed as being a member of the North Carolina Militia. He was living at the time in an area of Johnston County, North Carolina, which later became Wayne County (*Colonial Soldiers of the South, 1732-1774,* Murtie June Clark.

Land transactions of James Pate follow.

James received a royal land grant, 13 October 1784, of 195 acres along Stoney Creek (*Wayne County Deed Book 18,* page 333).

A 1789 deed for 305 acres in Dobbs County, in part, describes the property as lying on both sides of Stoney Creek. The name Elias Pate also appears in the deed as an adjoining land owner. This land was, no doubt, incorporated into Wayne County from Dobbs County in 1789 (*Wayne County Deed Book 1,* page 267).

The foregoing deed is significant in that it identifies two landmarks critical to this study. These are the Neuse River and Stoney Creek. This deed was granted in 1783 for property in Dobbs County, which became extinct in 1791, and was eventually recorded in Wayne County. It also is significant since it names an Elias Pate, a probable son of James Pate. The deed also mentions the name John Handley, who probably was a descendant of Bryant Handley, a prominent Stafford County Virginian whose family settled in the Neuse River basin. The name Bryant Handley was used as given names for a number of Pate children in North Carolina.

In my opinion, James Pate d. 1790 married Elizabeth Jernigan, daughter of David Jernigan. His children with Elizabeth Jernigan are believed to be:

James Pate Sr. 1740-1826
Daniel Pate 1745-1791
Isham Pate 1755-1840
Elias Pate 1760-1827
Thomas Pate 1769-1845
David Pate 1780-1868.

JAMES PATE, SR. D. 1826
SON OF JAMES PATE D. CA. 1790

Census and other records pertaining to James Pate, Sr:

1800 U.S. Census -- James Pate, Wayne County, page 699, no township.

Only the heads of household were named in the 1800 Census. All members of the household, including the head of household, were tallied by race, gender, age range, and status (either free or slave) in 12 columns.

James Pate, Sr. was born in 1740 in North Carolina. He died in 1826 at the age of 71 in North Carolina. He married (Mrs.) Mary Coor Ballard, 1755-1826, daughter of Thomas and Rachel Coor. Perhaps his children with Mary Coor Ballard were:

Henry Pate, b. 1782
Alice Pate, b. 1783
Vicy Pate, b. 1784
Winneford Pate, b. 1786.

On 5 Jan 1826, James Pate, Sr. made his Last Will and Testament. In his will, he named as legatees: Mary Pate, wife, Aley Pate, daughter, and his "three youngest children" -- Henry, Vicy, and Winneford. He named as executors: his son Daniel Pate and friend Bryan H. Pate. The will was witnessed by Shad Pate and Benagy Scott.

James Pate, Sr., no doubt, had a son named James Pate, Jr., but he was not mentioned in the will.

DANIEL PATE D. 1791
SON OF JAMES PATE D. CA. 1790

Census and other records pertaining to Daniel Pate:

> 1786 Tax rolls, Wayne County, 200 acres
> 1790 U.S. Census, Wayne County, page 150, New Bern
> 1791 Last Will and Testament, *Will and Inventory Book A*, Page 258.

In my opinion, Daniel Pate, 1745-1791, married Mary Davis in Wayne County, before 1775. I believe that he had three children, all born in Wayne County:

Charles Pate, b. ca. 1775 Thomas Pate, b.1776, d.p. 1791 Pearcey Pate, b.p. 1776.

Apparently, Daniel Pate was gravely ill when he made his last will and testament on 26 June 1791, and perhaps died the following day.

In his will, he named as legatees: Mary Pate, wife, Charles Pate, son, Thomas Pate, son, and Pearcy Pate, daughter. He named as executors: his son James Pate and wife Mary Pate. The will was witnessed by Elias Pate and (X) William Peacock.

Researchers are cautioned not to confuse this Daniel Pate, 1745-1791, with the Daniel Pate who married Mary "Polly" Mecoy in Craven County, North Carolina, on 18 July 1803.

ISHAM PATE D. 1840
SON OF JAMES PATE D. CA. 1790

The name Isham also appears as Isom or Isum in North Carolina records:

> 1786 Isum Pate, Wayne County tax roll - 60 acres
> 1790 Isum Pate, U.S. Census of Wayne, Co., p. 150, 16 "souls" including 13 slaves. 1791 - Isom Pate witnessed last will and testament of Daniel Pate.
> 1800 Isham Pate, U.S. Census of Wayne Co., p. 870, 9 souls, no slaves 1804 - Isham Pate bought 300 acres from his brother Elias Pate.
> 1810 Isom Pate, U.S. Census of Wayne Co., p. 251, 6 souls, no slaves.

Isham Pate apparently married Barbary Cummins about 1775. My research disclosed no other spouses. Evidence and confirmation of their marriage is provided in a Wayne County deed made on 4 May 1783, by "Isum and Barbary Pate" to Joseph Green (*Wayne County Deed Book 3,* pages 339-43).

In my opinion, the surviving children of Isham Pate and Barbary Cummins were:

> John Pate, b. ca. 1779
> Joseph Pate, b. ca. 1785, d. July 1847
> Bryant Handley Pate, b. ca. 1786, d. February 1856
> Rachel Matilda Pate, b. ca. 1790
> Shadrack Pate, b. ca. 1795, d. November 1854.

ELIAS PATE D. 1827
SON OF JAMES PATE D. CA. 1790

There were two men named Elias Pate in North Carolina during the period 1790 to 1830. One Elias Pate resided in Wayne County, and the other Elias Pate resided in Richmond County. Many Pate family searchers have merged these two men.

In my opinion, the Wayne County Elias Pate, son of James Pate, was born ca. 1760 and died in Wayne County, ca. 1827.

It also is my opinion that the Richmond County Elias Pate was born about 1790 and died before 1854 in Shelby County, Alabama.

To differentiate between the two men, brief summaries of the records for the Richmond County Elias Pate and the Wayne County Elias Pate are provided Pertinent records of the Elias Pate of Richmond County:

1800 Census No census record for Elias Pate in any state;

About 1805 Elias Pate married Nancy (Elizabeth) Brown in Marlboro County, South Carolina;

1812-1814 Muster Rolls Elias Pate 10th Company Richmond County Regiment; 1820 Census enumeration, Elias Pate Richmond County, page 170;

1821 25 July Will of Edmund Brown, testator of Marlboro County, South Carolina published. Will names daughter, Nancy, wife of Elias Pate, as legatee;

1827 Many Pate searchers hold that Elias Pate, who married Nancy Brown, died in 1827. If, in fact, Elias Pate of Richmond County died in 1827, he would not have appeared in the 1830, 1840, or 1850 U.S. Census enumerations;

1830 Census enumeration Elias Pate, Richmond Co NC, page 218; 1850 Census Slave schedule Shelby Co AL page 092;

1850 Census enumeration   Shelby Co AL. Page 255;

Elias Pate	64 W/M Farmer	NC 1786;
Elizabeth Pate	60 W/F	NC 1790;
James Pate	19 W/M	NC 1831;

1854 Probate of the Estate of Elias Pate, who died intestate, before Nov 1854. Filed in Probate Court Shelby County, Alabama. Recorded 28 Nov 1854. (*Probate Book L, Page 139*). The estate Adminstrators were George W. Pate (probably youngest son), and A. E. Hensley, gender and relationship to Elias Pate unknown.

Pertinent records of the Elias Pate of Wayne County:

1784 Deed to James Pate names Elias Pate as an adjoining landowner;

1790 Census Elias Pate Wayne County NC page 150 New Bern - 1 person in household; 1791 Elias Pate Wayne Co., witnessed LWT of Daniel Pate;

1804 Elias Pate deed. Elias Pate sold 300 acres to his brother Isham for "20 pounds specie", witnessed by James Pate

and Joseph Pate, Jr., in August 1804 (*Book 8, Page 80, Wayne County Deeds.*);
1810 Census Elias Pate Wayne Co. NC page 252;
1820 Census Elias Pate Wayne Co. NC page 479.

In my opinion, Elias Pate of Wayne County and his unidentified spouse had the following children, though with no birth dates and only one death date:

Elias Pate, d. 1805
Samuel Pate
Isham Pate
Stephen Pate
Charles Pate
William Pate
Daniel Pate.

THOMAS PATE 1760-1845
SON OF JAMES PATE D. CA. 1790

Some researchers suggest that Thomas Pate was a son of James Pate d. ca. 1790. I do not concur. In my opinion, Thomas Pate was born 1750 and was a contemporary of James Pate, not a son.
Census and other records pertaining to Thomas Pate:

1790 U.S. Census, Orange County, page 95, Hillsborough township
1800 No U.S. Census record of Thomas Pate
1810 U.S. Census, Wayne County, page 251
1820 U.S. Census, Richmond County, page 170
1840 U.S. Census, Richmond County, page 259, Rockingham township.

The 1790 U.S. Census indicates that Thomas Pate was born in 1750 in North Carolina, Volume 132, Page 102. *U.S. Bureau of the Census,* Washington, D.C., 1908.
The Thomas Pate in the 1810 census of Wayne County was age 16 to 25, which would place his birth 1775 to 1794, not 1750.

DAVID PATE 1786-1868
SON OF JAMES PATE D. CA. 1790

David Pate, of all the descendants of James Pate d. ca. 1790, is the best researched and documented. There are two significant facts to remember about this branch. First, this line moved from Wayne County to Bladen County, North Carolina about 1814. Second, this line then began, and continues, spelling the surname as "Pait", rather than Pate.

Samuel Thedford Pait, Sr., compiled and published in 1995 a 374-page book on the Pate/Pait family of Bladen County, North Carolina. The title was *David Pate and his Descendants 1780-1995*.

Pertinent census records for David Pate:

1810 U.S. Census Wayne County, page 252, 3 souls
1820 U.S. Census Bladen County, page 136, 9 souls
1830 U.S. Census Bladen County, page 65, 11 souls
1840 U.S. Census Bladen County, page 176
1850 U.S. Census Bladen County, page 103, site 12/12
1860 U.S. Census Bladen County, page 327, Elizabethtown township.

The marriages and children of David Pate were:
Marriage 1, Elizabeth Howell, b. 1782 in Waynesborough, Dobbs County. Married 1808 in Wayne County.
Their children were:

Charity PATE, b. 1810 in Wayne County
Stephen PATE, b. 1809 in Wayne County

Marriage 2, Ferabee BOYETTE, b. 1788 in Wayne County. Married 1812 in Wayne County.
Children were:

John PATE, b. 1813 in Wayne County, m. Charity Hester;
James PATE, b. 16 January 1815, Bladen County, m. Milbry Hester;
Hilary PATE, b. 29 September 1817, Bladen County, m. Annie Elizabeth Ivey;

315

Molly M. "Polly" PATE, b. April 1822, Bladen County, m. James
    L Gooden;
Jesse Cameron PATE, b. December 1824, d. 1903, Bladen
    County, also known as Pait, m. Huldah Brisson;
David Timothy PAIT, b. February 1829, Bladen County, d. 31
    January 1912, m. Anne Edwards.

Two significant contributions to Pate family history by Samuel
Thedford Pait, Sr., should be noted. First, Sam has been the guiding
force behind the establishment and development of the Pate-Pait
Historical Society in Bladenboro, North Carolina. Second, Sam
is a member of the Pate DNA Project and has been an avid supporter. The analysis of his DNA provides absolute confirmation of his
genetic links to his paternal ancestor, Thoroughgood Pate d. 1713.

TIMELINE FOR THOROUGHGOOD PATE

Born c. 1640 England – Died 1713 North Carolina

c. 1640 Birth in England, location and parents unknown.

1656 On March 25, Henry, Elizabeth, and Katherine Pate listed as headrights in a land patent for Henry Soanes. Patent was for 2800 acres in New Kent County for the transportation of 56 persons from England. It has been speculated that Elizabeth was Henry's wife and Katherine was their daughter. There are indications that Henry and Thoroughgood were related, perhaps brothers. They obviously arrived in Virginia about the same time and had some common associations disclosed in public records (as noted below). Interestingly, a Thomas Torrowgood was also listed as an emigrant in this patent. Source: *Cavaliers and Pioneers, Abstracts of Virginia Land Patents and Grants*, abstracted by Nell Marion Nugent, Volume Two: 1666-1695: Patent Book No. 4, page 337.

1657 In an inventory filed February 1, was listed as one of the 25 debtors of the estate of Giles Mode. Source: York County, Virginia Wills, Deeds and Orders Book III, page 22.

1658 On April 20, Howell Pryse sued Thomas Ligon because Thoroughgood Pate had escaped from his custody. Source: Charles City County, Deeds, Wills and Orders 1655- 1665, page 101. Likely left the James River area at this time.

1659 In an inventory filed December 16, was listed as a debtor, jointly with Arthur Dickson, of the estate of Stephen Page. Source: York County, Virginia Wills, Deeds and Orders Book III, pages 116-7.

1661 In an inventory filed February 19, was listed as one of the debtors (with Henry Pate) of the estate of Thomas Lund, a merchant. Source: Westmoreland County Deeds and Wills No. 1, 1653-1671, page 137. In Lund's will dated January 29, 1660, Henry Pate was given use of Lund land and the house for three years, and was appointed to care for the cattle. Westmoreland and Old Rappahannock counties adjoined, both fronting on the Rappahannock River.

1669 On October 30, listed as a headright ("Thorowgood Pate") in a land patent for William Taylor, who resided in Old Rappahannock County. Patent was for 1000 acres in Accomack County for the transportation of 20 persons from England. Patents wereoften filed many years after arrival of emigrants. Source: *Cavaliers and Pioneers, Abstracts of Virginia Land Patents and Grants*, abstracted by Nell Marion Nugent, Volume Two: 1666- 1695: Patent Book No. 6, page 266.

1684 On January 25, was a witness with Jeremiah Thornton to the will of Robert Prid in Rappahannock County, Deeds, Wills and Orders No. 6, 1682-1686, page 431. Thornton signed with a mark, while Thoroughgood signed his name "Thorough Good Pate". The scribe also used "Thoroughgood Pate" in the will's proving statement.

1685 On July 9, witnessed the sale of livestock by Gerrard Fawkes of Maryland to Edward Maddocks of Stafford County (Rappahannock River area). Source: Stafford County Deeds, Orders, etc.

1687 On May 20, Annie Sims, formerly the widow of Hugh Dowding but then the widow of John Sims, conveyed land left her by Hugh Dowding to Thomas Walker, Phillip Buckner, and Thoroughgood Pate, Stafford Orders, etc.

1687 On July 9, Stafford Court Orders reported that John Sims, on his deathbed, gave a horse named "Bold Colt" to Thomas Walton, Thoroughgood Pate, and Ralph Walker.

1687 In a Stafford County will of Thomas Odonnell, written 23 August and proved 18 September 1690, "Thur" Pate was given 50 acres. The will was filed in Northern Neck Land Office Warrants. Source: *Northern Neck Land Office Wills 1657-1784*, page 156.

c. 1690 First son Charles born. Sarah believed to be wife of Thoroughgood for the birth of all three known sons.

1690 On September 9, in Stafford County Court, confirmed debt of 500 pounds of tobacco to William Loxham.

1691 On October 7, filed suit against Henry Coldstream to protect his legacy in the Odonnell will. A non-suit was declared because he failed to appear, and was ordered to pay Coldstream 50 pounds of tobacco and costs.

1693 On February 10, William Loxham appeared in Stafford Court and presented a Power of Attorney signed by Thoroughgood Pate to authorize him to represent Pate. He testified that Pate owed him a debt for clerk and blacksmith work, and that he owed Samuel

Haywood a similar amount. Loxham assigned the debt Pate owed him to Haywood, relieving him of the debt to Haywood.

c. 1695 Second son John born.

c. 1698 Third son William born.

1703 Apparently living in Chowan Precinct of Albermarle County, North Carolina, before August 25. On that date, he and Sarah sold a tract of land in Green Hall to Nicholas Blackman, Deed Book W No.1, page 47. Both signed the deed by signature, not marks. His signature was written "Thoroughgood Pate".

1704 On February 3, purchased land patent from Thomas Luten. Source: Chowan County Deed Book W No. 1, p. 62.

1713 On September 3, inventory of estate of Thoroughgood Pate was filed in court. Source: *Secretary of State Wills* 1712-1722, page 74. No will recorded, nor other probate records. Assumed he died intestate.

1714 Chowan County Court appointed Nathaniel Chevin as guardian of William Pate for his education. Court record: "Nathaniel Chevin, esquire Godfather and Uncle to William Pate the son of Thorogood and Sarah Pate (the said. Thorogood being Deceased and ye said Sarah Incapable to Educate ye said Child)". Source: Deed Book B No. 1, Chowan County, North Carolina, pages 1-2.

1720 In will of Nathaniel Chevin, dated March 3, *Secretary of State Wills*, a 40-pound legacy was left to William Pate as "cousin", but perhaps was actually godson. St. Paul's parish registry is lost. Will also mentions Sarah, William's mother.

1723 On March 9, son Charles Pate of Albermarle County sold apparent Thoroughgood homesite of 126 acres, likely after the death of his mother Sarah. Land identified as the land purchased by Thoroughgood from Major Thomas Luten and descended to Charles as the heir-at-law of his deceased father. Source: Chowan County Deed Book C No. 1, page 637.

Note: This paper is primarily based on the research of Dr. Jim Peacock, but also on research by Audrey Parker Young and me.

COMMENTARY

This timeline clarifies Thoroughgood's life spent in Virginia and North Carolina. Though usually associated with North Carolina, he actually lived in Virginia for 40 to 45 years and only 13 years in North Carolina. The fact that he moved around so much could be the reason that he apparently married and had sons so late in life, assuming there were no earlier unknown marriages and/or children.

Another thing made clear is that all his debt problems were early in his life in Virginia (1657-1661). Apparently barely an adult (or maybe just passed as one), he may have gotten into debt through failed ventures. On the other hand, his fellow debtors were men of good standing, and their debts appeared to be only mercantile accounts receivable. The debts appeared on the inventories of the estates of merchants, which did not necessarily mean they were bad debts, just open accounts when they died.

His later associations disproved any imputations of being an irresponsible debtor. He was an heir on several wills and was a witness on other legal documents. Both he and his wife Sarah were literate, at a minimum capable of signing their own names.

It is my belief that he owned a lot of land in North Carolina that may have appeared only on records now lost. It is logical since his eldest son Charles, shortly after the death of Thoroughgood, was immediately active in a lot of land transactions, probably in his early to mid-20s.

Overall, this timeline makes it easy to chronologically follow Thoroughgood's trail and puts a new perspective and some new insights on his life.

A. J. Pate
Houston, Texas October 2015

EPILOGUE

This book will never be surpassed in the meticulous scholarship of Jim Peacock following decades of intensive research. However, Jim would be the first to state that there is still much to be discovered and revealed about this great American family. Not the least of which is to locate the family origins of Thoroughgood Pate himself in England.

Jim throughout this book clearly states whenever information is less than definitive, or when there are conflicting facts, inadequate documentation, or possible inaccuracy of his conclusions. These values were hallmarks of Jim's work shown by his unwavering dedication to accuracy, thoroughness, and careful labeling of citations and references to all sources quoted.

The door is still open for some future genealogist, perhaps yet unborn, to answer many of the open and unresolved questions of this family. This book is more closely focused on the family line of Charles Pate d. 1769, the oldest son of Thoroughgood Pate. There is much less detail and the record is incomplete on his two younger sons, John and William. There is likely more official documentation to be found on these two family lines which future research may reveal.

In the long run, there is always hope that more official records and long-forgotten family records will be discovered. There is also hope that new DNA technological advances can delve more deeply into the complexities of kinship beyond what can even be imagined today.

Donald Rumsfeld, former U.S. Secretary of Defense, once famously said: "As we know, there are things we know we know. We also know there are known unknowns, that is to say we know there are some things we do not know. But there are also unknown unknowns – the ones we don't know we don't know." Though spoken in a different context, this is a perfect description of genealogical research.

The more Pate males who join the Pate DNA Project, the greater the likelihood that new relationships and connections, previously unknown, will be revealed, now or in the future.

A. J. Pate
Houston, Texas November 1, 2017

Index

Pernicia H. (later Pate), 213–214, 218–219

Peter, d.p.1910, 211

Peter Alexander, 154

Phebe (Humphrey), 142, 162, 292

Pheobe (later Cloud), 145

Phillip, 307

Phoeby (daughter of Rev. William Pate, d.1841), 291–292, 294

Piercy Lucretia (later Brock), 178

Preston, 99

Priscilla (Lancaster), 231

Probate/Provitt, 181, 182

Prudence "Mitty" (Rogers), 179

Quina R., 154

Rachel (Covington), 204–205, 207

Rachel (later Davis), 146, 147

Rachel (later McCrone), 153–154

Rachel (Whiddon), 299

Rachel Florence (later Whaley), 181–182

Rachel J. (Hall), 100–101

Rachel Louisa (Van Landingham), 153

Rachel Matilda, b.ca.1790, 312

Rack E. (Cherry), 179

Randolph L., 115

Gen. Randolph McCall, 211

Rebecca (daughter of Charles Pate, d.1790), 59, 136

Rebecca (Fisher), 287

Rebecca (Franklin, later Snoden), 259, 268–269

Rebecca (later Kendrick), 95

Rebecca (later Pitts), 156, 158–159

Rebecca (later Railey), 251–252

Rebecca (later Wright), 171, 173, 177, 233

Rebecca (Randle), 104, 114

Rebecca, b.1604, 8

Rebecca, b.ca.1854, 297

Rebecca G., 260

Rebecca Jane, b.ca.1846, 133

Rebecca Jane (Cravey), 259, 262

Rhody, 192, 195

Richard (also known at Pattee), 13–15

Richard (in 1790 census), 307

Richard, b.ca.1826, 162–164

Richard, d.1657, 1, 4–5, 8–9, 15, 16, 22

Richard J., 216–217

Richard Washington, d.1867, 192–193, 198–199

Richmond (son of of Daniel Pate, d.ca.1878), 106

Richmond J., d.1881, 107

Richmond Love, b.ca.1815, 104–105, 109–110, 117, 118–119

Richmond Love, b.ca.1827, 114

Richmond Love, b.ca.1850, 118

Robert, 26

Robert (headright 1661), 18, 41

Robert (son of Elias Pate, d.1853), 95

Robert, b.ca.1877 (born Smith), 226–227

Robert, b.ca.1878, 130

Robert Bryant, d.1938, 179

Robert Carter, xv

Robert Thomas, d.1944, 212

Robert Washington (Richard?), 194

Roger, 13–15
Romella (Usher), 210
Rosa, 154
Ruby (later Bodkin), 293, 294
Rudolph, b.ca.1864, 277
Rudolph, d.1864, 273, 277–279
Ruth, 70–71, 72
Sabra (later Wright), 59, 82, 86,
    119–126
Sallie (Clements), 299
Sallie (married to Henry Thomas
    Pate), 210
Sallie (Whittle), 287
Sallie, d.1882, 211
Sallie Adams, 130
Sally (Campbell), 153, 154
Sally (daughter of John Asbury
    Pate), 154
Sally (later Cary), 16
Sally (McNair), 130–131
Samantha, 268–269
Samuel (son of Edward, d.1757),
    25, 54
Samuel (son of Elias Pate, d.1853),
    95, 314
Samuel (son of Samuel Pate,
    d.p.1840), 145
Samuel, 1730-1795, xi
Samuel, b.ca.1815, 105, 111
Samuel, b.ca.1852, 153–154
Samuel, d.1850, 32, 78–79, 82, 84,
    86, 87–103, 284, 285, 288–290,
    292–293, 301, 303, 307
Samuel, d.1850-1854, 92, 98, 100
Samuel, d.1870, 185, 218
Samuel, d.1920, 257, 258–259,
    261, 272

Samuel, d.p.1810, 57, 59–60, 68,
    77, 78–79, 82, 85, 92, 104, 131,
    135, 143, 145, 148, 152, 161,
    206, 235, 241–253, 292, 301
Samuel, d.p.1833, 246–248,
    284–290, 288–290
Samuel, d.p.1840, 145, 148, 152
Samuel, d.p.1848, 59
Samuel, d.p.1867, xi, 249, 254–
    255, 257–259, 271, 280, 282
Samuel A., d.ca.1910, 179
Samuel Bennett, d.1895, 299
Samuel Duncan, 105, 118
Samuel Hiram, d.1901, 208
Samuel Joel, b.ca.1850, 260
Samuel Levander, 99
Samuel R., d.1854, 92, 95, 100–
    103, 135
Samuel R. (married to Susan
    Fair), 101
Samuel Thedford, Sr., 305, 315–
    316
Samuel W., b.ca.1842, 297
Sarah (Baxley), 158
Sarah (Beckwith), 103, 115–116,
    139
Sarah (Chevin), xi
Sarah (Cliborn), 246, 251
Sarah (daughter of Charles Pate,
    d.1790), 59, 136
Sarah (Dunlap), 235
Sarah (Forehand), 227
Sarah (Henderson), 58, 136, 138,
    140, 236
Sarah (Hewitt), 279
Sarah (Howell), xi
Sarah (later Brown), 109

Winneford, b.1786, 311
Winnefred (Howell), 231
Winnefred Ann (later Gardner),
    179
Winnie (later Lancaster), 197
Winnie Huff, b.ca.1872, 114
Winnie Rebecca, 114
Winnifred (Howell), 178, 180–
    181, 220
Winnifred "Wine" (Stewart),
    82–84, 103
Woodrow, 154
Wynell, 154
Zachariah, d.1914, 280–281
Zacheus/Zachariah, d.p.1856,
    143–150, 155, 159–162, 184,
    263

Zebulon Vance, d.1941, 130–131
Zilla (Broach), 291
Zilphia (Pate), 181–182
[unknown forename] married to
    Samuel Pate, d.p.1833, 284
[unknown forename] (McElraw),
    290
[unknown forename] (Sweeny,
    married to Samuel Pate,
    d.1850), 86, 87–88
[unknown forename]
    (Weathersby), 292
[unknown forenames], vi, xiii–xv,
    32–33

Pates
Aaron, 21
Catherine, 21–22
Ezekiel, 21

Raunce, 21
Reubin, 21
William, 21–22

Adams
Angeline (later Pate), 211
Caroline Ann (later Pate), 130–
    131
Emily (Smith), 211
John P., 211

Julia (Newton), 211
Margaret (later Pate), 204, 211
Mary (Stubbs), 94
William B, 130
[unknown forenames], 204

Agerton
Leona (Flowers), 268

William Jesse, 268

Akridge
Abel, 268
Greenberry, 254
Hansford, 257, 269
Hardy, 257

Hugh, 257
James, 257
Neil, 257
Prudence (Parker), 257

Richard (sometimes Story), 296
Samuel (sometimes Story), 297
Sarah (Pate), 109
Warren Lumpkin (sometimes
Story), 297

William Jackson (sometimes
Story), 297
Winnie Elizabeth (later Wells),
226

Bruce
Phillip, 15

Bryan
Robert, 279

Buckner
Andrew, 41
Phillip, 41, 317

William, 43

Bull
Martha (later Pate), 290

Bullard
Drucella Ann (Bright), 97

George, 97

Bundy
Celia B., 208
Elijah, 208
Henry, 208
John L., 203–204, 208
Laura Jane, 208
Mary A., 208
Mary "Polly" (Pate), 203–204, 208

Nicholas Parker, 208
Sarah A., 208
Sherrod/Sherwood, 208
William, 203
William B., b.ca.1839, 208
Willis, 208

Burk
Arcadia (Cutts), 280

Thomas, 280

Burnett
Mary Ann (later Bright), 97

Bussy
Bridget (later Pate), 6

John, 5

Crumpton [Crampton]
Elizabeth, 167

Henry, 167

Jane, 167

Susannah, 167

William, 167

Cummins
Barbary (later Pate), 312

Curry
Jennett (later Wright), 123, 130

Curtis
Mary (later Pate), 236

Cutts
Adaline, 281

Arcadia (later Burk), 280

Charles Benjamin, 281

Cordelia, 280

Eliza Jane (Clary), 280

Elizabeth (Hailey), 280

Hezekiah, 280

Joel, 255, 280

Mary (later Milton), 281

Mary (Pate), 254–255, 280–281

Micajah, 280

Milbra (later King), 280, 282

Montgomery, 280

Olive, 280

Rhoda (West), 281

Samuel, 280–281

Sarah A. (Heath), 280

Susan (later Cutts), 280

William Porter, 254–255, 271, 280

Zachariah, 280–281

Dade
Francis, 41

Dale
[unknown forenames], 1

Dalloway
Alice (Pate), 8

John, 8

Daniel
Charity (later Pate), 218–219

Elizabeth, 219

William, 219

Daniels
Dicey (Phillips), 170–171, 172, 176, 191, 232–233

Harry, 233

Davenport
Lizzie (later Pate), 153–154

Davis
Aaron F., 146, 147, 160–161
Andrew (sometimes Floyd), 160–161
Betsy (Elizabeth?), 155
Calvin, 155
Catherine (later Knowles), 160–161
Drusilla (later Pate), 192, 195–197
Elizabeth (later Floyd), 160–161
Harriett, 155
James, 155
Jane (later Pate), 299
John, 147, 155, 164
Mary (later Pate), 311–312
Mary (sometimes Floyd), 160

Mary A. (Pate), 194
Mary Ann (Story), 297
Matilda "Martila" (Pate), 147, 155, 164
Matthew, 71–72
Obelia (later Pate), 216–217
Ora J., 155
Rachel (Pate), 146, 147
Rebecca (Bright), 97
Stephen, 155
William, 155, 195
Winnie (sometimes Floyd), 160
[unknown surname] (married to Rebecca Bright), 97

Davison
Ralph, 44

Deans
Amy Jane "Imogene" (Pate), 214–216
Anderson, 191–192
Buck, 216

Charlotte, 191, 199
Jerry, 214–216
Mary (later Pate), 175, 191–192, 197

Deas [Dees, Desse]
Ann C., 163
James W., 164
Terressa (later Pate), 148, 151, 153, 164

Patricia Ann (later Mordes), 155

Howett

Hoyt

Hubbard

Huckabee

Hudson

Huff

Hughes

Long
[unknown forenames], 74

Loxham
William, 42, 317

Lund [Lunn]
Christopher (father), 17–18,
39–41, 45
Christopher (son), 45
Katherine (Pate), 40–41, 44–45,
317

Robert, 17
Thomas, 9, 17, 36, 39–40, 42, 45,
47, 48, 317
William, 17
[unknown forenames], 26

Luten
Thomas, 50, 56–57, 319

Machelwain
Francis, 67

Maddocks
Edward, 41, 44, 317

Maguire
B.F., 237

Mancill
Gerald, 267

Mangram
Joseph, 88

Maphe
Robert, 39

Marchant
Isaac, 298

Mary Ann (Blanchard), 298

Martin
Edwin Wall, 118

Elizabeth (later Pate), 288

Rachel (Pate), 153, 154

McDaniel
Andrew J., 298
Clarkie Lucy (later Pate), 206
George, 286
Mary Ann (Blanchard), 298

McDonald John, 84
McDowell
Abbie B. (later Pate), 99

McElraw
[unknown forename] (married
Elijah Pate), 290

McGee
Archibald, 203

McGill
Allan, 194

Mary (later Pate), 192, 211

McGrath
Maggie (later Pate), 239

McGregor
Annie Jane (Pate), 130

John, 130

McInnis
John, 101

Martha (later Pate), 100–101

McKennie
Barnabus, 54

William, 168

McKenzie
A.A., 104

McKey
Arthur, 65

McKinley
J.A., 239
Sarah A. (Pate), 239

Miller
Fereby (Pate), 254–255, 281

Jincey (Mingo), 252

Milsap
Matthew, 103

Milshaw
Richard, 18

Milton
Mary (Cutts), 281

Mingo
Augustus, 252
Henrietta (later Pate), 252

Jincey (later Miller), 252

Mires
William, 70

Mitchell
Bathsheba "Bashaby" (Peacock), 192, 197
Bethany Ann (later Wells), 226
Elizabeth (later Weatherly), 101
Elizabeth (Pate), 181
Enoch, 182
James Caswell, 197

John A., 101
Louisa (Pate), 101
Martha Florence J., 102
Milbrey (Flowers), 268
Penelope "Penny" (Peacock), 192
Ransom, 268

Mitchem
Abraham W., xi, 266
Alcey Melvina, xi

Caroline "Callie" (Pate), iv, vi, 241, 266

Mitton
Anne (Pate), 6
Lewis, 8

Richard, 6
Ursula (Pate), 7

Mode
Giles, 17, 29, 32, 35, 48, 317
Jane (Haddon), 35

Nutt
Eliza (Wright), 123

Washington, 123

Oates
Joseph, 245

O'Bryan
Elizabeth (Wright), 124

William, 124

Oden
Susannah (Pate), 109

T.J., 109

Odom
John, 93
Maggie (later Pate), 208
Mary (later Pate), 204, 211
Mary (mother of Mary Odom
   Pate), 211

Philip, 211
Sabra (Wright), 211
Sarah Jane (later Pate), 204

Odonnell [O'Donnell]
Anna (Withers), 44, 45
Thomas, 9, 18, 39, 42–45, 48, 53,
   317

[unknown forenames], 26

Oliphant
Jesse, 244

Oliver
Catherine (later Pate), 97

Overinge
Edward, 5

Mary (Pate), 6

Overstreet
Jno., 35

Owens
Elizabeth (Pate), 2180-2250, 95
Elizabeth (Pate), b.ca.1861, 299

Jackson, 95
[unknown forename], 299

Retherford [Rutherford]
Thursey Ann (Pate), 152

Revill
Nathaniel, 143

Richards
Richard, 44

Richardson
Christopher, 44   Robert, 44

Rigdel
Joel, 88   Martha, 88

Rigdon
Diantha (Blanchard), 298   Elizabeth (Blanchard), 298
Elijah, 298   Jordan, 298

Risen
Dorothy (later Flowers), 264   John, 4
Roberson. see Robinson   Louvinia (later Howell), 231
   [Roberson] Roberts   Micajah, 298
Abigail (Lewis), 231   Myrtle (later Howell), 231
Cassandra (Apreece), 4   Richard, 4–5
Eleanea, 231   Sylvania (Blanchard), 298
Dame Jane (later Skipwith), 1–5

Robinson [Roberson]
Carol Ann (Moore), 305   Jessee, 224
Elizabeth (later Grant), 195   Levi, 251
Frank, 251   Mary "Polly" (Pate), 171, 172,
Gatsey (later Pate), 251, 252–253   175, 224, 232–233
Haywood, 177, 224   Penelope, 224
Henry, 224   Sarah (Deason), 251
Isaiah, 251   William, 224

Rogers
Prudence "Mitty" (later Pate), 178

INDIANA

LOUISIANA

MARYLAND

MISSISSIPPI

VIRGINIA

Accomack County, 17, 38, 317
Charles City County, 29, 35–36, 38, 48, 317
  Charles City, 29
Dismal Swamp, 26
Elizabeth City County, 30
Elizabeth River, 17, 40
Frederick County, 50
Gloucester County, 5–6, 9, 11, 15–16, 18–20, 22–25
Henrico County, 29
  Richmond, 187, 206, 300
Henry County Richmond, 219
Isle of Wight County, 20, 25, 54, 167
James City County, 29
  James City, 16, 29
James River, 14, 26, 30, 35–36, 38–39, 317
King George County, 16, 21–22
Lancaster County, 6, 15, 22, 25, 47
Loudoun County, 33
Lower Norfolk County, 17, 22, 40–41, 45, 47
Lunenburg County, 20, 25
Meherrin River, 167
Middlesex County, 16, 20, 24, 25
New Kent County, 16–17, 20, 24, 25, 38, 317

Norfolk County, 46–47, 50
North River, 15
Northern Neck, 11, 26, 33, 42, 46, 50, 53, 57, 59, 139, 293–294
Northumberland County, 22, 29
Nottoway River, 20, 25
Old Rappahannock County, 15, 16, 17–18, 20, 25, 29, 33, 36–38, 39, 45, 48, 317
Poropotank River, 14–15, 19
Potomac River, 17, 26, 33, 39
Princess Anne County, 46
Rappahannock County, 35, 38, 40, 41, 42, 47, 317
Rappahannock River, 17, 18, 21, 26, 36, 40–42, 47, 53, 317–317
Richmond County, 20
Southampton County, 25, 54, 239, 242, 317
Surry County, 18, 167
Warwick County, 29
Westmoreland County, 17, 29, 36, 39–40, 48, 317
York County, 17, 29, 35, 38, 48, 197
  Yorktown, 18, 24–25
York River, 15–16, 18, 29

ENGLAND

Bristol County Bristol, 18
Cambridgeshire Cambridge, 6
Chester County Hatherton, 5
Essex County Epping, 6
Huntington, County Washingly, 4
Leicestershire, 20

Brin, 4, 7, 15, 22
  Cotes, 1, 6
  Eye-Kettleby, 4, 6, 22, 46
Leicester, 1
  Osbaston, 6
  Sysonby, 6

WALES

Notes

www.ingramcontent.com/pod-product-compliance
Lightning Source LLC
Chambersburg PA
CBHW071950270326
41928CB00009B/1402